CW00421786

Dr Tony Moore is a writer, historian and academic based in
Melbourne. He has a PhD in Australian history from the
University of Sydney and is a lecturer at the National Centre for
Australian Studies, Monash University. Tony's career has spanned
political activism, documentary making at the ABC, journalism
and book publishing. He writes regularly on culture, history and
politics, and his last book was *The Barry McKenzie Movies*.

Dr Moore was awarded the NSW History Fellowship by the
NSW Government – Arts NSW to help research and write
Death or Liberty.

For Lizbeth

Rise like Lions after slumber
In vanquished number,
Shake your chains to earth like dew
Which in sleep had fallen on you—
Ye are many—they are few.

From Percy Bysshe Shelley, *The Mask of Anarchy*, written on the occasion of the
massacre at 'Peterloo', Manchester, 1819

* * *

'Freedom is more than a resolution—he is not free who is free alone.'

John Boyle O'Reilly, Irish political prisoner transported to Australia,
1868–1869

* * *

Sons of the South, make choice between
(Sons of the South, choose true),
The Land of Morn and the Land of E'en,
The Old Dead Tree and the Young Tree Green,
The Land that belongs to the lord and the Queen,
And the Land that belongs to you.

From Henry Lawson, *A Song of the Republic*, 1887

DEATH
OR
LIBERTY

Rebels and radicals transported to Australia
1788-1868

TONY MOORE

CONTENTS

INTRODUCTION: REMEMBERING AUSTRALIA'S POLITICAL PRISONERS

GROWING UP IN THE SUBURBS OF THE ILLAWARRA REGION OF NEW South Wales in the 1970s, my friends and I were frustrated that the exciting events of history seemed to pass us by. The great wars and revolutions that young minds hang on when they first turn to history happened elsewhere, in Europe, the Americas, Africa and Asia, while my own country appeared untroubled by violent conflict or even the clash of ideas. Later I would come to appreciate that in fact Australia had a robust, and at times bloody, history of dissent and a proud tradition of resistance to authority and privilege by the marginalised, the dispossessed and exploited, beginning with the country's Indigenous people, and the convicts transported here in chains. The stories of resistance are often closer than we realise.

What I did not know back at school was that only a few kilometres from home, in the West Dapto bush where my mates and I skylarked, lay buried a nineteenth century revolutionary named Joseph Marceau. The gravestone in the old Catholic cemetery masks more than it reveals, merely recording that Marceau, husband of Mary, died in 1883, aged 76 years. But the story of an earlier life full of derring-do, suffering and redemption may be pieced together, from convict records, from the memoirs of contemporaries and from family stories handed down to descendants still living in the region.

Joseph Marceau was one of fifty-two French Canadian 'patriots' transported to New South Wales for taking up arms against British rule in 1837 and 1838. The rebellion in the predominantly French-speaking province of Lower Canada was part of a succession of republican uprisings in Britain's Canadian colonies that culminated in armed raids across the border by radical insurgents from the United States, many of whom were also captured and transported as convicts to Australia. Marceau and his fellow French *patriotes Canadiens* were originally put to work on the shores of Sydney Harbour around Concord, an area that came to be known as Canada Bay. Eventually pardoned, all the French Canadians returned home, except for Marceau, who married an Australian girl, acquired land, and lived a quiet farming life in Dapto, an identity selling produce at the local markets, where he was fondly known as 'honest Joe'. He never talked about his past as rebel and convict, though he claimed to be the nephew of a famous French revolutionary, General François-Séverin Marceau-Desgraviers who stormed the Bastille and served with Napoleon. The failed revolution for which Joseph suffered the terrors of transportation—exile from everyone he loved, an odyssey to the ends of the Earth locked in the bowels of a wooden ship, the casual cruelties of the convict work gangs and the stigma of being branded a criminal in an alien land—was not in vain. The patriot risings helped persuade London to grant responsible government in Canada during the 1840s and made it easier for reformers to achieve self-government in Joseph's adopted homeland of New South Wales and other Australian colonies.

In Sydney's verdant Royal Botanic Gardens, hidden among subtropical shrubs, may be found a marker to another humble grave. A small plaque bears the name Joseph Gerrald, who died at the age of thirty-six in 1796, less than a decade after the penal colony was established. A makeshift memorial, erected in 1996 on the bicentenary of his death, reveals that Gerrald was one of the 'Scottish Political Martyrs' tried at Edinburgh and transported over the seas for sedition. His crime was to advocate democratic reforms to the British constitution, notably free speech and universal suffrage. Already ill with tuberculosis when sentenced, the young reformer could not be expected to survive the long voyage and died four months after arriving in Sydney. A sensitive and highly educated man, Gerrald's own words to the court on learning of his exile to New South Wales for fourteen years, inscribed on the plaque, provide an epitaph:

> ... whatever destiny awaits me, I am content. The cause which I have embraced has taken deep root, and must, I feel, ultimately triumph. I have my reward. I see through the cheering vista of future events the overthrow of tyranny, and the permanent establishment of benevolence and peace. It is as silent as the lapse of time, but as certain and inevitable.[1]

Sixty years after his premature death the legislative assemblies of New South Wales, Victoria and South Australia were elected by universal male suffrage, and by the late nineteenth century Great Britain's democracy was catching up with her colonies. Sadly, the tombstone identifying the precise site of Gerrald's burial in the gardens disappeared in 1807, but we do know it bore the inscription:

He died a martyr to the liberties of his country.

The understated resting places of the Canadian rebel and the British radical disturb our conventional understanding of the convicts as criminals—whether incorrigibles or victims of social injustice and unfair laws. The stories of Marceau and Gerrald suggest the use of transportation as a tool for political suppression, and a connection between the Australian colonies and the revolutionary ideas and movements sweeping Europe and the Americas. How many other political prisoners were transported to the Australian colonies? What led them to this fate? Did the Australian colonies become the British Empire's Guantanamo Bay?

* * *

This is the story of how the British Government banished to the ends of the Earth political enemies viewed by authorities with the same alarm as today's 'terrorists': Jacobins, democrats and republicans; machine breakers, food rioters, trade unionists and Chartists; Irish, Scots, Canadian and even American rebels. While criminals in the eyes of the law, many of these prisoners were heroes and martyrs to their own communities, and are still revered in their homelands as freedom fighters and patriots, progressive thinkers, democrats and reformers. Yet in Australia, the land of their exile, memory of these rebels and their causes has dimmed.

Death or Liberty brings together the stories of the political prisoners sent as convicts to Australia from all over Britain as well as parts of her empire, spanning the early days of the penal settlement at Sydney Cove until transportation ended in 1868. All Australians are aware of the nation's convict roots but few realise that transportation was a common punishment for protest, agitation, rebellion, dissent and riot directed against the British Crown and its representatives. In all approximately 3600 political prisoners were transported to the Australian colonies of New South Wales, Van Diemen's Land, Queensland and Western Australia, and to the isolated penitentiaries of secondary punishment such as Norfolk and Maria islands, Macquarie Harbour and the infamous Port Arthur. They included the Scottish Martyrs of 1794, the Naval Mutineers of 1797, the Yorkshire Weavers of 1820, the Tolpuddle Martyrs who formed one of the first trade unions for agricultural workers in 1834, the rural Swing Rioters and the machine-breaking Luddites, the North American rebels of 1837 and 1839, the Chartists from Monmouthshire in Wales of 1842, and over 2000 Irish rebels from 1798 to 1868, such as the United Irishmen, Whiteboys, Ribbon gangs, Young Irelanders and the Fenians. Some bold spirits broke free, hatching daring escapes, usually with American assistance, notably six Irish Fenians, who were rescued from Western Australia with great drama aboard the *Catalpa* in 1876, to the embarrassment of the British Empire.

In telling the stories of Australia's political convicts I ask who were these prisoners and what led them to take the radical actions they did? Why did the authorities so fear these dissenters and rebels and was transportation effective in halting dissent? What became of the political convicts in Australia and who escaped or returned home? Most crucially, what influence did these political activists in exile have on colonial life and politics, from the Castle Hill Rebellion to trade unionism and the early appearance of responsible and democratic government?

Death or Liberty adopts the 'history from the below' approach of E.P. Thompson, Eric Hobsbawm and George Rudé to understand the forces producing rebellion against authority. Studies by these scholars and others have shown how the uprooting of Britain's agrarian communities by the forces of capitalism, industrialisation and urbanisation and the expansion of Empire led not only to class division, social breakdown and crime, but also to revolution, riot and organised resistance. Social and labour historians have recast many political 'criminals' as progressive thinkers, democrats and reformers who paid the price for the advance of self-determination, universal suffrage, free speech and assembly, workers' rights and social justice. Transportation removed political threats from home and intimidated others who would contemplate dissent or rebellion. I examine the systematic use of this 'system' by British governments to suppress political movements over nearly a century, the experience of political prisoners in Australia and their impact on convict resistance, and the development of colonial political culture.

This history is sensitive to issues of class distinction in the eighteenth and nineteenth centuries. Many of the political exiles were well-connected, educated, charismatic leaders versed in the skills of organisation and oratory. Many more lacking formal education were self-taught working people who honed skills in articulating with their fellows as lay preachers in their churches, as union activists on the factory floor or through military command in the field. A significant minority of radicals transported to Australia were intellectuals and journalists, orators and publicists, who rehearsed as citizens of a new 'republic of letters' the ideas they would seek to make real through reform or revolution. As a consequence they have recorded their experience of exile in letters, pamphlets and memoirs. Their notoriety meant that newspapers and magazines in Australia, Ireland, Britain, Canada and America often reported their stories. They have left meditations not just on protest and rebellion, punishment and martyrdom, but on the conflict of nationalism and empire, the battles for liberalism and socialism and the right to fair pay and a vote.

The book is a chronological, character-driven and thematic narrative, with chapters based around different groups of political prisoners transported at particular times. Many of these groups—the Scottish Martyrs, the United Irishmen, the Tolpuddle Martyrs, the Canadian Patriots, the Chartists, the Young Ireland Martyrs and the Fenians—are today honoured in their countries of origin with memorials and celebrations as champions for the extension of democracy, workers' rights and of national self-determination. But here in Australia—with the possible exception of the Irish—there is little to commemorate their time on our soil or contribution to our history.

This problem of 'forgetting' may be due to the limitations of history conceived in purely national terms. The characters in this book moved beyond one nation to traverse the globe, contributing to the different places in which they lived, and even making a virtue of their status as 'citizens of the world'. A particular problem for a country with colonial origins is that many of the people who made a difference in Australia's past were mobile within a global empire as governors, soldiers, sailors, immigrants, explorers, scientists, missionaries, travellers and of course convicts. Furthermore, some of the freedom fighters exiled to the Australian penal settlements ultimately found refuge and belonging outside the Empire in the United States or France. Do we struggle to place the transported rebels and protesters into the Australian story because as exiles they are inherently transnational? Or does the manifest impact of the political convicts on their countries of origin and the patriotism inherent in their causes mean that they have been lost to Australian historical memory by the stronger claims of British, Irish, Canadian or American history?

Early in the twenty-first century eminent Australian historian Ann Curthoys observed that the 'globalisation' characteristic of our current age has in part prompted historians 'to pay far more attention than we have previously to all those processes, events, and themes that are best understood beyond the nation and which cross national boundaries'. She welcomed a new trend among scholars where 'the Australian historical experience becomes part of the study of relationships, networks, and connections, traced back and forth and indeed around the Empire as a whole'.[2] The people and movements in the history that follows are radical precisely because they struggled against the arbitrary boundaries and limitations of their age. As well as crisscrossing the borders of countries, colonies and empires, they pushed against entrenched social and civic barriers restraining political participation, classes, religions and ethnicities. The challenge in writing this book was to resist an anachronistic national narrative and instead recreate the mobility between countries and social groups afforded by empire, trade, war, diaspora and radical culture itself. Within this earlier stage of globalisation, Britain's exiled rebels should be understood not just for their role in the movements and communities they left behind, but in terms of the places and people they touched during their often involuntary journeys; their routes as well as their roots. Approached in this way, the stories of the political convicts reveal Australian colonies vitally connected to the world and the great causes of the age, participants in a system of imperial terror, yet champions of democratic innovation.

Death or Liberty was commissioned as an accessible narrative history, but one that is informed by the research and analysis of the many scholars who have worked in the fields of convict, imperial and radical history. As such it stands on the shoulders of giants, particularly George Rudé who undertook in *Protest and Punishment* exhaustive primary research giving names and lives to so many of Australia's political transportees, especially the less celebrated social protesters from rural and working-class communities. Like Rudé, I seek to connect the disparate stories of various political prisoners into a nearly century-long narrative, and discern continuities as well as differences. In undertaking this task I am indebted to the original investigative research work of scholars and writers who have already brought to vivid life particular groups of political convicts or their movements, with attention to detail and historical debates beyond the scope of this project. In particular I acknowledge Frank Clune's *The Scottish Martyrs*; Nancy Curtin's *The United Irishmen*; Anne-Maree Whitaker's *Unfinished Revolution*; Con Costello's *Botany Bay*; Joyce Marlow's *Tolpuddle Martyrs*; David Kent and Norma Townsend's *Convicts of the Eleanor*, *American Citizens, British Slaves* by Cassandra Pybus and Hamish Maxwell-Stewart; Tom Keneally's *The Great Shame*; Seán McConville's *Irish Political Prisoners, 1848–1922*; Blanche Touhill's *William Smith O'Brien and His Irish Revolutionary Companions in Penal Exile*; and Robert Hughes' *The Fatal Shore*.[3] Finally, I salute the thematic influence of cultural historian Raymond Williams from whom I borrow the idea of discovering new traditions, as a radical type of contemporary cultural change.

I have written this book so that twenty-first century readers, especially younger Australians, might learn the stories of the rebels, radicals and protesters who sacrificed their own freedom to help achieve the liberty, democracy and egalitarianism we enjoy today; so they may place in historical context today's detentions, wars on terror and movements of resistance. In our contemporary climate where laws are being tightened to curtail dissent in the interests of national security and economic growth, the chapters that follow seek to raise questions about the violence of both the state and its opponents, about enthusiasm for change and the instinct to conserve, about zeal, ruthlessness and idealism, to reveal the crucial place of hope, courage and sacrifice in human progress.

1

MARTYRS
TO
LIBERTY

TRANSPORTING RADICALS
IN THE AGE OF REVOLUTION

The enemies of Reform have scrutinised, in a manner ... unexampled in Scotland, every action I have performed—every word I may have uttered—Of crimes most foul and horrible, I have been accused—Of attempting to rear the standard of civil war, and to plunge this land in blood.[1]

THE SPEAKER WAS A TWENTY-EIGHT-YEAR-OLD LAWYER NAMED Thomas Muir standing before the High Court of Scotland in Edinburgh on 30 August 1793 to be tried on charges of sedition brought against him by the Crown. The prisoner in the dock was accused of 'wickedly and feloniously inciting, by means of seditious speeches and harangues, a spirit of disloyalty and disaffection to the King and the Established Government'. Furthermore he was charged with distributing 'seditious and wicked publications and writings', and 'reading aloud' from 'seditious and inflammatory writing, tending to produce in the minds of the people a spirit of insurrection'.[2] Muir would be the first political prisoner transported to Australia, one of five radical agitators to meet this fate in a series of notorious sedition trials held in Scotland in 1793 and '94. They are known to history as the Scottish Martyrs.

What had Muir actually done? Significantly he was charged with crimes of communication: writing, reading, publishing, speaking. Muir's crime was not taking up arms against the state, but taking words to the people. The right to free speech was on trial. In October 1792 he had been elected vice-president of the newly formed Glasgow Associated Friends of the Constitution and the People, one of many new societies forming around Britain to campaign for constitutional reform. Their aim was universal suffrage, the restoration of annual parliaments, equal electoral representation between cities and country and the reduction in the tax burden. Rather than humbly petitioning parliament or the sovereign as was customary, these new societies sought to build a movement for change by the modish methods of distributing information to the public, and bringing together supporters in representative gatherings that accelerated momentum, called 'conventions'. In December 1792 Muir played a leading part in a national Convention of Societies of Friends of the People held in Edinburgh. It was here before 160 delegates that he read the alleged inflammatory speech and distributed 'seditious' publications, notably the best-selling pamphlet *Rights of Man*, by outlawed radical Tom Paine. Muir's remarks were recorded by paid government informers, and on 2 January 1793 he was arrested and charged with sedition before the Sheriff of Midlothian and remanded in Tolbooth prison.

Born in 1765, Thomas Muir was a university-educated gentleman— the son of a respected and wealthy Glasgow merchant. He had handsome fine features, an aquiline nose, blue eyes and free-flowing hair in the French revolutionary fashion. As a youth he had brought innate intelligence to the advantages of wealth and social standing inherited from his family. Something of a prodigy, he entered the University of Glasgow when only twelve, and discovered a talent for satire that tested the patience of his teachers.[3] Nonetheless, Muir's gifts attracted a mentor, the liberal academic John Millar, who encouraged critical thinking and Enlightenment attitudes in his pupil. After earning a Bachelor of Arts he studied law at Edinburgh University where his gift for oratory established his reputation as both a legal advocate and an activist for parliamentary reform in Glasgow. Without any prior misdemeanour or blemish to his name, a man of such background and attainments could normally expect some leniency for a first offence. But these were not normal times.

Muir's fate lay in the hands of a jury of his peers and five judges, their Lordships Braxfield, Swinton, Esgrove, Dunsinnan and Abercrombie. Robert Macqueen, Lord Braxfield, the presiding judge on this high-profile political case, was an arch Tory, and an intimidating, wily presence.[4] In build he was more like a blacksmith than a law officer, with an uncouth manner, a broad Scots brogue and the red face of an intemperate drinker.[5] On hearing the charges Braxfield dispensed with any show of impartiality and told the jury that Muir's intention 'is plainly to overturn our present happy constitution: the happiest and most noble constitution in the world'. Turning to Muir's taste in 'seditious publications' Braxfield declared that 'the books which this gentleman has circulated have a tendency to make the people believe that the government of this country is venal and corrupt, and thereby to incite a rebellion'.[6] Lord Swinton threatened in a similar partisan vein that 'was hardly a line' in the charge sheet that 'did not amount to High Treason: and which, if proven, must infer the highest punishment the law can inflict'.[7]

Why was the world's greatest military and economic power, controlling an empire stretching around the globe, so alarmed by speeches and pamphlets? The immediate answer lies in the momentous events occurring just across the channel in France that had been ignited by the fall of the Bastille in 1789. The French Revolution had radicalised reformers across Britain, who joined local societies for the purpose of hastening constitutional change in favour of the people. The Edinburgh gathering called itself a 'convention', after the French parliament, and attendees styled themselves 'citizens' and 'delegates' in enthusiastic imitation of the Jacobin revolutionary buzz words. However, just as the overturning of the *Ancien Régime* kindled the hopes of British liberals, it filled many others, especially in the ruling class, with fear and horror. The government of William Pitt, a pragmatic politician who in an earlier incarnation as an 'independent Whig' had accepted the need for parliamentary reform, lined up with hard-line conservatives to denounce the incipient home-grown radical movement. In 1792 the French Convention passed a decree offering support to 'all subjects revolting against a tyrant'. The descent of the French Revolution into a reign of terror against the nobility persuaded Pitt to take measures to contain the contagion spreading across the channel, including the dispatch of spies and informers, tough censorship of publications and public speeches, and eventually the suspension of *habeas corpus*.[8] With the works of Paine in its sights, the government issued a proclamation in May 1792 prohibiting 'wicked and seditious writings' and empowering magistrates to comb the land for offending literature, authors and publishers. This was the net that would ensnare Thomas Muir and his fellow radicals.

One of the facts presented in the case against Muir was that he 'represent[ed] the Government of this country as oppressive and tyrannical', and the parliament as 'venal and corrupt' in comparison to the 'pretended existing Government of France'.[9] Arrested on 2 January 1793, Muir then broke his parole and fled to Paris in order, so he later claimed, to plead for the life of Louis XVI. Muir was a passionate Scottish nationalist, but his political *modus operandi* was fundamentally internationalist, forging links not just with English radicals, but also with republicans in Ireland, America and especially France.[10] However, the French king was executed by guillotine in

Place de la Révolution on 21 January 1793 to cries of '*vive la revolution*'. On 1 February the French Republic declared war on Great Britain, throwing Muir's international strategy into disarray.

Back in Scotland, Muir was pronounced an outlaw and struck off as an advocate. Granted a French passport by the revolutionary government he resolved to escape to the United States of America via Ireland, but made the mistake of returning to Scotland to farewell his family, where he was apprehended. The government at Westminster wanted an example made of this young man, especially to those prominent in the Edinburgh Convention; to teach a lesson to those who would stir up rebellion in the common people and embolden a foreign enemy in a time of war. The prosecutor in the case was to be the supreme representative of the Crown in Scotland, the Lord Advocate, Robert Dundas, brother of the Home Secretary in Pitt's Government, Lord Henry Dundas.

Unbowed by the impartiality displayed by his judges, Muir rose to defend himself, telling the court that:

> *I am accused of sedition; And yet, I can prove by thousands of witnesses,*
> *that I warned the people of the danger of that crime, exhorted them*
> *to adopt none but measures which were constitutional, and entreated*
> *them to connect liberty with knowledge, and both with morality.*[11]

Muir may have fared better with a diplomatic barrister and a show of contrition, but wanted to use the stage of the court to speak to the nation, thereby subverting the authorities' bid to silence him.[12] In a carefully argued three-hour oration, Muir claimed to be defending the customary rights of Britons and to be loyal to George III and parliament. Yet after insisting on his moderation, the idealistic reformer could not resist a defiant display of the firebrand radicalism that so alarmed conservatives. His crime, he asserted, was 'having dared to be ... a strenuous and active advocate for an equal representation of the People—in the House of the People. It is a good cause—It shall ultimately prevail—It shall finally triumph.'[13] The applause from his supporters had no effect on the jury who wasted no time finding Muir guilty of all charges. How could it be otherwise when all eleven men were chosen by Braxfield from members of a Scottish conservative organisation, an 'association of gentlemen', called the Life-and-Fortune Men, analogous to the Orange Societies of northern Ireland?[14] These men were already ill-disposed to Muir, having blackballed him when he sought to join their association. It was a convenient anomaly of the Acts of Union between England and Scotland that north of Hadrian's Wall juries could be rigged with impunity.

There followed a brief interlude during which the judges considered appropriate punishment, debating among themselves the relative merits of financial penalties, whipping, prison and banishment. Each had drawbacks: a fine would fall unfairly on the prisoner's family and keep him at large. Whipping was too 'disgraceful' to be endured by a man of Muir's 'character and rank'. Imprisonment would in time see him 'let loose' to 'disturb the happiness of *the People*', while standard banishment would merely export a 'dangerous' man to another, perhaps nearby country. Hanging was to be avoided, as it would create a martyr and provoke an outcry from more powerful reformers in the home counties of England, some of whom held seats in parliament. The British Government wanted Muir to be completely excised from the body politic, beyond contact with supporters and Britain's enemies. Since 1788 the courts had had at their disposal the means to make a person as dead, while mercifully sparing his or her life, by exiling them to one of the most isolated outposts on Earth—the newly established penal colony of New South Wales. From Botany Bay, escape, let alone communication with the outside world, would be well-nigh impossible. Lord Braxfield fixed his eye on the prisoner and passed the sentence that 'the said Thomas Muir be *Transported* beyond [the] Seas ... for the space of Fourteen Years', adding that should he return to Great Britain within that time 'he shall suffer Death'.[15]

The jury was shaken by the sentence's severity.[16] They expected a short prison spell at most for a man of Muir's social standing. According to eminent nineteenth century Scottish judge Lord Henry Cockburn this was the first time that transportation to anywhere in the British Empire had been used to punish sedition.[17] The common sentence duration for a transported criminal recidivist was seven years. Yet the Lord Advocate and his judges considered Muir a much greater threat to the realm than a common thief. Braxfield had been of a mind to transport Muir for the term of his natural life, but fourteen years' exile to the distant antipodean continent was effectively a life sentence. It is important to grasp the horror that transportation to

Botany Bay conjured in the mind of the late eighteenth century Briton who knew little of the world beyond their shore. The New South Wales colony was a mere six years old, and struggling with starvation. What little news reached home told of strange animals and vegetation, impenetrable forests and hazardous coastlines, a harsh climate and natives so savage that they had even dared to spear the governor. The east coast of Australia was as remote and alien in 1794 as the moon is for us today, except that we can see the moon.[18] For a man of educated and refined sensibility like Muir, there was the other horror of being submerged within his own country's so-called 'criminal class', in an upside-down society where common thieves, murderers and prostitutes were the majority. For a gentleman transported to New South Wales, hell really could be other people. Then there was the voyage, at least eight months in a crammed ship tossing about on barely charted oceans, risking disease, hunger, hostility from enemy craft or the vagaries of weather that could smash a boat into driftwood. Finally, the return journey at the completion of a sentence was beyond the financial reach of most, for they, and not the government, had to bear the costs of a berth on an infrequent ship. Cockburn, writing a generation later when the Australian convict system was operating full throttle, observed that 'a man transported was considered as a man never to be seen again'.[19] In these early days of the prison colony, transportation was looked upon with fear, as a species of living death.

Yet Muir was brave and composed when the sentence was pronounced, stating that '[w]ere I to be led this moment from the bar to the scaffold, I should feel the same calmness and serenity which I now do'.[20] He saved his last words before a British audience for the cause for which he had sacrificed his liberty, declaring:

> *My mind tells me that I have acted agreeably to my conscience and that I have engaged in a good, a just, and a glorious cause—a cause which, sooner or later, must and will prevail, and by a timely reform, save this country from destruction.*[21]

These prescient words, soon circulating in a pamphlet prepared by Muir, would inspire British democratic reformers down the generations.

The exile of Muir alone would not suppress the popular movement breaking out around the country. He was the first of a group of five political reformers to be arrested and tried in Scotland in 1793 and '94 for sedition and transported to New South Wales. The others were Thomas Palmer, William Skirving, Joseph Gerrald and Maurice Margarot. Like Muir all were educated, professional men. Palmer was a minister of religion who had attended Eton and studied arts and divinity at Cambridge. Skirving grew up in a prosperous family and applied his education at Edinburgh University to scientific agriculture. Gerrald was born in the West Indies to a wealthy Irish planter and educated in England at a prestigious public school. Margarot was the son of a radical European wine merchant of Swiss extraction based in London and had studied classics at the University of Geneva. Each of these men came to the reform cause through different routes, and to the attention of authorities for the leadership roles they assumed at the Edinburgh Convention and its aftermath.

The Reverend Palmer was an English Unitarian pastor and activist in the Society for the Friends of Liberty based in Dundee. He was tried in the Circuit Court of Perth on 12 September 1793 on charges of sedition for distributing a hundred copies of a pamphlet to 'various booksellers'. The offending publication, written by Scottish weaver George Mealmaker, warned against the recent clampdown on freedoms by a security-obsessed government. It asked '[i]s not the executive branch daily seizing new, unprecedented, and unwarrantable powers? Has [not] the House of Commons ... joined the coalition against you? Is not its independence gone, while it is made up of pensions and placemen?'[22] Judge Abercrombie condemned this document for its 'abundance of that party zeal' that is 'disgusting to all lovers of quiet and moderation'.[23] Found guilty of sedition and sentenced to seven years' transportation on 13 September 1793, Palmer countered that '[m]y life has, for many years, been employed in the dissemination of what I conceived to be religious and moral truths' and during the 'late great political discussions' he could not be 'an unconcerned bystander'.[24]

22

Skirving, Margarot and Gerrald were arrested on 5 December 1793 when they convened a second Convention of Friends of the People in Edinburgh, one year after the first, but now in a time of war. Skirving was active in the first Edinburgh Convention and was elected secretary to the second. His charges alleged he 'circulated a seditious handbill', 'made seditious speeches and motions' and 'endeavoured to reassemble' a convention disbanded by magistrates, all amounting to 'a crime of a heinous nature, and severely punishable'.[25] At his trial on 6 and 7 January 1794, Lord Braxfield, again presiding, castigated Skirving for holding such a meeting when 'this nation is engaged in a bloody war with France, consisting of millions of the most profligate monsters that ever disgraced humanity'.[26] The Solicitor-General's case against Skirving made much of the use of the French revolutionary terms 'convention', 'delegate', 'citizen' and the formation of various 'committees' by Skirving and his associates to argue that their intention must be regicide and seizure of power. Like Muir, Skirving was sentenced to fourteen years in New South Wales by the rigged Scottish courts. He replied that:

> *this sentence can only affect me as the sentence of man. It is long since I laid aside the fear of man as my rule ... I know that what has been done these days will be rejudged. That is my comfort, and all my hope.*[27]

He would not see his wife and eight children again.

The fourth man to be tried was the rambunctious Maurice Margarot. As a child he had been exposed to the conversation of radicals, who met at his family home in London and in 1792 he became active in the London Corresponding Society, pledged to publicise the cause of parliamentary reform and the idea that liberty was man's birthright.[28] As well as penning pamphlets and speeches on these themes, the silver-tongued Margarot spoke before the French National Convention, and was a mover and shaker at the second Edinburgh Convention. Knowing from the earlier trials that he was bound for Botany Bay and thus having nothing to lose, Margarot resolved to have some fun with the authorities and, like Muir, generate public support for his cause. Come the day of his trial, 13 January 1794, Margarot's opening play was to lead a procession of zealous supporters through the street up to the court steps, brandishing a 6-metre (20-feet) high 'tree of liberty' banner. This defiant gesture was the closest the Scottish Martyrs came to actual rebellion on British soil. Margarot was marked out by his Gallic appearance. Cockburn, a youth in attendance that day, observed that the 'popular idol in this scene was a little, dark creature, dressed in black, with silk stockings and white metal buttons, something like one's idea of a puny Frenchman, a most impudent and provoking body'. Even a sympathetic witness betrayed the Francophobia that greeted a man of Continental ancestry at this time.[29] The demonstration was met on a bridge by a line of city magistrates and the Lord Provost who demanded the 'rebels' retire. Just as the two lines converged a force of constables and sailors bearing batons rushed from nearby properties. Cockburn recalled that 'the houses vomited forth their bludgeoned contents; and in two minutes the tree of liberty was demolished and thrown over the bridge, the street covered with the knocked down, the accused dragged to the bar, and the insurrection was over'.[30]

In court, Margarot came out swinging, asking for definitions of sedition and treason, and comparing the trials to a 'State Inquisition', asking '[h]as not a man living under the British Constitution a right to examine the Constitution?'[31] Most controversially, he demanded that Lord Braxfield be disqualified from hearing the trial, on the grounds that at a recent dinner the judge had told guests he intended to send the accused to Botany Bay and give him a hundred lashes. While it appears that the bibulous Braxfield did indeed boast of his intentions over the claret, he refused to answer Margarot's questions on the indiscreet prejudgement. In complete disregard of their responsibilities to ensure at least the appearance of justice, the other judges hearing the matter endorsed Braxfield's decision to remain silent, and the trial proceeded as the Chief Justice prophesied, only without the lashes. Maurice Margarot was transported to New South Wales for fourteen years.

Joseph Gerrald was the last man to face trial, on 10 March 1794. Like Muir he was a young idealist just thirty years old with hair worn long as a badge of his radical principles. Freed by his inherited fortune to devote time and resources to political activism, he wrote and published the pamphlet *A Convention the Only Means of Saving Us from Ruin*, advocating an elected convention on the French model chosen by universal suffrage. At his arrest on the floor of the second Edinburgh

Convention he offered up a prayer before the scattering delegates to 'Thou Governor of the Universe' stating 'we are assured that no sacrifice is more acceptable to Thee, than that which is made for the relief of the oppressed'.[32] Although aware of the harsh punishment already meted out to the other defendants and suffering tuberculosis, Gerrald rejected a plan hatched by his friends to jump bail and escape to the United States, because he could not desert the followers he had inspired, insisting '[m]y honour is pledged; and no opportunity for flight shall induce me to violate that pledge'.[33] Gerrald pointed out to the court in his defence that all useful discoveries begin as 'innovations' that run the gauntlet of attempts at suppression, and that progress demanded new doctrines be at least tolerated. When he gave the example of early attempts to persecute Christianity and described Christ as a great reformer, Braxfield joked to his fellow judges in thick brogue 'Muckle he made o' that; he was hanget'.[34]

The jury was persuaded by the Crown's dangerous and flawed argument that to advocate any change to the constitution, such as universal suffrage, was inherently seditious, and as Gerrald admitted to such advocacy, he was guilty. Once again the jury were chosen from a conservative group avowedly opposed to reform, this time called The Friends of the Constitution. Leaving nothing to chance, Braxfield improperly instructed the jury that the accused was 'a very dangerous member of society, for I dare say, he has eloquence enough to persuade the people to rise in arms'. A talent for communication was deemed as menacing as the ideas expressed. Gerrald, coughing with his sickness, told the court that:

> [w]hatever may become of me, my principles will last forever ... whether I be doomed to drag out the remainder of my existence amidst thieves and murderers, a wandering exile on the bleak and melancholy shores of New Holland, my mind, equal to either fortune, is prepared to meet the destiny that awaits it.[35]

The judges obliged with fourteen years, which for a man suffering consumption was a death sentence.[36]

Convicted, the reformers were now offered to the public as traitors who had persuaded France that victory was possible. At Palmer's trial the prosecutor Maconachie alleged that '[i]f it were not for societies calling themselves "Friends of the People"' war would not have happened. Without the efforts of such malcontents, he argued, France would 'never have been so mad as to attack the British nation'.[37] While the government backed the Scottish judges, not everyone in Britain's factionalised parliament agreed. Outraged at the verdicts, influential Whig leader Charles James Fox rose in the House of Commons to criticise what he saw as a dangerous miscarriage of justice, declaring that 'so striking and disgusting are the whole features of this trial' that it made him fear '[i]f the day should ever arrive ... should the tyrannical laws of Scotland ever be introduced in opposition to the humane laws of England'.[38] He did not have to wait long. In the aftermath of the trials, Pitt's Government passed the *Seditious Meetings Act* and *Combination Act* restricting the right of subjects to hold public assemblies or to form organisations to agitate for political reform. Then in May 1794, the *habeas corpus* Acts were suspended in England and Scotland. An arrested suspect could now be detained indefinitely without trial.

Britain's war on France unleashed a form of national paranoia that is still recognisable today. The government of George III was fighting its own version of a 'war on terror', against the extremist ideology of France's ruling Jacobin party, which was characterised by the dictatorial Committee for Public Safety, manipulation of mob violence, ritualised beheadings of enemies, and a missionary zeal to spread revolution beyond its borders. Fearing the export of Jacobinism across the channel via home-grown supporters and publicists, Britain's leaders surrendered traditional liberties to fight revolution abroad and at home, erecting a regime of spies, censors, unfair trials and offshore imprisonment in a distant colonial outpost where the customary rights of free Englishmen did not apply. The Scottish Martyrs risked their own liberty to defend the liberty of others when it was most under threat. Maurice Margarot argued the belief in the inaugural address to the London Corresponding Society that liberty was 'man's birthright' until his death, and that 'his supreme duty' was to preserve that liberty, no matter the hazard.[39] Convicted and taken to prison hulks on the Thames the five men would now put this principle to the test.

An artist's stylised impression of the founding of the settlement at
Sydney Cove, Port Jackson in New South Wales.

The Scottish Martyrs were the first political prisoners to be
transported to Australia, but many more would follow, including:
hundreds of defeated rebels of the United Irishmen's uprisings of 1798
and 1803; assorted naval and military mutineers; waves of English rural
rioters and machine breakers, trade unionists and Chartists, between
1812 and 1848; North American freedom fighters from Upper and
Lower Canada (focused on Toronto and Quebec) and their armed
supporters from the United States, transported between 1839 and 1840;
dissidents from far-flung imperial possessions such as the West Indies
and the Cape Colony; and new generations of Irish rebels, including
thousands of impoverished land-war insurrectionists in the first half
of the nineteenth century, the gentlemanly leaders from the Young
Ireland movement of 1848 and the Fenians—antecedents of the IRA—
who arrived on the last ever convict transport, that arrived in Western
Australia in 1868. Some of the popular rebel and protest movements
took colourful names such as the Ribbonmen and Whiteboys in Ireland

and the Luddites and Captain Swing in England, the last two identified with fictitious folk leaders. Most of these 'politicals' did more than just read a speech or publish a pamphlet. They burned, broke or pillaged the farms and property of those they believed oppressed them, or rose in violent, bloody armed rebellion against the British Government or its colonial representatives. It seems the example made of the Scottish Martyrs was not the hoped-for deterrent.

In all, just over 3600 political prisoners were transported out of a total of approximately 162,000 convicts sent to Australia between 1787 and 1868, a ratio of one in forty-five.[40] This statistically significant figure was arrived at by social historian George Rudé who sifted through the court and convict records of individual prisoners for the entire period of transportation. In his scholarly work *Protest and Punishment*, he breaks this number down into place of origin, gender, offence, time period and, where possible, fate in Australia.[41] The largest nationalities among political prisoners were 2250 from Ireland, 1200 from England, Scotland and Wales, and 151 from North America. Only 120 were women, a much lower proportion than in the general convict population. From the perspective of the authorities, exile to Australia served as a safety valve for the build-up of political pressure, by excising the ringleaders, organisers and propagandists of dangerous radical movements and the rebellious, riotous or disloyal among the common people.

In the case of the Scottish Martyrs, transportation did more than remove seditious radicals and their dangerous ideas from British politics. Skirving and Gerrald would die shortly after arrival, while Muir and Palmer would perish journeying back—Palmer from illness and Muir from wounds inflicted in battle. The story of the Scottish Martyrs was in many ways typical, revealing many of the themes and issues that would re-occur among other groups of political prisoners transported to the Australian colonies.

The 'politicals' were a class apart from the other prisoners. The Martyrs, like many who would follow, were distinguished by education, wealth, connections within society and political support back home. There would be more well-to-do and even aristocratic political prisoners, and most others were respectable workers with trades or agricultural skills. Show trials were used by the authorities to teach a lesson about obedience, loyalty and control. The punishment itself was inhumane and hazardous to health. The Martyrs, like many who came after, were forced to endure poor sanitation, meagre rations and brutality from guards and ordinary criminals in the overcrowded hulks, and then suffered the voyage to New South Wales plagued with disease and threats of mutiny. Yet, once in the colony, their social status and celebrity guaranteed them privileges denied the ordinary criminal convicts, such as land grants while still under sentence, freedom of movement and communication, and exemption from forced labour and assignment. This would be a privilege granted to other gentlemen political leaders but not to working-class rebels. However, the diverging fates of the five Martyrs also illustrated the arbitrary nature of living in a prison, and the compromises with principle necessary to survive, and even thrive. Not surprisingly, men who held liberty and political agitation so dear could not resist meddling in the burgeoning politics of the colony, whether that be protesting the actions of the viceroy and military to the Home Office, or covertly stirring rebellion. The bold escape by one of the Martyrs on an American ship established a precedent that would continue throughout convict transportation, right up to the last political prisoners sent to Western Australia in 1868. Muir and his colleagues would not be the last radicals to exploit the theatrical potential of court, prison and exile for the performance of martyrdom. Like many of the literate political prisoners to come after them, Muir, Palmer and Skirving wrote moving accounts of their trials and punishment, distributed as pamphlets to rally supporters at home, but also to ensure that they would be remembered as martyrs to their cause. Finally, the five so-called Jacobins, like most of the protesters and rebels who came after them, fought for changes to the status quo that eventually came to pass, though seldom in their lifetimes.

Before exploring the Scottish Martyrs' transportation and lives as exiles in Sydney Town, we must take a step back and ask how a country, traditionally regarded as the freest in Europe, became so threatened by dissent that it was prepared to sacrifice cherished liberties and exile pamphleteers and protesters to the ends of the Earth? What compelled gentlemen of wealth and education to risk everything for the cause of reform? Why was the government so alarmed by ideas such as universal suffrage and one-vote-one-value that to us today seem the very essence of Westminster democracy? To answer these questions we must look beyond the immediate political catalyst of the French Revolution, to other revolutions that were changing irrevocably Britain's economy, society and empire.

* * *

THE AGE OF REVOLUTIONS

THE REFORM MOVEMENT TO WHICH THE MARTYRS BELONGED WAS born in the turmoil unleashed by the economic, agricultural, technological and social transformation in eighteenth century Britain that is known to history as the Industrial Revolution, but at root stemmed from the extension of the capitalist market system into all walks of life. In calling this period from the mid-eighteenth to the mid-nineteenth century the 'Age of Revolution', English historian Eric Hobsbawm, following Marx, understood that a revolution in how people made a living was the harbinger of political change.[42] Just as the coming of industrial capitalism tore asunder centuries-old feudal customs, village hamlets and traditional crafts and guilds, it created new categories of work, new forms of wealth, new urban centres, new social classes, new imperial possessions, new possibilities and new conflicts. In this capitalist revolution we can trace the origins of both the upsurge in crime that led to the establishment of a prison colony in New South Wales and the discontent that provoked sedition and even revolution from a succession of political rebels.

Capitalism grew out of the mercantilism of the Elizabethan period, turbo-charged in the seventeenth and eighteenth centuries by global commerce in commodities made possible by the expansion of trade routes across the Atlantic, Indian and Pacific oceans, the acquisition of trading posts, protectorates and colonies in discovered lands and the formation of joint stock trading enterprises such as the East India Company, to exploit these new markets. British trade, backed by growing naval power, led her to acquire an empire circling the globe, that by the late eighteenth century included colonies in North America, the West Indies, the Cape of Africa and Australia, as well as economic and political footholds in India and Africa. It is important when looking at colonial Australia to see it as part of an empire and international trading system in which people, goods and information circulated around the world. In the eighteenth and nineteenth centuries many British subjects, and those in the Empire's thrall, left the small communities in which their parents and grandparents were rooted to traverse the globe in sailing ships, as traders, sailors and soldiers, as administrators and free settlers and as slaves and convicts chained below decks. The glue that bound Britain's growing empire was trade in commodities and labour: tobacco from Virginia, sugar from Jamaica, tea from India and slaves from Africa. As well as a cheap source of labour and materials, the territories of the Empire provided profitable markets for goods manufactured in Britain, which were a spur to accelerated production.

The introduction of the factory system of manufacture in place of the old craft guilds was a great enabler of capitalism, even before the harnessing of new technology, notably the steam engine. One of the early factories, opened in 1769 and owned by potter Josiah Wedgwood, manufactured fine china closely resembling the oriental original in quality and decorated with the latest neo-classical designs. Rather than each item being made by the one craftsman, tasks were broken down into simple routines—repetitive tasks performed in a sequence to a strict time frame. Through this system Wedgwood, not a craft guild, controlled and customised every aspect of production and greatly increased output while reducing labour costs. The master, in his new role of capitalist, had turned craftsmen into a profit-generating machine. However, it was a machine still dependent on the power of human, beast, wind and water. The Industrial Revolution began in earnest in the late eighteenth century when Watt's steam engine was introduced to many British factories. This engine powered other new inventions that performed some of the routine tasks, greatly speeding up the production line, while humans continued to perform those tasks technology could not. Cotton was now spun into textiles on massive steam-powered weaving machines. Great industrial cities grew out of towns located near the coal seams needed to fuel the steam engines, and ports developed to ship in the raw materials and export the refined manufactures to the Empire and beyond. Britain experienced rapid growth in productivity, investment and profits. During the eighteenth century unprecedented fortunes were being made at home and abroad by a new class of entrepreneurs and mercantilists, investors and speculators who were well on the way to making Britain the workshop of the world. Together with accountants, bankers and university-educated lawyers, who managed the financial and legal integrity of commerce, these men of business made up what economists term capitalists and the French call the bourgeoisie. This economically ascendant class would support the cause of liberal political reform in the late eighteenth and nineteenth centuries.

At the other end of the social scale were the people who sold their labour to capitalists in factories, warehouses and mines. In the classic work *The Making of the English Working Class*, British social historian E.P. Thompson examined how this new class was formed as the old guilds and feudal relationships were replaced by the new capitalist bargain where labour power was sold for a fixed time.[43] The precursor to the creation of the English working class was the application of capitalist and scientific principles to farming—an agricultural revolution that greatly increased yield, profits and population, but dispossessed tenant farmers who were evicted from their smallholdings. Between 1760 and 1820 a succession of Enclosure Acts were passed by parliament fencing off land as the private property of squires and aristocrats, replacing the feudal arrangement that had allowed tenants access to common land in exchange for work and tithes. New model farms introduced methods such as crop rotation and agricultural machinery such as threshers, that required less labour and time. While some of the dispossessed found work as paid farm labourers, many sunk into landless and itinerant poverty, exacerbated by new poaching laws against catching game on both private and Crown land. The British commons was effectively privatised, and the customary rights of the common people to grow crops and vegetables, travel pathways and fish and hunt game made way for the new rights of private property. Conflict over wages, labour-saving machines, rising food prices and the abrogation of customary rights became increasingly common, and in times of particular hardship led to outbreaks of rioting and protest. In both Britain and Ireland participants in these rural uprisings would find themselves transported to Australia.

The privatisation of the land and extinguishment of traditional rights to share it was even more extreme on the imperial frontier—in new lands such as North America, and from 1788 in Australia, where Indigenous populations were removed at musket point. In New South Wales, for example, hunting grounds and tracks that had been walked by Aborigines for millennia gave way to fences, stock and homesteads. The human calamity of enclosure in Britain was in part allayed by the ready supply of 'virgin' land on the Empire's edge, that in Australia was stolen from the traditional owners under the self-serving legal fiction of *terra nullius*—the land belonging to no one.

The dispossessed of the British countryside flooded into the old cities like London and the new industrial towns in search of work. Many learned the discipline and trades of the industrial capitalist economy, working long hours for low wages in hazardous, often unsafe conditions. However, industrial workers found some solace in the collective life of factories, mines and construction sites, becoming over a couple of generations the proletariat described by nineteenth century radicals such as Robert Owen and Frederick Engels.[44] Workers tried to improve their conditions and wages by forming associations based on occupations or workplaces in the belief that in unity was strength. These embryonic trade unions were outlawed, and in the first half of the nineteenth century convicted union and Chartist agitators formed another group of political prisoners exiled to Australia.

In an economy suffering boom, bust and oversupply of labour many of the poor failed to find honest work, and took up the trades of the desperate—begging, prostitution, theft, robbery and extortion. The massive population shift from country to city was not unlike that occurring in the developing world today. Shanty towns sprang up and in the absence of the twentieth century welfare safety nets, public housing, town planning, sanitation or schools, degenerated into squalid ghettoes of the despised, deviant and debauched first sensationalised in William Hogarth's famous eighteenth century illustrations of the Georgian underclass. In the move from village to metropolis the old personal controls wielded by parson, squire and neighbours were replaced with the freedom of anonymity and the temptations of so much plenty just within reach. For alongside this poverty was conspicuous consumption by those profiting from empire and industry. Indeed, this was also an age of elegance in which ladies and gents promenaded the streets in fine clothes and filled their houses with luxury goods like Wedgwood's plates and silverware. Shop windows and warehouses presented as cornucopias brimming with produce for those with the money to buy. As new guilds of professional criminals emerged, the lanes and back streets of London and other cities were transformed into rookeries where delinquents and more seasoned criminals could bolt from view to dispose of their ill-gotten loot. In a sense the new criminal class of England had arrived at its own perverse caricature of the enterprise culture that drove the entrepreneurial bourgeoisie on which it preyed.

Blind to the connection between economic transformation and social deviance the propertied classes—new money and aristocrats alike—took alarm at the growth of an underclass out of control in both town and country that seemed to have forsaken honest toil and customary deference for sloth, gin and crime. 'Our people have become what they never were before, cruel and inhuman,' lamented author Henry Fielding.[45] Debates in parliament and the press railed in moral panic about the breakdown in order and an exaggerated threat from below that came to be defined by legislation and moralists alike as the 'criminal classes'. While not political in the sense of organised agitation, the delinquency and criminality of the lower classes was framed as a social problem that required governmental action. The workhouses run by parishes accepted only those who adhered to Christian moral principles and accepted harsh discipline, the so-called deserving poor. The rest of this social detritus would be dealt with by the criminal law.

New types of property produced by Britain's Industrial Revolution led to new types of theft. The old semi-feudal deterrent of hanging the odd felon was of no use to manufacturers, shopkeepers or consumers who wanted thieves caught and their property back. Surveying the application of punitive statutes to the 'vagabonds' of England, Marcus Clarke, author of *For the Term of His Natural Life*, had the radical insight that the law *makes* the criminal.[46] Robert Hughes calculated that between 1660 and 1819 187 new capital offences entered the statute books, six times greater than the previous three centuries. The feared increase in the criminal class was a self-fulfilling prophecy. These laws were mainly to protect property, not the person. The infamous Waltham *Black Act* of 1723 alone prescribed hanging for over two hundred offences, mainly forms of rural protest asserting customary rights, such as poaching fish and game, burning haystacks and writing threatening letters to landlords.[47]

Although the new statutes insisted on the death penalty, any attempt to actually hang all those convicted would make England a charnel house ultimately to the detriment of social order. As elegantly revealed by Douglas Hay in *Albion's Fatal Tree*, the imposition of the death sentence was a discretionary punishment more often observed in the breach.[48] It was in the gift of the Crown to exercise the Royal Prerogative of Mercy and spare the life of a convicted criminal, usually after it was formally requested, and proper obeisance was rendered to the Crown and local authorities who spoke on the felon's behalf. The judiciary itself could also commute a death sentence. By such interplays of mercy and gratitude the ties of obligation between classes could be repaired. But reprieve from the gallows meant a long incarceration as a prisoner of His Majesty, and as the new laws for property took effect the country's small number of gaols were swamped by the tide of commuted prison sentences. Transportation of criminals to colonies across the sea had begun in the seventeenth century, and evolved in the eighteenth century as a more humane alternative to the death sentence that removed the criminal with the finality of death, while cementing social control at home. This paternalist system of deference and clemency was particularly effective in the rural shires where it could compensate for fading feudal ties.

Transportation had a second use. It could provide forced labour for the Empire. Until 1776 many convicts were transported as indentured labour to the North American colonies, such as Georgia, where they worked on farms and plantations as well as public works. However, transportation to North America ceased with the outbreak of the War of Independence, never to recommence. Yet George III continued to grant mercy to the condemned, swelling the prisons to breaking point. The expedient of housing convicts in the hulks of decommissioned ships anchored in the Thames was no long-term solution, as the prison hulks

quickly succumbed to overcrowding and disease. The problem of what
to do with the growing population of convicted criminals led Pitt's
Government to establish a penal colony on the distant Pacific coast of
New Holland, mapped and claimed for George III in 1770 by Captain
James Cook. Only a handful of Europeans had ever seen this place named
New South Wales, but one of them who had, the wealthy naturalist
Sir Joseph Banks, was now Secretary of State. He persuaded Pitt that
Botany Bay, where he and his colleagues had foraged for specimens and
made fleeting observations of the elusive native people, should be the
site for the new settlement. Certainly its geographic isolation, off the
then trade routes, ringed by dense scrub, oceans and spear-wielding
'savages', made it just the spot for a colony of felons. While debate
surrounds possible strategic reasons for also choosing New South Wales,
the immediate cause for the arrival of the First Fleet through the heads
of Sydney Harbour on 26 January 1788 was the crisis in social control
brought on by the rapid transformation of Britain from a rural to an
urban-industrial economy.

As Manning Clark demonstrated, it is wrong to romanticise
Australia's convict transportees as poor unfortunates simply caught up
in an unjust system: the vast majority of convicts over the eighty-year
period of transportation were indeed incorrigible recidivists, earning
a living as criminal professionals and habituated to dishonesty and
casual viciousness.[49] By any measure, late eighteenth century Britain had
a crime wave on its hands. Nevertheless, economic and social conditions
did provide the context in which deviancy and criminality could thrive
among the poor, and in that sense Australia's involuntary settlers were
casualties of change. However, not all convicts were common criminals.
Here we come to the third use of transportation and the focus of this
book: as a safety valve for easing political pressures building up in
Britain, Ireland and other problem territories of the Empire. When
Robert Hughes claimed that there were 'only a few' convicts sent
out for 'political offences' he was focused on overt political crimes
such as treason and sedition, failing to count those transported for
their part in the waves of social protest that erupted in Britain and
Ireland in the first half of the nineteenth century.[50] Rudé's figure of
3600 transported political prisoners, or one in forty-five of all convicts,

is borne out by the records, and points to a significant crisis in authority and social harmony.[51] There were three broad categories of political prisoners transported to Australia. First, social protesters, drawn from poor rural or urban working-class communities who responded to economic distress (often caused by low wages, food shortages or the introduction of new technology) by rioting, organised acts of sabotage (notably machine breaking), forming associations such as trade unions or rising in more widespread insurrection. Secondly, nationalist rebels, usually republicans, engaged in often violent liberation struggles against British colonial control in their territory, most particularly in Ireland and Canada. Thirdly, political reformers, beginning with the Scottish Martyrs, who were inspired by the American and French revolutions, agitating to democratise the British constitution. These three types of political rebellion were of course connected, not least by their origins in the economic and political revolutions of the eighteenth century.

* * *

THE CAUSE OF LIBERTY:
A REVOLUTION POSTPONED

THE SCOTTISH MARTYRS WERE PLAYERS IN A POLITICAL CONFLICT between two very different ideas of liberty. The English had long boasted of their liberty under the constitution, relative to the absolute monarchies of continental Europe, with their standing armies and secret police.[52] In comparison to the France of Louis XIV or Prussia, Englishmen claimed with validity to be protected from arbitrary interference by the state in their lives and property. The boast 'Britons never will be slaves' meant liberty from government, guaranteed by the rule of law, explicit in which were rights such as equality before the law, search warrants, trial by jury, limited free speech and a constitution curtailing monarchy, composed of accumulated statutes, conventions and common law stretching back through the Bill of Rights of 1689, the Glorious Revolution of 1688, the *Habeas Corpus Act* of 1679 and the Magna Carta of 1215.[53] Indeed the rights of the free-born Englishman were said to have become a focus of resistance to the 'Norman Yoke' following the invasion of 1066 and have antiquity in the Dark Age councils of the Anglo-Saxons. This type of mythic liberty was rubbery enough to be all things to all people, and as E.P. Thompson has shown, was invoked by 'patrician, demagogue and radical alike', in causes as varied as '[p]atriotism, nationalism, even bigotry and repression', as well as piecemeal electoral reform.[54] Thus in the midst of the war with the French revolutionary government, English patriots could assert:

> *One nation is brave and free–*
> *Resolv'd to conquer or to die,*
> *True to their KING, their LAWS, their LIBERTY.*[55]

The idea of free-born Englishmen was inherently conservative. When elite reformers and ordinary protesters alike acted to protect the liberties of Englishmen they did so in deference to the law and custom, rather than an appeal to abstract rights or revolutionary change, defending rather than overturning the constitution. But by the late eighteenth century, the traditional, legalistic form of English liberty was failing to keep pace with expectations, and came under challenge—in both the American colonies and at home—from radical outriders of the new economy who began to associate 'liberty' with republican ideas of popular participation and the 'self-evident' 'rights of man'.

Unlike most convicts, the transported Scottish Martyrs came not from the lower class, but from the property-owning families who had built capital out of wholesale trade or scientific farming and had acquired wealth enough to send their sons to university, who in turn entered gentlemanly professions such as the law, the clergy and scholarship. Why would such men turn on the political status quo that had given them so much?

British industrialists, merchants and professionals enjoyed increasing economic clout in the eighteenth century, but they were locked out of political power, and this caused resentment, and also hope. While uprooting traditional communities, the individualism unleashed by laissez faire capitalism was also a liberating influence. Freedom in the marketplace proselytised by economist Adam Smith had a way

A cameo of Thomas Muir (1765–1799), who wore his hair long and
free in the French revolutionary style.

of encouraging the desire for other types of freedom, especially in the political sphere. The ideal of political liberty was articulated and developed by philosophers in France and Britain—by thinkers like Descartes, Rousseau, Voltaire, Hume and Paine—during a period of intellectual inquiry known to historians as the Enlightenment in which reason, not divine right or inherited title, was posited as the basis for authority. Rousseau argued in the *Social Contract* (1762) that 'Man is born free and everywhere he is in chains'. Spanning the late seventeenth and the eighteenth century, the Enlightenment sparked the modern movement for democratic reform we know as liberalism, which would not achieve all its aims until the twentieth century. In late eighteenth century Britain, such ideas became the talk of the new coffee houses where modish moneyed intellectuals like Muir, Margarot and Skirving gathered to discuss and assay the problems of the day. A radical community hungry for political change had emerged among the country's best and brightest.

From the outset this belief in political liberty came up hard against an entrenched political oligarchy that looked back to an earlier, pre-capitalist time. As so often happens, the political system had not kept up with economic and social change, and remained the bastion of older vested interests, notably the great landowners and country squires. While the assertion of parliamentary sovereignty over the monarch in the English Civil War and Glorious Revolution of the seventeenth century had made Britain the most liberal polity in Europe, it had atrophied, and even gone backwards, in the face of economic and demographic change during the eighteenth century. Indulging the popular romantic myth of the free-born Englishman, Margarot could argue with some conviction at the Edinburgh Convention that the 'tree of feudality' planted by the Norman conquest, but pruned by Magna Carta and the regicide of Charles I, was once again in bloom.[56]

The electoral laws of the late eighteenth century were a hangover from a century earlier when landed interests claimed a dominant role through their economic and military power. At the outbreak of the French Revolution in 1789 the majority of Britons could not vote for a Member of Parliament, and only a very small proportion of people could stand as one. Business people who were contributing so much wealth to the national coffers naturally wanted a say in how that money was spent, yet many in this class were locked out by restrictions on the franchise, and electoral rorting meant that many new industrial towns were unable to elect a Member of Parliament. According to Thomas Hardy—the tradesman made good who founded the reform group, the London Corresponding Society, in which Margarot was a leading figure—the majority of members in the House of Commons were chosen by only 12,000 voters. There had been no redrawing of electoral boundaries as populations had shifted over the previous century. Depopulated rural hamlets, termed rotten boroughs, continued to return a member to parliament, while new industrial towns had no representative. At the end of the eighteenth century the cities of Birmingham and Leeds (populations of 40,000 and 20,000 respectively) had no Member of Parliament, while the country electorate of Old Sarum returned two members despite having only seven voters.[57]

England and Scotland had shared the one parliament in Westminster since 1707, and the limitation of the franchise had passionate critics in both countries. However, the gerrymander was compounded in England by the *Landed Property Qualification Act* that had been passed by a newly elected Tory Government in 1710 to disadvantage their opponents, the more liberal Whigs, who received votes from urban businessmen. Henceforth, only men who owned land to the value of £300 in borough seats and £600 in the country could stand as candidates for the House of Commons.[58] Such men were the conservative heartland of the Tory Party and also powerful among the Whigs. This Act was a cause of particular grievance for the newly prosperous middle class of business and the professions, especially those residing in the boom towns that were remaking Britain. The innovation of the rule of law had been good for business, but now businessmen wanted a say over the making of that law. Their cause was initially advanced by the Whig party that, while dominated by great landowners too, had greater sympathy for mercantile and manufacturing interests. Local aristocrats wielded disproportionate control in rotten boroughs, giving an electoral advantage to the Tories. This influence was formalised in the so-called pocket boroughs, whereby the largest local landowner was entitled to sell a seat to a candidate and control how they voted in the House of Commons.

The power of government over the legislature was further strengthened by the abandonment of annual parliaments, weakening accountability to the electors.

While the conservatives in both parties who controlled the Houses of Lords and Commons encouraged the growth of capitalism and happily took their cut of the new wealth, they did not want to share power with the new men and those below them. Not unreasonably, the bourgeoisie wanted political power to correspond with their growing economic power, and to remake society in their own image. This is why the British radical movement of the late eighteenth century drew most of its supporters from the so-called middle classes of commerce and the educated professions. Reform was to be brought about in the name of the people, rather than by them. However, by the end of the century the liberal reformers would be joined by skilled craftspeople who were more critical of the connection between progress and capitalism, and in the nineteenth century the working class would develop their own union and socialist reform agenda as an alternative to middle-class liberalism.

Rebellion against the unrepresentative nature of British governance first began in 1776 in its outermost territories—among men of property in the North American colonies. The intransigence of the British Government when the colonists refused to pay taxes without representation sparked a liberal revolution we know as the American War of Independence. At the outset of that revolution the ideas of the Enlightenment were elegantly encapsulated in the Declaration of Independence, in a call to action drafted by Thomas Jefferson, that asserted:

> *We hold these truths to be self-evident, that all men are created equal, that they are endowed by their Creator with certain unalienable Rights, that among these are Life, Liberty and the pursuit of Happiness ...* [59]

It was during the American Revolution that Tom Paine emerged as a radical pamphleteer for the new radical form of liberty. He argued for a republic free of the Crown where the government derived its authority from 'the consent of the governed', to quote the *Declaration of Independence*. An inventor, businessman and one-time privateer of Quaker background, Paine moved to America in 1774 to seek his fortune, and joined the revolution against his homeland. His important contribution was penning the pamphlet *Common Sense*, which George Washington praised for having 'worked a powerful change in the minds of many men'. Paine's ideas would be influential in Britain and Ireland as well, where his book in defence of the French Revolution, *Rights of Man*, sold almost a million copies. His proselytising so worried the British Government that mere distribution of his works by some of the Martyrs was taken as proof-positive of sedition.

With the defeat of George III's forces, the constitution hammered out by the Continental Congress enshrined in the new republic many liberal principles. The United States of America would henceforth be a beacon to reformers, radicals and revolutionaries in Europe, especially in France and the vanquished superpower, Great Britain. While the most advanced democracy in the world, the United States remained compromised by the continuation of slavery and restriction of the franchise to men who owned property or paid taxes in many states. This was hardly surprising as the revolution's leading lights wanted freedom to pursue wealth and accumulate property, and slaves were a valuable form of property for plantation owners in the south. Furthermore women, with or without property, were excluded from voting or running for office. Nonetheless, with between 60 and 70 per cent of white men enjoying the right to vote after the revolution, the United States was the most democratic nation on Earth. While the British reformers of the 1790s were inspired by the American War of Independence and its new republican constitution they wanted to extend the right to vote to all adult men, regardless of their wealth or station in life. Some of their associates, notably Mary Wollstonecraft in *A Vindication of the Rights of Women* (1792), argued that universal suffrage must also be extended to women. They all agreed on the abolition of rotten and pocket boroughs and the property restrictions on standing as Members for Parliament. ·

* * *

THE WAR ON TERROR

IT WAS THE REVOLUTION IN FRANCE THAT BOTH INSPIRED THE British reformers to action, and provoked their opponents to use transportation to crush them and their organisations. Muir made passionate speeches defending the revolution in France.

In the spirit of cosmopolitan fraternity, when the British radicals looked to France they saw professional educated middle-class men like themselves finding common cause with the people against absolute monarchy, aristocratic privilege and feudalism. The leading French revolutionaries such as Robespierre and Danton were lawyers who claimed to speak on behalf of modernity, reason and enlightenment. English romantic poets also rallied to the banners and barricades of revolution in its first years. Journeying to Paris to observe the fall of the *Ancien Régime* firsthand, Coleridge 'hoped and feared', while an ecstatic Wordsworth enthused:

> *Bliss was it in that dawn to be alive,*
> *but to be young was very heaven!*[60]

It was in this spirit of idealism that young radicals like Muir and Gerrald forsook the powdered wigs of the older generation, and grew their hair long in imitation of the shaggy manes of the revolutionaries —a gesture as potent as the Che Guevara style of the student protesters of the late 1960s, that would give great offence to their judges.[61]

Even Pitt, keen to exact vengeance on Louis XVI for supporting the American revolutionaries, secretly financed the French revolutionaries in their struggle with the King—a contest analogous with England's own assertion of parliamentary supremacy in the Civil War and Glorious Revolution of the seventeenth century. However, as with the English struggle, moderates lost control of events in France. Instead, a republic was declared and a reign of terror unleashed on the aristocracy by Jacobin hardliners who dominated the new French National Convention. Now British values of moderation, class hierarchy and constitutional monarchy itself were under threat. As the revolution's Committee of Public Safety began to turn on its own leaders—the revolution devouring its own children—even the poets' enthusiasm began to cool. The aggressive resolve of the Jacobins in Paris to carry the flame of revolution to Europe's monarchies made war with Britain inevitable, and meant British radicals who promoted their goals of liberty, equality and fraternity could be committing treason.

Liberal historians have traditionally criticised this flirtation with French Jacobinism as a diversion from pragmatic parliamentary reform.[62] However in recent years historians Elaine McFarland and Nigel Leask have re-evaluated the Francophilia of the British radicals of the 1790s as symptomatic of a new cosmopolitanism forging closer links with reformers in other countries and internationalising radical politics.[63] The Society of the Friends of the People looked not only to France, but also to the United States, and closer to home, to the United Irishmen. Thomas Muir, taking advantage of his forced exile, would prove to be an exemplar of the globetrotting activist and propagandist, even calling himself a 'Citizen of the World'.[64]

For Tories and Whigs alike who rallied to the Crown it was self-evident that pamphleteers, rabble rousers and even poets who promoted the goals of the revolution were supporting terror, mob rule, even regicide. They need look no further than the writings and activities of the reformers' hero, Tom Paine, who returned to England in 1792, ostensibly to market a new invention, an iron bridge, and was immediately charged with sedition. The just-published *Rights of Man* had condemned Britain's monarchy and aristocracy as institutionalised plunder originating in a mediaeval 'banditti of ruffians' who overran the country, and mocked the much venerated Constitution as a 'sepulchre of precedent', whereby 'the rights of the living' were controlled by the 'manuscript-assumed authority of the dead'.[65] To British reformers accustomed to the constitutional approach, Paine's 'year zero' advocacy of revolution was alternatively a shock or an inspiration. To the government it was Jacobin treachery on British soil. Paine then confirmed the conservative propaganda by fleeing to France at the invitation of its National Assembly, where he was honoured as a hero of the Revolution and granted French citizenship. Paine was tried for sedition in absentia in England, and found guilty. Delegates from some British radical groups had attended the National Convention in France in November 1792, ahead of war being declared, supporting France's determination to use her arms to bring down 'tyrants' in Europe. War meant that the authorities could dangle threats of treason and the gallows. Braxfield warned Skirving at his trial that 'sedition ... [is] violating the peace and order of society', but 'when sedition has a tendency to overturn the constitution of this country it borders upon high treason'.[66]

Were the Martyrs really the dangerous revolutionaries and potential regicides alleged by the prosecution in their trials? The majority of British reformers were far more moderate than the revolutionary Tom Paine, believing liberty to be a national birthright compatible with the Crown and the Westminster constitution. Rising Whig leader William Pitt the Younger had himself championed the cause of electoral reform on his way up the greasy pole of Westminster politics. As Prime Minister he had earlier introduced a Bill to abolish rotten boroughs but this was defeated by vested interests in the House of Commons. Other pillars of the Whig establishment to advocate democratic reform included John Wilkes, who unsuccessfully introduced the first Bill for parliamentary reform in 1776. Even after the French Revolution, most reform advocates, including the Martyrs, believed that the constitution could be democratised while preserving the monarchy—what they called a 'crowned republic'. In the 1790s, some of the reform groups named themselves Friends of the Constitution to underline their loyalty to a system they hoped would continue to prove adaptable. Members of Muir's organisation swore 'adherence to the Government of Great Britain, as established by King, Lords and Commons'.[67]

Reformers believed that lack of democracy led to poor government by encouraging corruption. Margarot argued with precision in the London Corresponding Society that 'unequal', 'partial' and 'inadequate' representation resulted in oppressive taxes, unjust laws, profligacy with public money and limitations on liberty.[68] Far from embryonic socialists who wanted to redistribute property they were arguing for fiscal responsibility and to stop government 'picking their own pockets'. As men of some property, the Martyrs spoke for those who resented taxes imposed arbitrarily on the business and professional people without representation, an echo of the American complaint. As Margarot explained at his trial, 'I feel my pockets emptied with taxes; I feel my liberties taken one after another'.[69] They believed that the cavalier actions of government that hurt both the middle classes and the labouring classes with taxes and workhouses would be moderated if these groups were enfranchised. Logically, a parliament accountable to all voters would have to be mindful of the consequences of laws on all classes and 'diminish the weight of their taxes'.[70] In keeping with the reform movement's bourgeois inclinations, one of the main objections to the war with France was that it was bad for British business.[71] The Palmer/Mealmaker pamphlet argued that 'by [the war] your commerce is sore cramped and almost ruined', while the second Edinburgh Convention complained that the 'laudable industry' of the 'manufacturer' has been 'arrested in its progress'.[72]

There was a strong Christian dimension to the reform cause. Many activists, such as the anti-slavery campaigner and independent Christian MP William Wilberforce, were Evangelical Protestants. Muir was active in the Presbyterian church. One of the Martyrs, Thomas Palmer, was a clergyman who came to radical dissent through Anglicanism and the Unitarian rejection of the Holy Trinity. As well as questioning many of the metaphysical and mystical trappings of traditional Christianity, such as the Virgin Birth, Unitarianism advocated living an ethical selfless life according to Christ's example, which had radical implications. In the 1780s Palmer moved from writing tracts on religion to pamphlets supporting universal suffrage and parliamentary reform, without losing the evangelical impulse to preach what he saw as 'truth'. Skirving had also trained for the church, before making his career in academia and farming. Christian evangelicals found vindication for social justice and the equality of all people in the Gospels. Protestantism also provided ideological succour to both the work ethic and operation of the free market that was building British capitalism. In a speech to the second Edinburgh Convention on 19 November it was argued that the teachings of Jesus could alleviate national debt and help commerce and industry to prosper.[73]

Frank Clune, in his sympathetic study of the Scottish Martyrs, stressed the essential moderation of their platform in the context of Britain's tradition of constitutional evolution. However, consistent with most liberal historians he admonished their 'reckless flights of oratory and enthusiasm' that needlessly provoked the authorities despite the justice of their cause.[74] Thomas Muir was by nature a reasonable man, cautioning crowds against insurrection, and was described by

Cockburn as 'free of that wildness of temperament which sometimes inflames reformers into absurdity of project and ardour of disposition'.[75] Nevertheless his ideas, methods and affiliations were revolutionary in the context of the time.

Why did men of liberal disposition become known as British Jacobins? It did not help that some reformers seemed to side with the enemy and exhibit zeal for the French Revolution against their own government. The pamphlet published by Palmer warned Britons that '[y]ou are plunged into war, by a wicked ministry and a compliant parliament, who seem careless and unconcerned for your interest, the end and design of which is almost too horrid to relate, the destruction of a people, merely because they will be free'.[76] For Judge Abercrombie the worst aspect of this document was its publication

> *after the French Revolution had taken place [and] ... agitated the public mind; after unheard of crimes, unexampled in the history of nations had been committed ... after they had poisoned the minds of the lower order of the people; and after an alarm had been spread in this country.*[77]

At Skirving's trial the second Edinburgh Convention was admonished for dating minutes not by the Christian calendar, but from the date of the first Edinburgh Convention, in imitation of the French National Convention. Muir expressed solidarity with the French revolutionaries and exhorted people to read Tom Paine's *Rights of Man*, which not only supported the French Revolution but also predicted that the European monarchies would fall within seven years and be replaced by American-style republics. Worse still, ahead of the first Edinburgh Convention, Margarot had delivered a speech of congratulations from the London Corresponding Society to the French National Convention that predicted a progressive alliance of the people of the United States, France and Britain that would 'give freedom to Europe and peace to the world'.[78] It is difficult to determine whether Muir was really trying to plead for Louis XVI's life or was trying to escape, but during his ill-fated trip to Paris, he met with key revolutionaries such as Barras, la Fayette and even Paine.[79] To appreciate the danger attributed to such liaisons by conservatives, think of the alarm with which al-Qaeda connections are viewed today. Defiant demonstrations, dubious French connections and inflammatory literature suggest a strong, if naïve, identification with the Jacobins, and made it easier for their opponents to convict them.

The authorities were especially alarmed at any alliance between reformers and the lower classes. Braxfield admonished Muir for creating discontent in 'ignorant country people' against the current constitution.[80] Palmer's local Friends of Liberty association was 'composed chiefly of tradesmen and labourers'.[81] The second Edinburgh Convention made the mistake of calling on the 'rabble' 'by remembrance of their patriotic ancestors, who shed their blood in the cause of freedom'. This was a blatant appeal to Scottish insurgents such as Robert Bruce and William Wallace, who raised armies against the English. Such speeches threatened to take the movement beyond the polite debating societies of university towards the cross-class alliances that made for revolution in France.

Even worse from the perspective of the British Government, the conventions in Edinburgh declared solidarity with the Society of United Irishmen, an overtly republican and increasingly revolutionary group pledged to the granting of full political rights to Catholics and Presbyterians and ending English colonial rule in Ireland. Reading 'aloud' a letter from the United Irishmen in support of the Edinburgh Convention was one of the crimes of sedition brought against Muir. The 3000-word epistle praised the 'Reformers in Scotland' for 'openly, actively and urgently willing a Reform in parliament'. Muir was known to be critical of the 1707 Act of Union between Scotland and England, and his endorsement of the United Irishmen was seen as stoking the fires of Scottish nationalism, that would ultimately lead to the emergence of a United Scotsmen independence movement.[82] The Convention sensed the danger in Muir's letter and diplomatically declined to support the Irish radicals. Yet Muir continued to liaise with them, meeting with leading United Irishmen in Dublin and Belfast after he fled Paris.[83] Notwithstanding the legitimacy of the United Irishmen's grievances, this movement posed a real and present danger to British rule in Ireland, and with French support would lead a bloody rebellion in 1798. Savagely suppressed by the British, United Irish rebels were destined to provide the next and biggest wave of political prisoners transported to Australia (the subject of the next chapter). However principled or naïve their motives, seeking support for the Irish republican cause was a serious miscalculation on the part of Muir and other hardliners meeting in Edinburgh, making it easier for their opponents to discredit them as disloyal and seditious.

It is significant that the Martyrs' crime was sedition, not treason. They had not participated in armed insurrection, but fought with ideas and words.[84] However, the very effectiveness of Muir, Margarot and Palmer as users of media to promote their cause—whether publishing tracts, speeches, journalism and even poetry—instilled alarm in the ruling oligarchy.[85] Accordingly they were convicted for writing and distributing pamphlets, 'reading aloud' and 'poison[ing] the minds of the lower order of the people'.[86] As Leask has recently argued, the Martyrs thought of themselves as citizens of the 'republic of letters', an allegorical term used to describe the eighteenth century public sphere we call the Enlightenment, in which men—and some notable women like Wollstonecraft—wrote, discussed and debated ideas through a network of societies, journals, salons and coffee houses.[87] Believing that progress was brought about by the dissemination of ideas and information, reformers formed 'Corresponding' Societies to spread the word, rather than militias to storm the Bastille.[88] But with the political paranoia of the 1790s this republic of the mind came under pressure from the state, radicalising these liberal 'men of letters' at the same time that genres and technologies for communicating ideas were becoming more diverse, sophisticated and international. In language echoing today's debates about the internet, Muir asked the jury whether suppression of literature was even possible in an age where 'the works of Mr Burke and Thomas Paine, flew with a rapidity to every corner of the land, hitherto unexampled in the history of political science'.[89]

The media savvy of a literate young man such as Muir was not only very modern, but also revolutionary. This was because the publications circulated by groups like the Friends of the People were not 'authorised' at a time when the British Government regulated the content of journalism through a press licence—a tax designed specifically to shut down a burgeoning radical press. Furthermore, a range of severe punishments remained on the statute book as a warning to those who would print or disseminate dissent. Britain would not have a truly free press until the mid-nineteenth century. The popularisation of such illegal publications threatened to de-legitimise the bonds of deference that underpinned the agrarian hierarchy, and might encourage the people to rise up, as similar publications and oppositional journalism had done in the lead-up to the American and French revolutions. As media scholar John Hartley has argued, the creation of popular readerships in America and France by adversarial journalism stimulated the empowering idea of popular sovereignty.[90] In frustration at attempts to suppress publications, Muir told the court it may as well

> *bring an indictment against the alphabet itself, as it is the source of the evil you dread, as its parts form the components of sentences and paragraphs, which may contain the most dangerous sedition, and most horrible treason.*[91]

Unpersuaded by such arguments, Pitt's Government would introduce still tougher controls on free speech and the press. For the authorities it was not just what the radicals said, but how they broadcast their message and who received it. The oligarchy may have had cause to worry, as a dissenting and free press would march arm in arm with the advance of liberal democracy.

Even within the limitations on freedom of speech at the time, eminent jurist H.T. Cockburn argued that on the evidence presented, Muir should not have been found guilty of making seditious speeches.[92] He had promoted legal methods, condemned revolution and declared his preference for monarchy. Eventually, with the passage of the Great Reform Bill forty years later in 1832 these methods would prevail. However, in 1793 the landed oligarchy that ruled Britain was not about to surrender its prerogatives on the strength of reasoned arguments. Like the Communist Party elite of China today, the Whigs, and the Tories before them, were happy to see their country prosper from an economic and industrial revolution, but were not prepared to share power with the capitalists and workers behind the miracle or tolerate public expression of such a proposition. Braxfield was speaking for the ruling interests against the aspirations of the new rich when he smugly asserted at Muir's trial that

*[a] government in every country should be just like a corporation;
and in this country, it is made up of the landed interests, which alone
has the right to be represented ... As for the rabble, who have nothing
but personal property, what hold has the nation of them? ... They
may pack up all their property on their backs, and leave the country
... but landed property cannot be removed.*[93]

The Society of Friends of the People believed that all men should vote, and this extended beyond self-made entrepreneurs and professionals to the workers and unemployed, who lacked education, land and property. '[U]niversal suffrage ... Nothing can be so absurd,' scoffed Lord Swinton at Skirving's trial.[94] Conservatives such as Swinton and Braxfield would do whatever it took to protect their privileges.

The enthusiastic embrace of suppression by Pitt and his government can be explained by the immediate emergency of war, which for a time seemed to threaten national survival. The Prime Minister spurned the reform cause he had earlier encouraged and cut adrift men who looked at him to preserve, and even advance, British liberties. Again, the modern reader is familiar with leaders who sacrifice their early idealism to attain and hold power, and reformers who embrace conservatives to prosecute war. Indeed, this 'Pittite' coalition, forged in the heat of this war with revolution abroad and at home, would form the nucleus of a new Tory 'Conservative Party' following Napoleon's defeat.

The swift suppression of the British reform movement would radicalise as well as intimidate. Having tasted the batons of the court's hired goons, Margarot began to contemplate armed resistance. Writing from prison in the aftermath of his conviction, he wrote to a fellow Corresponding Society member advising that the poor should follow the example of the rich and form armed associations to protect their interests. However, the letter was intercepted by the Bow Street Runners (the antecedents of police) to be used in a case being prepared against Thomas Hardy.

In his scholarly examination of sedition trials in Scotland, Cockburn argued that because the Martyrs were subjected to 'political prosecutions, during a period of great political excitement', it was important for the court to have conducted itself 'calmly, impartially, and decorously'. However, instead the judges displayed bias and relished in the convictions, throwing the legitimacy of the verdicts into question.[95] Muir's jury of 'handpicked zealots for the status quo', to use Cockburn's description, set the pattern for the other trials. That it was harder to secure a guilty verdict for sedition from an English jury was demonstrated by the trial of Hardy who was acquitted on similar evidence. Liberal-minded opinion leaders in England, concerned that the Scottish Martyrs had suffered a miscarriage of justice, wrote letters to the press. William Godwin, earnest radical and husband of feminist Mary Wollstonecraft and father of Mary Shelley, advised the editor of the *Morning Chronicle* that '[t]his, sir, is a species of punishment scarcely precedented in the annals of mankind'. If punishment must be inflicted, he reasoned, better it be observed by one's countryman, but 'to transport me to the other side of the globe, that they may wreak their vengeance on me unobserved, is base, coward-like, and infamous'.[96] He condemned Pitt's 'atrocious despotism' for 'declaim[ing] against the French', while 'imitat[ing] them in their most horrible atrocities'.[97]

The Martyrs also had supporters at Westminster. Following the trials of Muir and Palmer, the prominent liberal-leaning Whig politicians Charles James Fox, Earl Stanhope, Lord Lauderdale and Anglo-Irish playwright Richard Sheridan criticised the severity of the sentences in parliament and demanded they be disallowed. Sheridan presented a petition that Palmer's verdict be struck out as *'illegal, unjust, oppressive,* and *unconstitutional'*.[98] Fox pointed out the clear hypocrisy that Pitt himself had once proposed similar reforms. However, the Home Secretary, Lord Dundas, was determined to make an example of the five men as a warning to others who might contemplate similar actions. Back in Scotland their example appears to have made an impression on her greatest living poet, Robert Burns, who following the trials of Muir and Palmer penned the rallying ode to Bruce's victory over the English at the Battle of Bannockburn, 'Scots wha hae wi' Wallace bled':

> *Lay the proud usurpers low!*
> *Tyrants fall in every foe!*
> *Liberty's in every blow!*
> *Let us do, or die!*[99]

BOUND FOR BOTANY BAY

WITH JUSTICE SEEN TO BE DONE, THE SCOTTISH MARTYRS WERE
taken in chains to the hulks moored on the Thames to await transportation
to New South Wales. Here they suffered the great indignity for men of
their social standing of labouring in work gangs with the other convicts,
on show for the public. With withering sarcasm Margarot thanked the
government for 'all the severities experienced … by your express orders:
bolts, padlocks, handcuffs, confinement in damp pestilential places along
with fellow felons, stinted ship allowances of provisions'.[100] Their place of
confinement, wrote Palmer, 'was continually wet and cold in the day time;
and in the night it was hot almost to suffocation by twenty-four persons
being put in a small place under close wooden hatchways unperforated by
a single hole'.[101] Due to the unhygienic conditions on the hulks, Palmer
became seriously ill, and feared for his life.

However, once at sea they were allowed privileges not available
to the ordinary felons. Transported together on board the *Surprize*, in
February 1794, Muir, Palmer, Skirving and Margarot were not chained
below decks with the other eighty-three prisoners, but were allowed cabin
accommodation and the freedom to move about the ship, on the orders
of Undersecretary of State Nicholas Nepean. Palmer was allowed to bring
along his servant, a young man named James Ellis, who sailed with him
and presumably attended to his master. Margarot was granted permission
to bring his wife, who shared with the children of free settlers, John
Boston and his wife. Unbeknownst to the authorities, Boston was a close
radical confederate of Palmer who had resolved to flee the government
crackdown and keep his friend company. Gerrald would not depart for
another year, enduring the rank conditions of the hulks with disastrous
consequences for his health.

Even before leaving port, Margarot set the pattern for his long
exile by writing to Home Secretary Dundas to clarify his status on
arrival at Botany Bay, wondering 'am I to be a slave, the transferable
property of the King of Great Britain, and be forced to labour under
the goad of a task-master? … or am I on landing there to be restored to
liberty?'[102] While no reply was forthcoming, Margarot was to enjoy both
fates—freedom of movement and forced labour during his time in New

South Wales. These were important questions for political prisoners and the day-to-day reality of their legal situation in the colony remained ambiguous in that any privileges they enjoyed were at the discretion of the governor. In fact, as 'gentlemen' it was understood that they would be allowed freedoms denied other convicts but the undersecretary of the Home Office had written to Lieutenant-Governor Francis Grose instructing him to 'keep a watchful eye' on the political prisoners lest they undertake action that is 'hostile to the peace and good order of your government' especially 'any publication of a seditious or dangerous tendency'.[103] This was effectively encouragement to spy on and censor the Martyrs. With regard to the Machiavellian Margarot this was prescient, if ineffective, advice.

Several months from England, a rumour accusing Palmer and Skirving of hatching a mutiny reached the captain, and the two were escorted at gunpoint to a cell where they spent the remainder of the voyage, stripped of all privileges. The alleged co-conspirators among a group of convicted soldier deserters were flogged and placed in 60 pound (27 kilogram) leg irons. Later, Muir was also detained after being caught in conversation with Skirving. However, it appears that the three were guilty of no more than discoursing in their usual political banter, and this was construed as plotting insurrection. The chief peddler of this plot was a convicted forger, John Grant, who had worked for Dundas in Scotland and may have been placed among the Martyrs as an agent-provocateur to bring them undone. Palmer and Skirving had no doubt he was a spy, and claimed he had spun a similar yarn about them on the ship from Scotland to London.[104] More mysteriously, we know from the letters and testimony of the three that they also believed Margarot to have accused them to the captain in order to maintain his freedom of the ship. They observed him 'paying his court' to the captain, 'unblushingly appear[ing] as his councillor [sic], friend and confident' and speaking with him 'in a confidential whisper'.[105] As a result Margarot was frozen out by his fellow Martyrs, and would spend the rest of his sentence 'in conventry' as Palmer put it. Hughes reasons that Margarot likely had a 'nervous breakdown' on the ship, but his future Machiavellian dealings with colonial authority suggest he decided to play a double game, whether to guarantee his survival, or to ensure he advanced to a position where he could wreak maximum damage on his gaolers.[106] Meanwhile, confined below decks in a makeshift cabin divided from the sixty female convicts by 'only a small wooden partition' the Reverend Palmer and Skirving endured five months 'in the midst of that infernal brothel' where 'the women were perpetually engaged in clamours, brawls and fighting', and trading sexual favours with the sailors.[107]

On arrival at Port Jackson, Palmer and Skirving were able to persuade Lieutenant-Governor Grose that far from being mutineers, they were the victims of a miscarriage of justice hatched by less honourable characters on board the *Surprize*. To the extent that there was trouble brewing, it was confined to the convicted soldiers with a history of mutiny in Canada who were embittered at being sentenced to serve in the New South Wales Corps. Together with Muir and the ostracised Margarot, the notorious Jacobins happily discovered they were to be treated as gentlemen in the colony. Only Britain's stratified class society, and the special nature of sedition as a political crime, can explain the special treatment afforded the Scottish Five relative to the harsh regime that confronted ordinary criminals from the working and so-called criminal classes. Not for the Martyrs the convict lottery of chain gangs, barrack accommodation, assignment to officers or free settlers and the ever-present threat of the lash. As per his instructions from London, Grose kept a close eye on them. He offered Palmer 'every indulgence' on condition he 'avoid on all occasions a recital of those Politicks which have produced in you the miseries a man of your feelings and abilities must at this time undergo'.[108] This was the paradox that ultimately wore them down: men who valued political freedom were confined in a place where all power was vested in one man and enforced by the motley gang of officers who commanded the New South Wales Corps. As long as they abstained from political agitation the habits of class deference and the gentlemanly code of conduct would shield the Martyrs from the excesses of military rule and extend to them some of the privileges enjoyed by the officers.

These included freedom to move about the colony and their own brick houses on the eastern side of the Tank Stream. As men of means they were allowed to purchase land for cultivation. Muir bought a 30-acre (12 hectare) farm from another convict on the north shore of Sydney harbour at what would later become Milson's Point. Palmer purchased

100 acres (40 hectares) of land to the west in what is now the suburb of Stanmore. Skirving bought 100 acres in modern-day Petersham, which he named new Strathruddie after the home in Scotland where he had left his wife and two sons.

Yet acreages and houses were of little use to either Skirving or Gerrald. Skirving had weakened on board ship, and his health continued to deteriorate on dry land. Gerrald was ailing from his tuberculosis on his arrival in November 1795 aboard the *Sovereign*, and the house he was granted became his hospice. He died on 16 March 1796, followed by Skirving three days later. Their commitment to reform had cost them their lives, and they were buried on alien soil as convicts rather than martyrs to a noble cause. Skirving was given the terse epitaph: 'A seditionist, but man of respectable moral conduct'.[109] Gerrald was remembered more generously in a book written by Captain David Collins, later first governor of Van Diemen's Land:

> *In this gentleman, the gifts of nature matured by education ... could not save him from a barbarous shore; where the few who were civilised must pity while they admire him ... Mr Gerrald breathed his last, glorying in being a martyr to the cause which he termed that of freedom, and considering as an honour that exile that brought him to an untimely grave.*[110]

Today a small plaque marks Gerrald's resting place in the heart of Sydney's Botanic Gardens.

As some of the most educated men in the colony, the Scottish Martyrs were an oasis of civilisation, whose society was valued by those seeking intellectual or cultivated conversation. Palmer was aware of this distinction, and could be condescending about the philistinism of the officer elite, writing that 'they are all aristocrats here from ignorance, and being out of the way, or desire, of knowledge'.[111] What did these university-educated observers make of their new home? A poem, attributed to Muir, described a place:

> *Where sullen Convicts drag the clanking chain and Desolation covers all the plain.*[112]

However, in happier moods both he and Palmer saw a land of bounty, if only it was rationally developed by an elected government in place of rule by governor and military. 'The reports you have had of this country are mostly false' enthused Palmer to a clergyman back in Britain, '[t]he soil is capital; the climate, delicious ... it will soon be the region of plenty, and wants only virtue and liberty to be another America'.[113] He judged the land 'to be rich in minerals, especially iron', and confessed to 'wonder and delight' at 'a new creation: the beasts, the fish, the birds, the reptiles, the plants, the trees, the flowers, are all new—so beautiful and grotesque ...'.[114] Palmer's humane disposition disapproved of what he considered a degeneration in relations between whites and the natives since the departure of the liberal-minded Governor Arthur Phillip. After hungry Aborigines had stolen wheat and skirmished with settlers, the government 'sent sixty soldiers to kill and destroy all they could meet with, and drive them from the Hawkesbury ... The dead they hang on gibbets *in terrorem*'.[115] More optimistically, the profitable business ventures of the officers of the corps and the more industrious convicts impressed Palmer: 'I never saw a place where a man could so soon make a fortune.'

While barred from politics the Martyrs were free to participate in the colony's embryonic economy. Rather than merely scrape out a living on their farms, they seized the entrepreneurial opportunities on offer. Muir had relatives purchase rum, tobacco and sugar from the Cape and Rio de Janeiro so that he had valuable commodities to barter for farm produce and livestock in the colony. Palmer was more ambitious and set about building a trading business out of the meagre resources he had at hand. With his friend, the free settler Boston, he formed one of Australia's pioneering trading firms, Boston and Company. The pair was nothing if not enterprising, building their own trading ship using instructions gleaned from a personal copy of the *Encyclopaedia Britannica*—the only one in the colony. The 30 ton *Martha* was sufficiently seaworthy for Boston and Company to open a regular trading route between Sydney and Norfolk Island. In this endeavour the encyclopaedia proved a treasure-trove for these entrepreneurial merchants, furnishing recipes for the sought-after commodities beer and soap. They constructed a windmill, made 'tolerably good wine' from a grape vineyard and began selling fish caught at Lord Howe Island.

In tending their estates and embarking on other enterprises, Muir, and especially Palmer, were being true to their bourgeois backgrounds and their commitment to freedom in trade as well as governance. They took pride in being able to feed themselves and others from their farms rather than draw on the government stores. But their business ambitions and laissez faire principles necessarily brought them into conflict with the officers of the New South Wales Corps, who as well as exercising military authority over them, also controlled a trading monopoly hostile to competition from new players. In letters home the merchant-officers of the corps were described as 'monopolists', 'plunderers' and 'hucksters'.[116] When the infrequent ships from Europe and the Americas called into Sydney Harbour to trade, only the officers of the corps were allowed on board to buy goods wholesale 'reselling them at 1000 per cent profit and more' according to Palmer.[117] Hard spirit was a most sought after commodity and sold at immense profit by the officers, earning them the notorious nickname, the Rum Corps. Profits were used to monopolise land and livestock, so by 1799 the corps' officers owned approximately 30 per cent of the cattle, 40 per cent of the goats, 60 per cent of the horses and 75 per cent of the sheep.[118] The trading prisoners were resented and harassed by the officers. A pregnant sow owned by Boston was shot by two members of the corps, and when he successfully sought damages of £500 in court, the military judge awarded only 40 shillings. During the trial an officer of the corps sought to blacken Boston's character by alleging that on the ship out to New South Wales, he had 'publicly drank to the murder of his King to the annihilation of the constitution of his country'.[119] '[T]hey have kept us poor' complained Palmer of the 'despotism and infamous monopolies' encouraged under Grose, who was himself an officer in the corps. Conflict continued as long as Boston and Company traded. Palmer, as a prisoner 'totally in their power', claimed to be the focus of the corps' 'rage', experiencing 'all the affronts and insolence they could heap upon me', and was alarmed at 'all the threats and violence of the conspiracy against me'.

True liberals, Muir and Palmer were as critical of the curtailment of economic liberty as they were of political liberty. In the face of the colony's food shortages, their letters were very positive about the economic potential of the new land, but they believed that the government-enforced

59

cartel had produced famine in paradise. 'Unless the changes were soon made the officers would make a princely fortune and the place would be ruined.' Development would require a free market and the introduction of elected parliamentary government in place of viceregal fiat and military rule. Thus, from its earliest days the Australian economy was divided between those capitalists who wanted open competition and those who sought lazy profits from state-buttressed cartels.

What of Thomas Muir, the youngest of the Martyrs? Not only did he remain true to his democratic political views, but judging by his later activities, it appears his exile radicalised him away from constitutional reform towards revolution. When discussing Muir's politics in Sydney, discussion hinges on a poem entitled *The Telegraph*, published in Britain under the convict's name in January 1796. Contemplating his exile, the poet reasons that:

> *The best and noblest privilege in Hell*
> *For souls like ours is, Nobly to rebel,*
> *To raise the standard of revolt and try*
> *The Happy fruits of lov'd Democracy.*
> *The sacred right of Insurrection there*
> *May drive old Satan from his regal chair*[120]

Often saluted as Australia's first published verse, the authorship of *The Telegraph* and its geographic origins are a subject of scholarly debate. Robert Hughes and other British authors accept that the poem is the work of the celebrated convict and composed in New South Wales.[121] But recently, Nigel Leask has argued that the poem, with its conceit of a Jacobin polity taking root in the Antipodes, is in fact a satire of British radicalism written in Muir's name by Tory wordsmith Reverend George Hamilton.[122] The poem's origins remain controversial but it was certainly read at the time as the words of the renegade radical. Assuming *The Telegraph* is the work of the Martyrs' enemies, as Leask's research indicates, it is a tribute to Muir's notoriety and the alarm that his proselytising continued to evoke. In the spirit of conservative wish-fulfilment, the poem has the exiled radical having second thoughts about the unforeseen dangers that might arise from 'spread[ing] the flame of freedom round the land' by igniting an uprising among the common people, using the metaphor of Aborigines losing control of a bush fire:

To clear the forest's dark impervious maze
The half-starv'd Indian lights a hasty blaze …
From Bush to Bush with rapid steps he flies
Till the whole forest blazes to the skies …
Till from a Rock he sees with wild maze
His Wife & Children perish in the Blaze.[123]

Robert Hughes saluted this work as the debut of the bush fire in English verse, but it is also a very early meditation on the political implications of a cutting-edge communications technology, the optical telegraph.[124] The poem suggests that even from exile in faraway Botany Bay, it may be possible to transmit seditious information back to Scotland. The optical telegraph was a new French invention employing a secret code to send messages instantly over vast distances between Paris and the countryside. Due to the telegraph's role in unifying the French republic it was an apt poetic metaphor for the transmission of Jacobin propaganda—not the last time new media would be connected with subversive politics.[125] For Leask the poem is important despite its origins, as it exposes the anxiety with which conservatives viewed the 'apparently unstoppable transnational mobility of radical ideology' and the specific fears that even transportation would not silence the Martyrs.[126] Muir lived up to these fears.

In the end Muir could bear living without political rights no longer and resolved to seek liberty in the United States. He executed a bold escape from captivity. When an American fur trading ship, the *Otter*, docked at Sydney Cove in 1796 he seized his chance, and reached a secret accommodation with the ship's captain, Ebenezer Dorr. On the night of the ship's departure, Muir rowed a small boat out through the harbour's heads, rendezvousing with the *Otter* in the open sea. From here Muir's derring-do became a swashbuckling adventure across two oceans to the far side of the world.[127] In the Pacific the ship visited the Polynesian islands of Anamooka, Niue, Tahiti and Motu. It is likely the *Otter*'s crew were the first Europeans to set foot on Motu Ko, Motu Kotowa and Pukapuka, and in the spirit of discovery the last island was named Muir.

Then the ship made for the northwestern coast of the North American continent to trade furs with the Indians, where a small landing party at Nootka Bay, including Muir, were for a time the involuntary guests of an indigenous tribe that wanted to trade their enemies' severed heads!

It had been Muir's plan to remain with the *Otter* until it docked in New York, but alarmed at the proximity of a nearby Royal Navy ship he secured passage on a Spanish warship which conveyed him to Monterey in Spanish California, where as a foreign national he was placed under the supervision of the viceroy, Don Diega Borica. Here things began to go wrong for the stateless exile, who requested that he be allowed to seek asylum in the United States, and was given to understand he would be conveyed through the Spanish heartland of Mexico and the Caribbean for that purpose. Escorted by ship to Mexico City and then Vera Cruz, it gradually dawned on Muir that he was a prisoner of the Spanish.

Ever the confident communicator, Muir addressed a letter to the world's most successful revolutionary, George Washington, requesting that the President grant him asylum. The aristocratic governor of Mexico, distrustful of a renegade British radical who might stir up trouble in his colony, intercepted Muir's letter to Washington, and kept him on a tight, if hospitable leash.[128] However, soon after when Spain entered the war as an ally of France, Muir was incarcerated in a Cuban prison worse than the wilderness of Botany Bay. Then, as now, the Caribbean island boasted a secure holding pen for prisoners of war with dangerous ideas. This was as close as Muir was to come to the American republic.

However, Muir's odyssey was far from over. The decision was made to transport Britain's most famous exile to Spain to stand trial, and he found himself on a frigate bound for Cadiz. It is not a little ironic that a man cast out of his own country for French sympathies should be transported back to Europe by France's allies to face punishment as a British combatant. Nearing the coast of Spain the ship was intercepted by a British squadron and battle ensued. Tragically Muir was hit by an exploding shell, losing his left eye. His face was so badly mutilated that a search party of British officers was unable to identify the still-wanted escapee, and he was left with the other anonymous wounded in a Cadiz hospital. On the Continent but still a prisoner of the Spanish, Muir was able to get a message to old associates in the French Government, who jumped at the opportunity to offer refuge to a celebrated radical fleeing British persecution. It now fell to no less a figure than Foreign Minister Talleyrand, the gadfly aristocratic courtier who would serve French leaders from Louis XVI to Napoleon, to secure his release and convey him to Paris in 1797.

Now a defector, Muir fluctuated between being a propaganda pawn and an adviser on French plans to invade Great Britain, until his novelty wore out. Muir had been critical of the tendency for the French Revolution to devour its own, but then his own country's constitutional monarchy was no less cruel to Muir. He had no reason to feel affection for the British state, and in the end he chose revolution over patriotism. However, in accepting from his French hosts the leadership of a revolutionary Government of Scotland in exile, Muir likely felt he remained patriot to his true homeland. As guest of the new directorate that had brought a measure of order from the chaos, Muir, now disfigured and wearing an eye patch, was able to enjoy a measure of liberty in the short time he had left. Weakened by his injuries he died a pauper in Chantilly in 1799 on 26 January, coincidentally the same date Australians would one day celebrate as their national birthday. Even though Muir's bid to find liberty ended in premature death at thirty-three, he was the first political prisoner to escape from the Sydney penal settlement and would not be the last to do so by American ship with the intent of finding asylum in the United States. His indefatigable quest for freedom would continue to inspire the cause for reform at home and among other rebels sentenced to Australia.

Palmer remained in the colony, keeping his nose clean of politics and giving the Rum Corps some healthy competition, until the expiry of his seven-year sentence. However, even when finally pardoned a free man in 1801, he faced the challenge of paying for his passage home. Buoyed by their earlier success as shipbuilders, Palmer and Boston purchased and renovated an old Spanish warship, the *El Plumier*, and set sail with Mrs Boston, the children and Ellis for England by way of the Dutch East Indies. This was a risky undertaking for amateurs, and the worm-eaten ship began to take water and sink off Guam, a remote Spanish possession near the Philippines. Awaiting Palmer and his shipmates on shore was the same Spanish hospitality that brought Muir to grief. Thrown into prison as enemy English, Palmer caught cholera, and died there in 1802, ironically for his nationality rather than his political views. His hosts were not yet finished with him. Learning of Palmer's radical past, the priests refused Christian rites, and had this fellow man of God buried on a beach in unhallowed ground reserved for common thieves and pirates. However, this was not to be the final resting place of the scholarly parson. In 1804 an American captain who admired Palmer's sacrifice for reform exhumed the body and laid it to rest in a churchyard in the city of Boston where his grave would be honoured by friends of liberty.

Only Maurice Margarot returned safely to Britain after serving his sentence. During his long fourteen years he could not resist meddling in politics. Robert Hughes believes he 'led a shadowy, ill-documented life as a double agent between the various colonial cliques'.[129] This is borne out by the known facts. Margarot kept Governor Hunter secretly informed about the wheeler-dealing of the New South Wales Corps' officers. He also reported on his one-time colleagues, the other Scottish Martyrs, to Governors Grose and King. At the same time he was writing back to the Colonial Office in London, and a paranoid King was convinced his superiors had Margarot spying on him. However, it also appears that Margarot had maintained his enthusiasm for liberty, and helped prepare the way for the local Irish rebellion of 1804 that climaxed in the Battle of Vinegar Hill (a serious challenge to authority, to be discussed in the next chapter). The exile had expressed the hope that New South Wales would break from Britain 'in the course of a few years' and King found evidence in Margarot's diary of 'some very elegant republican sentiments'.[130] For his assumed role in the uprising and being declared 'dangerous ... to the tranquillity of the colony', Margarot's sentence was extended—he was sent to Van Diemen's Land and then condemned to hard labour in the coal mines at Newcastle. Finally returning to London in 1810, seventeen years after he was first convicted, Margarot continued to surprise. While indigent and ostracised by the radical community, he appeared as a credible and influential witness in a parliamentary inquiry into transportation in 1812, making a strong case for its reform.[131] The ambiguous Margarot died in London in 1815, the last of the Scottish Martyrs.

CONCLUSION

IF THE POINT OF TRANSPORTATION WAS TO STOP THE 'SCOTTISH Jacobins' promoting their seditious ideas it did not succeed. Muir, Palmer and Skirving all produced widely circulated pamphlets that reinforced their status as martyrs for the cause of reform. Muir was reunited with the revolutionary government in France, providing the Directory with a public relations coup and valuable intelligence. Margarot promoted rebellion in the colony and later returned to England as an influential critic of the transportation system. However, with the exception of the wily Margarot, transportation certainly shortened their lives.

Muir had protested his moderation and loyalty to the monarch and constitution, yet he ended his days among Britain's enemies, helping to plan an invasion of his homeland. Had he been prepared to betray Britain for the cause of revolution as far back as 1793, or was he pushed into extremism by the harshness of his punishment, his exile and stateless wanderings as an escapee? With minor electoral reform, or even dialogue, it is likely that the Friends of the People and the Constitution movement could have been absorbed into the political mainstream and its loyalty guaranteed, but the oligarchy in control was not for turning, and the outbreak of war made concessions or negotiation impossible. At the other extreme, Margarot retired from the barricades to the backroom, where he played along with authority in order to have influence, even as a convict, while getting close enough to colonial insiders to inflict some harm, as with the Irish insurrection.

Today when nations such as Britain and Australia take for granted the democratic reforms for which Muir and the other Martyrs suffered it is tempting to dismiss the government that transported them as wicked reactionaries. However, it is important to understand that those in power, mindful of an earlier history of civil war, truly feared that home-grown revolution or invasion by France was possible, and even when Britain finally emerged victorious, conservatives like the Anglo-Irish statesman Edmund Burke still believed it 'was a close run thing'.

The mutilation and death in exile of Thomas Muir was a metaphor for the fate of the democratic movement in Britain. Other causes, such as the abolition of the slave trade in the Empire would be achieved in 1807 as the fear of revolution receded. However, ruthless wartime suppression, typified in the transportation of the Scottish Martyrs, set back the cause of parliamentary reform for over a generation. In the face of post-war reaction, their sacrifice would continue to inspire.

In Muir's last words to his judges before being taken to prison, he prophesied '[w]hen our Ashes shall be scattered by the winds of heaven, the impartial voice of future time will rejudge your verdict'. And so it came to pass. Fifty years after the Scottish Martyrs' exile to Botany Bay a monument was erected on Calton Hill, Edinburgh to honour their sacrifice for the cause of democratic reform, by then an unstoppable movement after the passing of the Great Reform Bill of 1832. Democrats in Britain would still have to wait more than another half century before achieving the universal manhood suffrage first demanded by the Martyrs, but at each incremental advance in the franchise, their sacrifice would be invoked. Yet in Australia, one of the world's oldest democracies, the Scottish Martyrs and their cause are neither mourned nor commemorated. Modern-day republicans do not acknowledge that pioneers of their cause were present here from the beginning of European settlement, a controversial but insistent part of our British birthright. This forgetting is even more surprising given the economic and cultural mark the Martyrs made on the infant colony and Australia's subsequent embrace of democratic innovations identified with the radical tradition: the successful agitation for colonial governments to be responsible to elected parliaments; the granting of universal male suffrage in New South Wales, South Australia and Victoria in the 1850s, long before the mother country; and the new Australian Federation's adoption of near universal suffrage with the extension of votes to women in 1902.[132] The democracy we enjoy today is neither natural nor inevitable, but had to be fought for by brave true believers against overwhelming opposition. Australians can be proud that the early days of white settlement were entwined in this struggle, and that some of the first fighters for modern democracy are buried in our soil. In this sense they are Australian martyrs too.

2

'DEATH OR LIBERTY!'

THE REBELS OF 1798 IN IRELAND AND AUSTRALIA

THE DEFEAT OF THE REBEL ARMY BY THE LOYALIST FORCES AT THE
Battle of Vinegar Hill in County Wexford on 21 June 1798 marked
a turning point in the uprising of the United Irishmen. Against the
odds, peasants and ordinary working people who had pledged to
establish a republican Ireland held their own for a month against better-
trained and armed soldiers owing allegiance to George III. However,
the rebels were now in retreat. Surrender seemed a matter of when,
not if, and commanders disagreed about whether to sue for peace or
fight on. Thousands of rebel soldiers had been killed at the hands of
loyalist troops. Atrocities were being committed by both sides, making
surrender perilous. Already United Irish commanders were being tried in
hastily convened military courts and executed for treason using mobile
gallows. Many more—between 325 and 500—would be transported to
the feared penal colony of New South Wales.[1] The rebellion had united
radical Protestants and Catholics in common cause for a republic, but on
the ground, under the cover of martial law, old hatreds were unleashed.
Government officers turned a blind eye to outrages perpetrated on
civilians, especially Catholics, by loyalist soldiers and the fierce sectarian
Protestant vigilantes known as Orangemen. Michael Dwyer, a Catholic
farmer turned revolutionary soldier, had a choice. He could surrender to
uncertain justice or join the small resistance force gathering in Wicklow
Mountains, just south of Dublin, under the command of another farmer
rebel, 'General' Joseph Holt, a Protestant sheriff turned revolutionary.

Dwyer, a native of Wicklow, had been at the centre of the rebellion
since it erupted at dawn on 23 May 1798, distinguishing himself at
the Battle of Arcklow in Wexford where the rebels had won an early,
morale-boosting victory. Dwyer had fought at the Battle of Ballyellis in
County Carlow on 30 June and at the recent rout at Vinegar Hill. He
now resolved to fight on with 400 other men, to keep alive the rebellion
until the arrival of a promised French invasion force to liberate Ireland. A
natural leader of men, Dwyer was promoted to the rank of captain in July,
and began a campaign that held down thousands of loyalist militia. Then
Holt, despairing that the French had abandoned Ireland, surrendered
on 10 November 1798 and was exiled to Botany Bay. Dwyer assumed
command and fought on. Hailed as the 'Wicklow Chief' for five long
years he would lead guerrilla raids on government troops from secret

Mid-nineteenth century anti-Irish propaganda by English
caricaturist George Cruikshank, depicting the United Irishmen at
Vinegar Hill in 1798 as a murderous priest-led rabble.

boltholes in the wilds of the mountains, humiliating the British Empire
in its own backyard.

❋ ❋ ❋

The rebels of 1798 were fighting to establish a democratic and non-
sectarian republic in Ireland, in part to advance the radical liberal principles
that had inspired revolutions in North America and France, and in part to
free their country from the burdens of a centuries' old English occupation.
The violent re-conquest of Catholic Ireland by Oliver Cromwell between
1649 and 1653 had been one of Protestant England's first steps on the
path to empire. Provoked by the Irish Rebellion of 1641, the puritan
warrior toppled the ruling Catholic Confederation on behalf of the
English Parliament, and fought a bloody war in which approximately
15 per cent of the population perished or fled into exile.[2] Estates and
farms were confiscated from the Irish gentry and freeholders and given
to Protestant settlers, many of them Cromwell's veterans. To guarantee
this land-grab in perpetuity, draconian Penal Laws were introduced in

1695, preventing Catholics from inheriting land and stripping them of civil and religious rights. By 1778 the Catholic majority owned a mere 5 per cent of land, with most in the hands of absentee English gentry and an oligarchy of wealthy landowners descended from settler soldiers, known as the Protestant Ascendancy.[3]

In the eighteenth century, Ireland was a separate country from Britain with its own government and parliament but it remained a colony. The power of the conquerors was manifest in a viceregal 'Administration' appointed by and answerable to London, and an Irish Parliament dominated by the Ascendancy, for which Catholics could neither vote nor stand. No Catholic could serve as a magistrate, judge, juryman, senior civil servant or military officer. Ireland's colonial status had opponents across the social divide, but its economic and legal inequities were borne most heavily by the Catholic tenant farmers and labourers who were in the thrall of landlords and their agents, and were said to be the poorest peasants in Europe.

The Irish-born Arthur Wellesley, 1st Duke of Wellington, who had served in Ireland, observed in 1829 that 'there never was a country in which poverty existed to the extent it did in Ireland'.[4] The Irish population doubled from 2.5 million to 5 million between 1767 and 1801, placing intense pressure on the country's unequally divided land to feed its people.[5] Most people in Ireland survived by tilling small rented allotments of an acre or so, on which they grew subsistence crops to augment meagre wages earned labouring for the landowner. Calories were insufficient and dependence on a single crop, the potato, meant famine whenever it failed due to weather or blight.[6] The peasants made do with mud huts but lived in constant fear of eviction by middlemen who bought mortgages and did the dirty work for landlords, siphoning off their cut in rent increases.[7] The emergence of this system in the eighteenth century allowed the landowning gentry to wash their hands of any obligations to tenants, breaking down feudal bonds of deference. Peasants might be evicted for falling behind or to make way for the enclosure of allotments into larger more profitable sheep or cattle runs. The introduction of enclosure, diminishing common rights, became a focus of rural protest in the 1780s. On top of rent, the Penal Laws also required that peasants pay tithes to the established Church of Ireland, the imposed version of Anglicanism. Eighteenth century Irish satirist Jonathan Swift mocked the inequality of

Ireland in his notorious pamphlet *A Modest Proposal*, which suggested that impoverished Irish could sell their children to the rich as meat, thereby easing their economic troubles.[8] The poor had their own ideas about how to respond to grinding poverty, low wages, high rents, evictions, hunger and the threat of starvation, and it was not a war of words. They banded together in local secret societies with colloquial names such as the Whiteboys, Right Boys, Defenders and Ribbonmen that used violence to wrest concessions from landlords, employers and especially unlucky middlemen and bailiffs they targeted in the dead of night.[9]

By the 1780s, thanks to a campaign by more liberal-minded members of the gentry sitting in the Irish Parliament, the laws forbidding Catholics to own land were relaxed. Some enterprising Catholic peasants began to purchase small freehold farms. One such family was the Dwyers who purchased 30 acres (12 hectares) at Eadestown in Wicklow in 1784 when their son Michael was twelve.[10] Although the boy helped his father tend sheep from a young age he had more schooling than most of his neighbours at a time when illiteracy was very high among rural Irish—due to the Penal Laws prohibiting education of Catholics. Like all Catholics, the Dwyers were discriminated against, but as small freeholders they had become comfortable by Irish standards, a late eighteenth century approximation of the hard-working, unpretentious people Australians call 'battlers'.

By way of contrast the Protestant farmer Joseph Holt, born in 1756, owned a large farm and was a respected, if minor, stalwart of the local establishment in Ballydaniel, Wicklow. He had a superior education and held significant law and order positions available only to middle-class Protestant landowners, including sub-constable and sheriff.[11] Holt was solidly built, prematurely bald with an intelligent, alert face set off by piercing eyes and a sharp eagle-like nose. A liberal man who valued his respectability, he kept aloof from the agitation of the United Irishmen and the land wars waged between poor Catholics and Protestants.

Michael Dwyer found work as an ostler, a skilled farm trade, while still an adolescent and grew into a strong, slim man with an intelligent, open face with large doe eyes. He married local girl Mary Doyle. The die of his life was cast at twenty-three years of age in 1795 when together with many of his relatives and neighbours he swore the secret oath of the Society of United Irishmen.

GEN. HOLT.

The Leader of the Irish Rebels.

'General' Joseph Holt (1756–1826), Protestant farmer from Wicklow turned United Irishman and rebel commander.

I [Michael Dwyer] do voluntarily declare that I will persevere in endeavouring to form a brotherhood of affection among Irishmen of every religious persuasion, and that I will also persevere in all my endeavours to obtain an equal, full, and adequate representation of all the people of Ireland. I do further declare that neither hopes, fears, rewards, or punishments shall ever induce me, directly or indirectly, to inform on or give evidence against any members of this or similar societies … [12]

Once forged, these intimate ties of family and locality became the United Irishmen's secret weapon. No county had more rebels transported to New South Wales than Wicklow, where 14,000 men swore the oath. The swearing of Dwyer and his clan was part of a covert recruitment drive by the United Irishmen after it abandoned hope of constitutional reform in favour of revolution. What was this radical movement? How did its vision for changing Ireland inspire ordinary farmers like Dwyer and Holt to take up arms against the government? Why did radicalism in Ireland, unlike Britain, move from debates and pamphlets to full-blown revolution in which tens of thousands would die? Quelling a full-scale armed revolution meant transporting the most rebellious men in Ireland en masse to the fledgling New South Wales colony, where their defiant spirit proved a cause of constant anxiety for authorities. What was the fate of the defeated rebels transported to Australia and what influence did they have on the new society? To answer these questions we have to retrace nearly a decade of agitation by the Society of United Irishmen and its allies at home and abroad.

✳ ✳ ✳

THE UNITED IRISHMEN

IT IS COMMON TO VIEW THE IRISH REBELLION OF 1798 anachronistically, through the prism of Ireland's twentieth century civil war and the 'troubles', as Catholic and nationalist. In fact, the Society of United Irishmen was founded in 1791 by educated and propertied Presbyterians in the northern Protestant stronghold of Belfast. They composed a democratic movement not unlike the English and Scottish Friends of the Constitution and the People, dedicated to the goals of manhood suffrage, annual parliaments, an end to the manipulation of rotten and pocket boroughs by large landholders and reduction in taxes. '[W]e gladly look forward to brighter prospects,' the United Irishmen declared, 'to a people united in the fellowship of freedom—to a parliament the express image of the people—to a prosperity established on civil, political, and religious liberty'.[13] Though Protestants they were non-sectarian radicals who had no time for the majesty of Kings or the Ascendancy Administration in Dublin and supported rights for both dissenters (as Presbyterians were known) and Catholics, both of which were politically marginalised by the status quo.[14] Presbyterians composed a sizeable minority of one-sixth of the Irish population and were concentrated in the northern counties of Ulster. Most were comfortable independent farmers like Holt or involved in textile weaving or, increasingly, trade and industry. As with the Scottish Martyrs, the United Irishmen were representatives of this new class, a bourgeois movement, made up of merchants, manufacturers and professionals aggrieved at the dominance of landed interests in the governing policy of Ireland, and their own political exclusion. Among its founders were Samuel Neilson, William Tennent and Henry McCracken.

These Belfast businessmen shared an entrepreneurial, self-improving urban culture far removed from the poverty and seasonal rhythms of Catholic peasant life. They were quickly joined by a group of Dublin Protestant merchants and professionals, notably Theobald Wolfe Tone, James Napper Tandy, John and Henry Sheares, Archibald Rowan and Thomas Emmet, together with bourgeois Catholics Dr William Drennan and Richard McCormack.[15] As in England and Scotland a taste of economic liberty in Ireland's two biggest cities was leading to demands for political liberty. Internationalist in outlook, they were inspired by the writings of Tom Paine, the American War of Independence and the French Revolution and were Ireland's first republicans. However, prior to 1795 the United Irishmen were pledged to achieving their goals through constitutional methods, and looked to supporters among the more radical English Whigs to persuade Prime Minister Pitt and the Irish Administration to embark on sweeping constitutional reform.

Left wing nationalist historian T.A. Jackson considered the Irish Rebellion of 1798 to be the first stage in a re-conquest of Ireland from the British colonisers, that would continue until well into the twentieth century. However, the United Irishmen are better understood as part of the liberal reform movement that grew out of the Enlightenment that had also inspired the constitution of the United States. The American Revolution had lifted its horizons beyond the economic and political grievances of the propertied men who led it, to declare itself a struggle for universal liberty, the equality of all, and the replacement of the arbitrary tyranny of Kings with republics as the best way to organise a modern state to achieve these goals.[16] United Irishmen historian Nancy Curtin has demonstrated that their republicanism valued 'civic virtue' in public life, and was critical of the corruption of this ideal by rigged, undemocratic assemblies and executives unrepresentative of the governed. As bourgeois reformers they argued for 'trade without restraints, for the removal of irksome civil disabilities, freeing individuals to succeed, and rewarding them for merit and achievement'[17]—radical goals in the late eighteenth century, intended to modernise Ireland. Rather than advocating land or property redistribution as socialists would in the next century, their social goals of economic and political liberalism and improved education were to advance the individual.[18] The republican ideal of virtue, they believed, could be established under the Crown, with the removal of oligarchic deformations to governance in Ireland and not originally conceived as anti-British, but rather as part of the birthright of all free-born Britons.

As with the Scottish Martyrs, the catalyst for the Irish radicals was the French Revolution. The United Irishmen media mouthpiece, the *Northern Star*, claimed France was 'the temple of universal liberty' and '[o]f all revolutions' its 'was the most glorious'.[19] However, the experience of revolution across the channel had deeper resonance in Ireland than in England or Scotland. The dissenting Presbyterians of Belfast cheered at news of the Fall of the Bastille, and supported the fall of the absolute monarchy.[20] Both France and Ireland were Catholic, and the progress of the revolution demonstrated that Papist peasants could surmount their provincial conservatism and intimidation by an authoritarian Church hierarchy to become citizens prepared to fight to defend the principles of liberty, equality and fraternity. In many ways, the disenfranchised poor peasantry suffering under Protestant landlords had more in common with the peasants oppressed by the decaying feudalism of Louis XVI's *Ancien Régime* than with England in the throes of an industrial and agricultural revolution. In Ireland democratic constitutional reform could not avoid religion. The demand for equal civil rights and universal adult male suffrage meant removing obstacles to the participation of Catholics in the political and economic life of Ireland.

The United Irishmen represented a clear and present danger to vested interests precisely because it set out to unite Protestants and Catholics and, after 1795, bourgeois intellectuals with working people of the countryside and towns. At its inception its founders sought to forge common ground with Catholic merchants and manufacturers who shared their interest in modernising Ireland's agrarian economy and liberating it from the shackles of English trade restrictions. Excluded from land ownership for many generations, an enterprising Catholic bourgeoisie had grown up in Dublin and other large cities straining at the bit to trade freely on the world market and develop a capitalist economy in which they, rather than the great Protestant landowners, would play a leading part. They shared with the Presbyterian radicals of the north the belief that the time had come when tax-paying men of property should have a say over how they were governed, regardless of religion. While Protestants, the Presbyterian elite had no love for the Anglican English Ascendancy that ruled through the Administration and its parliamentary puppets. The descendants of Scottish settlers, the Presbyterians, concentrated in Ulster, were known as dissenters because they disagreed with the officially established Church of England on points of faith, worship and Church governance, and were in turn excluded by Ireland's colonial elite. While relations between poorer dissenters and Catholics competing for scarce resources could succumb to bitter sectarian fighting, at the elite level the two marginalised communities began cooperating against the common enemy.

The United Irishmen's support for complete Catholic Emancipation was underscored in its infancy when the Protestant lawyer Theobald Wolfe Tone accepted the position of Executive Officer with the Catholic Committee, the official lobby group representing Catholic Ireland to the government. This committee had recently been wrested from the control of the more conservative collaborationist Catholic gentry and clergy by liberal business leaders seeking Catholic civil rights. They instituted parish elections for 240 members and transformed the committee into a Catholic Convention—effectively a parliament.[21] As a companion to Paine's *Rights of Man*, in 1791 Wolfe Tone wrote the pamphlet *An Argument on Behalf of the Catholics of Ireland*, which proved so persuasive among the northern United Irishmen that the Belfast chapter published 10,000 copies.

The United Irishmen wanted responsible government, dependent on majority support in the Irish House of Commons. However, under Ireland's colonial constitution the British viceroy and his Administration at Dublin Castle were answerable to Westminster (just like the governors in New South Wales) and not to the Irish Parliament. This was to ensure Ireland's rotten boroughs, even more corrupt than in Britain, were used to stack the Irish House of Commons with pliant placemen guaranteed to pursue policies that kept their country in the political and economic thrall of London. Of the 300 seats in the Irish lower house in 1798, 218 were pocket boroughs in the gift of the landed Protestant gentry, with election a mere formality.[22] Another eighty-one seats were corrupt rotten boroughs. Four great aristocratic families only had to combine to secure a majority and impose their will. Even so, the British Parliament could make laws for her colony, and reserved the right to override any Irish legislation, which had to go through the Privy Council.[23]

Without diminishing the political and religious causes of the Irish Rebellion of 1798, both Rudé and T.A. Jackson correctly traced its roots to discontent over the economic exploitation of Ireland.[24] While Britain underwent an industrial revolution and accelerated urbanisation, Ireland was kept an agrarian backwater, supplying raw materials to feed British economic expansion.[25] For example, Westminster charged heavy tariffs on imported woollen textiles manufactured in Ireland while the raw fleece could be exported to British factories duty free.[26] The British Government espoused free trade but restricted Ireland's freedom to trade with America and Europe, enjoying a parasitic relationship with its colony. Because Ireland's landed oligarchy invested heavily in Britain's economy, the Irish Parliament had done nothing to overturn this state of affairs. However, when a comparable trade monopoly imposed on the American colonies led them to declare their independence from Britain in 1776, Irish merchants of all religious faiths began agitating for greater trade autonomy. From the early 1780s disgruntled liberals among the Whig members of the Irish House of Commons took up the merchants' cause, and a Patriot Party led by Henry Grattan began agitating for enhanced Irish autonomy.[27]

French historian Alexis de Tocqueville observed that the most dangerous time for a corrupt and conservative government is when it embarks on half-hearted reform that encourages hopes of greater change than the old regime is prepared to countenance.[28] This happened in Ireland in the 1780s. Weakened by the American War of Independence, and anxious to keep Ireland loyal, the British Government acceded to some of the reforms demanded by this emerging nationalist alliance of urban business, liberal-minded Whig gentry in the Irish Parliament and the mainly Presbyterian Volunteer militia. Between 1780 and 1782 Ireland was granted greater trade and currency autonomy, some legislative independence and a relaxation of restrictions on Catholic land ownership. Such changes brought mobility to families like the Dwyers. While Britain baulked at further reform or rights for Catholics, a genie had escaped from the bottle. As a Whig MP, Jonathan Swift mobilised middle-class opinion against the Irish Tories in a series of published letters purporting to be from a draper, which localised many of the arguments used by the American revolutionaries against the Crown, concluding 'All Government without the consent of the Governed is the very definition of slavery'.[29] Henceforth, the Administration had to deal with a nationalist opposition in parliament backed by a vocal bourgeoisie, expressing itself through clubs and newspapers.[30] Then in April 1793 the tectonic plates of the Ascendancy shifted dramatically when, under mounting pressure from wealthy Catholics and their Church hierarchy, the parliament passed a Bill granting Catholics who owned freehold land the right to vote for the Irish House of Commons.[31] However, the Whig opposition would go no further, baulking in the face of the Ascendancy's intransigence at allowing Catholics to stand for election, and failing to push for parliamentary control of the Administration. Whig reform fatigue opened a space for the United Irishmen to argue for more radical change.

A commitment to Painite democratic principles and capitalist modernisation set the United Irishmen on a path of complete Catholic emancipation and anti-colonial national independence bound to be resisted by the landowning Protestant Ascendancy and its masters in London. The increasingly brutal opposition of the government and its supporters to any reform helped transform the United Irishmen from a constitutional to a revolutionary movement. By 1794 early hopes for a democratic Ireland under the Crown gave way to demands for a republic completely severed from Britain and its monarchy.

The influence of the United Irishmen during its early constitutional phase was magnified by an astute use of the press and other techniques of mass communication such as pamphleteering, lampoons, poetry and song-writing, that we would now define as agit-prop. Through ownership of newspapers, notably the *Northern Star*, the failings of the government could be exposed and public opinion won to the radical cause. Journalism provided a bridge to middle-class readers and (in the best tradition of the public sphere) helped build a constituency, first for reform and later for rebellion. The weaknesses of the Ascendancy regime were exposed and mocked in biting satire, such as *Billy Bluff and the squire, or a sample of the times*.[32] The Earl of Westmorland complained to Prime Minister Pitt that the United Irishmen 'set ballad singers in the streets', communicating their message to ordinary people so that 'this levelling spirit has gained much ground here'.[33] One song extolled the lessons of the French Revolution:

> *May French exertions never cease*
> *Till Europe shall reformed be,*
> *And union, liberty, and peace*
> *Succeed oppression's fell decree.*
> *Then every freeman's toast will be*
> *Union, peace, and liberty.*[34]

Many ballads drew on traditional Irish folk and drinking songs to spur ordinary people to rebellion:

> *The trying period is at hand*
> *Which must decide the cause,*
> *Whether we'll free our native land*
> *Or yield to tyrants' laws.*[35]

As convicts, the rebels would bequeath the Irish political ballad to Australian cultural radicalism.

The resolve of the Ascendancy to oppose United Irishmen's demands for reform was strengthened by the outbreak of war with France in February 1793. The Administration immediately created a large national militia, conscripting peasants to form a regiment in every county.[36] However, unlike the old Protestant Volunteer militias of the 1780s, this new force called up and armed Catholics as well. While ostensibly to repel a French invasion, the government in Ireland now had a large, if untrained, army to deploy against internal dissent. However, some in Pitt's Government, concerned about Catholic loyalty in the event of an invasion of Ireland, and the inability of stretched British military forces to adequately garrison the colony, advised further reform. Earl Fitzwilliam, a new viceroy associated with the liberal Whigs in Westminster, was appointed in January 1795 and forced the Ascendancy to accept a Bill allowing propertied Catholics to stand for parliament and take senior positions in the civil service. Such a concession might have stemmed the drift to rebellion but it was not to be. Ascendancy Tories complained behind his back directly to King George III, a staunch anti-Papist, and Fitzwilliam was recalled, along with his Bill. This was a defeat for Pitt's policy, and the new viceroy, Earl Camden, would prove an ally of the Ascendancy gentry in opposing Catholic rights and the United Irishmen.[37]

As in Britain, Irish subjects promoting revolutionary doctrines such as republicanism, or suspected of collusion with the French, could be tried for treason and sedition. The Society of United Irishmen had sent a delegation to the British national Convention of Societies of Friends of the People in Edinburgh where Muir read out their seditious letter and later made him an honorary member on learning of his fourteen-year sentence. Like many reform movements in Scotland and England, the United Irishmen had applauded the establishment of the French Republic. Then with the outbreak of war, radical groups sympathising with the French Revolution were banned, including the United Irishmen who were denounced as a 'desperate Jacobin conspiracy'.[38] Moderates departed, and the movement went underground and entered its revolutionary phase.

✱   ✱   ✱

REVOLUTIONARIES AND TERROR

THE AUTHORITIES' FEAR OF INVASION BY FRANCE AIDED AND
abetted by home-grown radicals was no paranoid fantasy. Sealing
the transformation from constitutional to revolutionary movement, the
United Irishmen leadership resolved in April 1794 to collaborate with a
French invasion of Ireland, effectively becoming a fifth column in a time
of war. Courting treason, the radicals let it be known to an undercover
French agent, the Reverend William Jackson, that should France invade
Ireland the rebel forces would rise at once to liberate their homeland
from the yoke of English rule. In a surprise attack, the French would
supply the arms, men and military expertise deemed necessary to defeat
Britain in the field. The arrest of Jackson later that month, and evidence
of his rendezvous with Wolfe Tone and Rowan, gave the government the
national security excuse to raid the Dublin chapter of the United Irishmen,
seize its documents and close it down. Pitt's agents intercepted a letter by
Wolfe Tone that Jackson was conveying to Paris, which stated that:

> The Government of Ireland is only to be looked upon as a
> government of force ... the moment a superior force appears it
> would tumble at once as [it is] founded neither in the interests
> nor the affections of the people.[39]

Nancy Curtin astutely notes that while this treasonous epistle confirmed
the worst fears of the British, the main effect of the Jackson affair was to
publicise to the whole country that the United Irishmen had the backing
of the triumphant French Republic, boosting the radicals' bona fides with
the common people.[40]

Once the leadership resolved to pursue a revolutionary course, a mass
base was needed to confront the government, and that required unity with
the labouring classes of town and especially country. From the beginning,
artisans and craftsmen in urban centres had been encouraged to participate
in the local chapters of the United Irishmen, and also formed their own
working-class groups, such as the Jacobin Club and embryonic trade unions.
However, what transformed the United Irishmen from being a radical
middle-class debating club, like the London Corresponding Society, into

an agent of revolution was its alliance with the Irish peasantry, especially the 'Defenders'. These local secret societies were a cross between a tenants' protection league, an agrarian trade union and banditti.[41] Irish historian Con Costello points out that centuries of exploitation and social conflict had left the Catholic tenant farmers with little respect for the institutions or laws of the state that were seen to favour rich Protestant landlords.[42] The Defenders first emerged in the early 1790s among Catholic tenant farmers from County Armagh in Ulster to protect themselves against the lower-class Protestant harassment meted out by the equally secretive Peep O'Day Boys (so-called because they would arrive at Catholic homes to commit outrages just before dawn) and the new Societies of Orangemen.

The latter had arisen among lower-class Presbyterians anxious about Catholics getting ahead at their expense. Their antecedents among the dissenter peasantry included local cells, such as the Oakboys, Hearts of Steel and Peep O'Day Boys, that opposed both enclosure and their Catholic competitors.[43] The Administration dog-whistled the Orange Societies into fervour in the 1790s. This was part of a divide-and-rule strategy to drive a sectarian wedge between peasant Protestants and Catholics, thus preventing the two groups coming together. Named in honour of William of Orange, these societies became fanatically loyal to the Crown and the Ascendancy government as both opposed Catholic mobility and countenanced violent outrages perpetrated by these very societies. No less violent, the Defenders had built on the tradition of rural resistance established in the previous two decades by the Catholic Whiteboys, who between 1761 and 1787 had waged a campaign of targeted terror—arson, vandalism, cattle maiming, assault, murder and stand-over tactics—against landlords and lease brokers to protect tenants' rights.[44] The Defenders' insurgency of the 1790s introduced greater militancy and discipline, characterised by nightly drills with secretly made pikes and ruthlessly enforced loyalty through retribution against informers. While called into being by economic distress, the Defenders also developed their own Catholic nationalism as a counter-ideology to the imperial Protestantism of their Orangemen adversaries.

Called upon by the big landowners and their agents to protect their persons and property, the Administration was equally ruthless in its attempts to crush the Defender groups. In disposing of the Defenders, the Administration could rely on the magistracy, composed of Protestant squires not usually well disposed to Catholic tenants. The magistracy relied on a network of local informers to assure convictions.[45] One hundred and sixty Defenders were sentenced to transportation prior to 1798, the first Irish political prisoners to be sent to New South Wales.[46] They were dispatched in the *Queen* in 1791, the *Boddingtons* and *Sugar Cane* in 1793, the *Marquis Cornwallis* in 1795 and the *Britannia* in 1796. This heavy-handed approach to banditry and insurrection had the unintended result of bringing the Defenders and United Irishmen together. Confronted with the Administration's partisan determination to destroy Catholic resistance while protecting Protestant landlords and the Orangemen, the Defenders began to lift their horizons beyond the land war to the radical idea of a French-style republic in which the concerns of Catholic peasants would count. Here were recruits for a national peasant army that the United Irishmen would need in the coming clash with government forces. New songs appeared, lamenting the plight of the tenant farmer:

> *I had a tyrant landlord, —base'*
> *Who knew my heart to Erin yearned,*
> *Even with the ground, my city did raze,*
> *And fired my substance dearly earned;*
> *Unmoved—remorseless now he sees*
> *My cottage falling, as it burns,*
> *My wife for mercy, on her knees,*
> *From him with ruthless frown he spurns.*[47]

Nevertheless, there was spirited debate within the United Irish leadership about the wisdom of recruiting the Defenders. Wooing peasants meant compromising middle-class liberalism with populist promises to redistribute land, and reduce rents, taxes and tithes.[48] Ballads aimed at the Defenders promised:

> *No longer the agents of power*
> *Will by our hard labour be fed;*
> *And the labouring poor of the nation*
> *Will then find plenty of bread.*[49]

An alliance with Catholics of property was one thing, but unleashing revolution among 'plebeian' Irish peasants might lead to anarchy or attacks on the bourgeoisie as had occurred in France, when extremists whipped up the levelling instincts of the mob. Rural Ireland was a violent society, in which disputes could end in vengeance and vendetta.[50] The bourgeois leaders were counting on the military discipline and secular republicanism of the anticipated French invasion force to keep order and restrain the sectarian excesses of their own Catholic peasants. Protestant prejudices aside, the United Irishmen embarked on the grassroots cultivation of support in the countryside and among the Defender group—the immediate context in which the Catholic battlers of the Dwyer clan swore their oath.

Any misgivings by some United Irishmen about unleashing a peasant revolt were cast aside when confronted by a series of provocative counter-measures undertaken by the Administration and its British backers. In 1796 the government formed a new mounted military force, recruited from conservative Protestant landowners—the yeomanry. That same year the parliament passed the controversial *Insurrection Act* to deal with 'outrages' committed by the Defenders and the looming threat of rebellion. This legislation greatly strengthened the state's power to quell disturbances or insurrection by removing traditional British rights, such as trial by jury. A man or woman could now be sentenced to transportation by two magistrates without trial by jury or adherence to the usual rules of evidence. It was reported to the Irish House of Commons that:

> *certain magistrates had privately conversed together, and without any information on oath or good evidence of any kind, at their own pleasure and without any Form of Law, did lay their hands on several fellow suspects and transport them.*[51]

Military courts were also established with sweeping powers, including the imposition of the death penalty. Counties suffering violence could be 'proclaimed' and subjected to night curfews and bans on assemblies. Administering 'unlawful oaths' was punishable by death or transportation. Particular forms of resistance, such as cattle maiming, were criminalised.[52] Then in November, following Britain's example, *habeas corpus* was repealed for all of Ireland. The immediate result was the execution, imprisonment or transportation of more Defenders. It became common practice to offer suspects pardons if they turned informer, provoking harsh retribution from the Defenders, typically assassination.

The United Irishmen's appeal in the countryside was greatly enhanced when a French force attempted to land on the west coast at Bantry Bay just before Christmas 1796. Peace treaties with several European powers left the French Republic free to focus on Britain. Wolfe Tone had fled to Paris following the exposure of his letter, and persuaded the French Government to send an invasion force of 15,000 men under the command of General Lazare Hoche. Victory in Ireland could knock Britain out of the war. Unfortunately for the rebels and the French, a week of inclement weather prevented the ships from landing any more than 400 troops who were picked off by the yeomanry. In fact, Hoche had erred in not getting word to the rebels that he was heading for Bantry Bay.[53] However, the commitment of the French to an invasion now seemed certain, boosting the United Irishmen's numbers and persuading the government to act before another force arrived.

Throughout 1797 more and more Catholics, disappointed by the failure of Fitzwilliam's Reform Bill, flocked to the United Irishmen's cause, especially in Leinster and Munster. William Orr, a Protestant United Irishman, executed later that year, declared:

> *all grounds of jealousy between us and the Catholics is now done away. [The ruling oligarchs] have denied us reform and them emancipation ... they have oppressed them with penal laws and us with military ones ... [T]here is nothing surer than that Irishmen of every denomination must stand or fall together.*[54]

Their recruitment drive was aided by a cultural campaign of pamphlets, ballads and journalism promoting the desirability of revolution.[55] At the harder end of the struggle, Defender gangs raided the homes of Protestant gentry to steal arms in preparation for the rising. More alarming for the government, the United Irishmen embarked on a strategy of winning over Catholic peasants who had been conscripted into the militia. One flyer bid the militia to allow Irish patriotism to 'awaken every noble and generous sentiment in your breasts, and never to turn your arms against your fellow men whose crimes are hatred to tyranny and oppression and a love of liberty'.[56] Billeting troops within local communities made them susceptible to the communities' grievances. General Bagwell reported that shopkeepers, and especially young women in Derry, had seduced fifty of his soldiers into swearing the United Irish oath.[57] The alliance of the radical bourgeoisie and the lower orders had lit the fuse in France and was the unity ticket that inspired most fear in the Protestant Ascendancy. Now the Administration sought to use its new powers to break this alliance apart by unleashing a reign of terror using the militia and yeomanry, beginning in Ulster. General Gerard Lake, an Ascendancy die-hard, declared martial law over that northern province and embarked on a brutal 'dragoon' campaign of executions and even torture, aimed at disarming the rebels. To deal with the United Irishmen's infiltration of the militia, the Administration ordered military executions to frighten the troops.[58] Four Monaghan militia men were identified by an informer as having recruited seventy of their comrades to the rebel cause, and were executed by firing squad in front of thousands of their fellow soldiers, who then had to inspect the bullet holes. The lesson did the trick. Lake reported that '[t]he decided aversion the Monaghan have taken to the United Irishmen is beyond all conception, and I am convinced if ever they are ordered to act against them, the carnage will be dreadful'. It was.

This policy of 'official terror' provoked rebuke from the new commander-in-chief, General Sir Ralph Abercromby, a British officer from Scotland answerable to both the viceroy and Pitt.[59] His priority was the repulsion of any French invasion of Ireland rather than dealing with local rebels. He was critical of Camden and Lake for dispersing the militia locally to protect the Ascendancy and carry out counter-insurgency. Abercromby acknowledged the Defenders' grievances, writing, 'I believe the lower ranks heartily hate the gentlemen because they oppress them, and the gentlemen hate the peasants because they deserve to be hated.'[60] On 26 February he circulated a letter to all officers proposing to end the terror, and claiming the militia was 'in a state of licentiousness that must render it formidable to everyone but the enemy'.[61] Abercromby feared that the abuse of martial law in 'disturbed' areas was throwing fuel on the sparks of rebellion. Like Fitzwilliam, Abercromby would not survive the wrath of the Ascendancy, and Camden replaced him with Lake, who had so distinguished himself in the brutalisation of Ulster. He quickly applied to counties Tipperary, Offaly, Laois and even parts of Wicklow the methods used to disarm the north—torture, burning homes and mass arrests to locate illegally made pikes and the men who would use them.

In preparation for the looming war, the United Irishmen established a secret national Directory, based in Leinster and modelled after the French Revolutionary Government. It was led by three men who would coordinate the uprising—the barrister Thomas Emmet and the Protestant parliamentarians Arthur O'Connor and Lord Edward FitzGerald. All three were men of property and education. O'Connor was a firebrand and his newspaper *The Press* dared to openly promote revolution. FitzGerald was a real coup. He had served with distinction in the British army during the American War of Independence, despite his sympathy for the revolutionaries, and was a scion of one of Ireland's oldest aristocratic families with a tradition of opposing the English conquerors. FitzGerald was also well connected in Westminster, being cousin and friend of radical liberal Whig leader Charles James Fox. By early 1798, informants claimed the United Irishmen had about 100,000 members and could count on that number again to join them in rebellion.

✳   ✳   ✳

THE RISING

AN UNDECLARED CIVIL WAR BEGAN ON 12 MARCH 1798 WHEN THE government swooped on a secret meeting of the Directory and arrested fourteen prominent leaders. O'Connor had already been apprehended and imprisoned in the Tower of London, and shortly afterwards Emmet and others were captured.[62] However, FitzGerald escaped to become part of a new Directory led by brothers John and Henry Sheares, and Samuel Neilson. Preparations for the rebellion continued unabated at the local 'barony' level under the command of colonels, who answered in turn to a county general selected from the colonels.[63] Impatient with waiting for the promised French invasion that was again postponed when Napoleon decided on an expedition to Egypt, the leadership made the fateful decision on 17 May to rise without them, and set the date of 23 May 1798. FitzGerald was designated as commander-in-chief of a rebel citizen army of some 280,000 potential insurgents.[64] His strategy was to make the most of their superior numbers by a surprise rising in Leinster and Ulster, signalled by the capture of the Dublin–Belfast mail coaches. Simultaneous with rebellion across the counties, 10,000 trained men under his personal command were to seize Dublin.[65]

However, on the eve of the rebellion the well-informed Administration launched a pre-emptive strike on the United Irishmen's new leadership, a second attempt at decapitating the rebellion. FitzGerald was captured en route to his troops on 18 May, subdued by a bullet in the shoulder and the blows of rifle butts. Mortally wounded, and denied medical assistance, Lord FitzGerald died in Newgate Prison on 4 June, robbing the rebellion of its most experienced strategist and the legitimacy of his ancient family name. The Sheares brothers and Samuel Neilson were arrested. Confusion reigned and central coordination fell apart, yet the coaches were seized at the appointed time. Next day, thousands of armed rebels crying 'Death or Liberty!' and bearing green flags appeared in Dublin, Meath, Wicklow and Kildare and the rising spread like wildfire through the midlands and the south. However, in the leaderless chaos Dublin was not taken. As the yeomanry and a garrison of 4000 secured the capital for the government, Dublin United Irishmen fled to rebel camps in Wicklow, Meath and Kildare. Next the rising spread to Wexford where the superior numbers of the United Irishmen gave the rebellion an important early victory. Alarmed at this turn of events, Camden's chief secretary, Viscount Castlereagh, warned London that

> *there never was in any country so formidable an effort on the part of the people ... our force cannot cope in a variety of distant points with an enemy that can elude an attack where it is expedient to risk a contest.*[66]

With thousands dead on both sides at the end of the first week, and no decisive victories, the de facto United Irishmen strategy was to spread the rebellion and hold territory until the French came. Unless Wexford was contained and the rest of Ireland pacified, Camden feared that '[e]ven a small body of French will set the country ablaze, and I think neither our force nor our staff equal to the very difficult circumstances they will have to encounter'.[67]

The arrest or death of the core United Irishmen leadership was a potentially fatal blow effectively robbing the rising of strategic coordination that was never replaced. However, local commanders took charge and against the odds led rebel armies to early success in the field. One such commander was Wicklow's Joseph Holt, who had come to the United Irishmen's cause later than Dwyer. In May 1798 he became a random casualty of the terror that gripped the countryside in the weeks leading up to the rising when government militia burned his home. Radicalised by this arbitrary abuse of power, he took the United Irishmen's oath and joined the rebellion. By June he was a colonel leading 960 'Wicklow Men' under the command of General Roche. When Roche proved a poor leader Holt took his place as commander of 11,000 Wicklow rebels and led them to victory at the Battle of Ballyellis.

Rudé's careful mapping of the rebellion demonstrates that its strength was in the country rather than the cities, especially in the southern, central and western counties, even though the origin and leadership of the United Irishmen was based in the big cities and the north, especially Belfast.[68] With Cork and Wexford the only cities involved, he characterised 1798 as 'essentially a peasants' rising' ranging over counties widely dispersed, but with the principal axis in Wexford, Wicklow, Kilkenny and Cork.[69] This mass rural mobilisation was testimony to the campaign's success in winning over the farmers, both Catholics and Presbyterians, exemplified by the rallying of Dwyer and Holt.

The rebellion was fought mainly by the rural labouring class, nicknamed 'croppies' because of their close-cropped hair, a French revolutionary fashion, which distinguished them from the ponytails and wigs of the wealthy and neo-classical Roman styling of the bourgeois radicals. The word also carried a sly dig about the potato crops the peasants lived on. To the Royalist forces, 'croppy' became the slang for all rebel Irish peasants just as the term 'round head' came to signify parliamentary soldiers in the English Civil War. The disparaging name would follow the Irish political prisoners to Australia. As well as winning members of the militia to the United Irish cause, women also played a frontline role, especially in fighting for villages and townships. Found among the 400 rebel dead after the defeat at Ballynahinch were two women clad in green, who had inspired the army as its standard-bearers representing the goddesses of liberty and reason.[70] As civilians, women bore the brunt of outrages, particularly rape, committed by men on both sides.

An early blow to the rebellion was the failure of Ulster to rise on 23 May, despite being the home of Presbyterian republicanism where the United Irishmen had first formed and still had its largest membership of about 49,000. Curtin reasons that the arrests, Lake's official terror in the province and anxiety about the excesses of the Catholic rebels of the South had cooled many Presbyterians' republican zeal.[71] Contemporary observers speculated that the outrages committed against Protestants in Wexford, in particular, might have broken the unity of the radical movement.[72] Furthermore, the experience of European countries liberated by Napoleon's armies and French attacks on American ships trading with Britain led some northern republicans to reconsider whether they wished to be saved by an increasingly imperial and authoritarian France.[73] Nevertheless, an Ulster force of about 7000 belatedly entered the fray under United Irishmen stalwart Henry McCracken in June, but suffered defeats at the Battles of Antrim and Ballynahinch.[74]

The deciding engagement of the rebellion occurred on 21 June, when a loyalist force of 10,000 under Lake attacked the rebel camp at Vinegar Hill, County Wexford. While there were 20,000 rebels, the loyalists had the advantage of heavy artillery, with which they bombarded the camp as they closed in. However, the rebels broke through enemy lines and fled en masse. The defeat at Vinegar Hill was a decisive turning point for the rebellion. Afterwards the initiative lay with the loyalists— rebel armies fought defensively while on the run. In the retreat, fleeing refugees, mainly women and children seeking protection in the camp, were indiscriminately mowed down by the loyalist cavalry and infantry— and left to rot. Wexford women in the camp were gang raped by the victorious soldiers, and in street-by-street fighting in the nearby town of Enniscorthy a rebel hospital was set on fire, the wounded burned alive.

Atrocities were committed by both sides throughout the war. Following the United Irishmen's defeat in the Battle of Antrim, suspected rebels were hunted down, slaughtered and buried in a mass grave.[75] When a rebel called out from a cartload of corpses he was buried alive.[76] The United Irishmen could be just as inhumane. The rebellion in Wexford took a nasty turn with the senseless sectarian killing of Protestants and the destruction of their property. Later, while the battle to retake Wexford raged, zealous rebels, intent on cruelling a negotiated peace between the two sides, broke into the prison and executed most loyalist prisoners, stabbing them with pikes and dumping the bodies in the river.[77]

Bloody and indecisive battles were fought at Connaught, Leinster and Munster, but ultimately poor central command and the superior power of the British and Irish military brought the United Irish forces to heel. Everywhere they were in retreat. Nevertheless, the rebellion might still be salvaged if the anticipated French invasion occurred swiftly. Senior United Irish commanders knew that Tandy's pleading had drawn success and two French expeditionary forces were on their way, one under General Humbert, and the other accompanied by Tandy and Wolfe Tone.

After the crushing defeat at Vinegar Hill, fleeing rebels from Wexford flocked to Wicklow where they were met by Joseph Holt's forces, who ambushed and defeated the pursuing British cavalry at Ballyellis. The Wexford rebels swelled Holt's Wicklow ranks to 13,000, from which he organised the smaller guerrilla force that Dwyer was asked to captain in the Wicklow Mountains. Curtin contends that too many United Irish defeats were the fault of romantic gentlemen generals obsessed with the doomed noble gesture on the battlefield rather than tactical withdrawal to fight another day.[78] Unlike these more conventional commanders, both Holt and Dwyer appreciated the rebel forces were no match for the well-trained red coats and militia on the formal battlefield, but that they would have an advantage launching surprise attacks from wooded mountains in country they knew well. This way cells of resistance could be sustained until the imminent French landing.

The Administration backed by British forces regained control and subdued the rebels in a savage fight-back led by Orangemen dragoons operating within and outside the government militia and yeomanry. In the heat of battle, loyalist forces extracted terrible slaughter on retreating armies, even after rebels had surrendered. Crushing the rebellion required that punishment be quick and severe. Beginning with the Wexford mop-up after Vinegar Hill, local United Irish commanders were quickly court-martialled and summarily executed, to dissuade renewed rebellion and as retribution for rebel atrocities, such as the massacre of Wexford Bridge where rebels butchered local loyalist prisoners. At the same time rape, murder, arson and other new atrocities were inflicted by loyalist soldiers on communities thought to have risen in rebellion. In this counter-terror, sectarian antipathy to Catholic peasants, especially that of Orangemen in the ranks, ran amok with little restraint imposed by local generals or the viceroy, Lord Camden. However, as the civil war entered its last phase London appointed a new viceroy, 1st Marquis Cornwallis, charged with calming down the excesses of loyalist troops. Cornwallis had tasted defeat himself at the hands of the Americans in the War of Independence and knew the value of clemency. He despaired of the Ascendancy reprisals, advising his superiors that

> [t]he yeomanry are in the style of the Loyalists of America, only much more numerous and powerful, and a thousand times more ferocious. These men have saved the country, but they now take the lead in rapine and murder ... The conversation, even at my table ... always turns on hanging, shooting, burning, etc ...[79]

Cornwallis immediately offered a general amnesty to ordinary soldiers who returned to their homes, but made clear that the ringleaders would face harsh retribution.

Into this atmosphere the French finally arrived, too late to save the rebellion. Humbert landed his 800 men at Killala, on the west coast on 22 August and declared his intention of liberating Ireland from the 'British yoke'. Unfortunately the other ships were delayed and only a few thousand rebels rallied to his brazenly formed Provisional Government of Connaught. Humbert then led a valiant march east towards Dublin, hoping to be joined by the United Irish forces of Ulster, but following the defeat at Antrim the north would rise no more. In September Humbert's army met a vastly superior force under Cornwallis at Ballinamuck, and was decisively defeated. The threat neutralised, the French prisoners were accorded the respect due to prisoners of war and shipped home. Not so the United Irishmen.

Wolfe Tone, captured with the remaining French ships, was tried for treason and sentenced to death. Rather than indulge the Crown with an exemplary execution he cut his own throat in his cell. Trials of the more than eighty United Irish leaders held in custody had begun in July as a lesson to the rebels in the field. Following the hanging of the Sheares brothers, Byrne and McCann, for high treason, the remaining prisoners, including Emmet, MacEven, O'Connor and Neilson, reached an accommodation with the government. In exchange for a detailed account of the aims and *modus operandi* of the United Irishmen and their uprising they were permitted to go into exile in America or France. So much for the men with status. On the ground local commanders and ordinary rebels continued to be executed for treason or sedition and up to 500 were transported to the New South Wales penal colony. Among them was Joseph Holt, who surrendered in November 1798.[80] Despairing of a further French landing force and any chance for the rebellion against overwhelming odds, Holt struck a deal—in exchange for laying down his sword he would not suffer the indignity of trial and sentencing as a prisoner, but instead go into voluntary exile with his wife and children, perhaps to the United States. When he learned that he was to be transported for life to Botany Bay 'he swore, blasphemed and inveighed most bitterly against this breach of his treaty'.[81]

Yet still Dwyer fought on, daring to raid Leitrim, Carlow, Limerick and Wexford, keeping a flicker of rebellion alive in the Wicklow Mountains, hoping for the promised French invasion. To the British Government, and the supplicant Irish Administration in Dublin Castle, Michael Dwyer was a renegade and a traitor committing acts of terror on the King's subjects. However, here was the classic case of one side's terrorist being another's freedom fighter. Dwyer's stubborn rebel stand, and the inability of the most powerful military force on Earth to bring him to heel, inspired the scattered, demoralised radicals and revolutionaries of the United Irish movement. He seemed to have a charmed life, narrowly escaping from British soldiers when cornered, or surviving a hail of enemy fire when others fell. Unable to demilitarise Wicklow, the government was forced to build barracks and roads for the campaign. The underground leadership made contact with Dwyer and conceived a plan to strike at the regime's very heart. On the ground the local Catholic peasants looked to him for protection from the vengeance of the army and Orangemen. They saluted him as the Wicklow Chief, one of their own who became a hero in the manner of Scotland's legendary resistance fighter William Wallace. Even when a price of £500 was placed on his head—a huge sum at this time—Dwyer remained at large, hidden among the people, immune to betrayal amid the counter-revolution, keeping alive hope for an Irish republic.[82]

Then, on 23 July 1803 this hope was dealt a near fatal-blow with the collapse of a carefully plotted United Irish coup d'état against the colonial Administration in Dublin. Dwyer's battle-hardened veterans, newly armed and awaiting the signal to attack the capital, learned to their dismay that the United Irish conspirators were ambushed as they made for Dublin Castle, and their leader Robert Emmet, younger brother of Thomas, executed. Anne Devlin, a cousin of Dwyer's who assisted in the plot, was tortured by a half-hanging, but refused to betray Emmet or inform on fellow rebels, even after her family were incarcerated. The coup's dismal failure left Dwyer with little choice but to surrender while he could still bargain from a position of strength. With his own father and sister in prison (and wife and children under arrest) and rebel friends facing the hangman's noose, Dwyer—still undefeated—decided to parlay terms with the British and perhaps secure exile for himself, family and compatriots to America. He surrendered on 14 December 1803 along with lieutenants Arthur Devlin, Hugh Byrne, Martin Burke and John Mernagh on the promise that they would be given pardons and passage to the United States.[83] The *Freeman's Journal* observed that

> *Dwyer, the noted Insurgent, was brought into town on Saturday evening last to the Castle ... He was dressed in country style, in a white frieze Jockey, and appeared to be somewhat inebriated. The noble captain was much displeased at the mob gazing at him and used some ruffianly and angry expressions.*[84]

'DEATH OR LIBERTY!'

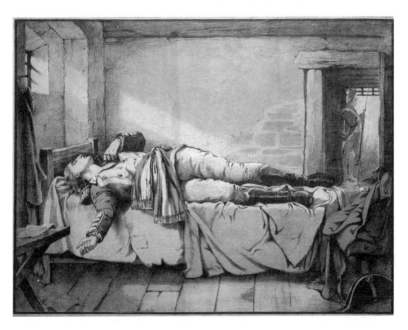

However, once he and his men were in custody they learned that they
had been betrayed. The Master of Kilmainham Gaol, Dr Edward Trevor,
informed Dwyer 'you will never set foot on American soil, to come back
when you like to raise another rebellion. You are to go to Botany Bay.'[85]
Charged with high treason, the Wicklow Chief and his men were to be
transported to one of the least republican places on Earth, the New South
Wales colony. The surrender of Michael Dwyer is commonly taken as
marking the end of the Irish Rising of '98, but there was one more bloody
Irish rebellion to come, a year later and half a world away in the outer
western Sydney district of Castle Hill where British troops would once
again hear the battle cry 'Death or Liberty!'

*   *   *

Why did the rebellion fail? The inability of the French to seriously
commit to an invasion meant the experienced Irish and British troops

would ultimately prevail, though at great cost in lives and casualties. The use of terror in the north by the government commander Lake and the elimination of the senior rebel command weakened the United Irishmen even before the uprising. The formation of the Orangemen and the excesses of some Catholics effectively divided the peasantry along religious lines, depriving the United Irishmen of overwhelming popular support in the countryside, especially in the north. In the end the union between Protestants and Catholics that lay at the core of rebellion proved weak under fire. There remained a tension between the United Irish quest for secular civic virtue and the Defenders' dream to retrieve their land and revive the Catholic Ireland of their forefathers. The two groups in the alliance often flew different flags—the United Irishmen green with a crownless harp and Defenders green with a yellow cross—and frequently bickered over goals and tactics.[86] The greater strength of the rising in the Catholic south and midlands meant the cosmopolitan, non-sectarian democratic revolution promoted by the middle-class United Irishmen became overwhelmed by an ethnic, peasant-based and anti-Protestant nationalism that would persist in the popular memory of the '98 Rebellion.

At the conclusion of hostilities 30,000 people were dead, including many non-combatants. Millions of pounds worth of property was reduced to smouldering embers. The immediate political consequence of the rebellion was the decision by Pitt's Government to constitutionally absorb Ireland into the realm of Great Britain. The rebellion and incursions by France demonstrated that as a semi-independent colony with its own parliament, Ireland offered a soft target to Britain's enemies. By an *Act of Union* taking effect on 1 January 1801, Ireland became part of the new United Kingdom. Its viceregal Administration was dissolved and the two parliaments were merged into one, with Ireland's Protestant MPs and nobility sitting in expanded Houses of Commons and Lords at Westminster. Pitt considered abolition of the Irish Parliament as the only way to curb some of the worst excesses of the Ascendancy that had wantonly stirred up rebellion by opposing reform, and even United Irishmen founder Archibald Rowan recognised that '[i]n that measure I see the downfall of one of the most corrupted assemblies I believe ever existed'.[87] However, despite the British Government holding out the prospect of enhanced rights for the Catholic bourgeoisie in the new union, they would not be allowed to sit in Westminster until 1829. By failing in its execution, the uprising had taken Ireland backwards, not forwards, now even more firmly under the thumb of the English. The extinguishment of these last vestiges of independence provoked the Dublin coup attempt of 1803 by the last remnants of the United Irishmen. However, the secular liberalism that had originally inspired the United Irishmen would grow ever stronger in the nineteenth century, making its mark in Britain, Canada and Australia and re-emerging in the Young Ireland movement of the 1840s.[88]

Rudé called the Rebellion of 1798 a 'near-revolution' because although losing its leadership at the decisive moment, the rebellion still came close to succeeding due to the rallying of ordinary farmers and working people who were prepared to fight for an Irish republic.[89] While the immediate result was the submersion of Ireland into Britain, the people now had a close-run rebellion and a legion of martyrs to inspire future generations. However, the other dream of uniting Protestant and Catholic in a common democratic cause was a casualty of the war, killed off by inflamed sectarian hatreds that would be carried by convicts, gaolers and settlers to Botany Bay. The defeat of the Rebellion of 1798 exacerbated other divisions in Irish society that would endure throughout the nineteenth century between liberal democrats and conservatives, republicans and loyalists, landed and bourgeois interests, landlord and tenant, employers and workers, unruliness and authority, and national and imperial belonging. These conflicts too would be imported into the social fabric of the Australian colonies.

* * *

REBELS TO CONVICTS

From the emerald island
Ne'er to see dry land
Until they spy land
In sweet Bot'ny Bay[90]

OLIVER CROMWELL, FOLLOWING HIS INVASION IN THE SEVENTEENTH century, introduced transportation to Ireland as a punishment. Irish prisoners were originally sent to the British plantations in the West Indies, and then to the North American colonies, following the *Transportation Act* of 1717, in order to 'deter criminals and supply the colonies with labour'.[91] After the British Parliament passed legislation in 1786 establishing the convict colony at Botany Bay, Ireland followed suit with an *Act for the Better Execution of the Law*, inaugurating transportation to New South Wales from Ireland.[92] Rudé calculated that of the approximately 39,000 Irish men and women convicts transported to the Australian colonies during the convict period, 2250 were political rebels or social protesters.[93] He divided the transportation of rebels and protesters from Ireland into five phases. First was the rural revolt that culminated in the secret Catholic Defender societies of the early 1790s, whose captured members were the first Irish political prisoners to be sent to Australia. Second but merging with the Defenders was the overtly political rebellion of the United Irishmen that continued in Wicklow and then Dublin, until 1803. Rudé's third phase is the prolonged and violent 'land and tithe war' that gripped agrarian Ireland, lasting from the end of the Napoleonic Wars until the 1840s. The fourth phase was the peasant resistance to the devastating potato famine of 1845 and the ill-fated Young Ireland Rebellion of 1848. The final group of Irish political prisoners to be sent to Australia were the Fenian rebels, who arrived in Western Australia on the last ever convict transport in 1868. The remainder of this chapter will consider the experiences of the Defenders and United Irishmen transported between 1795 and 1806, by far the largest group of political prisoners ever sent to Australia.

Even before the rebellion broke out there were 1186 political prisoners in custody, most of them Defenders. Records, such as they are, indicate that between 1798 and 1803 over 350 rebels were ordered to be executed and about 1000 sentenced to transportation or exile, to which can be added between 200 and 500 commuted death sentences.[94] For example, the United Irishmen commander Tom Lanagan, also known as Captain Steel, was saved from the gallows by the intervention of an aristocratic patron, and was transported for seven years instead.[95] Edward Gibbons, who had provided horses to French commander Humbert when he landed at Mayo, actually had the noose around his neck when he was informed that his sentence was commuted to transportation for life. It is impossible to know how many were executed illegally after battles without the benefit of a court verdict, and the figures for transportation do not tally with ships' records. Why? Approximately 318 transportees were sold to the King of Prussia to serve in his infantry and many more took up the option of service in the British army and navy.[96] John Malone, a soldier in the Royal Irish Dragoons who was found guilty of 'trying to entice others to desert to the rebels', was given 500 lashes and ordered to serve in the British army overseas for life.[97] James Lyons, a private in the Irish militia found guilty of defecting to the French in Mayo, was allowed to serve his life sentence in the army, but was mistakenly sent to New South Wales as a convict. A lucky few escaped the hulks. Edward Gibbons, having just avoided the gallows, escaped to France where he was made an officer in the Irish Legion, a republican army in exile.

How many Defenders and United Irishmen were transported? Numbers are difficult to quantify due to poor record keeping, the vagaries of military justice and the destruction of archives in Dublin's Four Courts by fire in 1922 during the civil war. On Rudé's calculations between 325 and 500 rebels were transported in the wake of the 1798 uprising, on six ships.[98] To this must be added the 160 Defenders sent between 1791 and 1797 on the *Queen*, *Boddingtons*, *Sugar Cane*, *Britannia* and the *Marquis Cornwallis*.[99] This makes an uppermost total of approximately 660 Irish political prisoners on either side of the republican insurrection of 1798 transported to 'Botany Bay'.[100]

The rapid build-up in the numbers of Irish prisoners in New South Wales over a very short time frame posed real problems for order in the colony. Bound to each other and their ideals by solemn oaths, they manifested a spirit of solidarity and defiance uncommon among the criminal convicts or the more individualist bourgeois radicals. Unlike the gentlemanly Scottish Martyrs, most were peasants, artisans or labourers. None of the top leadership of the United Irishmen, drawn from the urban bourgeoisie and breakaway gentry, were transported—most were hanged, imprisoned or exiled in Europe. Senior leader James Napper Tandy, whose death sentence had been commuted to transportation, was extended the further courtesy in deference to his age and rank of going into exile in France. More typically sent to New South Wales were rebel commanders of the second rank, local captains and chieftains, such as the independent farmers Joseph Holt and Michael Dwyer.

Captured rebels were dealt with either by the magistrates presiding at courts of assizes or by military courts martial, both operating under the *Insurrection Act* (renewed in 1799) that gave free rein to informers in contravention of the customary rules of evidence. Rudé characterised the punishment of accused rebels as 'savage, arbitrary' and 'vindictive' tempered by confusion 'so grotesque as to turn the tragedy into a comedy of errors'.[101] The severity and confusion of the punishment meted out is revealed in the treatment of three priests, none of whom were combatants.[102] Father James Harold was charged with complicity, had his house near Dublin burned by the militia and was transported for life. Father Dixon was sentenced to death on the say-so of an informer who accused him of administering a United Irishmen's oath, singing a rebel song and wearing a badge bearing the provocative slogan 'Erin Go Bragh' (meaning 'Ireland Forever'). He was reprieved from the gallows when the sentence was commuted to transportation to New South Wales. By virtue of hearing confession, Father Peter O'Neil was accused of participating in the murder of an informer, and the presiding general at his court martial ordered the priest flogged with a cat-o'-nine-tails laced with pieces of tin to secure the names of the guilty parishioners.[103] He later recalled:

> *My back and the points of my shoulders were quite bare of flesh ...*
> *After a pause a wire cat was got; the first lash, as it renewed my pains,*
> *made me shake the triangle, indeed a second infliction penetrated my*
> *loins and tore them excruciatingly.*[104]

Despite receiving 257 lashes, O'Neil refused to betray the confidentiality of the confessional, and was sentenced to be transported. Although the priest was pardoned by a Court of Inquiry, it did not arrive until after his transport ship the *Anne* had left, and once in New South Wales the Irish authorities refused to issue the pardon because they did not want him to return.[105] Unfortunately such miscarriages of justice were not uncommon. In some cases, leaders escaped from custody while pardoned men were transported by mistake to New South Wales, and rarely did a record of sentence duration accompany the hapless prisoner, to the annoyance of officials in Sydney. Governor Hunter complained to London that

> [t]he manner in which the convicts are sent out from Ireland is
> so extremely careless and irregular that it must be felt by these
> people as a particular hardship, and by government as a great
> inconvenience. Every ship [of] that country have [sic] omitted to
> bring any account of the conviction or terms of transportation of
> those people they bring out.[106]

As a consequence, many political prisoners languished as convicts long after the expiry of their term. The next governor, King, blamed the administrative shambles on convictions 'mostly by Courts-Martial prior to the time when the proceedings of such Courts were sanctioned by law', or summarily 'before magistrates who exercised their powers under the Insurrection Acts, and whose proceedings were, in the disturbed state of the country, not recorded'.[107] Thus, the Irish political prisoners posed a problem for the bureaucrats at the helm of the convict colony from the moment they disembarked.

* * *

A WHIFF OF MUTINY

THE REPUTATION OF IRISH POLITICAL PRISONERS IN SYDNEY FOR insurrection was not helped by the reports of attempted mutinies on many of the ships transporting them to Australia. The *Sugar Cane* was six weeks out of Ireland when rumours reached the captain that prisoners had sawn off their chains as part of a plot to take control of the ship, with the connivance of aggrieved sailors and marines. A convict who escaped his chains was executed and the alleged ringleaders flogged. A conspiracy was also discovered on the *Boddingtons*, in which 'all the officers were to have been murdered, the first mate and the agent excepted, who were to be preserved alive for the purpose of conducting the ship to port, when they likewise were to be put to death'.[108] This account came from a convict informer, as did most allegations of mutiny. Following similar accusations, a group of Defenders on board the *Marquis Cornwallis* suffered a particularly violent retribution. Sailing from Cork in 1795 carrying 222 convicts, including ninety Defenders, the *Marquis Cornwallis* was a month at sea when the captain learned that the Defenders and some of the military were plotting to seize control. Nearly fifty suspects were whipped and placed in handcuffs, thumb screws and leg irons. The ringleader, one Sergeant Ellis intended for the New South Wales Corps, was so severely flogged that he died leg-ironed to a fellow conspirator nine days later. In Ireland, Defenders had dealt swiftly and savagely with traitors in their midst, and when some of them below decks tried to strangle the convict who betrayed their mutiny the guards fired into the melee, killing ten and injuring many more. It was later revealed at an inquiry that female convicts planned to strike a blow 'by preparing pulverised glass to mix with the flour of which the seamen were to make puddings'.[109] On arrival in Sydney in February 1796 the convicts of the *Marquis Cornwallis* were identified by Judge-Advocate David Collins as

> *for the most part, of the description of people termed Defenders, desperate and ripe for any scheme from which danger and destruction were likely to ensure, the women were of the same complexion ... what an importation!*[110]

The captain was exonerated.

While the seditious character of the Defenders was blamed for these troubles, other investigations suggested that poor on-board conditions contributed to discontent among both convicts and crew. When the *Britannia* docked in Sydney in 1797 authorities learned that one in seventeen convicts had died—a total of ten men and one woman. An inquiry convened by an appalled Governor Hunter found that short rations and brutal punishment had caused the deaths. Not for nothing did Robert Hughes describe the *Britannia* as one of the worst hellships in convict history.[111] Paranoid about mutiny in the aftermath of the *Marquis Cornwallis*, the ship's master responded to rumours by ordering James Brannon be given 300 lashes one day, followed by another 500 the next! Fellow prisoner Patrick Garnely was told by the master, 'I will not hang you, it is too gentle a death, but I will cut you to pieces', and he died after enduring 400 lashes with a 'cat' containing horse skin designed to tear deeper into the flesh.[112] Of the ten who died during the trip, six died directly from floggings and two who had also been flogged perished from thirst after being refused their water rations and left to drink their own urine. The woman who died on the voyage is said to have committed suicide. In the case of the *Britannia*, the ship's officers were discharged from the service. Not surprisingly, many of the disembarked prisoners despaired and fled into the bush, suffering further flogging, with two hanged upon capture.[113]

One of the most notorious mutinies involved United Irish rebels transported on the *Anne* that departed Cork in 1800. The ship was part of a convoy, but became separated just after leaving Rio. During a routine fumigation of the convicts the cry 'Death or Liberty!' rang out as one prisoner seized the ship's master. The deck erupted in riot while thirty prisoners seized weapons from the armoury and attacked officers. However, a convict was shot dead and order restored.[114] To teach a lesson, the leader of the mutiny, a United Irishman from Limerick named Marcus Sheehy, was executed by firing squad, the only transported convict to suffer such a fate at sea, as all others were hanged as per regulations.[115] The other mutineers, including a United Irish captain from Tipperary, Philip Cunningham, were brutally flogged and on arrival in Sydney incarcerated at Norfolk Island. Cunningham, a stonemason, had revived the United Irishmen's organisation in the south of Ireland in 1799, harassing the yeomanry and rescuing prisoners in a smaller scale version of the Wicklow operation. Captured and transported for life in October that year, he was one of the leaders of the mutiny on board the *Anne*. Another thirteen prisoners had perished on this ship, suggesting a regime of overcrowding, poor hygiene and inadequate rations may have driven the men to revolt.

Although Joseph Holt had freedom of movement about the convict transport *Minerva* on which he journeyed to Sydney, he later complained that '[i]f I had known the misery of this vessel, no lord or lady would have influence enough to induce me to surrender'. He had purchased passage for his wife and children, so enjoyed some comfort compared to most crew and convicts. It may have been the birth of another child during the journey, but Holt claims in his memoir that he resolved to retire from rebellion. Gaining the captain's confidence, Holt was given supervision over the convicts, and in that capacity was able to render his comrades valuable service, such as regular recreation on deck. This made all the difference to their survival chances.

Not so lucky were the Irish prisoners on board the *Hercules* and *Atlas*, two ships of shame that arrived in Sydney weighed down with the stench of death. Not long after the *Hercules* had passed Cape Verde on 29 December a large group of convicts attacked the guards and seized the quarterdeck. An hour and thirteen dead prisoners later the mutiny was suppressed. When the leader, Jeremiah Pendergast, was identified he was shot dead there and then by the ship's master, without due process. A Vice-Admiralty Court investigating the mutiny found that the prisoners had endured dirty conditions and overcrowding in order that more room could be made for cargo to trade in Sydney. Worse still, fumigation of vermin had not occurred, and convicts were cheated of the correct water and food rations by use of loaded weights.[116] As a result another thirty prisoners had died on the 209-day journey, and the remainder who disembarked in Sydney were described as emaciated. Costello speculates that the fact that eighty-four of the prisoners on board, veterans of the uprising, had life sentences would have exacerbated the desperation of the starving, cramped prisoners. In this instance there was some justice, with the master, Luckyn Betts, found guilty of manslaughter and fined the not inconsiderable sum of £500. The corner-cutting and squalid conditions on the private contract transports was again brought to the attention of the Navy when the *Atlas* arrived in Sydney having lost 68 men and two women to typhus and dysentery. Some of the dead were still lying chained in their bunks and four more perished on arrival, while twenty were hospitalised. An investigation found that the high mortality rate resulted from 'the want of proper attention to cleanliness, the want of free circulation of air, and the lumbered state of the [ship's] prison and hospital'.[117] As with its sister ship, the prisoners had been packed in tight to make way for imported goods. This time the only punishment was to forbid the master to unload the cargo he had prized above human lives.

According to Holt's published account of his exile in Australia, when the *Minerva* docked at Port Jackson, he was greeted by a rotting corpse, more skeleton than man, left hanging from a gallows atop a hill.[118] What manner of place had the Irish rebels been sent to? Much of the historiography of convict Australia falls into one of two traditions. The first, stretching from convict ballads and Marcus Clarke's gothic masterpiece *For the Term of His Natural Life* to Robert Hughes' *Fatal Shore*, condemn the harsh regime of the cat-o'-nine-tails, chain gangs and brutal gulags, such as Norfolk Island and Macquarie Harbour. A more optimistic interpretation of conditions facing convicts in the penal system was first expounded by academic historian John Hirst in the 1980s. He argued that 'convict society in New South Wales was a much happier and humane one than traditional judgements have allowed'.[119] With reference to administrative control, working life and economic opportunities he demonstrated that most convicts were able to negotiate a measure of freedom, and even advancement. Rather than a brutalised society, early New South Wales was

> *much more a normal British colony which had convicts as part of its labour force and which had always preserved crucial legal rights and economic opportunities for convicts and ex-convicts.*[120]

For Hirst the assignment system, whereby convicts worked for private individuals, far from resembling the American model of slavery, still guaranteed the convicts rights and protection as subjects of the Crown.[121] James Boyce has recently applied a similar approach to the early history of Van Diemen's Land, drawing on evidence that in the colony's first two decades convicts enjoyed considerable economic and administrative freedom as hunters and shepherds.[122]

Where do political prisoners generally, and the Irish rebels in particular, fall in this debate? Over the eighty years of transportation convicts sentenced for political crimes might experience either the gulag or a fair go, depending on when they arrived, their crime and sentence, how they behaved and most importantly their education, skill and social class. The New South Wales colony was a tougher prospect prior to the 1820s, when punishments were harsher and there were fewer free settlers, less capital for investment, a smaller market and therefore limited opportunity for assignment to private employers. When Hughes claimed that 'Australia was the official Siberia for Irish dissidents' he was referring to 'the turn of the [eighteenth] century' when most of the United Irishmen arrived.[123] In Van Diemen's Land conditions became tougher over time because the abolition of assignment in 1839 meant that all prisoners were funnelled through the harsher 'probation' system serving two years on government road gangs. Convicts with skills were in demand and found better berths than mere labourers. Educated prisoners, especially those with medical, legal, engineering, clerical or even pedagogical expertise, were sought after for service to the government. Due to the high incidence of lawyers, teachers, clergy, writers, organisers and propagandists in their ranks, political prisoners tended to be better educated than convicts specialising in theft or crimes against the person. Through the 1820s, '30s and '40s the colonial economies reaped a rich harvest of vital trade and agricultural skill due to the transportation of rural and urban working-class social protesters, particularly the Swing Rioters from southern England, the North American Patriots and the Chartists. Their economic journey and the extent to which they fared better in Australia than at home will be explored in the next chapter. Political convicts might also possess military prowess, bearing and sometimes rank which could be beneficial to the government if channelled into policing rather than rebellion. In a society sensitive to the nuance of class, status and hierarchy convicts with bourgeois or (in rare cases) aristocratic background could expect to be treated less harshly than the majority of lower-class convicts and be extended some of the privileges of free settlers. This was certainly the case with the scholarly and gentlemanly Scottish Martyrs and later with the leaders of the Young Ireland Rebellion of 1848. How were the Irish rebels of 1798 regarded and treated when they arrived in New South Wales?

* * *

FIRST IMPRESSIONS

THE IRISH WERE TREATED DIFFERENTLY FROM OTHER PRISONERS. Thanks to the mutinies aboard the *Marquis Cornwallis* and *Britannia*, Governor Hunter regarded the Irish Defenders as 'turbulent', 'worthless' and 'horrid'. Displaying Protestant bigotry he could not abide the 'credulous ignorance that an artful priest may lead them to every action that is either good or bad'.[124] With the contempt that conquerors sometimes have for the conquered, officials in Sydney disdained the Irish peasants among the prisoners for their poverty and illiteracy, their 'Papist' religion and the tendency of some to speak in their ancestral Gaelic. The official Church of England chaplain, the Reverend Samuel Marsden, dismissed the Catholic prisoners as 'composed of the lowest Class of the Irish nation; who are of the most wild, ignorant and savage race that were ever favoured with the light of civilisation'.[125] Captain David Collins, later lieutenant-governor of Van Diemen's Land, described the Irish prisoners as 'a race of beings (for they don't deserve the appellation of men) so extremely ignorant'.[126] Collins had grown up the son of an English major general in Ireland as part of the Protestant Ascendancy, and was betraying its prejudice against the Catholic peasantry—one that coloured the official attitudes to the rebel convicts in the colony. Reviled as traitors and barely human, the Irish prisoners composed what Robert Hughes termed 'Australia's first white minority'.[127]

As a consequence of the complete marginalisation of Catholic peasants in Ireland, their poor nutrition and scant education, the rebel prisoners presented as illiterate, ignorant and superstitious. Ignorance could be fatal. Some Irish prisoners who had never travelled further than their villages believed that if they escaped into the bush it was possible to walk to China. Fifteen to twenty who arrived on the *Queen* bolted into the scrub, with most starving to death.[128] Six other escapees from the *Britannia* were caught and hanged. One Irish bolter who made it through the bush to a settlement thought he had reached China, asking an officer of the New South Wales Corps 'what has brought your honour to China all the way?'[129] What emerges from the escape attempts, the many folk ballads and laments, and even the eventual rebellion, was the Irish prisoners' deep longing for home. In the early 1800s this was not mere homesickness or nostalgia, but an urgent desire to get back to Ireland to join the fight that leaders such as Dwyer and Emmet were keeping alive.

Letters from the governors make clear their concern that such a rapid build-up of seditious Irish political prisoners must threaten the stability of the colony. 'If so many Irish are sent here,' complained Governor Hunter, 'it will be impossible to keep order.'[130] His successor, Governor King, was aghast at the arrival of the *Anne* from Cork in 1801, carrying:

> *137 of the most desperate and diabolical characters that could be selected throughout that kingdom, together with a Catholic priest of the most notorious, seditious, and rebellious principles—which makes the numbers of those who, avowing a determination never to lose sight of the oath by which they are bound as United Irishmen, amount to 600, are ready, and only waiting an opportunity to put their diabolical plans in execution.*[131]

Unfortunately for both the governor and the diabolical prisoners, prior to 1817 free settlers were still thin on the ground, so most went to work for the government on a handful of farms, public works and services, exacerbating the concentration of numbers that made the authorities anxious. Rudé demonstrated that whereas later groups of protesters and rioters would be dispersed across the countryside through the assignment system, the United Irishmen were massed together.[132] While private assignment, as Hirst has shown, allowed convicts greater freedom and usually better conditions, work for the government meant a tougher punishment regime under military overseers, cramped living conditions and shorter rations.[133] It was no accident that the Castle Hill Rebellion was planned and executed on the government farm at Parramatta.

Despite their alleged ignorance, the Irish political convicts manifested a spirit of defiance that not only frustrated authorities, but leveraged a degree of space and dignity. The rebels had at their disposal a repertoire of resistance that ranged from the soft protest of humour, songs and speaking Gaelic to the hard defiance of plotting, violence and insurrection. The Irish prisoners were impatient with obedience and servility among their own, one resident observing that a 'man who endeavours to reform, or to give satisfaction to his master is barely tolerated, while he who has been subjected to excessive punishment at the penal station is considered a hero'.[134] In this way solidarity was used to enforce resistance to authority and the go-slow. In the context of New South Wales' own fledgling Protestant Ascendancy, attending the Catholic Mass became both a marker of Irish national identity and a cover for assembling. The very insolence and mob-mentality that earned the Irish prisoners rebuke and punishment also won them a thin slither of autonomy within the system. Rudé made the important point that political prisoners were able to manifest cohesion only where 'the crime for which they were transported had given them a sense of identity as a group'.[135] The oaths, drills and battles experienced by the Defenders and United Irishmen had forged such an identity. It helped the rebel prisoners transform their numbers into strength. The mere fact that governors and the New South Wales Corps were worried about a rebellion indicated that the rebels had changed from vanquished foe to threat. Irish solidarity was despised by English officials, but also feared.

While representing a clear and present danger to the authorities, the Irish rebels also provided the colony with much-needed agricultural and craft skills. Unlike the general convict population of recidivist criminals, the Irish political prisoners were ordinary working people, with a weighting among the men towards tenant farmers, rural labourers and trades and a smattering of professions, clergy and military personnel. Among the seventy-six rebels on the *Minerva* in 1799 were to be found a teacher, an army officer, two lawyers, a Catholic priest and Protestant clergyman, and a large number of tradesmen, including a blacksmith, an apothecary, a silversmith, cotton printer, jeweller, soap maker, gardener, butcher, coppersmith, an iron-founder and a number of carpenters, millwrights and wheelwrights, stonemasons, distillers, bakers and weavers.[136] This diversity reflected the cross-class coalition that the United Irishmen were able to assemble. Other ships brought Defenders and United Irishmen from rural districts accustomed to agricultural or pastoral work. This skill base presented authorities in Sydney with a paradox. While the Irish rebels appeared insolent and seditious, many were very promising from an economic point of view.

More promising still was the small minority of educated United Irishmen transported after the Rebellion of 1798. Joseph Holt came the closest to the gentlemanly status of Muir and his colleagues. However, there were other educated rebel leaders transported, including Captain St Leger, Captain William Alcock, James Meehan, medical doctor

Bryan O'Connor, two teachers William Maum and Farrell Cuffe, the Protestant Reverend Henry Fulton and the three Irish priests. Governor Hunter observed of the *Minerva* and *Friendship* contingent that '[m]any of those prisoners have been either bred up in genteel life, or to professions, unaccustomed to hard labour'.[137] The unwritten rules governing social hierarchy meant that despite 'determined abhorrence of the crimes', Hunter's administration could not 'divest ourselves of the common feelings of humanity so far as to send a physician, a former respectable sheriff of a county (Holt), a Roman Catholic Priest, or a Protestant clergyman to the grubbing hoe or timber carriage'.[138] While such men might be executed, to put them to hard labour would threaten to overturn the class-based social order.

Holt was given a land grant to live on and farm with his family, and as an experienced farmer was employed for wages to manage the property of settler William Cox, who he had befriended on the *Minerva*. Over the long term he prospered, making a success of the farm, and growing his own property through further grants and purchases. As a Protestant gentleman capable of combining rebel political ideals with social respectability, Holt had no difficulty adapting to colonial society. In Sydney he appeared to maintain his shipboard resolve to keep aloof from the seditious shenanigans of lower-class convicts. However, the privileges extended to some of these rebel gentlemen in Sydney were withdrawn at the slightest accusation of collaboration in any seditious plotting. It did not bode well for Holt when the always-suspect Maurice Margarot paid him a visit. In 1800, Holt was arrested and detained for a period, while false rumours of his complicity in a plot were investigated. Thus they lived in continual anxiety, marked men due to their high profile as former leaders, vulnerable to an army of convict informers.

* * *

PUNISHMENT

THE OVERWHELMING MAJORITY OF IRISH REBELS SENT TO NEW South Wales were skilled and unskilled manual workers, not educated property owners and professionals. Rather than receive land grants they would do hard labour and be vulnerable to the full range of physical punishments. In dealing with disobedience and rumoured conspiracies to foment rebellion the penal system had at its disposal a hierarchy of punishments.

Until the 1830s floggings were routinely prescribed for all transgressions by prisoners. Refusal to work, laziness, disobedience to an employer, drunkenness and disorderly behaviour were all floggable offences, suggesting that the authorities used the whip as they would on a beast of burden, to extract as much labour as they could. What shocks the modern reader is the number of lashes that were inflicted in one session on a single individual, and the damage inflicted on the convict's body by this punishment. It is worth remembering that this same punishment was mandatory in the army and navy, reflecting a far more draconian society.

For Robert Hughes flogging served a simple existential purpose: to break a man's spirit by breaking his body.[139] Another use of flogging, as we saw with Father O'Neil, was to extract information. A magistrate as well as Anglican clergyman, Samuel Marsden is not remembered as the whipping parson for nothing. Charged in September 1800 with discovering and suppressing a rumoured plot by Irish prisoners to plunge the colony into rebellion, the Reverend Marsden resorted to the cat-o'-nine-tails to extricate the whereabouts of an alleged stash of pikes from his tight-lipped suspects. Informants claimed the pikes were intended to dispatch soldiers while still sleeping in their beds.[140] 'We have not been able to come at any pikes yet ... I think there will be sufficient evidence ... to justify some severe examples of punishment.'[141]

Five of Marsden's plotters received 300 lashes, and another four got 100. One of these men, twenty-year-old United Irishman Patrick Galvin transported on the *Minerva*, was flogged to near death. Joseph Holt observed the young rebel's bravery in the face of this torment:

He was tied up next to receive 300 lashes. The first hundred were on the shoulders, and he was cut to the bone between the shoulder blades, which were both bare. The doctor then ordered that the next hundred be inflicted lower down, which reduced his flesh to such jelly that the doctor ordered him to have the remaining hundred on the calves of his legs. During the whole time Galvin never whimpered ... He was asked where the pikes were hid. He said he did not know, and that if he did he would not tell. 'You may as well hang me' he said.[142]

Marsden acknowledged that 'though a young man he would have died upon the spot before he would tell a single sentence'.[143] Such a method of interrogation amounted to torture. As preacher, landowner and law officer, the Reverend Marsden had free rein in the colony to indulge his puritanism, his avarice and his sadistic streak. Although a disciple of the anti-slavery evangelical reformer William Wilberforce, Marsden succumbed to the gaoler's temptation to hold prisoners in contempt and to abuse his power over them.[144] A colleague on the bench wrote that 'I have known him to order 500 lashes, and the punishments afflicted by his authority were more severe than those of any other magistrate in the colony'.[145] Informants alleged Marsden was on a hit-list to be killed at the outset of the uprising, so his treatment of the suspects was not just business—it was personal.

A keen Protestant proselytiser, Marsden had a prejudiced view of Catholics, claiming 'they are dangerous members of society ... They are extremely superstitious, artful and treacherous' and 'fond of riot and cabals'. He was suspicious of Catholic worship as a ruse to conspire and viewed their clergy as unworthy competitors, arguing that they attended Mass only 'to recite the miseries and injustices of their punishment ... and to inflame one another's minds in some scheme of revenge'.[146] So it is not surprising that for his alleged part in the conspiracy Father Harold was forced to stand next to the tree to which the others were tied and 'attend and bear witness on the said several sentences being severely carried into execution, as a peculiar mark of infamy and disgrace'. Holt described the flogging of Maurice Fitzgerald, an accused farmer from Cork, by two flagellators, a right- and left-handed man:

I never saw two threshers in a barn move flails with more regularity ... The very first blow made the blood spout out from Fitzgerald's shoulders … I have witnessed many horrible scenes, but this was the most appalling sight I had ever seen. The day was windy, and although I was fifteen yards to leeward from the sufferer, the blood, the skin, and flesh blew in my face as the executioners shook it off their cats … [Fitzgerald] never uttered a groan, the only words he said were 'Flog me fair, do not strike me on the neck'.[147]

Marsden's methods elicited no evidence of pike manufacture, but he concluded on the basis of informers' testimony that

unwarrantable consultations and seditious meetings have been assembled by several of the disaffected Irish convicts, tending to excite a spirit of discontent which was fast ripening to a serious revolt and consequences the most dreadful.[148]

As further 'severe punishment' eighteen of the United Irish suspects, including Galvin and Father Harold, were to be sent to Norfolk Island—a penal station of secondary punishment in the Pacific Ocean, 1675 kilometres (1041 miles) northeast of Sydney. Such was the extent of King's paranoia that Irish prisoners were about to plunge Parramatta into revolt that a further thirty-four suspects rooted out by Marsden soon joined their countrymen on Norfolk. Betrayed by an escaped convict who was to spread news of a Sunday uprising from farm to farm, the plotters were sentenced to be 'transported to some secluded isle belonging to the territory, there to remain for the term of their original sentences, employed in hard labour, and ordered to the strictest discipline to reduce them to due obedience, subordination and order'.[149]

Banishment to harsh penal stations became the favoured punishment to deter convicts from committing further crimes in the colony. At the time that the Irish rebels were transported to New South Wales, Norfolk Island was the principal destination for recalcitrant offenders and the seditious. Its 35 square kilometres (13 square miles) were thick with tall Pacific pines that the Royal Navy hoped could be harvested for ships' masts. When the timber proved insufficiently flexible, it was left to the commandant James Morisset to cement the island's reputation as one of the British Empire's harshest prisons, infamous for liberal reliance on the 'cat' and the noose to bring inmates into line. When some of the United Irishmen at Norfolk were caught planning an uprising, the two ringleaders, twenty-four-year-old John Woologhan and forty-year-old Peter Mclean, were executed just before Christmas 1800. An official inquiry into the incident found that

> [t]heir intention was forcibly to have made themselves masters of the island, and for that purpose they have prepared a number of pikes. The officers were to have been put to death, they even proposed to murder the women and children.[150]

Norfolk was soon joined by penal stations at Moreton Bay, the Hunter coal mines, Port Macquarie and Van Diemen's Land, all used to quarantine the Sydney settlement from dangerous prisoners. The Irish convict and balladeer Frank MacNamara (Frank the Poet) is said to have immortalised the brutality of these outposts in the song 'Moreton Bay' (though its provenance is obscure). The Derwent and Port Dalrymple in Van Diemen's Land were settled in 1803 to absorb some of Sydney's convicts and to secure the island against the French. As well as the incorrigible Maurice Margarot, the rebel leaders Martin Burke, Denis McCarty, Richard Dry, Holt and Dwyer would all cool their heels in Van Diemen's Land for alleged conspiracies. As Van Diemen's Land became more populous, Sarah Island in the isolated Macquarie Harbour and later still Port Arthur would come online as geography-aided maximum-security prisons conceived to terrify the general convict population out of re-offending.

For the Defenders and United Irishmen, New South Wales was indeed a gulag. While former rebel officers did not escape incarceration in the more extreme penal stations, they did escape the more brutal punishments—floggings, solitary confinement, the treadmill, working in chains—that were casually inflicted on Irish political prisoners from lower-class backgrounds. Given the clear class bias in physical punishment it is interesting that recourse to the lash declines as political and economic rights are extended down the social scale in the 1830s and '40s.[151] In the late eighteenth century black-African slaves were still whipped, maimed, branded and bred as property, and clearly peasants and manual workers, subjects of the King but yet to become citizens, were not accorded the same human rights as the bourgeoisie and gentry. Likewise common soldiers and sailors could be flogged for misdemeanours. The bodies of mere subjects could be treated with impunity by the Sovereign and his agents.

Rudé placed hanging at the apex of the hierarchy of punishment used to keep convicts in line.[152] In the first two decades of transportation the death penalty applied to political offences committed in the colony, as well as to serious crimes against the person and property. Following the two alleged insurrectionists on Norfolk Island the next political prisoners to be hanged in Australia were the ringleaders of the Castle Hill Rebellion that broke out among former Defenders and United Irishmen in 1804.

✳ ✳ ✳

REBELLION

THE REGIME OF PUNISHMENTS ENDURED BY IRISH PRISONERS MIGHT create the impression of pitiful victims of British tyranny. However, this would be wrong. The floggings, banishments and executions were an indication of official paranoia, but also of the imprisoned rebels' determination to resist and, if possible, effect an uprising or escape. Despite the floggings and banishments, plotting continued among the Irish of Parramatta and Toongabbie. In the aftermath of the Marsden Inquiry and the Norfolk Island troubles, King begged London to transport

> *no more men of a violent Republican character, and particularly priests (of whom we have three) … If more Irish Republicans are sent I do not know what will be the consequences. They have hitherto kept us in a constant state of suspicion.*[153]

In order to prevent the Irish republicans gathering to conspire or rebel, King issued a proclamation bearing similarities to the *Insurrection Act* issued in Ireland ahead of the 1798 rising. Meetings of twelve or more prisoners could only occur with permission. Holding two meetings in defiance of this law and failing to disperse when ordered to do so would be punishable by death. Prisoners administering seditious oaths would be sentenced to 1000 lashes, a penal station or working in a chain gang.[154]

Nevertheless, unskilled Irish labourers continued to be worked and housed en masse at the government farms of western Sydney, where it was possible to swap news of Ireland, whisper plans and schemes, and even construct home-made weapons, such as the deadly pike. According to Holt, by 1804 plans for a western Sydney uprising were well advanced among the Parramatta United Irishmen. The former rebel general claimed in his memoir that he advised their leaders against taking the course of insurrection, telling them 'you saw in Ireland that even there you could not depend on each other, and I am sure it would be worse here. An insurrection will only add to your misery, or bring you to the gallows'.[155] Assuming this is a true account of Holt's position, this meeting—and the plotters' hopes for his support—would serve to connect him to the conspiracy. The leaders had also met with Margarot, who is believed to have used his relative freedom of movement to help organise the rebellion.[156]

The worst fears of the colonial government finally came to pass when the republican battle cry 'Death or Liberty!' broke over the bush at Castle Hill on 4 March 1804. The spark was belated news of Emmet's attempted coup and the hope that they might seize a ship and take it home to fight in a renewed rebellion. Hence the other rallying call, 'A Boat Home'.[157] The leader of the rebellion was Philip Cunningham, veteran of '98, the United Irish mutineer from the *Anne* who had been sent to Norfolk Island. As a stonemason his skills were in demand and he was brought to Sydney where he became overseer of government stonemasons at the farming settlement of Castle Hill, northwest of Parramatta, where 474 convicts were concentrated by 1804.[158] Notwithstanding this responsibility, Cunningham craved liberty and tried to escape on a French ship, suffering 100 lashes when caught. Resolved on an uprising, Cunningham succeeded in maintaining secrecy and loyalty (the password was St Peter), so that the authorities were not alerted until the very eve of the rebellion, when it was too late to stop. At 7 pm on Sunday 4 March convict John Cavenagh set his hut alight, the sign that the uprising had begun.

Constables and one of the loathed floggers were overpowered with some viciousness, and muskets, ammunition, axes, scythes, swords and grog were seized from the store and nearby farms. Cunningham assembled the rebel convicts on Toongabbie's Constitution Hill, and dispatched columns to collect arms and men for an attack on Parramatta, and then Port Jackson. Initial raids in the Hills district had secured the rebels about a third of the colony's armoury. Australian historian Andrew Moore has noted that Cunningham deployed the tactics used by the United Irishmen in the Irish Rebellion of 1798: massing forces on high ground and seizing weapons from the enemy.[159] First, rebel prisoners at Parramatta were to set fire to John Macarthur's nearby Elizabeth Farm to draw the garrison out, and signal to the local prisoners to rise up and seize arms and the town.[160] Farmhouses were soon ablaze around Castle Hill and buoyed by the euphoria the Irishmen enjoyed their night of freedom together, swigging stolen grog and singing forbidden rebel songs, while they waited for news of Parramatta's rising.[161]

But the rebellion was betrayed. A messenger, John Griffen, whose mission it was to spread word of the rebellion to the neighbouring districts, turned informant, so that Parramatta, Winsdor and the Hawkesbury failed to rise.[162] Once alerted, the Parramatta garrison secured the streets, and news was dispatched posthaste by horseman to the governor in Sydney. Fearing attack, Marsden and the Macarthur family, who were dining together, led an evacuation of Parramatta by boat down the river in darkness. Elizabeth Macarthur described the 'alarums and excursions' that erupted when

> ... our servant burst into the Parlour pale and violent in agitation, 'Sir' says he, looking wildly at Mr. Marsden, 'come with me,' 'and you too madam,' looking at me ... he told us that the Croppies had risen, that they were at my Seven Hills farm and that numbers were approaching Parramatta ... We then learnt that Castle Hill was in flames. The fire was discernible from Parramatta. It was recommended that as many Ladies as chose should go to Sydney, as constant intelligence was brought into the Barracks of the near approach of the Irishmen who were expected every minute to enter the town. The number was reported to be 300.[163]

Governor King arrived in Parramatta first, and that very night proclaimed martial law (for the first time in Australia), declaring 'the Districts of Parramatta, Castle Hill, Toongabbie, Prospect, Seven and Baulkham Hills, Hawkesbury and Nepean to be in a STATE of REBELLION'.

Meanwhile, the New South Wales Corps, under its commander Major George Johnston, marched through the night from Sydney to Castle Hill and began pursuit.

When word failed to arrive of a Parramatta rising, Cunningham decided an attack would be folly, and marched his men to Windsor where he hoped to rendezvous with prisoners from the Hawkesbury ahead of an engagement with soldiers. However, before they reached their destination the New South Wales Corps, who were in rapid pursuit, routed the rebels. Against a rebel force of about 270, Major Johnston commanded a force of twenty-nine soldiers and fifty militia with vastly superior fire power.[164] However, to improve his odds he resorted to deceit, riding ahead under flag of truce to parley, buying time for the corps to catch up with the rebels. With their ranks lined up behind them, Cunningham and his lieutenant came forward to discuss terms with Johnston, falling into his trap. On one account, when asked their demands, Cunningham replied 'Death or Liberty ... and a ship to take us home'. At that, Cunningham found a pistol pointed at his head, and Johnston ordered his troops to fire at the assembled rebels.

In battle the corps performed well and thanks to machine-like discipline and superior firepower routed the rebels. Without a leader and ill-trained, the rebels fled before the advancing ranks of red coats armed with muskets and bayonets, loading, firing, then reloading.[165] Soldiers and militia killed between fifteen and twenty, captured forty and confiscated twenty-six muskets, four bayonets, two swords, a pitchfork and a pistol.[166] Despite his capture, Cunningham was wounded by sword, and some of his men were killed despite surrendering. While the corps had speedily suppressed the rebellion, Johnston's victory was sullied by his abuse of a flag of truce to capture Cunningham—a dishonourable ploy contrary to the gentlemanly codes of war that bound a British officer. That he did so is likely a measure of the contempt he had for a man of Cunningham's class and nationality and the desire to make a quick example to the rebels. King rewarded Johnston with a land grant of 2000 acres (809 hectares). Ironically, next time arms were raised against the government of the colony—the so called 'Rum Rebellion' against Governor Bligh—it would be Johnston and the corps leading the mutiny and lauding liberty and the fall of tyrants.

Next came the retribution, and it was swift. Cunningham was hanged that night without trial in the government store in nearby Windsor. Eight other leaders of the rebellion were found guilty of treason and went to the gallows. Their bodies were left hanging in chains for weeks in different sites around Sydney as a warning to others who might contemplate rising against lawful authority in His Majesty's colony. Some of those hanged were English convicts, confirming the authorities' worst fears that the Irish political prisoners could contaminate the wider criminal population with their republican treason.[167] Nine other rebels were sentenced to a flogging, of either 200 or 500 lashes. A much larger group of about forty believed to be ringleaders, including Margarot, were sent to the Newcastle mines at Coal River, Norfolk Island and Van Diemen's Land. This time the dragnet caught Holt, who King believed was 'principally concerned in these proceedings'.[168] Despite protestations that he opposed the rebellion he was convicted of sedition on the information of informers and was stripped of privileges and sent to Norfolk Island where he served nineteen months. Holt later recalled of his new prison that 'the usage I have seen men receive exceeds in cruelty anything that can be credited'.[169] Henceforth, political prisoners would be scattered through assignment and internal exile and kept on the move in growing colonies, rather than concentrated where they could influence others.[170]

While King thought the punishments commensurate with the rebels' crimes, he did have pause to reflect that

> *excepting a brutal violence to one individual, no act of atrocity marked the conduct of these deluded people ... Not a blade or grain of wheat was injured, nor was any property except arms, ammunition, and a few trifling things invaded.*[171]

The aim of the Castle Hill rebels was not vengeance, looting or to inaugurate a republic of thieves in the Pacific, but, as their battle cry had it, 'Death or Liberty and a ship to take us home', in order that they might reverse the verdict of the Battle of Vinegar Hill. Historians Anne-Maree Whitaker and Andrew Moore consider the prisoner's rising in the grey-green scrub of Castle Hill, so far from emerald Ireland, to be the last chapter of the rebellion that had begun in 1798.[172] Aptly the surviving rebel convicts named the raised ground near Rouse Hill where they were forced to make their stand 'Vinegar Hill', after the fateful battle back home where so many of their comrades had died for an Irish republic. The name stuck, though it appears on no map. Moore laments that Cunningham has not had the attention he deserves as an Irish martyr and Castle Hill has little recognition in Ireland. Perhaps an uprising of convicts led by a humble working-class man was considered insufficiently heroic?

Building on Whitaker's scholarship, historian of the Irish political convicts Ruan O'Donnell has began the process of reconsideration, arguing that the Castle Hill Rebellion was 'the most serious insurrectionary challenge directed against the Australian state'.[173] It dwarfs the rebellion at the Eureka Stockade on the Victorian goldfields in 1854 because the small size of the Sydney settlement and the large mass of convicts relative to free settlers and soldiers meant the government was vulnerable if all the prisoners rose. Unlike the Rum Rebellion of 1808, which was a coup that left the authority of the Crown and the convict system intact, the Castle Hill rebels rejected the legitimacy of both, and were pledged by oath to oppose British colonialism, whether in Ireland or New South Wales. Disembarking in Sydney in the aftermath of the uprising, Sir Henry Brown Hayes, an officer and gentleman of Cork transported for abducting and marrying an heiress, caught sight of the Castle Hill rebels still hanging on the gallows and recorded, 'me thought I smelled the bones, and heard the groans of dying patriots'.[174]

While denied the promised land of America, Michael Dwyer, like Holt before him, was extended privileges befitting his status as a commander. He and the other Wicklow leaders languished in prison until July 1805 when they received orders to board the ship *Tellichery* for transportation to Sydney.[175] Despite being charged for treason, the Crown honoured part of the original agreement, and allowed Dwyer to be exiled for life rather than be tried and sentenced as a prisoner. The Secretary of State looked favourably on his written request to take his family, in which Dwyer argued 'there is nothing so distressing to the parents as parting of their children, especially me, who had the misfortune to forfeit them and their country'.[176] When the *Tellichery* sailed in August 1805, Dwyer and his lieutenants—John Mernagh, Hugh Byrne, Martin Burke and Arthur Devlin—were not only allowed to take their families, but were given the freedom of the ship and allowed the dignity of wearing their own clothes, much to the chagrin of the officers guarding these notorious prisoners.[177] Like Holt, Dwyer claimed to have now drawn a line under his career as a rebel, promising his captors to 'forever exclaim against any man or men if I hear any of them speak or act against the government'.[178] Unfortunately for Dwyer his reputation had preceded him to Sydney.

By the time the Tellichery arrived in Sydney on 15 February 1806 the brutal suppression of the Castle Hill Rebellion had done much to quieten down unrest among the Irish convicts. This did not stop Governor King's suspicion of this fresh batch of republican Irish, and he immediately complained to London that

> *I cannot conceal that the arrival of the five United Irishmen, who appear to have been considerable leaders in the late rebellion in Ireland, without any conviction, added to the number of disaffected of that class here already, will call forth the utmost attention of the officers of this colony.*[179]

Nevertheless, in deference to Dwyer's status as an officer he and his colleagues were each granted 100 acres (40 hectares) of land to farm at Cabramatta in south western Sydney.[180] King informed his superiors in London that, 'I have allowed them to become settlers, with the encouragement generally given to free settlers from England. How far these indulgences will operate on their apparent turbulent dispositions time will show.'[181] By the terms of their exile they were 'to be subjected to all the laws and discipline [of the penal colony] and any further indulgence was to be earned by their good behaviour'.[182] However, like Holt, Dwyer would constantly arouse suspicion and was closely watched. He was destined, like so many others in the colony, to fall foul of King's successor, Governor William Bligh.

One year into his exile in May 1807 Dwyer and close colleagues were arrested by Bligh who suspected them of plotting rebellion. Dwyer was accused of saying that 'all Irish will be free in this new country',

which he did not deny, and of planning to lead a march on Government House at Parramatta, which he said was a lie. Tried for sedition, the men were acquitted for lack of evidence and the inability of the prosecution to produce any weapons. Convinced of Dwyer's guilt, Bligh overrode the verdict, stripped him of his settler status and banished him to Norfolk regardless. Despite being a one-time renegade rebel, Dwyer was popular with some of the officers of the New South Wales Corps, perhaps because of his military bearing, or because he was a sociable man's man who enjoyed telling a yarn over a drink, or three. This act of seemingly arbitrary justice became one of the Rum Corps' many grievances against Bligh. Dwyer would spend six months on Norfolk and then a further two years in Van Diemen's Land where Martin Burke was also sent. A reprieve came when the New South Wales Corps overthrew Bligh in the Rum Rebellion. The military government of Major Johnston brought Dwyer and Burke back to Sydney as free men and restored their land. Significantly Governor Macquarie confirmed these pardons and by 1810 Dwyer had rejoined colonial society, once more a romantic exile rather than a convict.

✻   ✻   ✻

GETTING ON IN AUSTRALIA

WHATEVER THE LENGTH OF THEIR SENTENCES, MOST IRISH POLITICAL prisoners, like the vast majority of convicts, would spend the rest of their days in the colony.[183] The British Government did not want rebels back in Ireland and refused most petitions to return. Furthermore, the cost of returning was beyond the financial means of most on first gaining their freedom. However, many former Defenders and United Irishmen stayed because they were able to build a better life in Australia. In what ways did they prosper in this new country?

Rewards, as well as punishments, were built into the system to encourage obedience and self-improvement while efficiently harvesting labour. An absolute pardon allowing an immediate return home could be granted by the government back in London, usually when political expediency required clemency for an individual or category of political convict. While this discretion was not exercised in the case of transported Irish rebels it was extended more often to the English rural protesters and Canadian Patriots of the 1820s, '30s and '40s where it became part of the machinery of social control and deference.[184] The local governor also had the power to grant pardons, in reward for exemplary behaviour or the need to promote vital talent for the service of the colony. King was particularly generous with pardons for high-profile gentleman political prisoners, especially if they possessed essential skills.[185] Wexford United Irishmen captain Henry Alcock was pardoned for good behaviour despite being a rebel leader. Father O'Neil, the priest flogged in Ireland, was pardoned and allowed to return home in 1802, and was offered £200 by King to remain as a teacher. After his seven-year stint on Norfolk even Father Harold was pardoned in 1808, and returned to Ireland.[186] Young Paddy Galvin, who had suffered at the hands of Reverend Marsden, received a pardon in 1810 and made his home in New South Wales.

After serving his prison term on Norfolk Island things began to look up for Holt. Sent from Norfolk to the new colony on the Derwent in Van Diemen's Land, Holt, ever the gentleman, hit it off with the lieutenant-governor (and fellow Irish Protestant), David Collins. On his return to Sydney he was pardoned by Bligh, despite being caught distilling alcohol illegally. Over the years he increased his land holdings and by 1810 had more than 200 acres (80 hectares), on which he grazed a flock of 400 sheep plus cattle and horses. His now married son farmed a further 100 acres (40 hectares).[187] In 1811 Holt received a free pardon that meant he was free to return to Ireland at his own expense. He sold his farm for the significant sum of £1800 and left for Ireland with his wife aboard the *Isabella*, while his adult children remained in New South Wales. Even for those with sufficient income to afford passage to Europe, the journey across the globe was perilous. The *Isabella* was wrecked off the Cape of Good Hope, but the Holts managed to make it safely to a nearby island. Returning to Ireland the former rebel commander received a hero's welcome and became a publican and farmer near Dublin, dying in 1826 at the ripe old age of seventy. In regular contact with his children half a world away, Holt came to regret leaving Australia, believing, despite his early travails, that he was on the way to greater wealth and social position than he could ever hope for in Ireland.[188]

Certainly, thanks to the availability of land (at the expense of the Aborigines), the rapid establishment of industries such as whaling, the growing export trade in wool and other staples and the shortage of skilled labour, it was possible for the humble and the well-off, the emancipist and the free settler to advance their prospects. The developing economies of New South Wales and Van Diemen's Land could appear especially bountiful in comparison to so poor a country as Ireland that seethed with land hunger and rural violence in the decades following the Napoleonic Wars. While Hughes is correct in his assertion that 'the Irish in Australia saw themselves as a doubly colonised people', especially in terms of religion and culture, it was also true that an enterprising and hard-working Irish political prisoner could make a go of the new land.[189] Holt's estimation of the opportunities available in the convict colonies was borne out by the social mobility enjoyed by some of his fellow rebels who stayed.

First, let us turn to the rebel officers and other professionals. Captain Alcock had his sentence reduced and was appointed to the prestigious post of the colony's assistant engineer. James Meehan was assigned to the Surveyor-General, Charles Grimes, and after his pardon began a meteoric career in that profession. As acting Surveyor of Lands he was paid a huge salary of £182 a year and had the responsibility of exploring and surveying much of Van Diemen's Land. Promoted to Deputy Surveyor-General by Governor Macquarie in 1812, Meehan mapped many new townships in Sydney, and acquired 1140 acres (461 hectares) at Ingleburn in southwestern Sydney, where he retired with a pension of £100 in 1823.[190] Governor King came to revise his suspicion of the Catholic clergy, concluding that regular worship 'had a most salutary affect on Irish Catholics', improving their morality and quietening them down. Accordingly, he gave permission for regular Mass in a proclamation of 19 April 1803, and provided Father Dixon with a salary of £60 per annum to provide this service.

What of the majority of rural tradespeople and labourers, most of them Catholics, who composed the rebel rank and file? If Australia seemed a land of opportunity to the Protestant squire Holt, how much more could it offer to Catholics who were discriminated against and kept in insecure peasant tenancy back in Ireland? As early as the 1790s a parole system had been introduced that rewarded good behaviour and work ethic by freeing a convict from compulsory labour to sell his or her services to employers for a wage. While able to move about to find work, the so-called ticket-of-leave man was required to report regularly to authorities and could only live in a prescribed district. Other carrots in the gift of the governor included granting well-behaved convicts land, permission to marry and, later, under Governor Macquarie assistance in bringing out families to settle—an early version of a family reunion migration program.[191]

On the basis of analysis of petitions, memorials, musters and census roles, Rudé concluded that most Defenders and United Irishmen in the Australian colonies 'spent comparatively peaceful and uneventful lives'.[192] From 1806 at least fifty received land grants of between 30 and 135 acres (12 and 55 hectares). Some ex-prisoners lost land and others expanded through industry, bloody-mindedness or luck. What follows are examples of what some ordinary prisoners achieved after gaining their freedom.[193] Michael Bryan, who was granted 40 acres (16 hectares) by Macquarie, eventually owned 540 acres (219 hectares) at Seven Hills in northwest Sydney. James Byrne increased his land from 40 to 200 acres (16 to 81 hectares) and Thomas Bryan from 100 to 306 acres (40 to 124 hectares) between 1820 and 1828.[194] John Lacey, a young Dublin ironworker, was permitted to bring out his wife and child and was given a land grant of 100 acres (40 hectares). By 1828 he owned an estate of 1080 acres (437 hectares) in western Sydney.[195] Equally impressive, Andrew Doyle from Wicklow was allowed to bring out his wife and by 1828 had built a small land grant at Toongabbie in Sydney's west into 1220 acres, grazing 130 head of cattle. More typically, the cobbler Patrick Mason prospered at his trade, and eventually purchased 100 acres and cattle.

Then there were former convict rebels who through industry, talent and no doubt ruthless ambition became vital cogs in colonial business life. Denis McCarty, a United Irishman and farmer from Wexford, was made a constable at New Norfolk in Van Diemen's Land in 1808, and acquired a farmhouse sufficiently grand for Governor Macquarie to be his guest. A budding entrepreneur, McCarty bought a schooner, traded up the Tasmanian and New South Wales coast, discovered coal and won the tender to build a road between New Norfolk and Hobart, doubtless with the assistance of assigned convict labour. His fee was 2000 acres (809 hectares). Litigious in defending his interests, McCarty imported a rebellious spirit into business, Van Diemen's Land Governor William Sorell describing him as 'one of the most turbulent and insubordinate men in the Settlement'.[196] In 1820 McCarty was drowned in the Tamar River in suspicious circumstances.[197] Acknowledged for his 'speculative turn', Denis McCarty was a pioneer in what would prove to be a long line of Australian rent-seeking developers.

Richard Dry, a Protestant woollen-draper, was given a life sentence and endured banishment in Van Diemen's Land for supposedly plotting insurrection. He liked the island colony, became a storekeeper and married a 'currency lass' born in Australia. Pardoned with a grant of 500 acres (202 hectares) he took to farming and sheep grazing and eventually owned 12,000 acres (4856 hectares). Branching into commerce and trade, Dry was a founder of the Cornwall Bank in 1828 and in 1837 established the Tamar Steam Navigation Company. This one-time United Irishmen revolutionary ended his days a respected leader of Launceston society, and his son, a fervent anti-transportationist, was knighted.[198]

Edward McRedmond was an illiterate labourer from County Offaly when he joined the Rebellion of 1798, but in Sydney established himself as a small trader. Pardoned in 1809 with a grant of 135 acres (55 hectares) and a spirit and wine licence his ascent was rapid. He made his fortune as leaseholder of the road tolls between Parramatta and Sydney, which he invested as a shareholder in the Bank of New South Wales, established in 1817.[199] In 1840 when he died, McRedmond had five houses and land at Bathurst, Annandale and the Hawkesbury.[200] This involuntary immigrant's rise from nothing through a combination of grog, land, tolls, banking and undoubted entrepreneurial flair and hard work is a familiar Sydney story to be repeated through the generations.

These prisoners from humble backgrounds had become employers, landlords and captains of business. They are remembered as nation-builders, not rebels. They doubtless did better economically than they would have in Ireland, even if it was at the cost of their freedom for a significant period of their lives. The land hunger that had driven them to violent insurrection was for many put right in Australia, though at the expense of the Aborigines, whose common land was being carved up as part of a new conquest.

The prisoners of '98 would leave their mark on Australia in other ways. The United Irishmen were cultural as well as political rebels. They owed their appeal to a sophisticated and colourful marshalling of journalism, pamphlets, poetry and especially songs for the republican cause. By tapping into and shaping Irish romantic nationalism the United Irishmen became part of the cultural DNA of their homeland and some of their culture of resistance seeped into Australia's folkways. In *The Australian Legend*, social historian Russel Ward placed great weight on the nomadic bush worker of colonial Australia as the essence of a new democratic national type that had begun to shape labour movement politics and the creative arts by the 1880s and '90s.[201] He acknowledged the influence of rebel ballads and exile laments sung by Irish political prisoners on the popular culture of a still-forming nomadic rural working class, composed in part of ex-convicts. The transportation of the rebels left a hole in the Irish psyche that was filled by laments such as 'The banished Defender ... in cold irons, in Van Diemen's Land'. Later generations of Irish prisoners could find solace singing nineteenth century anthems to '98, such as 'The Croppy Boy', that recalled:

> *It was early, early in the spring*
> *The birds did whistle and sweetly sing,*
> *Changing their notes from tree to tree,*
> *And the song they sang was Old Ireland free.*[202]

These 'treason songs' and many written later were carried by waves of Irish prisoners 'to be sung', as Hughes put it, 'in many an Australian humpy and rum shop' throughout the nineteenth century.[203] Local songs appeared early. William Maum wrote seditious poems, or 'pipes', about Governor King, while Laurence Davoran, a lawyer sentenced for life, came to attention during the Rum Rebellion for writing a song in defence of Governor Bligh.[204] By the late nineteenth century the bushman romanticised by popular journals such as the *Bulletin* was said to exhibit an anti-authoritarian 'larrikin' streak that had its roots in convict resistance. This anti-authoritarianism was channelled into the nascent union movement for contemporary struggles against the bosses and the colonial governments that backed them. In this new era of class war and Australian nationalism the stories and songs of the Irish rebels joined the legacy of Eureka and the verse of Henry Lawson to provide a vocabulary of republican resistance to help de-legitimise British imperialism. Back in Ireland songs critical of transportation were still being written as late as 1917, when in the aftermath of the Easter Uprising the 'Ballad of the '98 Heroes' remembers 'the treacherous foe ... sent Dwyer to Botany Bay'.[205]

What of Michael Dwyer who, like Holt, was made a target by his reputation and endured eternal banishment? The ups and downs of his career in the colony makes for a morality tale illustrating how far talent and enterprise could take a man, and how easy it could be lost. Reintegrated into Macquarie's Sydney, Dwyer found his leadership qualities were in demand, and he became a constable of the Georges River District in 1810. The former outlaw was now an enforcer of the law. This was not as unusual as might be expected. As well as McCarty, both James Lyons and Martin Burke joined the constabulary, suggesting these rebel captains were regarded as moderating influences on the alleged excesses of their fellow countrymen. While Irish rebels who became constables could be ostracised as traitors to their United Irishmen's oath, Dwyer remained popular as a folk-hero and was respected by Irish and English alike. In these years he increased his land holdings with the acquisition of 610 acres (247 hectares) at Pittwater, and became active in the Catholic community, contributing to a building fund to erect St Mary's Cathedral in Sydney. Mixing business with pleasure, Dwyer also became the landlord of a western Sydney pub, the popular Harrow Inn, a major business undertaking which appealed to his risk-taking nature and gregarious personality. As publican, the former revolutionary-turned-policeman would regale patrons with rebel folk songs and the exploits of his band of brothers at large in the Wicklow Mountains.[206] Then, in 1820 Dwyer was promoted to Chief Constable of Liverpool, an influential and respectable position of authority in the rapidly expanding colony. Michael Dwyer would not be the last Irish-Australian to chart a course through politics, the Catholic Church, the constabulary and the liquor trade, but in his case the balancing act proved overwhelming. Not a year into his new job he was dismissed for public drunkenness and mislaying important documents. This misfortune led to the collapse of his business venture when a creditor sought to get back £2000 she had invested in the pub. Even though he had to sell his land to pay off his debts, Dwyer was compelled to spend a week in debtor's prison. There in the fetid cells the former Wicklow Chief contracted dysentery, from which he died on 23 August 1825. Having borne seven children Mary Dwyer would live until 1861, seeing another failed Irish rebellion, her daughter marry a bank manager and a grandson become Dean of St Mary's Cathedral.

But Dwyer's legend did not die with him. As the nineteenth century wore on, the '98 rebellion, shorn of its radical democratic ideals, became sacred to new generations of Irish nationalists seeking independence from the English. With the approach of the rebellion's centenary in 1898 commemorative monuments were erected and marches held throughout Ireland and the diaspora.[207] While the rising had failed, it was a noble defeat in a worthy cause—a brave but doomed stand like that of the 300 Spartans against the Persian Empire at Thermopylae, a blood sacrifice that legitimised the struggles of the successor independence movement, the Fenians. Captured by Catholics who forgot the anti-sectarian vision of the Presbyterian leaders of the United Irishmen, popular memory of the rebellion and propaganda now elevated its Catholic captains and peasant defenders. Catholic hero Dwyer was called into service once more.

At the climax of the Irish-Australian commemoration of the 1798 rebellion in 1898 the remains of Dwyer and his wife were disinterred from the small cemetery near Sydney's Central Railway station, and reburied with great ceremony at Waverley Cemetery, beautifully situated on a hilltop overlooking the Pacific rollers. Here in this more suitable place of homage, a memorial was unveiled in 1900 attracting huge crowds to esteem the legacy of the 'Wicklow Chief', the title inscribed on Dwyer's grave. It remains one of the largest monuments honouring an Irish rebel in the world and a place of pilgrimage for true believers.[208] In 2003 a statue of Dwyer was unveiled in his birthplace, the Glen of Imaal in Wicklow, to honour the bicentennial of his surrender. Yet in Australia, popular memory of the rebel hero faded as the Irish became assimilated into the very heart of the nation.

CONCLUSION

IT IS IMPORTANT TO SEE THE PROGRAM OF THE UNITED IRISHMEN and the '98 rebellion as part of the international movement for liberal democratic change that led to a middle-class revolution in North America and France, the suppression of radical reform groups in Scotland and England and war in Europe and beyond between the old monarchies and republicanism. The failure of Emmet's Dublin coup, the transportation of Dwyer and his men and the uprising in Castle Hill were the last acts of the United Irishmen's revolution. With the end of the wars with France, and the passing of fears of an invasion, His Majesty's subjects in Ireland, unlike those in England and Scotland, did not recover their civil liberties. Ireland remained under the thrall of emergency laws and a paramilitary constabulary that Rudé characterises as a form of military occupation.[209] Following a relatively peaceful decade during which Ireland was politically integrated into the United Kingdom, insurrection would break out once more in the 1820s, in a wave of violent rural protest over land, food prices and Church tithes. With the Irish Rebellion of 1798 now an inspirational memory, new champions would emerge for Catholic emancipation, universal suffrage, land reform, Irish independence, even a republic. Many would be exiled to Australia.

Returning to the debate between Hirst and Hughes it is apparent that not only were both the gulag and the social escalator operating in the early decades of the penal colony, but a prisoner might sample both during their sentence. In the decade following the arrival of the first Defenders before the governorship of Lachlan Macquarie and the expansion of the assignment system, the Irish political prisoners received more sticks than carrots. The overwhelming majority of Irish rebels sent to New South Wales were unskilled and skilled manual workers, not educated property owners and professionals. Rather than land grants they would do hard labour on government farms and public works and be vulnerable to the full range of physical punishments. Under the control of inquisitors such as Marsden, justice and punishment could be arbitrary and cruel. For those rebel prisoners unlucky enough to be sentenced to one of the outposts of secondary punishment reserved for hardened re-offenders and the seditious, such as Norfolk Island, transportation did indeed become a hell-on-earth. However, the many who behaved and worked hard could expect to find employment and even become landowners on attaining parole and completing their sentences. These prospects for self-improvement were particularly attractive to poor Catholic prisoners, who faced economic marginalisation and legal impediments back home. Rebel prisoners from humble backgrounds doubtless did better economically than they would have back in Ireland, even if it was at the cost of their freedom and dignity for a significant period of their lives. The transported rebels of '98 provide the first examples of two Irish traditions that took root in Australia—a spirit of resistance to English authority and an ambition to prosper. In some fields of Irish achievement, notably working-class politics, the two traditions would eventually merge.

The solemn oaths of the United Irishmen, in which members swore never to betray their comrades, came to the penal colony as convict solidarity, a collective identity conferring strength on the otherwise powerless. Solidarity entered colonial workplace culture and in latter generations was expressed in trade unionism, its strategy of collective bargaining, and in the Australian Labor Party (ALP). Working-class activists of Irish Catholic background would play a disproportionate role in the ALP, leading governments and helping to civilise Australian capitalism. The United Irish prisoners bequeathed to Australia its first popular republican movement, and its first rebellion in the name of liberty. In 1988 on the probable site of Vinegar Hill, former prime minister Gough Whitlam, himself a martyr to the intransigence of colonialism in Australia, unveiled a monument honouring the rebels who died there in defence of the republican ideal.[210] Yet, when the modern republican debate was launched in Australia by Paul Keating, a street-smart and visionary prime minister of Irish Catholic ancestry, no mention was made of the republican convicts who were brought here in chains. The lawyers and intellectuals of the Australian Republican Movement pitted dry and somewhat elitist constitutional arguments against the majesty and mystery of the monarchy, forgetting their nation's own history of republican martyrs and heroes. Uninspired and locked out by republican appeals to the law rather than the land, to the head rather than the heart, the people did not rally, and the British Crown still sits at the apex of the Australian polity.

3

PROTEST FROM BELOW

BRITISH REBELS OF FIELD AND FACTORY

Arise, men of Britain and take your stand! Rally round the standards of Liberty, or forever lay prostrate under the iron hand of your land and money-mongering taskmasters! … Transportation has not had the intended effect on me, but after all, I am returned from my bondage with my views and principles strengthened. It is indelibly fixed in my mind that labour is ill-rewarded in consequence of a few tyrannising over the millions … I believe that nothing will ever be done to relieve the distress of the working classes unless they take it into their own hands.[1]

THESE WORDS BELONG TO GEORGE LOVELESS, A PLOUGHMAN FROM Dorset, delivered in 1837 after suffering exile in Van Diemen's Land. Four years earlier he had come together with five fellow labourers under a sycamore tree in the small village of Tolpuddle to form a Friendly Society of Agricultural Labourers. They could not have imagined how this small gesture would change their lives irrevocably—and in time the lives of working people throughout Britain and the Empire. In order to raise their wages from 6 to 10 shillings so that they might feed their families, these six working men formed the first trade union among agrarian workers. While trade unionism had began in the hurly-burly of the great industrial and commercial cities, the appearance of worker solidarity in the rural heartland of Southern England struck at ancient paternalist prerogatives of deference and control that predated capitalism. It also exposed the gulf between middle-class liberalism and emerging forms of radicalism based on working-class solidarity; between the free market beloved of capitalists and new demands that the state intervene to protect the weak, to provide what Australians would later call a 'fair go'. Thirty years before Elizabeth Gaskell explored the culture clash between industrial and agrarian England in her novel *North and South*, the radically modern cause of workers' rights had established a beachhead on the country estates of Dorset. The small action is remembered not because their new union waged a militant or violent campaign against their masters, but because the government, in its zeal to strangle trade unionism in its infancy, made first martyrs, then heroes, of the Tolpuddle labourers.

FROM LITTLE THINGS, BIG THINGS GROW

WHEN WE THINK OF RURAL SOUTHERN ENGLAND IN THE EARLY decades of the nineteenth century many of us picture the ordered and genteel country life depicted in the novels of Jane Austen. While social hierarchy, distinction and prejudice were key concerns of Austen, she was principally concerned with the divisions within what was called 'Society'. This was an interconnected elite headed by 'gentlemen' in possession of wealth, education, manners and leisure underwritten by income derived from inherited landed property (generating wealth through pastoralism, agriculture and tenants), military or naval commissions, old professions or connections to an even wealthier landed aristocracy. New wealth based on commerce or manufacture was still condescended to as 'trade', even though it was making Britain the wealthiest and most powerful nation on Earth. The stain of being *nouveau riche* could be washed off by obtaining a landed estate through investment, marriage into the old elite or both. When the lower orders make an appearance in *Pride and Prejudice*, *Emma* or *Persuasion* as tenant farmers, tradesmen, rural labourers, domestic servants and coach drivers they are fleeting, largely silent stereotypes, suitably deferential, doffing caps and tugging forelocks, as they see to the needs of their masters and betters. The image conjured is one of social harmony, where different classes know their place and masters and landlords exercise authority over workers and tenants in the spirit of *noblesse oblige*.

However, such an image is a romantic myth, testimony to the social blinkers which directed the critical gaze of Austen to her own social set, and the subtle gradations within this provincial elite. For beyond the country houses, ballrooms and sitting rooms of the leisured class, England's green and pleasant land was being torn apart by economic distress, new technology, social conflict and a cycle of riot and repression. In the decades following the Napoleonic Wars, English agricultural workers rose again and again to destroy machines like threshers, burn farms to the ground, attack the hated workhouses and threaten farmers with violence in order to raise wages, lower rents and guarantee employment. Austen's fictional world is without connection to the convict colonies of Australia, yet many, many hundreds of agricultural labourers and village tradesmen were transported from the home counties for various forms of what

136

George Rudé termed 'social protest', that was characterised by riot, arson and machine breaking. This cycle of protest by the poor lasted from 1812 through to 1848, the so-called Year of Revolution and engulfed both city and country. However, it was rural protest that supplied the largest proportion of political transportees. In 1830 alone, over 500 agricultural labourers were sentenced to New South Wales and Van Diemen's Land. This was the year of the Swing Riots, a wave of rebellion that swept through England's bread basket in defiance of the new capitalist relations and technology that were remaking the agrarian economy as surely as the Industrial Revolution transformed craft manufacture.

However, it was not the tumult of the Swing Riots (and its suppression by the means of mass exile to the other side of the world) that brought the rights of working people and the cruelty of transportation to the attention of the British public. It was the much smaller stand taken at Tolpuddle in 1833 by Loveless and his five neighbours, not in anger or violence, but in defence of a new idea 'that union is power'.[2] But this idea was not to be tolerated. From such little things, big things grow.

At the centre of the Tolpuddle incident stood George Loveless—humble ploughman, father of three and devout Methodist. He was thirty-seven years of age in 1834 when the men were taken into custody, and the natural leader of the group by dint of bearing, intelligence and a commitment to self-improvement and community activism derived from his Wesleyan faith. Three of the other Tolpuddle Martyrs were practising Methodists, but religion was not the only tie that bound them. Three of the six were relations of Loveless. James Loveless, twenty-five, was the younger brother of George, and married with two children. Joining them was their brother-in-law Thomas Standfield, and his son John, at twenty-one the eldest of six children. These relatives, with their natural solidarity, formed the leadership core—what labour historian Joyce Marlow calls 'a pre-formed central committee'.[3] They were joined by James Brine, twenty-one, and James Hammett, twenty-two, both Anglicans who would later marry into the Standfield and Loveless families respectively, cementing the bonds still further. With the exception of George Loveless

THE TOLPUDDLE MARTYRS

JAMES BRINE   THOMAS STANDFIELD   JOHN STANDFIELD   GEORGE LOVELESS   JAMES LOVELESS

A contemporary drawing of the Tolpuddle Martyrs upon their return
from Australia. James Hammett is not shown as he did not return
home for another two years due to an assault charge.

and Thomas Standfield they were young men, and none had ever strayed
far from Tolpuddle. Only one of the six, Hammett, had ever been in trouble
with the law, having served four months' imprisonment for pilfering three
pieces of iron. The other five were regarded as honest, hard working and of
abstemious habits, though forever barred from 'respectable' Dorset society
due to their status as common labourers.

While class background provides an immediate context, historians
of the Tolpuddle incident are in agreement about the centrality of the
Methodist religion to George Loveless's identity and to the political
worldview he brought to the founding of the Friendly Society. His brother
James and in-laws Thomas and John Standfield were all committed
Methodists in a part of the world where this religion was not so common.
Loveless complained 'of men that were persecuted, banished, and not
allowed to have employ if they entered the Wesleyan Chapel at Tolpuddle'
where Methodism 'is considered as the sin of witchcraft'.[4]

Loveless was no mere follower in his faith, but an enthusiastic lay
preacher, who spent much of his free time moving about the countryside
proselytising the Gospel to his fellow workers and their families. This
distinctly British form of Protestantism had emerged only recently, in

the late eighteenth century, inaugurated by the Wesley brothers in part as a critique of the ostentation of the government-sanctioned Church of England and also as a grassroots faith relevant to the needs of ordinary people. By contrast the established Church was very much, as its status suggests, the plaything of the establishment. Just as Methodism dissented from the Church of England on key matters of worship, so too did it suggest a different role for working people to the cap-doffing subservience promoted by a church mired in the hierarchical perspectives of the gentry who dominated its clergy and congregations. By preaching justice between men on Earth alongside the consolations of paradise in heaven, Methodism could encourage a social conscience, and provided the ethical framework for Loveless's brand of community activism. To those who cautioned 'that the working man ought to remain still and let their cause work its way' because 'God in his good time will bring it around for him', he responded in defence of social agency:

> *I believe that God works by means and men, and that he expects every man who feels an interest in the subject to take an active part in bringing about and hastening on so important a period ...*[5]

A Methodist lay preacher like George Loveless, drawn from the ranks of working men and speaking in the local vernacular in humble, unadorned chapels, was a democratic innovation of the new denomination that bore little resemblance to Austen's social-climbing, craven Anglican minister Mr Collins, who constantly curries the good favour of his patroness, Lady Catherine de Bourgh. Prior to schism with the Anglican Church in 1784 when the first Methodist clergy were ordained, the Wesleyan revival relied entirely on lay preachers, and throughout the nineteenth century they continued to run services, conduct sermons and take the Gospel out to the people. The refreshing, and to some threatening, message at the heart of the new religion was that the laity was as valued as the clergy.[6]

However, Methodism was no revolutionary creed.[7] It upheld Christ's New Testament injunction that taxpayers should 'render unto Caesar the things which are Caesar's'. Methodism's social conscience was tempered by respect for the institutions of government and society, and strict adherence to Christian moral codes. This gave some Methodists the wriggle room to

Machine breakers demolishing machinery in a textile factory driven
by anxiety that the technology would make their jobs redundant.

support the status quo. But, for others, especially in conservative areas
like Dorset, dissent in religion was translated into criticism of society's
inequities and the desire to improve the condition of those at the bottom
of the heap. In rural areas of the south, Methodists stood out as a
minority in a way they did not in the industrial north and the capital, and
discrimination against them by Anglicans may have fuelled discontent.

While not formally educated, Loveless had become an accomplished
reader, and thought deeply about the relationship between his religion
and society. He would later write a theological pamphlet critiquing the
Anglican Church's fusion with the government. In her history of the
Tolpuddle Martyrs, Joyce Marlow argued that Loveless balanced a strong
commitment to his faith's democratic social practice with the belief that
the state was ordained by God, and therefore Methodists must obey the
laws of the land.[8] This meant only peaceful and legal means could be

employed to improve the lot of working people. Such convictions made Loveless a reformer rather than a wild-eyed radical.

Methodism also provided working people with a code for living that strengthened their capacity for self-government and organised activism. It stressed self-improvement, self-reliance and self-discipline, which translated to working-class life meant abstinence from the 'sins' of alcohol and gambling, fidelity in marriage, domestic prudence and a valuing of literacy to facilitate Bible study. For George Loveless, Methodism had been akin to a community university, introducing him to reading, men of inspiration and to a world of ideas. Methodism's belief in self-help and self-control dovetailed with unionism's injunction that as a disciplined group workers could bargain with employers as equals. Methodism's democratic emphasis on lay preachers able to take the word of God beyond the Church to the people was one seedbed for union activists. Addressing their neighbours in local halls, barns and fields, preaching gave devout men of ability like Loveless the opportunity to enhance their skills at writing, organisation and oratory. George's younger brother James, the second-in-command in initiating the Friendly Society, was also a lay preacher. Not surprisingly, working-class Methodist lay preachers would furnish a steady supply of British labour movement leaders in the second half of the nineteenth and early twentieth centuries, notably Keir Hardy. Through self-determination and moral living, working-class Methodists in Britain and later the Australian colonies hoped to attain something that had long been the privilege of their employers—respectability.

Far from rebels, the six Tolpuddle men had kept well clear of the recent wave of rioting that had ripped at the social fabric of rural Southern England.[9] Three years earlier in 1830 thousands of farm labourers distressed by unemployment, the enclosure of land and falling wages had embarked on a frenzy of machine breaking, arson and demands for money and higher pay with menace, across more than twenty counties in a bid to restore what they considered their customary rights. Over 500 of these so-called Swing rioters were transported to New South Wales and Van Diemen's Land, the largest contingent ever exiled from England in one go, conveniently enriching the colonies with much-needed agricultural wherewithal. Swing was the climax of almost two decades of rural discontent, a series of spontaneous guerrilla actions to slow down or turn back the Agricultural Revolution that had exposed malingering vestiges of feudalism to the calculation of market forces and the cold iron of machines. George Rudé considered the Swing Riots to be the last dramatic hurrah of the old pre-modern form of protest from below, where peasants looked back to traditional ways of rural life before the disruptions of enclosure, the market economy and new machines.[10] However, rather than lead to an improvement in working conditions, the Swing Riots merely served to harden the resolve of the new Whig Government, the rural gentry and their larger tenant farmers to crush future disorder before it could get out of hand. While the Tolpuddle action was the antithesis of disorder, its very quality of disciplined organisation made it a more potent threat to employers and the state.

*　*　*

THE TOLPUDDLE TRAP

THE RATIONAL GEORGE LOVELESS SAW THE FUTILITY OF unfocused mob violence of the Swing variety, and understood that the market and scientific agriculture were here to stay. He was less interested in restoring ancient feudal obligations between masters and servants than in the new model of trade unionism emerging in the industrial cities of the north. In the face of declining wages and tougher parish charity for the poor, the six men decided to look forwards, rather than backwards; to take control of their working lives rather than beg for crumbs. However, Loveless had not reckoned with the implacable opposition of local landowners to the idea that mere labourers could join together to collectively bargain for better wages and working conditions. In its very 'city-like' modernity, the formation of a Friendly Society of Agricultural Labourers was far more threatening to the power structure of rural England than the primitive peasant anarchy of the Swing Riots. The Tolpuddle episode would prove to be a turning point in lower-class protest, a moment when the still-forming English working class decided to get organised rather than mad, to harness the potential power of solidarity. The drama that began at Tolpuddle would also prove to be a turning point for the British state, because in its zeal to crush unionism, the government provoked a public backlash, exposing in a dramatic fashion the limits of transportation as a way of silencing opposition.

A respected man in the district, George Loveless had already represented Dorchester workers in a series of meetings in 1832, where he tried to persuade local farmers to provide a fair minimum wage. An almost Dylanesque contemporary folk song collected by Joyce Marlow captured the wage stress of the 1830s:

> *Come all ye Britons, where'er you may be,*
> *I pray give attention and listen to me*
> *There once was good times, but they've gone by complete*
> *For a poor man lives now on Eight shillings a week*

> *The 'Nobs of Old England' of shameful renown*
> *Are striving to crush the poor man to the ground,*
> *They'll beat down their wages and starve them complete*
> *And make them work hard for Eight shillings a week.*[11]

In the aftermath of Swing many farmers had found it politic, or humane, to raise wages, but not in Dorchester. The Great Reform Act was passed in 1832 bringing wide-ranging changes to the electoral system that had remained virtually unchanged since the late 1680s. Loveless may have felt it was the right time to press for local change. While most agreed to an increase to 10 shillings a week those in Tolpuddle refused to go higher than nine, and then maliciously lowered wages to seven and threatened to go down to a parsimonious 6 shillings. Such an income was unsustainable, especially for men with little children too young to earn themselves. So in October 1833 the Tolpuddle men came together secretly to plan a union on the model advanced by 'utopian socialist' reformer Robert Owen.

In 1833 Owen had established the Grand National Consolidated Trades Union in London, close enough to be talked about in the rural south. Loveless had 'seen at different times accounts of Trade Societies', and perhaps Owen's recently published *Address to All Classes in the State.*[12] Now he sought the advice from Owen's union about efforts by workers to establish trade unions in London, Birmingham and other industrial cities in the north, where strikes for better pay and conditions were becoming more common. Two union delegates came from London and addressed a group of about forty interested workers, a large group for such a small village, suggesting enthusiasm for the idea. The Dorset men agreed to form an agricultural branch of the national organisation. The plan was to recruit all local farm labourers as members in order that they could withdraw their labour as one, to bring the employers back to the bargaining table. The other purpose for the Friendly Society would be to prudentially pool dues for distribution to members in times of unemployment, rising prices and other calamities, 'a kind of Agricultural Savings Bank' as their lawyer would later put it.[13] The delegates provided the men with general rules for running a trade union, relating to office holders, three-monthly elections of management committees, finances and methods to ensure secrecy, such as passwords.

Significantly for Loveless, and the fate to befall him, the rules were explicit that 'the object of this society can never be promoted by any act or acts of violence, but, on the contrary, all such proceedings must tend to injure the cause and destroy the society itself'.[14] The Friendly Society therefore complied with Methodist obedience to the government, especially as unions had been made lawful in 1824 with the repeal of the Combination Acts of 1799–1800. Members would pay a fee of one shilling and a subscription of one penny per week.

Such was the discontent over falling wages that many local workers agreed to join the Friendly Society. It was hoped that the Society would grow large enough to cover Dorset and be incorporated into the national union body. But how could they ensure that the members of the Friendly Society acted as one rather than break ranks at the first whiff of resistance from employers? Loveless and his leadership group agreed to impose a solemn oath on themselves and other members bounding them to adhere to the rules of the Society. Based on the union model, they devised a ceremony of initiation that mixed modern union rules with quasi-religious rites, culminating in the swearing of an oath never to reveal the Society's members or activities, kissing the Bible and contemplating a 2 metre (6 foot) painting of a skeleton, the traditional symbol of death. The Oath said in part:

I do before ... God and this most loyal lodge most solemnly swear that I will not work for any master not in the Union ... and if ever I reveal any of the rules may what is before me plunge my soul into eternity.[15]

Pointing at the skeleton James Loveless bade them to 'Remember thine end'. It must be remembered that unlike Loveless and his relatives, many farm labourers were barely literate and understood the world through religion and superstition. The ritual of initiation, comparable to the ceremonies of traditional lodges such as the Masonic Order and the more recent Orangemen and White Boys of Ireland, was a hangover from the not-so-distant days when unions were banned, and was deemed necessary for solidarity in a hostile environment. Yet, the swearing of this oath, carried out in secret with sinister overtones in a room at the home of Thomas Standfield on 9 December 1833, would be their undoing.

Despite the veil of secrecy, in a small village community the labourers' actions quickly came to the attention of the local magistrate, a wealthy landowner named James Frampton who had earlier rebuffed Loveless's pay claims. In rural England, as in Ireland, magistrates remained a force to be reckoned with, literally holding the power of life and death over the majority of the local population. Magistrates kept the central government informed on the state of the King's Peace in their little piece of the realm, and in the absence of a national police force they kept that peace by swearing in constables and warrants, supervising gaols and administering the courts and summary punishments.[16] But magistrates were far from neutral officials administering the law without fear or favour. They were drawn from the old landed oligarchy, and were themselves political and economic players jealous of their ancient prerogatives and keen to press new advantages as employers and landlords enabled by the laws of the market.[17] Frampton, an employer ideologically antithetical to unionism, was a canny class warrior masquerading behind the robes of the magistracy. He had acted decisively to quell riots in Dorset during the recent Swing disturbances where other magistrates had wavered, and he remained vigilant against dissent.[18]

Unions may have established themselves among manufacturing workers and miners in the industrial north and even in London, but were unknown in the home counties of rural Southern England, and local landowners like Frampton were determined to keep it that way through a network of spies. Tipped off about the Friendly Society, he intimidated Edward Legg, one of the labourers who attended the initiation, to inform about all that had taken place and name names.[19] But how was he to proceed given that unions were no longer illegal? The well-connected Frampton went straight to the top, writing in January 1834 to the Home Secretary, Lord Melbourne, in the Whig Government of Earl Grey. The Whigs may have abolished slavery in the British Empire and championed the Great Reform Bill that cleaned up the old rotten boroughs and extended the franchise to the better-off urban middle class, but the government lined up firmly on the side of the prerogatives of property in the emerging class conflict between employers and labourers. Melbourne believed that 'the resolutions and acts of the trades unions ... amount to a conspiracy to control their masters', and considered those trying to raise wages in the north of England 'the most formidable difficulty and danger with which we had to contend'.[20] The Home Secretary was a scion of a fashionable Whig family, who in youth had evinced the morality and style of a Regency rake and in middle age found solace in private pleasures and misanthropic cynicism.[21] Determined to make a stand against the growing working-class movement, Melbourne, who was soon to become prime minister, took a special interest in the Tolpuddle case, and helped Frampton weave a legal web to trap the six agitators for the felony of swearing an illegal oath.[22]

Having rejected advice that he re-enact the Combination Acts as politically impossible, Melbourne sketched out a sneaky path to the same end. An Act of 1817 (a period of post-war protest) made members of societies swearing secret oaths 'not required by the law' guilty of belonging to 'unlawful combinations' as defined in an older wartime Act of 1799.[23] Most significantly for the Tolpuddle matter, both Acts amplified a prohibition on 'unlawful oaths' sworn in the armed forces legislated in 1797 following the Royal Naval Mutinies within the fleets anchored at Spithead and the Nore. Both 'mutinies' were in fact strikes by sailors and some officers for improved wages and conditions, but the Nore dispute, on the Thames, escalated into overtly political demands that the King dissolve parliament and make peace with France, or suffer a blockade of London.

Twenty-nine ringleaders were hanged and another fifteen, mainly Irish, were transported to New South Wales.[24] Over the decades of peace the 1817 law had fallen into disuse, then obscurity, but Melbourne thought its powers could be revived for the new class war.[25] It might be legal for unions to seek to raise wages, but not to impose oaths on members.[26] It was essential that all three Acts be fused in any indictment, for only the 1797 *Mutiny Act* stipulated that the penalty for swearing an illegal oath was transportation. Winding back the social clock required winding back the law to the eighteenth century. If this arcane and harsh chain of anti-sedition legislation conceived in the heat of war and mutiny could be made to apply to unions, the government had a weapon to put them out of business. The Tolpuddle Friendly Society would be the test case.

Striking at oaths that bound men to act as one appealed to the Whig version of individual liberty, for what could be more unfree than compelling the individual conscience to submit to the will of the collective. This antipathy to compulsory solidarity has remained the nub of a liberal problem with unions ever since. Then, as now, it failed to take account of the far greater power and wealth of the individual employer vis-à-vis individual employees as the reason that workers seek to equalise their bargaining power through unity. Nor does the abstract individualist critique of collective bargaining recognise the backing of the state that capitalists and landowners could usually rely upon, an unfair 'collectivist' advantage amply demonstrated by the role of the apparatus of government in the Tolpuddle case.

Leaving nothing to chance, Frampton posted a caution around the environs of Tolpuddle on 22 February warning that any 'mischieving and designing persons' administering or taking an Unlawful oath 'will become guilty of felony and liable to be transported for seven years'.[27] Frampton wanted to ensure unionists not plead ignorance of the law, but Joyce Marlow has argued the notice erred in describing unions as 'Illegal Societies' when they were not, and in assuming any unionist in Britain would think an oath they had been taking for years was unlawful.[28] Besides, the initiation had taken place before the warning was issued.

At dawn on 24 February 1834 a constable was dispatched by Frampton to bring in the six men Edward Legg had accused of swearing the oath. Loveless was first to be apprehended. He had just farewelled his wife Elizabeth and was en route to work on a neighbouring farm when he was stopped by a constable and told, 'I have a warrant for you, from the magistrates'.[29] Reading the warrant he was surprised at the charge of participating in the swearing of an illegal oath, but informed the constable he would accompany him, 'To any place wherever you wish me.'[30] Loveless's journey would be a long one, to the ends of the Earth, before he again greeted his family as a free man. In short order George's brother James, Thomas and John Standfield, James Hammett and James Brine were rounded up, leaving their wives and children despairing as they were marched 11 kilometres (7 miles) from Tolpuddle to Dorchester.

Hauled before Frampton, the men were identified by Legg and learned that they were charged with a crime punishable by transportation, a prospect terrifying to a group of ploughmen who had never been outside Dorset. Loveless replied in all honesty that they did not know they were breaking a law. The six men were refused bail, had their heads shaven and were locked in the dank, cold cells of Dorchester Gaol.[31] Simple men without connections, they were treated as convicts from the start, in violation of the presumption of innocence, in order to break them. George Loveless later wrote, 'I had never seen the inside of a jail before, but now I began to feel it—disagreeable company, close confinement, bad bread, and what was worse, hard and cold lodging.'[32] Here the constabulary set about interrogating the men, hoping one would crack and turn Crown witness.

Judging George Loveless to be the leader he was offered a deal: disown the union, tell all in court and go free.[33] In effect, Loveless had the choice of betraying his comrades and returning to his family or suffering transportation. The canny magistrate knew if Loveless gave in, his reputation with the men would be in tatters, neutering the county's leading union advocate as surely as if he were exiled to Botany Bay. However, the prisoner was made of sterner stuff, and replied, 'No; I would rather undergo any punishment' than 'betray my companions'.[34] All six would stand trial. So seriously was the matter taken by the government that Melbourne sought the advice of the government's highest law officers, the Attorney-General and the Solicitor-General, in preparing the indictment.[35] If proved, the convoluted felony of swearing an illegal oath would provide authorities with the precedent to suppress unions throughout the land.

The men were tried at the Dorchester assizes in March 1834. They first confronted a grand jury charged with deciding whether the complex indictment stitched together from various statutes by Melbourne was valid. This jury of magistrates and the legally qualified demonstrated that the law was indeed a family business, because it included Frampton, his son Henry, his stepbrother, and Lord Melbourne's brother-in-law![36] The judge, Mr Baron Williams, advised the grand jury that the swearing of unlawful oaths imposing secrecy was an offence, even if the society in question could not be proven seditious. He had been a Whig MP, and knew where his loyalty lay. Once the grand jury agreed that there was an indictment to answer, the trial began in earnest before a petty jury, made up of small farmers who Loveless surmised were beholden to the big landlords.[37] There were no workers or Methodists among them. As well as prising evidence of the oath, complete with the drama of priest-like smocks and the skeleton, out of witnesses Edward Legg and another informant John Lock, the prosecutors hammered home the connection to the old *Mutiny Act*—guilt under the newer legislation relating to oaths would result in punishment no more severe than a fine. The crucial fact was swearing the members of the Friendly Society to secrecy. Because unions were not illegal, the prosecution successfully mounted the subtle, circular argument that the six men were guilty of 'administering an oath not to reveal a combination which administers such oaths'.[38] As Marlow explains in her trial study, the indictment was within the letter of the law, if not its spirit.[39] Various papers, including a rule book committing members to secrecy and a list of members' names, that included the six defendants, sealed their fate. Before the jury retired a statement by Loveless written on behalf of the six defendants was read to the court:

> *My Lord, if we have violated any law, it was not done intentionally; we have injured no man's reputation, character, person or property; we were uniting together to preserve ourselves, our wives and our children, from utter degradation and starvation.*[40]

In summing up, the judge revealed his Whiggish political colours, railing that if unions were allowed to persist 'they would ruin masters, cause a stagnation in trade [and] destroy property'.[41]

Despite a spirited defence by counsel paid for by the Grand National Consolidated Trades Union, all six were found guilty, and each of the Tolpuddle labourers was sentenced to seven years' transportation. How could it be otherwise before a jury of employers in conservative Dorset where unions were feared as a social contaminant from the industrial north, when all the resources of the government were deployed against six simple men? As George Loveless was escorted from the court to begin a journey in chains that would take him first to the hulks, then to Van Diemen's Land, he passed to the assembled crowd a piece of paper on which he had written:

> *God is our guide! from field, from wave,*
> *From plough, from anvil, and from loom;*
> *We come, our country's rights to save,*
> *And speak a tyrant faction's doom:*
> *We raise the watch-word liberty;*
> *We will, we will, we will be free!*
>
> *God is our guide! no swords we draw.*
> *We kindle not war's battle fires:*
> *By reason, union, justice, law,*
> *We claim the birth-right of our sires:*
> *We raise the watch-word, liberty*
> *We will, we will, we will be free!*[42]

These lyrics may have already enjoyed circulation in radical circles, but through this simple gesture Loveless had sent into the world a clarion call that would inspire supporters throughout Britain. The 'Song of Freedom' on their lips, they would prove ceaseless in their efforts to free the Tolpuddle men.

✻   ✻   ✻

WHAT HAD CHANGED IN ENGLAND TO MAKE THE PROPERTIED classes so afraid of ordinary farm workers? Why was the government determined to throw the weight of the British state at these humble men and exile them to the Australian colonies? To answer these questions it is necessary to go back two decades before the Tolpuddle union was formed, to the closing years of the Napoleonic Wars when Britain, reeling from the tempo of economic transformation and the merciless cycle of boom and bust, entered a period of social instability in which middle-class radicalism was joined by the new threat of protest from below.

✱ ✱ ✱

THE ANGRY DECADES

GEORGE RUDÉ DISCERNED A FORTY-YEAR CONTINUUM OF BRITISH social protest beginning with the first great wave of machine breaking by workers inspired by the (mythical) King Ludd from 1812 and concluding with the last mass demonstrations by the Chartists in 1848, the Year of Revolutions in Europe. While some of these movements, such as the Cato Street Conspiracy and Chartism, sought constitutional change, most wanted redress of economic grievances, and hoped for an improvement in their social situation. While middle-class radicals were sometimes involved, the chief actors were ordinary working people seizing the initiative without bourgeois or aristocratic mentors, either resisting the market economy or seeking to improve their position within it. In the earlier period, protest was shared between the countryside and the city, but by the 1840s it was largely concentrated in the industrial centres of the north. Rudé also mapped a transformation of protest over time, from the more traditional rural resistance of rioting, arson and spontaneous destruction of property, such as houses and machines, to increased organisation and the use of modern tactics of strikes and petitions.[43] The exception is the continuation of rural rioting in the Scottish highlands, following a later wave of enclosures.[44]

What links these outbreaks of riot and militancy across geography and time is the growing demand by working people to have a say over their economic and political destinies and their attempts to secure a greater share in the wealth and liberty they had helped create. These protests were the first skirmishes in a new class war between capital and the emerging working class, and prefigure the rise of an organised

labour movement and the emergence of a socialist political challenge to conservatives and liberals in the second half of the nineteenth century. As E.P. Thompson demonstrated in his definitive work, the English working class was formed in the turbulent decades between 1790 and 1830 not simply by the Industrial Revolution, but because of the emergence of 'class consciousness', '[t]he consciousness of an identity of interests as between all these diverse groups of working people as against the interests of other classes'.[45]

This class awareness is manifest in the emergence of new working-class industrial and political institutions such as trade unions, and also in new cultural practices, from self-education to forms of recreation and entertainment expressive of solidarity.[46] The riots of the Luddites, the articulate stance taken by George Loveless and the Chartist petitions are different points in workers' gradual realisation of their potential power as a class.

Another common thread is the government's recourse to transportation to punish these protesters. At the beginning of the nineteenth century, protesting as we understand it was a felony punishable by death or, more commonly, transportation. By sifting through court records and the convict indents in Australia, Rudé categorised the type and number of British social protesters who were transported.[47] These included: forty-two Luddites in the years 1812–13 and 1817; fourteen participants in the 1814 Pentrich Rebellion; nineteen weavers from Scotland's Radical War in 1820; five of the Cato Street Conspirators that same year; over 500 Swing protesters in 1831, and twenty-six Bristol rioters the same year; seven from the Welsh Industrial Riots of 1831 and 1835; the six Tolpuddle Martyrs in 1834; five from the Welsh Rebecca Riots of 1842–43; three rebels from the Battle for Bossenden Wood in 1838; and 102 Chartists from 1839 to 1848.[48] The Australian colonies performed the dual role of a terrible place of exile with which to deter would-be rioters and unionists and a safety valve for discontent, removing troublemakers and rabble rousers from local communities and robbing nascent movements of their leaders. Working-class agitation would not cease with the Chartists, but they were the last popular working-class political protesters to be transported from England, Scotland and Wales.

Ireland also had her own spike in transportation of social protesters during the hard years between the defeat of the United Irishmen rising at the end of the eighteenth century and the Young Ireland Rebellion of 1848. However, in a country predominantly rural and effectively under British occupation, the protests over rent, tithes and land continued the sectarianism, gang violence and anti-colonial dimension of the Defenders, and should be distinguished from the machine breaking and unionism of a rapidly industrialising England. The story of the decades-long Irish land war, the devastating impact of the famine of the Hungry Forties, and the merging of protest with the nationalist Young Ireland rebels of 1848 and the Fenian republicans of the 1860s will be examined in Chapter 5.

Overlapping with the rise of social protest was the advance of the radical liberal program that had led to the exile of the Scottish Martyrs in the 1790s. In the decades following the war with France these seditious proposals for electoral and parliamentary reform moved from the radical fringe to the centre of mainstream political debate, culminating in the passing of the Great Reform Bill by the Whig Government in 1832. However, it would be wrong to imagine that constitutional reform was achieved without struggle, or that the middle-class radicals and their Whig supporters were able to wring concessions from a recalcitrant parliament and Crown without working-class agitation. In many ways the escalation in working-class protest was a consequence of their exposure to radical political campaigns, and frustration at the limitations of the bourgeois liberal program that delivered the franchise and the right to sit in parliament to the urban middle class, while leaving property-less working people without political rights. Working-class radicals took away from the Reform Bill agitation that they had different interests and goals from the liberals, stemming from their different position in the economy.

Drawing comparisons with their propertied employers, ordinary toilers like George Loveless reasoned that, 'Labour is the poor man's property, from which all protection is withheld. Has not the working man as much right to preserve and protect his labour as the rich man has his capital?'[49] Indeed, bourgeois individualists, who defended the liberty of the market and of employer entrepreneurs, often had opposing interests to the workers of factory and field, who thought in collective terms, and looked to the government to guarantee fair wages and rents and charity in time of need. Those seeking an intellectual defence for this collectivist agenda could find it in the same book that inspired radical liberalism, Tom Paine's *Rights of Man*, which E.P. Thompson reminds us was also 'a foundation-text of the English working-class movement'.[50] This is because Paine, despite his enthusiasm for commercialism, outlined a progressive program for graduated income tax and state intervention in the market to ameliorate the most exploitative or anti-social effects of capitalism.[51] Through ideas such as age pensions and public education, Paine anticipated the social democratic agenda implemented in the West in the late nineteenth and early twentieth centuries, and not surprisingly a significant number of middle-class radicals would sympathise with the plight of workers in the decades after the Napoleonic Wars. But sympathy was not enough. Unionism emerged out of the realisation that unless compelled, employers and politicians would do nothing, as Loveless observed:

> *never no, never will (with a few honourable exceptions) the rich and the great devise means to alleviate the distress, and remove the misery felt by the working men of England … the labouring classes must do it themselves or it will be left undone.*[52]

British workers would need their own movements and methods.

Rudé divided these decades of social discord into three phases. First were successive breakouts of spontaneous riots and anti-industrial movements that erupted from the end of the Napoleonic Wars into the 1820s. Second was the turbulent 1830s, which marked a change from the 'primitive' protest of the Swing Riots to the almost modern trade unionism of the Tolpuddle Martyrs. The third and final phase spanning the late 1830s through the '40s was dominated by the overtly political Chartist challenge.

The upsurge in social protests towards the end of the Napoleonic Wars must be seen as the culmination of a longer process of capitalist transformation. One result of the agrarian and industrial revolutions in the late eighteenth century was the growth of new manufacturing cities in the Midlands and the North of England within proximity of mines, ports and rivers. Towns like Manchester, Birmingham, Leeds, Sheffield and Liverpool became magnets for landless farm labourers seeking work and an improved standard of living. In this process of accelerated urbanisation, towns burst their old borders to gorge on nearby rural communities, belching factory smoke and staining rivers with refuse. Shanty towns were hastily erected on their peripheries amid great piles of slag and dust, ingesting craftsmen and ploughmen, seamstresses and milking maids, farm labourers and shepherds, book keepers and engineers, traders and hawkers down the maw of modernity. Not surprisingly working-class resistance would begin in these cities, where the bonds of mutual obligation between classes were weak and the workers, concentrated in large numbers, gradually came to sense the strength that lay in unity.

Nor was the countryside immune from change. The war economy of the early nineteenth century led to the further extension of market methods into the agricultural sector in the rural south. More and more common land was enclosed, tenants came to rely on wages rather than subsistence plots for survival, and new machines yielded greater output using less human labour. However, during the war with France the army and navy's hunger for food for their men and wool for uniforms masked the impact of enclosure and new technology on employment. Then, as the long war drew to a close, Britain's economy went into recession. Napoleon's defeat proved a mixed blessing as demobilised soldiers and seamen returned to their villages and cities, swelling the numbers of those looking for work, needing to provide for themselves and perhaps a family, their horizons broadened and expectations heightened in the service of their country. There was insufficient work for the veterans, especially in the country, due to both mechanisation and the recession. There were also food shortages that in turn led to rapidly rising prices.

At different times there were other immediate factors encouraging protest. The outbreak of revolution in France and elsewhere in Europe in 1830 and again in 1848 influenced the mood for change in Britain. Both years coincide with widespread civil disorder and protest from below. A change of government, notably the election of the Whigs with a mandate for reform in 1830, seems to have raised national hopes and expectations, unintentionally fanning long-smouldering discontent that ignited in the Swing Riots. The growing popularity of Methodism among industrial and rural workers helped the building of an organised labour movement by enhancing literacy, self-discipline and commitment to social justice. However, the most direct provocation for unrest from working people was a downturn in the economic cycle. Rudé's mapping demonstrated that incidents of riot, machine breaking and incendiarism in both city and country coincided with periods of exacerbated economic hardship when work was scarce and food prices increased.[53]

* * *

PRIMITIVE PROTESTERS

UNEMPLOYMENT AND THE RISING COST OF LIVING SPARKED THE first great wave of protest from below, beginning with the Luddites. From 1811 to 1813 workers concentrated in the hosiery and textile industries of the Midlands and the North, in the old declining manufacturing regions of East Anglia and in industrial Wales embarked on a campaign of protest against economic and technological change distinguished by the tactic of machine breaking. The government in London was so alarmed at this cycle of destruction that it declared a state of emergency, suspended *habeas corpus* and sent 12,000 troops into York and Leicester.[54] Eight rioters were killed by soldiers, and to demonstrate that the wilful destruction of property would not be tolerated a further thirty were hanged and forty-two eventually transported to Australia.[55]

Of all the nineteenth century social protesters, the Luddites are the best known, remembered for destroying machines and popularly criticised as misguided opponents of inevitable progress. To this day the word Luddite is used negatively to chastise someone resistant to technological innovation. This is unfair, as Luddism was actually a positive strategy to assert a measure of worker control over production.[56] Rather than rejecting technology, Luddites resisted the proletarianisation of crafts and agricultural work, whereby skilled tasks were broken down into a series of smaller, routine jobs performed to the rhythm of steam-powered machines. The Luddites had well-grounded concerns about the loss of jobs to labour-saving new technology, but they also resented how capital equipment enhanced employer control over their work speed and the product of their labour. These artisans wanted to put the man back in manufacture. While machine breaking has been dismissed as a backward reaction to progress, it was in fact a canny way for workers to leverage some bargaining power vis-à-vis employers, a form of organised assertion of collective strength that pre-figures trade unionism. As Hobsbawm and Rudé have argued, sabotaging machines should be seen as a rational tactic for inconveniencing employers during an earlier phase of industrial capitalism when strikes were not organisationally feasible.[57] Out of such collective resistance, working people, especially those brought together in large numbers in mills, mines and docks, began to develop a consciousness of themselves as a class with different, often opposing, interests to employers. Machine breaking commonly associated with the Luddites would persist right through the first half of the nineteenth century, especially in the more backward agricultural sector, reaching its climax in the Swing Riots of 1830.

In 1812 food scarcity and high prices in the immediate aftermath of the war led to food riots in Sheffield, Nottingham and Carlisle, followed by major demonstrations in London against the new Corn Law in 1815. Representing a decisive shift from free trade to protectionism, the Corn Law was the first of many import tariffs raising the price of home-grown grain, enriching the great landowners. The army had to protect parliament from angry mobs unable to afford bread.[58] Then the following year a serious wave of rioting broke out in the agrarian districts of East Anglia protesting the combination of high bread prices, low wages and unemployment, with animosity directed at threshing machines blamed for taking jobs. Of the more than eighty people tried, five were hanged and another nineteen had their death sentences commuted to transportation. Their crimes were typically demanding money, food and goods from farmers and shopkeepers, or increases in their wages. Rudé cites the example of Richard Rutter, a forty-year-old unemployed labourer excluded from Poor Law relief because he had sufficient property to fail the means test. After leading a crowd to the home of John Horsely, where he demanded £5 and then on to the White Hart Inn in Ely, where he attempted to extort a wage of two shillings plus flour and beer, Rutter was sentenced to fourteen years' transportation. With the Spa Fields Riot in London, a march of unemployed 'Blanketeers' in Manchester (mainly weavers so-called because they carried blankets) and an ironworkers' strike in South Wales, 1816 was a volatile year.

For Rudé, Luddism was a 'primitive' form of protest, sharing features with other primitive movements such as the Swing and the Rebecca Riots.[59] These looked backwards to imagined pre-capitalist relations between masters and servants, rather than forwards, and were thus prevalent in rural areas where market forces and technology were still to be firmly entrenched, or among urban workers with strong craft traditions predating industrialisation. Primitive protest was a working-class variation of the same species of romanticism that inspired poets of the early nineteenth century such as Blake and Shelley to conjure images of England's 'green and pleasant land' rid of 'dark satanic mills'.[60] Some protesters and radicals joined with romantic poets in the hope that a new 'Jerusalem' might be built by returning to a rural Arcadia, hence revolution implied revolving back to an idealised organic past.[61]

Some in the governing class shared the prejudice that the cities encouraged vice and corruption among the lower classes. New South Wales' governor, William Bligh, for example, dismissed Sydney Town as a cesspit of greed, and instead idealised and encouraged the small farmers of the Hawkesbury as the colony's future. Rural romanticism idealised a golden time before industrial capitalism when Britons were organically connected to the land and each other. This romanticism was still strong in the late nineteenth century in the writing of utopian socialists like William Morris who believed a workers' revolution would revive mediaeval craft guilds and return England to an agrarian way of life.[62] In a less articulate, more naïve form, this nostalgia for the pre-modern connects the Luddites, the weavers from Scotland's Radical War and the Rebecca and Swing Riots, and is even present in some of the more radical policies of the Chartists. The reality was that the older agrarian way of life condemned most ordinary people to dire poverty. However, in the early nineteenth century what was popularly remembered in the countryside was that the poor had enjoyed common rights and protections prior to enclosure, capitalist farming, and the notorious Black Act banning traditional customs, such as catching game. Capitalism and industrial revolution would progressively lift living standards throughout the century, but was initially experienced as dislocation, deterioration and pauperisation, leading to crimes like poaching and theft, but also to protest.

Primitive protest was often spontaneous and given to ill-disciplined crowd behaviour. It favoured the destruction of property, usually that owned by parsimonious employers, or public buildings or local infrastructure associated with punitive charity, private levies or taxes, such as the hated workhouses, turnpikes or tollgates. Rioters' favourite targets for destruction were farmhouses, threshers, barns and ricks in the country, and mills and 'frames' and boilers in manufacturing centres. Such destructive acts were so widespread in the decades after the Napoleonic Wars that laws were passed to protect these specific forms of property from attack. The crime of arson was a popular way to destroy property, though it was not uncommon for men to simply dismantle a house, or disable a machine with hammers. Not surprisingly 'pulling down houses' was made a crime punishable by death. Sometimes the rioters coerced the employer or farmer into carrying out the destruction. Other ways that protesters sought to intimidate employers, landlords and local authorities that were quickly outlawed as felonies included cattle maiming; assaults on peace officers (the precursors to police); sending threatening letters making demands in relation to wages, rent, food and machines; conspiring to raise wages; and the administration of unlawful oaths.[63] Many of these crimes were punishable by hanging but it was more common to transport those found guilty.

While they might have a local leader from the community, these early protest movements often had a fictional leader, a figure possessing mythical qualities. Thus, the Luddites took their name from the invented leader Ned Ludd. Two decades later, the rural rioters who swept through the wheat belt of Southern England were said to be commanded by the dashing Captain Swing, a larger-than-life character who never existed. In a land that could trace its rebel lineage back to the Celtic Queen

Illustration of the yeomanry attacking the meeting of workers and
their families in St Peter's Fields, Manchester on
16 August 1819, sardonically mocked at the 'Battle of Peterloo'.

Boadicea, sometimes a folk-heroine was needed. The Rebecca Riots of 1842–43 took their name from a mythical matriarch, whose daughters were actually male farmers and labourers riding on horseback dressed as women, destroying the hated turnpikes and tollgates.[64] Like the legendary Robin Hood, who stole from the rich and gave to the poor, modern folk-heroes buoyed ordinary people in the belief that their actions were guided by wise, brave leadership, and also helped intimidate authorities who were paranoid about conspiracies. In reality, many of the early social protest movements had no leader at all, their spontaneous formation in response to a crisis or grievance resulting in a collective leadership that Hobsbawm and Rudé call 'primitive egalitarianism'.[65] Fictional captains thus become symbolic of the many acting as one, so that each protester is Ned Ludd, Rebecca's daughter or Swing.

One of the more colourful protests from below in the early nineteenth century was the Pentrich Rebellion in June 1817. In a bold action straight out of Robin Hood, charismatic leader Jeremiah Brandeth and his band of men tried to seize Nottingham Castle. Dubbed the Nottingham Captain, Brandeth had the support of armed and trusted rural workers from the villages of Pentrich and South Wingfield. As well as labourers this proletarian guerrilla force included skilled workers, such as stocking weavers, miners, iron-founders and a stonemason—people who felt their craft skills were under threat. As head of a 'North Midlands Committee' Brandeth planned to spark an uprising throughout the Midlands, and was cooperating with other cells. Betrayed by a spy they were overwhelmed by government troops. Brandeth and his two lieutenants were hanged. Of the thirty-five men apprehended and tried for high treason, fourteen were transported to Australia. Rudé's research indicates that most of the convicted were younger men aged twenty-one to thirty-seven.[66]

Workers were also capable of assembling peacefully to protest for improved wages and conditions. In 1819 Manchester's weavers staged a mass rally in St Peter's Field, signalling their peaceful intent by encouraging a festive atmosphere, with picnics and playing children. Yet authorities took this mass gathering as a threat to order, and mobilised the local Lancashire Yeomanry Cavalry to disperse the crowd. Instead the yeomanry demonstrated contempt for human life born of class prejudice, riding into the unarmed families with razor-sharp sabres raised. So furious was their attack that eleven people were slaughtered and almost 400 people wounded. There was an immediate outcry. While the terror unleashed by the loyalist yeomanry and British Army in Ireland had evoked little grief in Britain, the 'Peterloo Massacre', as it became known in ironic comparison with the Battle of Waterloo, outraged middle England, and was swiftly condemned by Whig and Tory politicians. The young poet Percy Shelley set in verse radical hopes that the outrage might awaken the English people to action:

> Rise like Lions after slumber
> In vanquished number,
> Shake your chains to earth like dew
> Which in sleep had fallen on you—
> Ye are many—they are few.[67]

Peterloo was indeed a harbinger of the class conflict to come, and taught working people valuable lessons about how ruthless the state could be in protecting the prerogatives of the propertied classes. Despite the outcry, Peterloo would not be the last time troops would be used against the people.

This first phase of protest came to a climax in 1820, a year of financial crisis in Britain, with attempted rebellions in London, Scotland and Yorkshire. The incident in the capital is known as the Cato Street Conspiracy. Harking back to the aborted gunpowder plot of the seventeenth century, a cell of radical republicans conspired to plant explosives to blow up the British Cabinet.[68] Five were executed and five transported. E.P. Thompson considered the backlash by the state against this treason the start of 'the most sustained campaign of prosecutions in the courts in British history'.[69] This was expedited by the passage of the 'Six Acts' in 1820 that greatly enhanced the state's power to suppress drilling, meetings and seditious libel, the last aimed at a burgeoning radical press.

Scotland had two rebellions, one in the lowlands where working people demanded the right to vote among other constitutional reforms and another in the rural highlands over clearances and enclosure.[70] Although the insurrection in the lowlands had a political focus—hence the name 'Radical War'—it involved radicalised skilled workers rather than bourgeois liberals, notably weavers, miners and cobblers. Hailing from towns near Glasgow grappling with the accelerated changes of industrialisation, the source of their discontent was as much economic as political. Its leaders reasoned that if they had the vote they may not be so vulnerable. Of the eighty-eight charged with high treason for conspiring to subvert the constitution, twenty-five were sentenced to hang and nineteen transported to New South Wales, seven for life. In line with the exemplary sentences prescribed for treason, one of the executed leaders, a stocking weaver named James Wilson, who denounced his 'mummery of a trial', was hanged, drawn and disembowelled as a warning to other worker radicals.[71] However, harsh penalties did not deter a wave of machine breaking in Yorkshire, led by radical weavers with links to the insurrectionists in Glasgow. In the end thirteen who were sentenced to hang were transported to Van Diemen's Land.

Beginning in 1820 the British Government embarked on a process of law reform, which limited the use of the death penalty. That year the notorious *Black Act* was repealed so that poaching was no longer a capital offence. Sending threatening letters also ceased to attract the death penalty. The Combinations Laws, prohibiting organisations like trade unions, were repealed in 1824. In 1827 the energetic Tory Home Secretary Sir Robert Peel systematically cleaned up the criminal law, removing the death penalty from all capital crimes where the court had seldom imposed a death sentence.[72] However, fearful of protest from below and cognisant of the need to protect property rights, the law-makers were careful to preserve the death penalty (and the mitigating punishment of transportation) for riot, machine breaking, destroying buildings, burning haystacks and cattle maiming.[73] Rudé calculated that Peel's reforming crusade against the gallows, coupled with his establishment of effective police forces in the cities in 1829 (nicknamed Bobbies after Sir Robert), had the effect of doubling the number of convicts transported to the Australian colonies, from 2149 in the years 1824–26 to 4160 in 1828–30.[74]

The use of police in preference to troops against protesters meant that rallies and riots were much less likely to escalate and resulted in arrests and trials rather than casualties. Nevertheless, troops would still be needed in moments of crisis, such as the Swing Riots. The death penalty was further curtailed by civilising law reform in the 1830s and '40s. Significantly, the most popular protest crimes—rioting, machine breaking, cattle maiming and robbery with threats—ceased to be punishable by hanging in 1841. However, along with murder, piracy, burglary and robbery, hanging was still available for burning a house with people living in it. Of course as capital offences were weeded out, transportation increased. Reluctance to impose the death sentence for political offences is reflected in the fact that the fifteen people sentenced to hang for treason or arson between 1842 and 1848 escaped the gallows, with nine transported to Australia instead.

* * *

THE LAST PEASANTS' REVOLT

THE CLOSEST ENGLAND CAME TO REVOLUTION WAS THE SWING Riots of 1830 that swept through the wheat-growing farms of South West England like an Australian bush fire. Rudé considered these riots, often known as the last 'Peasants' revolt', to be 'the most explosive in modern British history'.[75] The protesters sent threatening, often barely literate, letters demanding higher pay and lower rents and went on night-time rampages from farm to farm, burning produce and homes and extorting money and promises of improvements in wages from intimidated employers. However, what distinguished the Swing Riots was the widespread destruction of agricultural machinery, notably threshers, across thirty counties. Although the Luddite campaign of resistance happened in 1812, it is the Swing Riots that singed machine breaking into popular memory. The riots spanning August to December 1830 provided the largest number of English political prisoners ever transported to Australia.[76]

What were the immediate causes of this outbreak? The first labour historians who examined the Swing rising found its cause in the enclosure of land and the consequent dispossession and impoverishment of labourers who had always had their own plot and access to common land.[77] Between 1770 and 1830 English peasants lost close to 6 million acres (2.4 million hectares) of common land to enclosure.[78] This was land on which they grew their own subsistence crops, grazed their livestock, gathered wood for warmth and cooking, and came together as a community for meetings and festivals. Common land also allowed villages to share in communal harvests. Enclosure was a privatisation of the people's property that dwarfs the sell-offs of public utilities in the 1980s and '90s. By eliminating self-sufficiency in food, enclosure reduced landless labourers to complete dependence on wages paid by squires and the larger landlords. By increasing yields from the land and the prices for produce, enclosure provided the great landowners with an excuse to massively increase the rent burden paid by tenant farmers and their workers. For E.P. Thompson the escalating extraction of rent during and after the Napoleonic Wars exposed enclosure as 'a plain enough case of class robbery, played according to fair rules of property and law laid down by a Parliament of property-owners and lawyers'.[79]

While enclosure was undoubtedly a significant grievance among the 1830 Swing rioters it is far from the whole story. A later generation of social historians, led by Hobsbawm, Rudé and Thompson, emphasised the resistance of agricultural workers to their proletarianisation and pauperisation as capitalism tightened its grip on agricultural England.[80] Specific grievances arose from this that are apparent from the targets attacked by the rioters. Both cyclical unemployment and a long-term decline in jobs for farm labourers were blamed on new farm machinery, specifically the threshers. Periodic wage reductions joined rising food prices and rent increases to make it difficult for property-less agricultural workers to feed their families, and drove many men to take drastic, violent action. 'We don't want to do any mischief,' explained one labourer who participated in the Swing Riots, 'but we want the poor children when they go to bed should have a belly full of tatoes instead of crying with half a belly full.'[81] Wage rises and lower rents dominate in the demands rioters made on employers and landlords, both in letters and face to face.

Instead of a minimum wage, Britain's approach was to top up low wages with charity, tempting employers to drive wages lower still.[82] From 1795 changes to the old Poor Law, known as the 'Speenhamland' system, meant that the state, through the local parish, was to make up the difference when prices rose and wages fell, depending on a worker's family circumstance.[83] Unemployment and declining income left workers at the mercy of local charity, and here they came up against the parsimony, piety and industrial discipline of the Poor Law 'workhouses'. The system was stretched to breaking under pressure from enclosure and demobilised soldiers after the Napoleonic Wars, and the governors of Poor Law relief became ever harsher and discriminating in deciding who would qualify as 'deserving' for relief.[84] One sympathetic magistrate observed that:

> [t]he poor in the Parishes of the South of England ... have been ground into the dust in many instances by the Poor laws ... Instead of happy peasants, they are made miserable and sour-tempered paupers ... Should you wonder they are dissatisfied?[85]

It is no accident that rioters targeted the hated workhouses where those without means were forced to earn bare sustenance through praying and aimlessly walking the treadmill. However, old folk habits, like love of ale and aversion to sermons, excluded many of the working families of England from the cold charity of the workhouse, condemning them to near starvation as the 'undeserving poor'.

Finally, the wider political climate in 1830 was charged with change and possibility. That year revolution once again swept through France, ridding the country of the Bourbon King Charles X and reviving hopes in liberty, equality and fraternity among middle-class radicals and ordinary people across the channel. These hopes seemed borne out in July 1830 when the Whig Party won a general election on a reform platform that appealed to the middle classes, ending many years of Tory rule and the government of the Duke of Wellington. While the new prime minister Earl Grey had in mind concessions to the liberal agenda of the bourgeoisie rather than any romantic ideas of winding back enclosure and capitalism, many of the landless poor may have hoped for a better deal.[86]

While the Swing rioters were seeking redress of clear and present economic hardship, radical agents provocateurs may have contributed to the clamour for an improvement in living standards. While the radical press had up until this time largely focused their sympathy and agitation on social division and immiseration of the poor in the industrial cities, Hobsbawm and Rudé have noted the influence of middle-class radicals in the countryside, notably William Cobbett, a journalist and activist who had moved from the bourgeois emphasis on extending constitutional rights to a quasi-socialist agenda of wealth distribution and workers' right to a living wage.[87] Cobbett insisted that 'the labourer must have his belly full and free from fear, and this belly full must come out of his wages and not from benevolence of any sort'.[88] The worker's dignity as a human being demanded a fair day's pay for a fair day's work, and not cold charity.

But what was fair? Cobbett calculated the basic dietary requirements of a labourer with a wife and three children, 'the bare eating and drinking', and this proved to cost twice the average wage.[89] Rural labourers' 'dwellings are little better than pig-beds, and their looks indicate that their food is not equal to that of a pig'.[90] The slaves of the West Indies, Cobbett concluded, were better fed, clothed and housed than the labourers of England.[91] His newspaper, *The Political Register*, was credited by the Attorney-General in 1831 to have had 'a prodigious effect' on working people throughout Britain, encouraging them to band together 'in great societies' to purchase copies and disseminate their contents by means of reading them out loud 'in many places where the poor are in the habit of resorting'.[92]

It is important not to fall victim to the same nostalgia for pre-enclosure rural life that stirred the protesters, radicals and romantic poets. For centuries life for farm workers had been cursed by harsh weather, pestilence, poor sanitation and the cavalier prerogatives of the great landowners and squires. By breaking down the old bonds of mutual obligation that tied peasants to great landowners and substituting wages and the cycle of boom, bust and unemployment, the Agrarian Revolution left labourers with little to lose. The temptation of many to break the law is illustrated by an interview with a farm labourer undertaken by Cobbett:

> *'How do you live upon half a crown a week?'*
> *'I don't live on it',* said he.
> *'How do you live then?'*
> *'Why ... I poach, it is better to be hanged than to be starved to death.'*[93]

The resort to riot was undertaken with the same grim choice.

Unlike the commercial and industrial cities, rural England was poorly served by locomotives, making communication difficult and communities isolated. Nevertheless, following the first outbreak of machine breaking in Kent in August 1830 the Swing Riots spread rapidly. Joyce Marlow argued that Swing had its 'spontaneous combustion' in Kent because it was a county close to the radical influence of London, and also a part of England near France, then in the throes of revolution.[94] The riots passed over Surrey and spread westward through the grain-growing heartland of Hampshire, Wiltshire, Berkshire and Dorset.

Typically of primitive protest, the rising was said to be led by Captain Swing, a commanding romantic rebel on horseback, fanning the spark of revolt from county to county, inspiring the long-suffering labourers into insurrection. It seems certain that this rumour, passed from village to village and reported in the press, helped the riots move very quickly from Kent until they extended to over half of Southern England. The myth of Captain Swing gave peasants the confidence to rise up, and the prospect that they would be seen as faceless foot soldiers following orders rather than ringleaders. Menacing anonymous letters that were sent to landowners in the lead-up to physical confrontations were often signed in the name of Swing. However, there was no brave nightrider leading the peasants into revolt. Rather the rioting was spontaneous and haphazard but irresistible owing to the deep discontent that had built up over decades. *The Times* quoted a magistrate who observed that '[t]he insurrectionary movement seems to be directed by no plan or system, but merely actuated by the spontaneous feelings of the peasants, quite at random'.

Not quite random. What is remarkable is how common were the features of the various riots, the targets, the methods and the demands across disparate counties, demonstrating the *systemic* nature of agrarian social exploitation in Southern England.

Across counties the protests adhered to a common pattern. Villagers hurriedly met and leaders emerged who brought order to proceedings. A group then marched to the homes of farmers, squires and sometimes the local nobility and Anglican clergy where they presented their demands, sometimes peaceably but often with threats of violence or destruction of property. It was common for ricks to be burned and the hated machines to be targeted and destroyed. Swing was the greatest bout of machine breaking in British history. Violence against the person was far less frequent, and usually directed at the functionaries who had immediate control over local labourers and their families: overseers, and Poor Law administrators. No one was killed by the rioters. Even *The Times* praised the 'admirable' 'conduct of the peasants', which compared favourably to the bloody uprisings in France.[95] Perhaps the newspaper was relieved that the state retained its monopoly on killing?

It was not uncommon for the rioters to extort money while engaged in these home invasions. Typical were a group of Berkshire labourers from Kintbury, who roved from farm to farm destroying agricultural machines and demanding money for performing this service. In the minds of the protesters it appeared just that masters would reward them for taking the initiative of restoring the customary employment relations.[96] More crucially, machine breaking was a way the workers bargained for improved wages from a position of strength. William Oakley, a skilled wheelwright and carpenter who was leading the Berkshire men, addressed the magistrates at Hungerford Town Hall with explicit wage claims, demanding 'We will have 2s. a day till layday and half a crown afterwards for labourers and 3s. for tradesmen, and as we are here, we will have £5 before we go out of the place or be damned if we don't smash it.'[97]

One-off fees for smashing machines were adjusted according to the means of the employer. Although £2 was the common charge in Kintbury, Lord Craven was relieved of £10 by Oakley's offsider Francis Norris, who had collected £100 by the time of his arrest. Both Norris and Oakley were sentenced to transportation for life, to Van Diemen's Land and New South Wales respectively. Historians David Kent and Norma Townsend stress that in demanding that employers pay money for the privilege of having their machines wrecked, the farm invaders were following the customary practice of 'collective begging'.[98] As part of this practice, the takings were evenly distributed between the men.[99] The charging of a fee and the transaction were frequently conducted with civility, rather than menace, though intimidation was implicit and those subjected to such night visitations would have harboured fears for the consequences for not paying up.

As mentioned, threatening letters, sent to employers and notables ahead of any organised deputations, were another feature of the protests. Hundreds bearing the name Captain Swing found their way to key players in local power structures.[100] In November 1830, a fifty-year-old Winchester farmer, John Boyes, was transported for seven years for 'demanding money with menaces' and 'conspiring to raise wages', leaving behind a wife and ten children. Isaac Looker sent a letter to fellow Haxford farmer John Rowland threatening '[i]f you goes to sware against or a man in prison, you have here farm burned down to the ground and thy bloody head chopt off'. This missive, typical for its poor literacy and violent imagery, was sufficient evidence for Rowland to be transported for life. However, his son Edward claimed he wrote the letter and was transported instead.[101] As the riots moved from east to west in November, Henry Williams, a twenty-one-year-old tailor and lay preacher in Herefordshire wrote anonymously to a prosperous farmer John Monkhouse, demanding he destroy his own machines: 'Remember in Kent that have set ('with fire') all that would not submit and you will serve the same ... so pull down your Thrashing Maschine or els Bread or Fire without delay. For we are 5 thousand men and will not be stopt.'[102] The overtly political tone of these threats saw Williams sentenced to fourteen years' transportation.

The most rebellious counties were Wiltshire, Berkshire and Hampshire. The riots lasted four months but by Christmas 1830 they were petering out. This was partly due to the moderation of the protester's aims but also to the harshness of the government's crackdown. The English winter with its bitter cold was also settling in, dampening even the most insurrectionary spirits.

For Rudé and Hobsbawm, Swing was the last great protest calling for the reinstatement of traditional rights.[103] They stress the conservatism of the Swing rioters, who wanted to wind back the clock, not go forward. In threatening letters and torch-light confrontations with employers the bands of disgruntled workers were demanding customary rights they believed the farmers had disregarded. For this reason the rioters made little attempt to hide their identities and displayed no shame. They believed right, and public sentiment, would be on their side. The aggrieved farm workers naïvely looked to the common law of England to protect their rights, but they had been superseded by new statutes that made such forms of protest as 'collective begging' punishable by death or transportation. The labourers' yearning for an older moral economy was shared by many of the smaller farmers and squires for whom they worked. These smaller landowners often found new technology and model farming a mixed blessing. There are documented instances of farmers happily cooperating with the demands of rioters, or adding their names to demands for rent reduction.[104] They sympathised with the protesters, complaining that they too suffered from escalating rents charged by the great aristocratic landlords and had to pay Church tithes—burdens they had no choice but to also pass on to their tenant labourers. Even some magistrates sympathised with the wage claims of their local labourers, but not James Frampton in Dorset, who read the riot act and called in the local yeomanry.[105]

While some landowners and members of government feared the riots were a rehearsal for the regime change occurring across the channel, the Swing movement had no revolutionary intent.[106] The protesters maintained their customary faith in the Crown, hopeful that their grievances would be listened to and that the government would act to improve their lot. Naïvely they hoped for a legally enforced minimum living wage, an act that would restore the old notion of mutual obligations. A printed pamphlet discovered by Joyce Marlow makes clear the economic limit of the goal: 'All we ask, then, is that our wages may be advanced to such a degree as will enable us to provide for ourselves and our families …'[107]

However, such an intervention in the market was anathema to the free market liberalism of the new Whig Government, and their bourgeois supporters. Confronted by the rising, conservatives and liberals found common cause in the defence of employer prerogatives and the restoration of order. The change of government from the Tories to the Whigs would mean a great deal for the cause of constitutional reform, but both aristocratic parties were as one on the need to restore order in the countryside, and to use the full powers of the law to make examples of those who challenged the authority of the state and the rule of property.[108]

The protesters' old-fashioned faith in the Crown was answered with disdain and cruelty as the new Home Secretary, Lord Melbourne, created Special Commissions to expedite the harshest punishment on the rioters. Kent and Townsend calculated that 1976 protesters were apprehended and tried, across thirty-four counties in ninety different courts.[109] Notwithstanding that in four months of protest no one was killed, 252 people received death sentences, with nineteen being sent to the scaffold. An incredible 505 were transported to the ends of the Earth for sentences of seven or fourteen years, while 644 were imprisoned in England.

Why the mass exile? In part because the rising had happened not in the industrial cities where the new factory-based working class was uppity, but in the rural south, where the gentry sat atop a more static social hierarchy and the farm workers at the bottom traditionally knew their place. However, transportation must also be seen as an expedient to permanently rid the countryside of the malcontents and rebels so that the southern rural social order might settle back to its old ways. Finally, as was the case in the late eighteenth century, the supposedly reformist government together with conservative landowners were seized with the fear that the revolution in France was being imported to Britain, borne by home-grown radicals like Cobbett stirring the peasants into discontent and insurrection.[110]

Thanks to court records, newspaper reports, the convict indents created on arrival in Australia and the official colonial files for each prisoner (regularly updated by the colonial convict departments until sentence and parole was completed), we know quite a lot about the transported Swing rioters.[111] Most had never been outside their village. At an average age of twenty-nine they were older than the usual convicts, and more than half were married.[112] As well as the many farm workers, a large proportion were skilled artisans, such as carpenters, millwrights and blacksmiths. Robert Hughes argues that this aristocracy of labour, better read and informed, were just the sort to lead other villagers in demanding their rights. With their trades' skills they were also just the sort of convicts in demand in the colonies.[113] The majority of Swing prisoners were transported on two ships, the *Eleanor*, bound for Sydney, and the *Eliza*, that took her human cargo to Hobart. Kent and Townsend have painstakingly gone through all the English and Australian records of the men who came to New South Wales on the *Eleanor*, and brought their stories to life in forensic detail in the scholarly history, *The Convicts of the Eleanor*.

The authorities were determined to make examples of the protesters. When Tisbury bricklayer Thomas Abery was found guilty of machine breaking at Salisbury, even a reference from the local Lord Arundel testifying to the defendant's work ethic and bravery (displayed in repairing Salisbury Cathedral) did not stop him being transported.[114] The crackdown on the Swing rioters became an excuse to arrest known agitators. Joseph and Robert Mason were brothers from Sutton Scotney, Hampshire, aged thirty-one and twenty-four, who were market gardeners and small holders, rather than labourers, and leading agitators in the villages of central Hampshire.[115] They were respectable men who regularly attended Church and read the Bible, but they were also regular readers of Cobbett's *Political Register*, having found in the Christian message an injunction to fight for social justice in the here and now.[116] Like the Loveless brothers in Dorchester, they were Methodists, a faith that preached the dignity of working people. They belonged to a local Radical and Musical Society, whose members played a disproportionate part in the Hampshire rising, giving the riots in their area more political focus. Led by cobbler Enos Diddams, the Society was a mix of craftsmen, labourers and small farmers who were influenced by Cobbett's ideas.[117]

Just prior to the riots in October 1830 the Mason brothers had drawn up a petition from 'the working and labouring classes' asking for the right to vote and be represented in parliament, and making the explicit connection between their indigent and exploited condition and their exclusion from political power.[118] The petition adapted the traditional radical program to working-class concerns, asking for lower taxes but also complaining of the tithes paid to the Church of England, and the poaching laws that forbade the poor hunting game for subsistence. After collecting 177 signatures from local villagers, Joseph Mason delivered the petition to the King while he was in Brighton—a gesture that led *The Times* to ridicule his radical Society as 'Hampshire bumkins'.[119]

With the outbreak of the Swing Riots, Hampshire experienced some of the most extensive and prolonged protests. Sifting through the evidence, Kent and Townsend demonstrate that the Masons' radical group played a key part in coordinating a strategy of strikes and machine breaking. For example, a letter from Diddams was read to workmen at Sutton Scotney instructing them to walk off the job, and break the 'sheens' the farmers used for threshing wheat.[120] Not surprisingly the brothers were arrested in the aftermath, accused of leading a large crowd around Barton Stacey, East Stratton and Micheldever, and were charged with 'demanding money' for machine breakers at East Stratton. In mitigation, Hobsbawm and Rudé suggest the Masons were voices of moderation and modernisation during the Hampshire rising, keeping the protesters non

-violent, on message and organised.[121] They appointed a treasurer, kept accounts of damaged machinery and ensured employers they confronted paid up on the basis of their means. When the crowd stopped at a pub, Joseph Mason scrupulously took records and paid for the drinks out of the money collected from employers.[122] Nevertheless, their crimes against the laws protecting property were manifest, and the brothers were found guilty and transported. Other workers who had signed the Masons' petition were arrested and tried, including John Silock, a twenty-seven-year-old ploughman.[123]

Kent and Townsend's research indicates that alongside known 'bad characters' the authorities singled out radicals and working men with some education for exile to Australia.[124] The Masons' 'superior education and intelligence' made them more dangerous to authorities, and the jury was instructed that this elevated the seriousness of their crimes.[125] They did not go quietly. In an address to the court one of the brothers claimed that anyone in the vicinity of the riots dressed in worker's garb, even the judge, would have been found guilty.[126] From the ship *Eleanor* at Portsmouth they wrote letters stressing that their punishment had not dimmed their fervour for political change, and bid their neighbours get them released should Britain be blessed with a reformed parliament or revolution.[127] The brothers were separated by authorities, Robert being sent to Van Diemen's Land on the *Eliza* and Joseph taking the *Eleanor* to New South Wales.

Of the 505 Swing protesters transported only two were women. Elizabeth Parker, a labourer of twenty-four from Gloucestershire, was first sentenced to four months' prison for machine breaking, but was retried in 1832 and transported to Van Diemen's Land for life.[128] However, many more women suffered as a result of the resort to transportation on such a grand scale, plunged into grief and poverty through the loss of husbands, fathers, sons and brothers. Families without breadwinners became destitute, beggars at the mercy of the parish and landlord. *The Times* described a harrowing melee outside the Wiltshire Special Commission, when:

> [t]he cart for the removal of the prisoners was at the back entrance
> to the court house and was surrounded by a crowd of mothers, wives,

sisters and children … The weeping and wailing of the different parties … was truly heart rending. We never saw so distressing as spectacle before, and trust the restored tranquillity of the country will prevent us from seeing anything like it again.[129]

Tranquillity would prove illusory. The exile of the Swing protesters, many of them the natural leaders and risk takers in their neighbourhoods, left deep scars on rural communities that took many years to heal. There was more social protest to come, in the country and the cities, and more mourning of loved ones exiled across the seas. Never again would the peasants rise up as they did under Captain Swing in 1830. Mass transportation had taught those left behind the terrible price of rebellion.

✱ ✱ ✱

ON THE UPSWING IN EXILE

WHAT BECAME OF THE SWING CONVICTS IN AUSTRALIA? Joseph Mason judged his fellow prisoners on board the *Eleanor* to be 'for the most part men of honest principle'.[130] Many had skills in high demand in colonies that were starved of labour and accustomed to convicts with an urban, criminal background. The arrival of the *Eleanor* in Sydney on 26 June 1831 with her cargo of agricultural labourers and skilled tradesmen was good news to landholders looking to make a go of their property. They began to lobby the convict department for preference in the assignment of convicts.[131] African slavery was about to be abolished throughout the Empire thanks to the efforts of the abolitionists and evangelical independent MP William Wilberforce, but in Sydney a new landed oligarchy hungry for unpaid labour was bidding over the Swing convicts.

Van Diemen's Land was said to be a much harsher prison, its name itself conjuring a hellish demonic land in the minds of simple men. A rural folk lament from the period, sang by those back home as much as those in chains, captured the dread and the drudgery of enforced servitude awaiting the exiles:

We labour hard from morn to night, until our bones do ache,
Then everyone they must obey, their mouldy beds must make.
We often wish, when we lay down we ne'er may rise no more.
To meet our savage Governors upon Van Diemen's shore.[132]

The savage governor awaiting the men was George Arthur, a stern disciplinarian, who brought a feral if freer convict colony to heel in the name of order, giving his name to a new type of prison built on an impregnable peninsula, Port Arthur. Notwithstanding the loss of liberty and being wrenched from their country, family and friends, how much did the *Eliza* convicts suffer in Van Diemen's Land? Assigned as a market gardener to an educated and generous settler, Richard Dillingham seems to have found a cornucopia, explaining in a letter to his parents that:

> *I want for nothing ... As for tea and sugar I could almost swim in it ... I am allowed ... plenty of tobacco and good white bread and sometimes beef sometimes mutton sometimes pork. This I have every day. Plenty of fruit puddings in the season of all sorts ...*[133]

Though technically working for nothing but rations, the convict lottery was able to throw up more generous masters that rewarded good workers. While the Swing exiles lost their liberty, they found in the colonies, thanks to the assignment system then in its mature stage, a state-guaranteed system of master–servant contract that gave them a level of security, rations and income in many ways superior to what they could expect in England.[134] The obligation to pay assigned convicts was removed in 1823, but its practice continued, especially for skilled convicts. It seems that none of the Swing convicts were politically troublesome in Australia.[135] This makes sense, as most were ordinary, if aggrieved, workers rather than activists, and may have wanted to just keep their heads down and get on.[136] However, not all Swing convicts had a good time of it. Thomas Cook, a nineteen-year-old attorney clerk, who was transported for fourteen years for signing a threatening letter in the name of the legendary Captain, clearly had a hard time in New South Wales, which he later wrote up as *The Exiles Lamentations*.[137] Even the well-fed Dillingham complained about his 'want' of liberty.[138] Some fell into a cycle of petty offending. Both women transported, Elizabeth Studham and Elizabeth Parker, clocked up numerous charges in the colony, ranging from prostitution, drunkenness, disorderly behaviour and even assault to theft.[139]

The tide was slowly turning the transportees' way in England. While warning that Swing was 'a dangerous precedent', *The Times* had misgivings during the trials about the deeper causes of the uprising, especially the greed of the great landowners:

> *Let the rich be taught that Providence will not suffer them to oppress their fellow creatures with impunity. Here are tens of thousands of Englishmen, industrious, kind-hearted but broken-hearted human beings, exasperated into madness by insufficient food and clothing ...*[140]

The settling into government of the Whigs and the eventual passing of the Great Reform Bill in 1832 allowed a relaxation in fears of imminent revolution. Indeed, as Thompson argues, by exposing profound inequalities in the countryside, the Swing 'revolt' discredited the moral authority of the rural gentry, and encouraged middle- and working-class people in the cities to agitate to lessen the aristocracy's hold on parliament. By so doing the Swing rising hastened the achievement of long-delayed political reform.[141] In this changed atmosphere the government decided that a judicious deployment of mercy might help re-establish the bonds of *noblesse oblige* in the countryside and placate urban radicals and liberals outraged at the harsh sentences. In 1835, 220 of the seven-year prisoners sent to Van Diemen's Land were offered pardons, and in 1837 those on fourteen-year and life sentences were also pardoned.

How many Swing convicts tried to return to England? It was necessary for most pardoned convicts to earn their own passage home, which took time. In the end very few took a ship back. Many more, enjoying an improvement in their economic position and status not available at home, elected to remain and make the most of the opportunities available in a new land. Few of them committed second offences in the colonies.[142] Some brought their families out as a vote of confidence in their new home. Tracing the lives of various emancipated Swing convicts in Australia, Kent and Townsend revealed that about 20 per cent of Swing transportees acquired modest farming land—an ascent up the social ladder—(made possible by the forced removal of Aboriginal peoples from their ancestral lands), that would simply have been out of their reach in rural England where so much land was already taken.[143] Some who had returned to England had second thoughts and returned to the colonies with their families as free immigrants. Rudé calculated that approximately 20 per cent of Swing convicts had descendants in Australia in the second half of the twentieth century. Transportation to New South Wales would come to a halt in 1840 and a decade and a half later a new constitution would extend political rights to working men in New South Wales that their fellows in England would not attain until 1884. Although Hughes found no evidence of 'any overt kind of political activity' by the Swing protesters in Australia, perhaps they had an influence in their communities, reflecting on their past suffering, using the ballot box to secure the standard of living and economic rights denied them in England?[144] With manhood suffrage the serious business of building a 'working man's paradise' in the one-time convict colonies would begin.

* * *

THE LAST RIOTS

BACK IN BRITAIN, SWING WAS NOT THE END OF THE OLD-STYLE primitive rebellion, with two significant uprisings occurring in England and Wales in the late 1830s, and eruptions in 1848 in the rural hinterland of the Scottish highlands. The so-called Battle of Bossenden Wood of 1838 was a peasant uprising in rural Kent. It was led by a charismatic leader John Nichols Thom who exerted a cult-like control over local villagers from Boughton under Blean, not far from Canterbury. Under the name of Sir William Courtnay, Thom claimed to be a saviour who could absolve his followers from mortal sin. Rudé points out that while almost mediaeval in its religious fanaticism, the rebels had very modern grievances, notably a severe economic recession in Kent.[145] The fifty or so armed men who rallied to Thom's standard were out-of-work labourers, and a smattering of disgruntled under-employed tradesmen and small farmers, not unlike the Swing protesters. Most were completely illiterate and unable to feed their families due to the economic downturn. Thom won their support by vowing to overturn the New Poor Law of 1834 that excluded so many from parish support. In the battle that ensued with soldiers and constables near Boughton Hill, eight labourers were shot dead, including Thom. An army officer was also killed, and nine of the rebels were tried for murder. Three of the surviving ringleaders—William Wills, Thomas Mears and William Price—received death sentences but were instead transported to Australia, arriving in Van Diemen's Land in March 1839.

The Rebecca Riots in North and West Wales, while associated with the beginnings of the Chartist agitation, also bore the marks of pre-modern protest. Labourers and impoverished farmers went about the countryside destroying property that symbolised taxes and levies, notably turnpikes and tollgates. To hide their identity from authorities they wore women's clothing, and claimed to be led by a female rebel named Rebecca. The protests in Wales lasted a long time, from 1839 to 1843, and climaxed in a daylight attack on the loathed Carmarthen workhouse. While many people were arrested and sent to prison over the years for Rebecca activity, only five men were transported. Rudé revealed that one of these was David Davies, known as 'the Singer' for his contribution to the chapel choir. He and fellow rioter John Jones, colourfully referred to as 'Johnny of the Big Barn', were both sentenced to transportation for twenty years for adding firearm offences to property destruction, and arrived in Van Diemen's Land in January 1844.[146]

The last old-style peasant uprising occurred in the Scottish highlands in 1848 where capitalist agriculture was pushing into the last pockets of the country. The Scottish rioters who were transported in 1848 were resisting land clearances in the districts of Sunderland and Inverness and protesting at rising food prices in the northwest of the country.[147] For Rudé these outbreaks on the 'Celtic fringe' of Wales and Scotland represented 'a final desperate upsurge of the old village community against the dissolution of old ties and the new values that capitalist commercialism brought in its train'.[148]

The swift and harsh judicial suppression of the Swing rioters did not bring machine breaking to an end, though it moved from the rural south to the industrial heartlands of the Midlands and North and South Wales. Machine breaking tore through factories in Manchester, and in the coal collieries of Durham and South Wales, climaxing in violent riot in the Welsh industrial town of Merthyr in 1831. There were other spasmodic outbreaks during the 1830s, notably at Beck's Steam Factory in Coventry in 1831, threshing-machine destruction in Leicestershire in 1837, and destruction of factory machines in Lancashire in 1839 and Staffordshire Potteries' industries associated with Chartism, to be discussed ahead. However, these events in the late 1830s did not spread because workers in England were becoming accustomed to the new technology and discovering more effective ways to bargain with employers, especially in the cities, where shop floor unity was becoming more commonplace. The lesson that the Tolpuddle agricultural labourers drew from the experience of city-trade unionists was a simple yet powerful one: in unity is strength.[149]

* * *

TOLPUDDLE TO CHARTISM

THE CONTRAST BETWEEN SWING AND TOLPUDDLE, SEPARATED BY a mere three years, illustrates the shift from what Rudé terms 'primitive' or 'archaic' forms of protest seeking to restore customary rights in a traditional rural society, to a 'modern' movement to secure economic and political rights within industrial society.[150] The Swing protesters and most who came before were demanding the rights of free-born Englishmen, rights that in folk memory had been suppressed by the Norman Conquest. Beginning with Chartism in the 1840s, protest in Britain increasingly took on the modern form that would predominate in the West in the late nineteenth and twentieth centuries.[151] Spontaneous riot gave way to organised movements. Violence, machine breaking and arson gave way to unions governed by written rules of association, permanent leaders, formal memberships, petitions, marches, rallies and collective bargaining. These changes were all features of the Tolpuddle case and the mass movement that emerged to secure the martyrs' justice. As such Tolpuddle represents not just an important historical moment in the struggle by trade unions for legitimacy but also a moment of symbolic transition for the English working class from rejection of the industrialising economy to demanding a say over how it operated.

The last threshing machine was destroyed in 1837. Leaders emerged from the rank and file of protest groups to form a quasi-professional cadre of political activists. Most significantly, the goal shifted from hoping to restore a pre-industrial world of work to reforming the conditions and living standards of working people within industrial and even agrarian capitalism. At an existential level, workers simply became accustomed to using technology and began to defend the new suite of skills associated with industrial and farming machinery. More deeply, a new form of socialism was emerging that eschewed nostalgia in favour of a modernist belief in progress.

The 'Song of Freedom', which George Loveless thrust into the throng after he was sentenced to transportation, asks supporters to 'raise the watch-word liberty' but this was a different idea of liberty to that promoted by bourgeois radicals. It was liberty from the market rather than from the state, a freedom from the unequal power of employers to be won through collective action rather than individualism. This new liberalism would gather strength in the second half of the nineteenth century, nowhere more so than in the Australian colonies.

❋   ❋   ❋

'SONG OF FREEDOM'

AS LOVELESS WAS ESCORTED FROM COURT WITH THE OTHER FIVE Tolpuddle convicts, the earnest Wesleyan could not have divined that within a short time he would be first a martyr, then a celebrated 'working class hero' to unionists and radicals in dire need of the cultural legitimacy that martyrs and heroes can confer.[152] In passing sentence Judge Williams had cared not one iota for the proven good character of the defendants.[153] However, in singling out George Loveless and his friends to teach unions a lesson, Home Secretary Lord Melbourne and the government had miscalculated.

The men had the right stuff for martyrdom. Whereas the victims of the Swing crackdown were an undifferentiated mass of prisoners, missed in their communities but difficult to conjure with, the Tolpuddle Martyrs were only a handful of individuals with names and biographies who could be digested easily via the newspapers. Like Jesus's twelve apostles, so too were the stories of the Tolpuddle Six memorable.[154] Not only were most of them of unblemished character with solid work records, they were led by an articulate man who, buoyed by his religious faith, exhibited loyalty and nobility in the face of harsh treatment. Loveless was no mythical King Ludd or Captain Swing, but a flesh and blood leader whose words were recorded in court and whose simple dignity was reported in the leading newspapers of the day.[155] As Tolpuddle historian Joyce Marlow observed, here was a modern rendering of David and Goliath.[156] His flourish with the 'Song of Freedom' caught the imagination of the press and public alike. He and four of his fellow exiles would later write memoirs, putting their side of the case to the judgement of history, and ensuring they would be honoured as secular saints of the labour movement, even if they later sought to escape its embrace.[157]

But when the terrible sentences were delivered, the men's first thoughts would have been for wives and children, parents and siblings who they feared would be lost to them forever. What if the authorities harass them? How would they earn enough for food and rent? Would they be thrown on the cold charity of the Poor Law and workhouse? The martyrs left behind families whose palpable suffering evoked not just popular sympathy, but campaigns to raise funds to keep them from penury. Because of the close ties of kinship and the social and religious obligations that make a small community tick, the removal of the six men would have had a devastating impact on the lives of their families and left a deep hole in the life of Tolpuddle. Diana Standfield not only lost her husband Thomas and son John, but also her brothers George and James. Frampton wasted no time refusing parish assistance to this mother of five, telling her, 'You shall suffer want. You shall have no mercy, because you ought to have known better than to have allowed such meetings in your house.'[158] The other wives met with the same discrimination. This petty vindictiveness played into the hands of Frampton's opponents. Looking after the wives and children was a happy confluence of righteousness and political savvy on the part of the national union organisation and the various support groups.

After a brief spell on the Thames' hulks, clothed in grey, coarsely woven convict uniforms, and fitted with heavy irons to their feet, James Loveless, Thomas and John Standfield, James Hammett and James Brine were speedily embarked for Sydney on the *Surrey* in March 1834. Due to illness and perhaps because he was the leader, George Loveless was separated from the other five and entombed for several months back in Dorchester Gaol, before being conveyed in clanking chains to the fetid below-decks of a hulk.[159] He was destined to remain isolated, and rather than follow his brother and friends to New South Wales, was transported on the *William Metcalfe* to the harsher regime of Van Diemen's Land. Just before departing England, Loveless wrote to his wife thanking her 'for that kind attention you have ever paid me', and bidding her:

> *Be satisfied, my dear Betsy, on my account. Depend on it, it will work together for good and we shall yet rejoice together ... I shall do well for ... the Lord ... will be my support in life and death.*[160]

Arriving in Sydney in August not all five unionists were equally lucky in the assignment lottery. Not only did the Tolpuddle convicts' reputation precede them to Australia, but among many men of property and authority their crimes were exaggerated out of all connection to reality, confusing them with the Swing rioters. On first meeting James Brine, his new master on the Hunter River gleefully declared, 'You are one of the Dorchester machine-breakers, but you are caught at last.'[161] The prejudices of the home counties squirearchy had clearly taken root among the Australian squattocracy. Indeed, many large landowners in Australia had immigrated so as to continue to enjoy in the colonies agrarian privileges that were under pressure from industrial capitalism at home. The Tolpuddle labourers found themselves subject to masters trying to recreate Southern English society in districts like the Hunter.

Thomas Standfield, in his mid-forties, had a hard time as an assigned shepherd near Maitland. His son described him as 'a dreadful spectacle, covered in sores from head to foot, and as weak and helpless as a child'.[162]

Standfield was forced to sleep outside in a 'watch box', without protection from the night weather, and had to walk 6 kilometres (4 miles) for his daily rations, also at night.[163] As marked men they did not have an easy time. When Brine needed replacement shoes and a blanket his master told him:

> *I will give you nothing until you are due for it. What would your masters in England have had to cover them if you had not been sent here? I understand it was your intention to have murdered, burnt and destroyed everything before you, and you are sent over here to be severely punished, and no mercy will be shown you.*[164]

Shortly after disembarking, James Loveless was forced to walk to his assigned farm over 322 kilometres (200 miles) from Sydney.[165] John Standfield did well out of the lottery, assigned to a kindly master on a farm at Bolwarra in the Hunter, but a few miles from his father.[166] Hammett also landed on his feet, literally. He walked all the way to Queanbeyan to work on the farm of the soon-to-be famous explorer and Aboriginal 'protector' Edward John Eyre.[167] It could have been worse for the men. The year the unionists arrived 3000 floggings were inflicted in New South Wales, yet they all managed to leave with backs untouched.[168]

George Loveless arrived in Van Diemen's Land on 12 September 1834 to take his lowly position in the redemptive regime of Governor Arthur. As was the practice there and in New South Wales he was examined for identifying features and again interrogated about his felony, by a magistrate and Arthur himself, no less. When asked 'what object had you in view' for forming the union, Loveless replied 'to prevent our wives and families being utterly degraded and starved' and followed with the logical answer 'I had no idea whatever that I was violating any law … I cannot see that a man can break a law before he knows that such a law is in existence …'.[169] Apparently the governor was impressed by Loveless's account, as he immediately rescinded an order from London that the prisoner should work in irons on a road gang, and instead assigned him to the safe berth of the viceregal farm.[170] Arthur's change of heart accords with the governor's belief in reform through reward and punishment. Loveless endured a week in the chain gang, in order that he appreciate the relative freedom of servitude as a shepherd and cattleman on the governor's farm. However, he was still vulnerable. A year into his sentence, when nine cattle in his charge escaped, Loveless found himself before a magistrate for neglect of duty. This time he defended himself, and escaped fifty lashes by persuading the court he was overloaded with duties.[171]

In his account of Van Diemen's Land, Loveless recorded the privations of convict life, the floggings, the deaths, the callous overseers, a slave regime worthy of Pharaoh.[172] He pronounced Arthur's beloved snakes-and-ladders system of reform a failure, for it only hardened and embittered those in its thrall. Of the assignment system he observed a grim game of chance where:

> [s]ome few get kind masters who consider the prisoners are men ...
> But the greater part are so situated that, bad as government usage
> is, they are far worse off; treated like dogs, worked from the dawn
> ... till the close of day, often half naked, and all but starved.[173]

'Nothing can be more absurd,' he concluded, 'than to suppose that you can keep down the conquered for any length of time, by pouring out on them judgement without mercy.'[174] Nor did he spare the bush landscape, which was all 'gloom and dreariness'.[175] It is likely the ploughman was homesick for the neat, hedged fields and 'dewy meads' of Dorset.

The Tolpuddle labourers may have been notorious rebels in the colonies, but back home they had become a national cause. The Tolpuddle case had such an impact at the time, and remains a commemorated event in trade union history, because the government overplayed its hand. The prosecution's case would prove to be a house of cards, its clever connections too easily demolished by skilful orators in the common sense court of public opinion as well as in parliament. To transport the men to Van Diemen's Land and New South Wales when unions were technically

Following pages: The 35,000-strong demonstration to Copenhagen Fields, Islington on 21 April 1834 carrying a petition to the government bearing 200,000 signatures demanding the Tolpuddle Martyrs be pardoned.

legal, using a noose of sand based on unrelated statutes about swearing secret oaths, smacked of vindictiveness, injustice and even desperation. Far from cowering, the emerging union movement in the cities went on the offensive, securing friends in high places, including parliament.

The judgement and sentences won the Tolpuddle 'unionists' supporters from across the nation, not just from the usual radical suspects writing for papers like the *Republican*, the *Poor Man's Guardian*, the *True Sun* and Cobbett's *Political Register*, but from reform-minded Whigs and liberal newspapers, who would normally take the side of employers. In London, a Tolpuddle defence committee was quickly formed, with the dual purpose of campaigning for pardons to free the men and raise money to support the transportees' wives and children. As the trial and fate of the Tolpuddle men became better known, support also came from unexpected quarters. Fair-minded editors in the conservative press feared that a miscarriage of justice had occurred that undermined the integrity of the British justice system.[176] The anti-union *Morning Herald*, for example, wanted an honest up-front fight with their adversaries, not a 'side wind' puffed by clever lawyers.[177]

The counter-offensive against the sentences began almost immediately. In the hope of keeping the six from ever leaving England, a Grand Meeting was held in London numbering around 10,000 'in favour of the Agricultural Unionists convicted at Dorchester'. Crowd puller Robert Owen headlined. A succession of public meetings were held throughout England and over the next few years, petitions carrying anywhere between 20,000 and 250,000 signatures were presented to King William asking that the Dorchester labourers be pardoned. The urbane and educated 'conscience constituency' of the capital had signed on to the labourers' cause in symbolic solidarity with working-class unionists who were organising in the northern cities.[178] On 21 April 35,000 people marched on Whitehall to present a 'monster' petition to the Secretary of State for delivery to the King.[179] The carefully organised rally, climaxing in a mass gathering at Copenhagen Fields, Kings Cross, was notable for union banners held high, the colourfully costumed tradesmen, and its discipline—the modern display of union power was taking shape. Nevertheless, the King and his ministers were unmoved.[180]

The Tolpuddle case attracted the attention of one of Westminster's leading reformers, the Irish nationalist and parliamentarian Daniel O'Connell, who for a time put aside his own campaign for the independence of his homeland to lend his talents to righting the injustice he believed had befallen the unionists. Perhaps he thought he could fan the popular sympathy for the English labourers towards Irish autonomy?[181] While there had been an outcry at the banishment of the Scottish Jacobins and a lament in Ireland at the fate of the exiled rebels of '98, there was no organised movement for liberation of transported convicts to compare with the Tolpuddle Martyrs. Radical MPs Thomas Wakley and Feargus O'Connor, the Chartist leader, took up the labourers' cause in the Commons, and presented the petition to parliament. Reform-minded Whig Lord John Russell lent his considerable authority to the case for a royal pardon. Radical papers began conducting opinion polls to show the majority favoured the labourers' return.[182] The organised movement in parliament and on the ground to secure a pardon for the unionists set the standard for latter-day movements to secure the release of political prisoners, such as French officer Alfred Dreyfus exiled to Devil's Island, Nelson Mandela in South Africa's Robben Island Prison, the Birmingham Six wrongly accused of IRA terrorism, and the Australian David Hicks, sent to Guantanamo Bay.

In the end it was the unintended consequences of the Crown's flawed indictment against the Tolpuddle six that broke the government's resolve. The reanimation of the *Mutiny Act*'s banning of unlawful oaths was turning into a Frankenstein's monster. O'Connell and other opponents of the law cannily pointed out that the Act must criminalise all unauthorised oaths, including those by conservative societies such as the Orangemen, the bulwark of loyalist Protestant representation in northern Ireland. This was embarrassing for the government as no less a peer than the King's son, the Duke of Cumberland, was a Grand Master of an Orange Lodge, and he was not alone among the nobility.[183] *The Spectator* wryly asked 'were the Dukes of Cumberland and Sussex aware that they were liable to a transfer for seven years from Kew and Kensington to the pickpocket capital of the world?'[184] In fact, the only society excepted by the *Mutiny Act* was the Masonic Lodge.[185] Amid demands in parliament and on the street that the Orange Lodges be closed down, the government relented on the issue of pardons.

Unlike the case with the uncoordinated protest of Swing, the use of transportation to neutralise the threat of trade unionism had failed. Rather than silence a new idea, the terror always implicit in transportation amplified it. By turning six ordinary men into martyrs, transportation had sown a whirlwind of outrage throughout Britain. Public opinion weakened the Whig resolve, and as Wakefield tabled yet another petition on 14 March 1836, Lord John Russell, who had succeeded Melbourne as Home Secretary, rose in the House of Commons to announce that, 'His Majesty has been pleased to grant a free pardon' to each of the Dorchester labourers. Furthermore the government offered the unprecedented olive branch of paying the labourers' fares back to England. The back flip resounded across the sea to the Australian colonies, where governors jumped to orders to incrementally pardon the six men and to secure their passage home. In Van Diemen's Land, Governor Arthur lived up to his reputation for efficiency and quickly informed George Loveless of his good fortune. Loveless was soon on his way back home, arriving in London on 13 June 1837.

Yet, whether out of malice or incompetence, the New South Wales administration of the relatively liberal Sir Richard Bourke dragged the bureaucratic chain, so that the scattered men continued to labour for their masters in ignorance, learning about their freedom by accident. The Standfields, Brine and James Loveless did not set sail until September 1837, and the unfortunate Hammett, caught out on an assault charge, languished in the colony another two years before prising his passage from his hosts. This was a final indignity on a noble man, for decades later it was revealed that Hammett had not actually been present the night the oath was taken. It was his younger brother John who had partaken in the ceremony. However, John's wife was pregnant, and James, himself a member of the Society, took the rap for his brother in an act of self-sacrifice.[186]

The unions emerged from the Tolpuddle case with new friends in parliament and a new-found legitimacy as players in industrial society. Due to changing community standards of what constituted appropriate punishment, banishment to the Australian colonies could no longer be relied on to bury a political problem.

The Tolpuddle Martyrs returned to an England in which Chartism was beginning to stir, and were called upon by the movement's organisers to help inspire working people to action. There was an official welcome home rally on Kennington Common, London in April 1838, with the five men who had returned riding in an open carriage ahead of a procession 6000 strong, marching with union banners as the band played 'See the Conquering Hero Comes'.[187] George Loveless's pamphlet *The Victims of Whiggery* was invaluable propaganda, sold at meetings and snapped up by Chartists who drew moral strength from the unionists' triumph over adversity. A number of the Tolpuddle veterans spoke on Chartist platforms to cheering crowds of working people.

At a mass meeting near Tolpuddle in November 1838 George Loveless, an authentic working-class hero, was elected by popular acclaim to be a delegate to the national Chartist Convention, but he did not attend.

After a time in the limelight and then as farmers together on land purchased for the martyrs by the union movement, the tightly bound Loveless, Standfield and Brine families decided to leave their notoriety behind and start afresh in Upper Canada, a province of the Empire that enters our story in Chapter 4. George and Elizabeth Loveless left in 1847 and in this new land prospered as farmers at Siloam, Ontario, where they built a Methodist Church. Loveless eschewed politics for devotion to his religion and family, and became a pillar of a community that knew nothing of his convict past.[188] George and Elizabeth's graves stand side by side in the yard of their Church and bear the Biblical quotation, 'These are they which came out of great tribulation and have washed their robes and made them white in the blood of the lamb'.[189]

✻ ✻ ✻

THE CHARTER

CHARTISM AROSE IN RECOGNITION OF THE FACT THAT THE economic suffering of working people in both city and country required a political solution. Unions could only go so far in ameliorating exploitation when government sided with employers and landowners. Why would it not, when these classes voted for and comprised the parliament and government? Only if working people were represented in the House of Commons would governments take seriously their concerns. Only if workers were full political citizens would they enjoy their traditional liberties as British subjects. The courts were supposed to protect these liberties, but the Tolpuddle case showed that the judicial system favoured one class over another, and that politics was necessary to achieve justice. Chartism was both a platform for the political emancipation of working-class and lower-middle-class Britons and a new mode of activism to achieve that goal.

For Rudé, Chartism was the watershed between primitive and modern forms of protest.[190] As a movement it lasted from 1837 to 1849, and while strongest in urban centres, especially the industrial cities of northern England and south Wales, it was the first national mass workers' movement.[191] Its essence was a campaign for a 'People's Charter'—a modern democratic supplement to the original bulwark of English liberty, the Magna Carta. The Charter was a six-point plan for democratic political reform that updated and expanded the radical program from the late eighteenth century to enable the participation of working people in the British polity. Top of the list was suffrage for all men twenty-one and over, followed by electorates of equal size, voting by secret ballot, abolition of the property qualification for election to the House of Commons, payment of Members of Parliament so that working men could stand, and annual elections of parliament to make it more accountable to the people. Most of these had been part of the program of the national conventions of the 1790s, in defence of which the Scottish Martyrs were exiled.

By the end of the 1830s the Charter had become the organising focus for disparate working-class protest associations around industrial Britain and a beacon of hope for change. The Charter was three times presented to parliament, in 1839, 1842 and 1848—each time accompanied by 'monster petitions'. In preference to riot and violence the Chartists focused on the very modern campaign tactic of collecting signatures in support of the Charter nationwide, and presenting them to parliament at the climax of a great gathering in London and a procession to Westminster. Petitioning Crown, Lords and Commons had a long history, but the mass movement petition was recent, perfected

The Six Points
OF THE
PEOPLE'S
CHARTER.

1. A VOTE for every man twenty-one years of age, of sound mind, and not undergoing punishment for crime.

2. THE BALLOT.—To protect the elector in the exercise of his vote.

3. No PROPERTY QUALIFICATION for Members of Parliament —thus enabling the constituencies to return the man of their choice, be he rich or poor.

4. PAYMENT OF MEMBERS, thus enabling an honest trades-man, working man, or other person, to serve a constituency, when taken from his business to attend to the interests of the country.

5. EQUAL CONSTITUENCIES, securing the same amount of representation for the same number of electors, instead of allowing small constituencies to swamp the votes of large ones.

6. ANNUAL PARLIAMENTS, thus presenting the most effectual check to bribery and intimidation, since though a constituency might be bought once in seven years (even with the ballot), no purse could buy a constituency (under a system of universal suffrage) in each ensuing twelvemonth; and since members, when elected for a year only, would not be able to defy and betray their constituents as now.

The Charter—the six demands were: 1) universal manhood suffrage; 2) secret ballots; 3) abolition of the property qualification for voting; 4) wages for MPs; 5) equal electoral constituencies; and 6) annual parliaments.

during the agitation to free the Tolpuddle six. Despite the peaceful tactics of the early Chartists, the movement was deemed a threat by the government. In the face of indifference from the parliament, divisions emerged among Chartist leaders, between those who favoured 'moral force' and those who believed opposition should be met with direct, even violent, action. Not surprisingly, on those occasions when Chartist demonstrations degenerated into riot, many of the more zealous activists found themselves transported to the Australian colonies.

Chartism emerged from the failure of the Great Reform Act of 1832 to enfranchise working-class Britons who had played their part in the reform cause.[192] By 1831 Lord Grey's Whigs, as the traditional liberal-leaning party, decided that parliamentary reform could be delayed no longer, and had better be led from the top, than seized by revolution from below. Radical working-class groups had been mobilised by bourgeois reformers, principally in the industrial north, to bring pressure to bear on recalcitrant conservatives.[193] In 1831 workingmen bore the brunt of criminal sanctions for protests in London, Birmingham, Gloucester and Bristol as part of the Reform Bill agitations. Of the more than 100 people tried for Reform Bill protests, only twenty-seven were transported, but on Rudé's calculations these were mainly skilled working people, such as bakers, butchers, blacksmiths, brick makers, carpenters, cabinet makers, brewers, shoemakers, stonemasons and domestic servants.[194] Urban working-class participation in the reform agitation not only helped politicise a mass base for the radical cause, it nourished hopes for political representation that were ultimately frustrated.

These working-class radicals, like the Scottish Jacobins of the 1790s, wanted to send their own people to Westminster, but the Reform Act only extended the vote to the propertied middle class. While most rotten rural boroughs were eliminated, new industrial cities duly afforded representation (as radicals and liberals had long wanted), and the property qualifications for voting were relaxed and standardised, working people (and indeed the lower middle class) remained shut out. To vote it was necessary to own or rent county land or urban properties of a value simply too high for most working men to qualify. This was deliberate, as both Whigs and Tories, landed interests and the bourgeoisie, were wary of 'mob rule' by people with insufficient investment in the country, by which they meant the status quo from which they profited. While the reforms increased the size of the electorate by more than 60 per cent, only 653,000 adult males (approximately one in five) were able to vote for the House of Commons after the passing of the Act.[195] Women remained disenfranchised. Even with these limitations, conservative landed interests in the House of Lords only passed the Reform Bill after Grey's Whigs secured a sweeping mandate in an election in 1831, after which King William IV reluctantly agreed to create sufficient Lords to break the deadlock.

If working people wanted the vote they would have to break from the liberals and organise it for themselves. Chartism was inaugurated in 1837 with the formation of the National Charter Association, an organisation that Rudé considered the 'nucleus of a worker's party', a precursor to the British Labour Party. However, the movement is better seen as a coordinated countrywide network of different local organisations, drawing strength from community roots. For example, a leading light on its first national committee was William Lovett, a representative of the London Working Men's Association. The Charter was published in May 1838 and the numbers attracted to the first rally at Kersal Moor, Lancashire in September 1838 demonstrated its appeal. Chartism's activists were drawn from skilled tradespeople and the lower middle class who had aspirations to participate in politics and the education to lead. Women workers played an important role as activists, despite the decision to leave female suffrage off the Charter. As with Tolpuddle, people with humanist religious convictions, especially Methodists but also Catholics, played a prominent part.

Unlike the older protest movements, Chartism had coordinating committees and permanent, elected leaders comparable to the calibre of George Loveless, such as Feargus O'Connor, editor of Ireland's *Northern Star*, sometime MP and advocate of the Tolpuddle unionists—a far cry from mythical everyman figureheads like Ned Ludd. Rudé considered Chartism to be both a forward-looking and backward-looking movement, reflecting its dual support from an industrial working class in rapidly growing cities, and from craftspeople in the declining weaving and other traditional manufacturing industries of England's West Country and the West Riding of Yorkshire.[196]

Despite the alarm that Chartism provoked in both conservatives and liberals within the propertied classes, the movement was not revolutionary. Rather it was reformist and utilitarian, seeking the greatest happiness for the greatest number of people by modifying the existing constitution. Petitions recognised Westminster and the monarch as the legitimate authority. The Charter did not call for a republic. Like the original bourgeois liberals the Chartists wanted to curb the power of the executive, but their notion of the good society was one where the majority ruled to improve the lot of the many, not the exercise of individual liberty. Rather than obsessed with abstract principles, Chartism was a pragmatic 'knife and fork ... bread and cheese question'.[197] This accorded with the then ascendant ideas of political philosopher Jeremy Bentham. The Chartists' vision was collectivist not individualist, a foretaste of British Labour's democratic, Fabian socialism and the twentieth century welfare state.

Government fears of Chartism were fanned when a convention of fifty delegates came together, meeting first in London, and then Birmingham, to draw up a strategy. As with the radical conventions of the late eighteenth century, this smacked of an attempt to create an alternative parliament. The hint of treason was not helped when firebrands among the delegates proposed extreme measures, including a mass withdrawal of bank deposits and a month-long general strike. While the goals of Chartism were reformist rather than revolutionary, there were leaders and activists who insisted that more radical direct action, including 'physical' force, was needed to persuade an intransigent parliament that in June 1839 had refused to accept the first petition. Encouraged by local extremists, agitation escalated into the old-style attacks on property, notably a violent rebellion of ironworkers and miners in Newport, Monmouthshire, Wales in 1839 and the Plug-Plot Riots in 1842. These eruptions provided the bulk of the 103 Chartist prisoners transported to Australia.[198]

The Welsh uprising was led by Chartist radical John Frost, assisted by William Jones and Zephaniah Williams. Frost was a well-to-do draper and one-time mayor of the Welsh coal hub, Newport.[199]

Amid a tense atmosphere triggered by the arrest of Chartist Henry Vincent, Frost led an angry group of marchers through industrial working-class communities of south Wales, gathering supporters before converging on the Westgate Hotel, Newport. Here the local business owners and landed elite had chosen to make a stand, aided by sixty soldiers. Intelligence had it that the Chartists planned to take the town and sever Welsh communications with London, a signal for a national uprising. The Chartists tried to force their way into the hotel, shots were exchanged and a bloody pitched battle was joined. Frost's men stood little chance against the disciplined, well-armed troops, and retreated, leaving twenty-four miners and ironworkers dead and more than fifty wounded. Confusion on the ground among the Chartists was matched by confusion as to their true strategy. The alleged conspiracy to spearhead a national Chartist rebellion was later denied by Frost, though Chartists in other parts of Britain claimed that success in Newport was to be their signal to rise.[200]

Altogether twenty-nine Chartists faced court for the attack. Frost, Williams and Jones, along with five others, were tried for high treason, found guilty and sentenced to be hung, drawn and quartered—the traditional traitor's execution. However, a huge public outcry eventually led to their transportation instead. Fifteen other Chartist rebels were also transported for disturbances in 1839, especially rioting in Birmingham.

According to Rudé the Battle for Newport was one of the last 'blood baths' of working-class protesters in Britain.[201] Henceforth, in confronting Chartist protest with force, the government relied on police rather than the military. A police force had long been opposed by British liberals worried about the use of permanent police by absolutist regimes on the continent. However, the London 'Bobbies' were so successful at actually arresting law breakers that by 1839 the innovation had been extended to other places. This meant Chartists more often than not faced police wielding wooden staves rather than the bullets and bayonets of troops. Furthermore, the most popular protest crimes—rioting, machine breaking, cattle maiming and robbery with threats—ceased to be punishable by hanging in 1841. However, hanging remained available for treason or for arson endangering people. Of course as capital offences were weeded out, transportation increased. The increasing reluctance to impose the death sentence for political offences is reflected in the fact that the fifteen people sentenced to hang for protest-related treason or arson between 1842 and 1848 all escaped the gallows, with nine transported to Australia instead.[202]

An economic depression in 1841 had a devastating impact on wages and employment and led to a series of strikes with Chartists at the helm. This meant that workers were refusing to work unless the aims of the Charter were implemented. In May 1842 in the midst of this industrial action a 'monster' petition bearing over three million signatures was tendered to parliament, only to be once more rejected. The *Northern Star* complained bitterly that:

> *[t]hree and a half millions of the slave-class have holden out an olive branch of peace to the enfranchised and privileged classes and sought ... EQUALITY BEFORE THE LAW; and the enfranchised and privileged have refused to enter into a treaty! The same class is to be a slave class still. The mark and brand of inferiority is not to be removed ... The people are not to be free.*[203]

Out of this frustration a series of violent strikes swept through the industrial heartlands of Staffordshire, Cheshire, the Midlands, Lancashire, Yorkshire and lower Scotland in the summer of 1842. Factory-floor confrontations became nasty, with physical threats and attacks on foremen and, most notoriously, industrial sabotage on a large scale. Harking back to Luddism, gangs of protesters seized control of factories by force and compelled workers to remove plugs thereby disabling the steam boilers, bringing machinery and production to a halt—hence the name Plug-Plot Riots for this wave of sabotage.

The Peel Government, steeled by the determination of the gung-ho Duke of Wellington, dispensed with police and sent in the troops, backed by cavalry, to break the strikes. Frontline leaders Feargus O'Connor, Thomas Cooper and George Harney were arrested, along with almost 1500 protesters and strikers. Most were let off but of the 245 brought to trial for the 'Plug-Plot' riots, 146 were imprisoned and a total of seventy-two transported to Van Diemen's Land.[204] These Chartists were the largest single group of industrial workers to be exiled to Australia.

The government doubtless thought their crimes were self-evident enough to avoid a repetition of the public outcry that accompanied the clearly wronged Tolpuddle Martyrs.

If the Tories thought the use of transportation and the gallows would quell Chartist agitation, they were mistaken. However, after the Plug-Plot crackdown, more legal and imaginative methods were employed. Chartist leaders who met the property criteria began standing for the House of Commons, including Harney and O'Connor, the latter elected in 1847. This anticipated the election of working-class Labour MPs later in the century, first in the Australian colonies and then in Britain, in the hope of establishing a pro-reform block of votes. More laterally, and in the spirit of self-improvement, O'Connor reasoned that if lack of land and property excluded workers from full citizenship, then the Chartist movement should help them acquire land. Taking a leaf out of the capitalist book, he formed the Chartist Co-Operative Land Company (later the National Land Company), in which workers could buy shares, and the funds were used to purchase land that was subdivided for housing. Shareholders chosen by lot were granted purpose-built homes in these new Chartist estates that still stand in Oxfordshire, Worcestershire and Gloucestershire. O'Connor astutely judged that workers did not just want equality of rights, but aspired to the security and autonomy that came from owning a stake in society. While undermined by a parliamentary inquiry into its financial sustainability, mutual building societies like the National Land Company would be established in Britain and the Australian colonies in the second half of the nineteenth century. These societies purchased and subdivided land, constructed modest homes and lent money to working-class families. Land-hungry, home-loving, hard-working Chartist immigrants to Victoria and New South Wales would drive the colonies' home-ownership levels to the highest in the world during the 1860s, '70s and '80s, laying the foundations for Australia's characteristic working-class suburbia.

The Chartist campaign again exploded into national prominence and violent confrontation in 1848. This was the year when France once more seethed with revolution, and Karl Marx and Friedrich Engels wrote *The Communist Manifesto*, advocating a proletarian revolution to overturn capitalism. 'There is a spectre haunting Europe,' they prophesied, 'the spectre of Communism', and began establishing links with various working-class movements in different countries to work towards a socialist revolution.[205] Their millennial predictions carried some weight as first Paris, then Berlin, Vienna and parts of Italy succumbed to revolution. Chartism did not quite fit the Communist bill. Marx rejected the liberal reformism and support for parliaments that most of the Chartists advocated, but did concede that once granted, universal suffrage would result in government by and for the working-class majority. However, he did not believe the bourgeois state would give workers the vote without a revolution.

With authority in crisis on the Continent, O'Connor called together the biggest mass meeting yet on Kennington Common, with estimates of numbers varying from 50,000 in the press to 300,000 by the organisers. As a precaution against a European-style insurrection, the government deployed 8000 soldiers into London and swore in 150,000 special constables. However, the meeting proved peaceful. Not so in industrial Manchester, where Chartist rioters stormed a workhouse, clashed violently with police and caused mayhem in the city for three days. Also parts of Scotland, especially Glasgow, endured outbreaks of violence.

A final petition was submitted to parliament but was again rejected. At this point some in the leadership, notably O'Connor's opponent Ernest Jones, had planned to call a national assembly to demand Queen Victoria dissolve parliament until the Charter was legislated, but support for what would amount to treason was ebbing. Perhaps transportation had succeeded in cowering some of the radicals?

As a result of violence and seditious plotting in 1848, sixteen Chartists were transported to Van Diemen's Land.[206] Seven Scots were found guilty of various rioting offences, but nine English Chartists were tried in Liverpool and London on more serious charges of sedition and 'levying war'.[207] It was alleged that five of the accused were 'republicans' who plotted an uprising against the government, to take place on 15 September 1848. They were a mixed group of tradesmen, led by William Cuffay, a tailor and son of a freed West Indian slave. The notorious scheme became known as 'the Orange Tree conspiracy' after the pub where they met, and its architects received life sentences.

The Chartists were the last British political prisoners to be sent to Australia, and some of the 102 prisoners from the years 1839 to 1848 fared well in exile.[208] Assessing the Welsh Chartists on their arrival in June 1840, the governor of Van Diemen's Land, Sir John Franklin, considered John Frost sufficiently dangerous to confine him at Port Arthur, the penal station of secondary punishment cut off from the rest of the island.[209] Here the Chartist leader impressed his gaolers and was appointed clerk to the commandant, and later worked as a schoolmaster. Conditionally pardoned in 1854 he journeyed to New York, and returned to England with a full pardon in 1857. Zephaniah Williams and William Jones remained in the colony. Williams did well, bringing out his family and enjoying success first as a prospector and coal-mine owner and then as a publican.[210] The seventy-two 'Plug-Plot' and eighteen assorted northern rioters arrived in 1843 and served out their sentences in relative obscurity, and apart from two, these working men remained in the Australian colonies. Of the fifteen Chartists transported for offences in 1848, the nine English conspirators were granted the privilege of immediate tickets-of-leave—likely in recognition of the overtly 'political' nature of their crime, while the riotous Scots had to endure probation stations and work gangs. Pardoned in 1856, William Cuffay enjoyed success as a Hobart tailor, and has the distinction of being the only Chartist prisoner to return to political activism, as a leading campaigner for workers' rights in Tasmania (Van Diemen's Land was renamed in 1856).[211]

Back in England, Chartism declined rapidly after 1848. Sapped by ongoing divisions between reformists and hardliners, the energies of Chartists flowed into other, local organisations, and into self-advancement through immigration to Canada, the United States and, ironically, Australia. By the late 1840s the eastern colonies were losing their fearsome reputations as hell holes, and many Chartists, keen to escape the class inequalities of the old world, hoped that as free immigrants they might remake their lives in a new society.

* * *

CONCLUSION: THE WORKING-MAN'S PARADISE?

REVOLUTION MAY NOT HAVE OCCURRED, BUT THE GENTRY LIVED IN continual fear that it might. Transportation was the chief weapon of counter-revolution in the first half of the nineteenth century, and from the perspective of the state it must be judged an overall success. Troublemakers and agitators were removed and discontent given a safety valve as the most riotous land- and wage-hungry workers found new opportunities in the Australian colonies. While the Swing exiles lost their liberty, they found in the colonies, thanks to the assignment system then in its mature stage in both colonies, a state-guaranteed system of master–servant contract that gave them a level of security and income in many ways superior to what they could expect in England. Many working-class protesters remained in Australia. Furthermore, on completing their sentences many, thanks to their marketable skills, enjoyed an improvement in their economic position and status not available at home, and within two decades would enjoy political rights that working men in England would not attain till 1918. However, the limits of transportation as a form of political death became apparent with the Tolpuddle episode, when overreaction evoked a popular and elite backlash. As the Empire and the world became more integrated by improved communications and transport it was not so easy to silence radicals by sending them to the ends of the Earth. By the 1830s an organised and respectable radical movement was able to mobilise public opinion in defence of martyred reformers and rebels, while in a shrinking world Australia was no longer out of sight, out of mind.

The protest movements from the end of the Napoleonic Wars to the last Chartist agitation of 1848 represent the slow emergence of working-class agitation and organisations in town, then country. Often working men and women were enlisted by liberal middle-class reformers to help push for the political reform of the old aristocratic-controlled constitution, culminating in the passing of the Great Reform Bill of 1832. However, this reform only extended political rights to vote to the propertied middle class, and stopped well short of granting even voting rights to working people. The alliance between proletarian and bourgeois, worker and boss was always riven by contradictions, not least working-class preference for collective protection of wages and conditions over the liberals' commitment to individualism and the free market. The conflict between Whig liberals and working-class self-assertion came to a head in the Tolpuddle trial where the government attempted to wind back and crush trade unionism. The public furore at the transportation of the Tolpuddle Martyrs demonstrated how transportation could backfire, amplifying rather than silencing dissent. The state's overreaction led to a Pyrrhic victory in which unionism was legitimised rather than suppressed. Clearly public opinion about worker organisations and the right to protest was changing.

Working-class protest then entered a more modern phase climaxing in the demand for working-class political rights, a struggle lost in Britain in the 1840s, but speedily won in the Australian colonies. The Chartists were the last English political protesters to be transported. The move from riotous violence to organised activism also saw a commensurate moderation in punishment on the part of the state. Rudé observed that 'as protests became more muted and lost its thrust, the army, the hangman, and the penal colony could, without much danger, be phased out in turn'.[212] Within the Australian colonies the movement against transportation gathered pace, ending in New South Wales in 1840, and in Van Diemen's Land in 1853.

Through the transportation, then mass immigration of working-class Chartists, the utilitarian cast of their politics influenced the shape of colonial and then Australian politics. The great Australian historian W.K. Hancock observed that '[w]ithin ten years of the discovery of gold, practically the whole political programme of the Chartists was realised in the Australian colonies'.[213] In the struggle for a new constitution in New South Wales, told with great style by historian Peter Cochrane in *Colonial Ambition*, liberal reformers seeking a democratically elected Lower House drew on the traditional rhetoric of free-born Englishmen, but took the details of their program from the radical Chartists.[214] Two of the most radical leaders of the Constitutional Association established in 1849, John Dunmore Lang and Edward Hawksley, were profoundly influenced by Chartism. Hawksley had edited the Chartist journal *Citizen* in Britain, and in Sydney launched the *People's Advocate* as the radical voice for constitutional democracy.[215] Distancing the cause of self-government from the radicals in the early 1850s, the politically canny leader of the liberal tendency, Henry Parkes, astutely used the spectre of British Chartism to argue that wise democratic reform from the top could avoid such social strife.[216] Political scientist Hugh Collins perceived a neat fit between Jeremy Bentham's utilitarian ideas about representing the will of the majority, influential among colonial liberals, and 'Chartist doctrines of the colonial democrats seeking a legislative check upon gubernatorial authority and the privilege of wealth'.[217] They were implacably opposed by the oligarchy of wealthy landowning squatters, who dominated the Legislative Council that advised the governor.

Hoping to perpetuate the landed prerogatives of pre-reform England in the colony, the 'squattocracy' wanted a restricted franchise for the proposed legislative assembly, and some, such as demagogue politician turned Tory, W.C. Wentworth, even advocated an hereditary antipodean House of Lords to check colonial democrats.[218] Derided by democrat journalist Daniel Deniehy as a 'Bunyip Aristocracy', the pastoralists backing Wentworth, such as James Macarthur, envisaged a plantation economy based on cheap convict labour, but they were swimming against the tide. Sydney's bourgeois merchants and working-class artisans had a different vision for New South Wales: of a diversified economy making its own manufactured goods and providing skilled employment. The two classes came together as an irresistible political force for reform and by 1858 New South Wales had a popular Lower House, elected by universal male suffrage and secret ballot, boasting short parliaments, equal electoral districts and, from 1889, payment of MPs. While still balanced by an oligarchic Legislative Council selected on a limited franchise, self-government in Australia had embarked on a Chartist experiment, with the British Government's acceptance.

Across the Murray River in Victoria on 3 December 1854, the Ballarat gold miners rose in rebellion over the imposition of licence fees and fought a pitched battle with troops at the Eureka Stockade. The demands they put forward were those of the Chartists. In the capital, Melbourne, one witness later described an atmosphere of 'political excitement and turbulence', invigorated by 'combative Chartists from Glasgow, Clerkenwell, and Chelsea, brim-full of schemes for the reformation of mankind in general and the people of Victoria in particular ...'.[219] By 1857 all the aims of the Charter, bar annual parliaments, were instituted in the new democratic constitution of Victoria. Indeed, Victoria has the distinction of being the first jurisdiction in the world to introduce secret ballot, known elsewhere as the 'Australian ballot'. The

Chartist program was in turn adopted in the constitutions of Western Australia, South Australia and Tasmania, and the new Federation improved on the Chartists' points by extending the vote to women in 1901.[220] Sensitive to the interests of the working-class vote, liberal colonial governments passed legislation establishing free, compulsory education for all children and schemes providing small land grants, known as selections, to low-income earners who wanted to make a go of farming and be their own bosses. The selection acts owe something to the Chartist National Land Company idea, and while the harsh Australian climate undid the hopes of many small farmers, many other Chartist immigrants made a success of cottage ownership in the growing cities. 'Budding radicalism', far from 'withering in the antipodes' as Robert Hughes argued, was blooming, but they were peculiarly native flowers.

In the increasingly volatile area of industrial relations, the Chartist influence was clear. The Chartist convict-turned-colonial-activist William Cuffay played a leading role in the campaign of the late 1850s and '60s to reform the punitive Masters and Servants Acts in favour of workers.[221] The Hobart *Mercury* observed in Cuffay's obituary that 'being a fluent and an effective speaker he particularly distinguished himself in the agitation for the amendment of the masters' and servants' law'. He 'was always popular with the working classes' and 'contributed in a great degree to the settlement of the masters' and servants' question on a satisfactory basis'.[222] In the rough democracy of the new colonies the son of a slave and convicted republican conspirator could become a respected labour leader.

After the defeat of the unions in the great strikes of the 1890s the labour movement resolved, in the manner of the Chartists, to seek representation in colonial, then Federal parliaments, to press for working-class interests. The Australian Labor Party inherited the Chartist social program and joined with sympathetic Liberal governments to introduce this agenda. Historians John Hirst, Hugh Collins and Neville Meaney have noted the continuity with Chartism of novel reforms from the late nineteenth century and first decade of Federation, notably the erection of architecture for the arbitration and conciliation of industrial disputes, centred on the principle of a legally enforced minimum wage based on the cost of living.[223] A minimum living wage had been the chief demand of the Swing protesters and the Tolpuddle Martyrs who were transported to the Australian colonies. With a secure income, more and more workers could feed their families, pay the rent, save and even purchase their own home, or become owner-builders on the new subdivisions on suburban fringes of the cities. State governments aided this process, funding public housing estates for low-income earners to rent, and eventually buy, beginning with the Sydney garden suburb of Daceyville in 1912, which like O'Connor's National Land Company, awarded houses through a lottery. By the mid-twentieth century, the dreams of working-class radicals had become the Great Australian Dream of a suburban, home-owning democracy.

How ironic that it was in the land described by George Loveless as '[h]ell' and a land of slaves, that these important social reforms were first achieved.[224] Even more ironic that it was Australian Liberals, such as Alfred Deakin and Henry Bourne Higgins, who implemented these measures, with the help of Labor. For in the Australian colonies free-market liberalism had taken a different course. Through converts such as Victorian intellectual and government minister Charles Henry Pearson and media proprietor David Syme, New Liberalism had embraced state intervention as necessary to preserve Australia from class conflict, to foster manufacturing and to ameliorate some of the anti-social aspects of capitalist modernity.[225] Other elements of what journalist Paul Kelly has termed the 'Australian Settlement' included age pensions, tariff protection from cheap imports and immigration restriction to exclude cheaper 'coloured' labour—the notorious xenophobic White Australia Policy that racially limited the rights and bounty of citizenship to those of British stock.[226] Whatever their merits to us today, at the time all these measures were the fruits of universal suffrage, and argued for on the grounds that they would protect the living standards of working people. The cause, for which so many nineteenth century protesters were transported, had become legitimate. Visiting French intellectual Albert Metin described the practical experimentation of the Australian polity in the years after Federation as 'Socialism without doctrine', but the working-class locals would come to call it the 'fair go'.[227]

How did the cause for which nineteenth century working-class protesters fought fare in Great Britain? A new Liberal Party emerged from the wreck of the Whigs in the 1850s and sponsored further widening of the franchise, which finally passed as the Second Reform Act in 1867 granting the vote to most adult males. Women over thirty had to wait until 1918 and again until 1928 until they received equal voting rights to men. From the late nineteenth century a new Labour Party supported by the urban working class, forged from an alliance of unions and Fabian intellectuals, supported Liberal governments in reforms to improve the conditions of workers. By 1895 the once dangerous goals of the Swing rioters, the Tolpuddle Martyrs and the Chartists had become sufficiently safe that the Prince of Wales, later Edward VII, is said to have declared 'we are all socialists nowadays'.[228]

Each year in July, leaders and members of British trade unions gather in the town of Tolpuddle, Dorchester within sight of the still-standing sycamore tree, to honour the six labourers transported to Australia. Workers, union officials and assorted Labour luminaries come together, not in solemn mourning of the suffering of George Loveless and his comrades, but in a spirit of festivity, donning nineteenth century costumes, watching plays, enjoying a ploughman's lunch and a pint of beer while singing along with Billy Bragg to old folk songs. They have been remembering Tolpuddle and its martyrs like this for over a century. In April 2009, to mark the 175th anniversary of the Copenhagen Fields monster rally to free the Dorchester labourers, thousands again marched, bringing London traffic to a standstill. Sadly in Australia—the working man's paradise that led the world in adult male suffrage, the eight-hour working day, the establishment of a Labor Party, and a national Labor Government—few remember the Tolpuddle men who for a time lived and toiled among us. Nor do we yet as a nation commemorate the many unsung rebels of field and factory, who for their passionate belief in the 'fair go' were exiled to our shores.

NORTH AMERICAN PATRIOTS VS THE EMPIRE

CANADIAN REVOLUTIONARIES IN EXILE

HUNTING THE BRITISH LION

IN NOVEMBER 1838 THE BRITISH PROVINCE OF LOWER CANADA (*Province du Bas-Canada*) exploded in rebellion for the second time in as many years. The Nationalist radicals among the French-speaking majority rose up to rid the colony of the English minority who had ruled France's former North American territories since 1763. The uprising was mobilised by *'L'Association des Frères Chasseurs'* (the Association of Brother Hunters), a revolutionary secret society pledged to restore sovereignty to the French *habitants*—settlers from France and their Canadian-born descendants. In the rural southern shire of Beauharnais, local command was thrust upon François Xavier Prieur, described in the press as 'a cultured young man of high intelligence'.[1]

Prieur was a fifth-generation French-Canadian born into a farming family from the heavily forested northeast of Lower Canada. Contrary to the British prejudice critical of the supposedly backward rustic French peasantry, the young man did well at school and proved to be a talented entrepreneur.[2] Leaving home and the land, he built up a successful trading store in the southwestern town of Saint Timothée in the years before the rebellion. Prieur later described his youthful self as 'a sincere lover of my homeland' who had 'read something of the heroism of our forefathers', meaning the French settlers who fought the British for control of Quebec in the North American theatre of the Seven Years' War (1756–1763).[3] He became a fervent French-Canadian nationalist, persuaded by the speeches and writings of the radical politician Louis Joseph Papineau and was thrust into the community of anti-British *Patriotes Canadiens* that included the brothers Wolfred and Robert Nelson, Louis-Hipolyte La Fontaine, Denis Viger, Édouard-Étienne Rodier, Jean-Louis Beaudry, George-Étienne Cartier and Côme-Séraphin Cherrier.[4] Prieur recalled 'join[ing] up with all the faith, all the self-abnegation, all the delight even that one can put into a cause to which one is sincerely devoted'.[5]

Papineau and many of the radical *patriotes* sat in the popularly elected Lower Canadian Assembly, but real power resided in the British lieutenant-governor appointed by London, his cabal of hand-picked advisers who administered the colony as the Executive Council, and the Legislative Council, a larger appointed body representative of

211

François Xavier Prieur (1814–1891), a merchant who as a young idealist in 1838 became a French-Canadian rebel seeking to liberate his people from British rule.

British interests. This oligarchy was known colloquially as the 'Châteaux Clique'. At its apex stood the hard-line Sir John Colborne, decorated commander who played a large part in Napoleon's defeat in the Battle of Waterloo, and a lieutenant-governor from 1829. In 1837 a bitter standoff between the Assembly and the governor provoked the first rebellion by French nationalists against British rule. While the uprising was swiftly suppressed, the grievances were left to fester as the rebel leaders suffered courts martial and the scaffold. *Patriote* leaders fled to the United States, and elected fellow exile Dr Robert Nelson commander and President of the coming republic. They then began organising a secret army, the *Frères Chasseurs*, to relaunch the rebellion. In February 1838 Nelson issued a Declaration of Independence for Lower Canada, from the safety of his refuge in Vermont, that proclaimed:

> *... whereas we can no longer suffer the repeated violations of our dearest rights, and patiently support the multiplied outrages and cruelties of the Government of Lower Canada ... WE, in the name of the people of Lower Canada ... SOLEMNLY DECLARE:*
> *1. That from this day forward, the PEOPLE OF LOWER CANADA are absolved from all allegiance to Great Britain and ...*
> *2. That a REPUBLICAN form of Government is best suited to Lower Canada, which is this day declared to be a REPUBLIC.*[6]

Despite these grand and inspiring words, the *Chasseurs* held their fire until November. Then, as rebellion again swept through the province, Prieur faced a moral dilemma. A devout Catholic wrestling with his conscience, he chose the nationalist cause over the dictates of the Church, that demanded parishioners obey lawful authority.[7] Still, Prieur tried to lead the local rebel militia by Christian principles, distinguishing himself by moderation and civility in dealing with the English officials and gentry, and resisting those who would use the rebellion as a pretext to settle petty grievances.[8]

At this point Prieur was joined by a senior *Chasseur* officer François-Marie-Thomas Chevalier de Lorimier, who had just crossed into Lower Canada from the United States, where he had been in exile with other *patriote* leaders since the 1837 rebellion. Of noble lineage and some political influence, de Lorimier had been a local notary (Justice of the Peace) and brought a mantle of legitimacy to the local struggle.[9] Unfortunately the Beauharnais *patriotes* were inadequately armed, with only 'six iron-bound wooden cannon', a 'hundred sporting guns', mostly antiques from the eighteenth century, and an assortment of pikes and scythes. However, they were confident of imminent assistance from the neighbouring United States, where de Lorimier reported American sympathisers recruited into the *Chasseurs* were poised to cross the border.[10]

As prearranged, on the night of 3 November 600 rebels mustered at Beauharnais, occupied the landed estate of Edward Ellice and next morning at 6 am captured the passenger steamer *Brougham*.[11] Officials and government sympathisers in the parish were placed under protective custody, and the *patriotes* awaited orders from the provisional revolutionary government that was to be established by Dr Nelson. These orders would never come, for the quixotic Nelson had crossed the border without the promised reinforcements or arms and, with only local rebels at his disposal, abandoned the planned offensive against Montreal, and retreated to the backwoods of Odelltown. Meanwhile, in place of the anticipated Americans, several hundred British troops and Canadian volunteer militia advanced towards Beauharnais. Prieur and de Lorimier marched 200 men to face the enemy and massed with other *patriotes* at Baker's Camp on the Chateauguay River. Here their force of 500 under the elected commander Dr Perrigo prepared to meet 'a troop superior in numbers, well disciplined and armed to the teeth'.[12]

At the first battle on the morning of 9 November the *patriotes* prevailed and put the Queen's soldiers to flight. Their triumph was to be short-lived as the main rebel force under Dr Nelson was overwhelmed later that day at the Battle of Odelltown by the superior numbers and arms of the government. Many were killed or captured but Dr Nelson escaped across the border before the fighting had ended. News was received of a force of 1200 government regulars and volunteers, including cavalry and artillery, advancing on Beauharnais. At the last moment Prieur was persuaded to abandon an 'impossible resistance' that would 'spill blood uselessly', and 'bring down on our parishes the vengeance of a powerful and implacable enemy'.[13]

The uprising had failed, and as the rebels withdrew to their farms and families, Prieur tried to escape across the border into the United States. 'Here ends my career as a soldier and as company commander,' he later recalled, 'and begins that of fugitive, of accused committed for trial, of prisoner condemned to death, and of exile amongst convicts.' He found his house in 'smoking ruins ... totally destroyed', for to teach the rebels a lesson, the British army embarked on a campaign of arson, burning the homes of suspects and anyone who helped fugitives like Prieur.[14] Still, close friends and even complete strangers sheltered him as he sought to evade the soldiers. On the run, tired and hungry Prieur was finally betrayed by some of his fellow *patriotes* who were promised pardons in exchange for his whereabouts and evidence that he was one of the masterminds. Captured by British soldiers, he was conveyed to the Pied-du-Courant Prison at Montreal with other alleged ringleaders from around the province to await trial for treason. Here he met Leondre Ducharme, a classically educated rebel like himself, though most were ordinary workers and farmers.

With British subjects baying for the rebels' blood, treason trials began in November 1838. A succession of trials by military court martial were held for 108 prisoners, one after the other, through the festive season of 1838 and into the New Year, with Prieur facing the court with de Lorimier and ten others from his district on 11 January 1839. The proceedings before a court of fifteen British military officers 'took place in English, a language that the majority of us understood not at all'.[15] Far from being hailed as martyrs, the accused endured 'abuse and insults' from the 'rabble' that 'invaded the approaches to the court'.[16] Despite pleas for mercy by influential witnesses who were grateful for his restraint and humanity in the crisis, Prieur was found guilty of treason, and along with his eleven co-accused, was sentenced to death.[17] Prieur, who endured the suffering of his mother in court 'succumbing under the weight of her grief', noted that most of his condemned companions 'were fathers of families whose wives and children were already homeless, as a result of the destruction of their property by fire'.[18]

The first executions began on 19 December with the hanging of a twenty-two-year-old law student Joseph Duquette and Joseph Narcisse Cardinal, a solicitor. The young student needed to be hanged twice, after his rope was incorrectly knotted, and he became tangled on the fall and smashed his head.[19] Henceforth the scaffold did a brisk and more efficient trade. In February de Lorimier and Charles Hindenlang were told to prepare themselves for execution. Chosen to share a cell with de Lorimier, Prieur 'prayed with him' and observed as he wrote a last letter, a political testament distinguished by optimism for the future:[20]

> I die without remorse; I desired only the good of my country through insurrection and independence; my opinions and my actions were sincere, and have not been stained by any of the crimes which dishonour humanity … In spite of so many misfortunes, my heart still retains its courage and its hopes for the future; my friends and my children will see better days; they will be free.[21]

Hindenlang was a young Frenchman of Swiss Protestant background, who as a *Chasseur* officer had accompanied Dr Nelson into Lower Canada via the United States and fought with the *patriotes* at Odelltown. According to Prieur he was 'generous but fanatical … the result of that revolutionary education which was still current in France, and which was spreading throughout Canada'.[22] Hindenlang went to his death without the solace of faith in God or an afterlife that sustained many of the *patriotes*, but found vindication in the republican cause for which he was about to forfeit his life.[23] His last words before ascending the gallows were:

> [t]he cause for which I am being sacrificed is noble and grand; I am proud of it, and I have no fear of death … Canadians, my last good-bye is this old cry of France: 'Long live Liberty long live Liberty, long live Liberty'.[24]

It was only after twelve of his fellows had already been hanged and the agony of waiting many months for his own name to be called that Prieur learned on 25 September 1839 that his sentence, and that of fifty-seven of his fellow condemned rebels, was commuted to transportation to Australia for life.[25] The prisoners, most of whom had never journeyed beyond their parish, had scant time to console loved ones, for they were to embark on this odyssey to the other side of the world 'the next day'.[26] As frantic parents, wives and children invaded the gaol to say 'a farewell that was believed to be for ever', Prieur lamented the shame and bitterness of

> *respectable men, fathers of families, banished for life amidst the convicts in another hemisphere, not for atrocious crimes, but for giving way to the impulses ... of an ill-directed patriotism.*[27]

Yet his own mother calmly assured her son, 'You will come back again'.[28]

In the same month that the French *patriotes* had risen up in Lower Canada, the neighbouring province of Upper Canada was under attack from a covert foreign enemy seeking to import revolution from the republic on the other side of the St Lawrence River. On the evening of 12 November 1838 a young American farm labourer named William Gates boarded a schooner at Sackets Harbor, New York State. Together with another 100 men he intended to cross the St Lawrence to Prescott, on the British side of the Canadian border. The boat was met by the steamer *United States*, and towed a mile onto the river to rendezvous with yet another boat crammed with men that was attached to the mysterious convoy. Stowed on both schooners was a significant quantity of guns, ammunition and provisions. The mission of the armed Americans was to liberate Upper Canada, a colony that frontier idealists like Gates genuinely believed was 'ripe for shaking off the yoke of British bondage'.[29] In the same vein, another young democrat on board, Daniel Heustis, reflected that Upper Canadians had arrived at their '1776' moment and were poised to 'throw off the yoke that was on their necks, as our fathers had done when the yoke oppressed them'.[30] As the vessels glided along the river in the 'bright moonlight evening', Gates imagined the welcome the men would receive from 'our Canadian neighbours', who were 'struggling for that freedom which we were enjoying, and which with a little aid they would be successful in securing'.[31]

Secrecy was paramount, for this force of 'patriots' was a private citizen army, acting in contravention of their government. The schooners were detached near Prescott but Gates' vessel drifted a mile down the river, landing at Windmill Point. The force dragged their artillery up a steep hill and took possession of an imposing windmill and its adjoining buildings. Atop the 18 metre (59 foot) high stone structure they festooned the patriot flag, which featured an eagle and two stars on blue.[32] Unfortunately for the invasion plan, the other schooner became stuck on a sand bar where it was immediately menaced by the steamer *Experiment*, one of two British gunboats patrolling the river.[33] The Americans managed to fire first, from a 5 kilogram (12 pound) gun, loaded with a cannon ball and grapeshot, killing eleven and crippling the British boat before making their getaway back to the United States. The hasty retreat of this schooner carrying half the men and most of the supplies spelt disaster for the insurgent force at the windmill.[34] Once it reached the American side of the river the schooner was seized by the US Army, robbing Gates and his colleagues of much needed soldiers, ammunition and the commander General Birge. 'We were a small band of about two hundred and fifty souls,' Gates lamented, 'yet our hearts fainted not, though deserted by friends and left on foreign soil ...'[35]

Pluck aside, the invaders' situation went from bad to worse the next morning, when an 'innumerable host' of British troops lined up into battle formation in front of the windmill, blocking any escape. Gates described:

> *their columns ... filling up in the rear till the river banks, fields and woods, appeared live with red coats ... displaying their numbers to as great advantage as possible and with what pomp and parade they were masters of, to strike dismay into the bosoms of our little band.*[36]

This army was the 83rd Regiment joined by local volunteer militia and numbered about 2000.[37] Rather than be intimidated by the arithmetic, the motley crew of frontiersmen resolved to meet the red coats in battle.

To understand why these Americans had decided to take on the might of the British Empire, it is necessary to go back to the uprising of 1837. While Upper Canada had been in the grip of a constitutional crisis akin to that in Lower Canada, the outbreak of rebellion in the capital of Toronto in 1837 was a shock to imperial authorities, for this was a colony settled by British immigrants and assumed to be steadfastly loyal. Although the red coats quickly dispersed the rebels, their leader, William Lyon Mackenzie, made it safely across the border into New York State where he joined with other refugees from both provinces in agitating for American intervention to reignite the Canadian revolution. Gates explained how Americans in the frontier states immediately sympathised with the Canadian rebellions and 'could but feel their hearts burn within them to go and give them aid':[38]

> *Meetings were held in all quarters. Resolutions and speeches glowing with patriotism and valor, were read, spoken and published. The friends of Canada took greater courage and flattered themselves that truly the time and the hour had come for her redemption.*[39]

While the US Government had no intention of provoking war with the British, many of her citizens, enthusiastic to banish British 'tyranny' from the North American continent and keen for glory, had other ideas.

Across the border states covert militaristic societies of 'patriots' were hastily formed, bounded by secret oaths and disguising their hostile purpose by calling themselves 'Hunting Lodges' and using code words derived from this shared pastime. This was an Anglo-American version of the French-Canadian *Chasseurs* movement being promoted in American states bordering Lower Canada. One of its symbols was an illustration of an American bald eagle, talons tearing at the British lion. Gates explained that these societies attracted '[m]en of all classes, ages and distinctions— those of influence and station, as well as those who were poor and illiterate' and by early 1838 'the "Hunters" were swelled to many thousands in number'.[40] At only twenty-two years old, Gates was one of the first to sign up, joining the local Cape Vincent Hunters Lodge in the aftermath of the failed Toronto rebellion in November 1837. 'I felt the spirit stirring my youthful blood in sympathy for the downtrodden of Britain's rule,' he later reminisced. 'I could not remain an idle spectator in such stirring times.' But he would have to cool his heels for almost a year of border raids and skirmishes before his lodge launched its night-time invasion across the St Lawrence.

To lead their stand at the windmill, the Americans voted unanimously to confer command on Colonel Von Schoultz, a Polish émigré with military experience from fighting in that country's ill-fated struggles for self-determination and praised by Gates as a man of 'noble bearing' and 'cool self-reliance' who 'knew no fear'.[41] As the two sides took their positions, a large crowd of spectators took vantage points on the American side of the river to cheer on the patriots. In the first battle, the 'Hunters' demonstrated their marksmanship on the advancing British infantry. Gates, admittedly a biased combatant keen to accentuate the valour of his inexperienced comrades, claimed that:

> *I saw some twenty acres almost literally covered with the fallen, and*
> *though I felt but little sympathy for them, the groans and imprecations*
> *of the wounded and dying were heart rendering to hear.*[42]

He estimated British casualties numbered 300 compared to thirty on the American side, but actual loyalist dead was only thirteen.[43] With huge reserves of men the British quickly recovered the advantage and forced the Americans to retreat to the windmill, where they were besieged. Next morning an injured patriot, twenty-five-year-old carpenter Stephen Wright, surveyed the misty battlefield 'studded with the bodies of the dead':

> *A mist curtained the sun—and mist gathered in the eyes of many*
> *of our comrades, as we thought of the weeping mothers, agonized*
> *sisters, and the heart-broken wives that had been made in the short*
> *space of a single day.*[44]

Less poetically, pigs were gorging on the corpses.[45] During a truce to bury the dead, Von Schoultz indicated the Americans would only surrender if they were treated as prisoners of war—a condition the British commander Colonel Dundas refused, considering the invaders to be no better than bandits and pirates.

By the dawn of the second day of the siege, with the British firing volley after volley from heavy artillery at the windmill, it was becoming clear that there would be no reinforcements from either the United States or the Canadians that the Hunters had come to liberate. Far from rising in support of the Americans' stand, Upper Canadians were present at the battle as local militias backing up the British regulars. The situation became more desperate when it was revealed that the Americans' doctor had failed to bring medical supplies to treat their wounded. Von Schoultz called for volunteers to cross through enemy lines to procure medicines, and Gates joined Aaron Dresser and two others on the risky mission. Finding a small damaged sailing boat they set off on the river, only to be spied by the British steamer *Coburg* and the craft strafed with bullets. Gates realised their position was hopeless and the four men surrendered and were taken on board the patrol boat as British prisoners—despite the fact that they were now technically in American waters.[46] The men were stripped of possessions, handcuffed and 'surrounded by some fifty soldiers' who threatened that the prisoners were to 'be hung to the yard arm', or used as 'targets for the most gracious majesty's loyal militia'.[47] However, the prisoners were taken to nearby Fort Henry instead, where they were soon to be joined by compatriots from the windmill.

On the third day of the siege the Americans realised there was no chance of escape by land or water, and accepted Colonel Dundas's terms of unconditional surrender. As the surviving 160 Americans, now prisoners, filed out the British regimental band struck up a mocking version of 'Yankee Doodle Dandy'.[48] Twenty patriots had died. According to Gates his comrades hoped that by avoiding further bloodshed they might earn 'some little degree of the enemy's clemency'.[49] However, the British and Canadian militia had suffered high casualties and were in no mood for mercy.

The Battle of the Windmill was the climax of a year of raids on Canadian soil by American insurgents seeking to provoke a republican revolution against British rule. Like the other 'invasions', the action at the windmill was ill-conceived and poorly executed. The men lacked discipline, and the leadership proved less interested in military tactics than glorious gestures.[50] For Stephen Wright, the young carpenter from New York State, the patriots' 'leaders proved themselves utterly unequal to the task of directing or guiding the men under their control', making a debacle of their landing and fatally compromising the mission.[51] But at root the invasion failed because idealists like Gates, Heustis and Wright wilfully misread the popular mood in Upper Canada. A handful of Canadian radicals, like François Xavier Prieur in Lower Canada, looked to the 'Hunters' as liberators. However, for the vast majority of loyal Canadian subjects and the British Government these extreme democrats were nothing more than 'pirates', viewed with the same disdain as modern-day terrorists. While many Canadians certainly wanted more control over their government, they wanted reform within the monarchical system and bonds of empire, so a revolution was never likely.[52] When the anticipated popular uprising failed to materialise, the Americans, often ill-led and inadequately armed, stood little chance against crack British regiments. In raid after raid the over-confident Americans found themselves outnumbered, outgunned and outmanoeuvred and thrown back behind their borders. The retreating men were often cut down without mercy, and many were captured and imprisoned, where they were subjected to the tender mercies of the British justice system.

To legally arm itself against the American incursions, the Upper Canadian Government had passed the *Lawless Aggressions Act* in January 1838 making 'piratical invasion' by citizens of a foreign power a felony punishable by death or transportation.[53] This was first used against Americans captured in the Battle of Short Hills in June 1838 and was the legislation under which 140 of the prisoners captured at the windmill were to be dealt with in courts martial beginning in December 1838.[54] Far from taking issue with the British Government for this cavalier treatment of Americans, President Martin Van Buren reacted to the Short Hills incident by declaring that any citizen invading Canadian territory could expect no legal protection from the US Government.[55]

Von Schoultz stood trial almost immediately and was executed eight days later. In short order ten other patriots from the windmill were found guilty and hanged by the end of 1838. Gates claimed that while officers were each given a day before the court, the remaining men were tried perfunctorily in batches of about fifteen.[56] All, including Gates, were condemned to hang, though the practice was to keep the men in limbo about their sentence until execution was imminent. They waited on death row for weeks, then months in the Fort Henry cells 'dispirited, emaciated, weak in body and sick at heart', not knowing if they were to die or be pardoned.[57] Then in late September 1839 the condemned men were chained, marched to the water and conveyed by river steamer with convicted rebels from Toronto Gaol to Quebec, where they joined François Xavier Prieur and the other prisoners from Lower Canada on board the ocean-going naval ship, *Buffalo*. They had exchanged the gallows not for freedom, but for its very opposite.

Many today think of the United States of America as an arrogant superpower courting hubris and compromising its self-proclaimed ideals fighting a 'war on terror', in which enemy combatants and suspected terrorists have been detained without trial, and even tortured, in maximum security prisons beyond the reach of America's democratic laws. In our post 9/11 world, the word 'patriot' has connotations of President George W. Bush's *Patriot Act*, a twenty-first century American version of the *Lawless Aggressions Act*, deployed against terrorists outside and inside the country's borders. Yet American citizens were once on the other side of the divide, radical democratic insurgents seeking to liberate the supposedly tyrannised subjects of the British Crown in Canada. These actions by citizen militants were undertaken within an idealistic tradition, promoted by their leaders, to evangelise government of the people, by the people, for the people. Few today are aware of the high price some of these American 'patriots' paid for forming secret armies and crossing the rivers and lakes separating the United States from Canada to promote revolution. For they were transported for life to Van Diemen's Land, the British Empire's maximum security prison at the ends of the Earth, to a nineteenth century version of Guantanamo Bay.

✳ ✳ ✳

PRISONERS OF EMPIRE

IN ALL 151 NORTH AMERICAN REBELS WERE TRANSPORTED TO THE Australian colonies on life sentences between 1838 and 1839. Fifty-eight were the French Lower Canadians, and ninty-three were caught in Upper Canada, 75 per cent of whom were United States citizens.[58] Many of the Upper Canadian convicts were also Americans who had settled in the province or were recently arrived Irish or Scots.[59] The Lower Canadians were all captured in the rebellion of November 1838, while the Americans and Upper Canadians were caught in three American raids that took place between June and December 1838, at Short Hills, Windmill Point and Windsor.[60] One would die on the ocean journey to Australia, and many more after arrival. Throughout their incarceration and transportation the prisoners remained divided by ethnicity and the province in which they were captured and tried. The French-Canadians were intended for the isolated prison of secondary punishment, Norfolk Island, part of New South Wales, while the Americans would go to Van Diemen's Land.

George Rudé examined the North American rebels transported to Australia briefly in *Protest and Punishment*, and distinguished Canadian and American historians have examined in detail the rebellions of 1837–38, the British response and the role of the Hunters' Lodges.[61] However, the definitive academic history of the American convicts' travails in Canada and Australia is a recent work by Australians Cassandra Pybus and Hamish Maxwell-Stewart, *American Citizens, British Slaves*. This carefully researched and elegantly written history examines in forensic detail the primary sources relating to the patriots' military actions, capture, trial and exile in Van Diemen's Land. As such it is the first close scholarly analysis of the convicts' published journals that compares the prisoners' own accounts against official records, letters, newspaper reports and many other documents to understand more accurately the experiences and motives of both rebels and empire builders, prisoners and gaolers.

What manner of men were the North Americans transported to Australia? Blood, marriage and parish, as well as sharing a deep faith in the Catholic religion, bonded many of the French-Canadians to each other. The Americans, by contrast, were a scattering from all the different incursions into Canada and hailed from different border states or were US immigrants to Upper Canada from a variety of origins. However, the shared experience of the Hunters' Lodges and incarceration on land and sea forged solidarity. Like most political prisoners transported to Australia, very few had ever been in trouble with the law and were ashamed and alarmed at being classed as common criminals.[62] An examination of the convict indents, the records made when the prisoners arrived in Australia, reveal that the Canadian convicts were mainly skilled manual and lower clerical workers, or subsistence farmers. Artisan occupations listed included blacksmith, joiner, carpenter, baker, painter, carriage maker, wheelwright and weaver—all respectable trades that were the economic backbone of local communities. Not surprisingly, given the economic staples in both Canadian provinces as well as the US border states, there was a good representation of farmers and agricultural workers, such as Gates. But there was also a peppering of merchants like Prieur, a surgeon, the articled law clerk Linus Miller and even the self-identifying 'gentleman' Ducharme.[63] The plethora of journals produced by the Canadian rebels is a testimony to the education and even literary flair to be found within the cohort.

The transportation of political prisoners from corners of the Empire other than Britain and Ireland was not so rare, and was an extension of the use of this punishment against criminals in subject colonies, as research by both Rudé and Pybus and Maxwell-Stewart shows. The British penal colony on the Andaman Islands off the coast of Burma received prisoners from the Indian Mutiny of 1857, the Mapilah revolt and later the Gadhr independence movement.[64] The Australian penal settlements were an important weapon in the suppression of dissent on the edge of Empire, receiving rebel slaves from the West Indies, unruly Khoi from the Cape Colony and Maori militants from New Zealand.[65] Like many of these exiles the French-Canadians were non-British subjects of Empire. But the transportation of citizens of another sovereign country at peace with Britain was new, designed to project fear of her terrifying deterrent across the border as a warning to any other Americans tempted to invade the Empire's territory.

All those transported were originally condemned to death. The transportation of the rebels in lieu of the gallows had the advantages of demonstrating British clemency to the world while still providing a terrible deterrent to Canadian firebrands and American zealots hoping to carry on the fight. The decision to transport the Americans and Upper Canadians was the handiwork of the lieutenant-governor of Upper Canada, Sir George Arthur, who in his prior viceregal position was principal architect of the system of punishment in the colony of Van Diemen's Land. Arthur had personally questioned the inmates at Fort Henry, whom he allegedly called 'buccaneers, pirates and ruffians', and received petitions for clemency on behalf of several of the American and Upper Canadian prisoners on death row.[66] This included one humbly handed to him by William Gates' mother, signed by many of the prominent men from the prisoner's home of Jefferson County asking Arthur to spare his life.[67] The British Colonial Secretary, Lord Glenelg, also requested that executions cease. Twenty-nine prisoners had been hanged since the outbreak of rebellion and nineteen of these executions had occurred in Upper Canada. Prevailed upon by both the government in London and his own better instincts, the severe lieutenant-governor, who had given his name to the infamous penitentiary Port Arthur in Van Diemen's Land, judged that transportation to the feared island he had governed for thirteen years would teach a lesson about the price of disloyalty, deter further American 'piracy' on Britain's territory, and placate public opinion baying for blood. A letter from the British ambassador in Washington confirmed that transportation was viewed with terror by Americans, in part because its chains, floggings and forced labour smacked of slavery.[68] For Daniel Heustis, a patriot captured at the windmill, it was a 'punishment worse than death'.[69]

But in transporting the rebels Arthur faced the legal problem that prisoners, political or otherwise, could not be transported directly from one colony to another, but must go to London for processing by the convict department via the hulks. Already an ordinance exiling eight leaders to the Caribbean colony of Bermuda had been disallowed by the British Attorney-General. As a result the first fourteen patriots to be transported, a mixture of Americans and Upper Canadians captured in the Short Hills raid, were shipped to the London hulks before being sent to Van Diemen's Land. Here, to the government's chagrin, the prisoners had their cause taken up by radicals in parliament, resulting in some having their sentences reviewed in public court—though the Canadian sentences were confirmed and the prisoners duly transported.

To avoid a repetition of such radical grandstanding in the cause of Canadian independence, Arthur plotted with allies in the Colonial Office to circumvent the law, dispatching the remaining convicts directly from the Canadian colonies to Australia, ensuring that at no time did they set foot on land where the legal rights of free Englishmen might be enforced. By this subterfuge 137 men on board the *Buffalo* who had endured courts martial, including François Xavier Prieur and William Gates, were denied the right to have their sentences scrutinised in an open civilian court in London, and the chance, however slim, of an acquittal. These manoeuvres would be later challenged but by that time the prisoners would be already absorbed into the convict system on the other side of the world, a long way from the scrutiny of London's gentlemen radicals. It is ironic that American political prisoners caught bearing arms on foreign soil suffered a nineteenth century version of what the Bush Administration termed 'rendition', where laws intended to protect prisoners' rights were circumvented by conveying them through territories where popular sovereignty was void.

With the manacled prisoners dispatched onto the Atlantic Ocean from Quebec aboard the *Buffalo* on 28 September 1839, the authorities in Canada may have assumed that they had heard the last of these failed rebels. But in the case of the Canadian rebellions the pen would prove mightier than the sword. No fewer than two French and seven American prisoners wrote and published extensive journals of their experiences, of battle and trial, journey and exile. The prisoner-pamphleteers were the Americans William Gates, Daniel Heustis, Robert Marsh, Linus Miller, Samuel Snow, Benjamin Wait, Stephen Wright and the French-Canadians François Xavier Prieur and Leondre Ducharme. These accounts ensured that the underdogs' version of history was told in their lifetimes and beyond. They also provided the most detailed individual records ever produced of convict life in Australia and are, according to Pybus and Maxwell-Stewart, 'the largest collection of convict narratives in existence'.[70] Despite the obvious propaganda intent, together they paint a persuasive picture of the petty tyrannies, cruelties and corruption encouraged by the transportation 'system'.[71]

✳ ✳ ✳

PATH TO REBELLION

THE REBELLIONS IN CANADA BROUGHT TO NEAR BREAKING POINT a matrix of tensions related to the rights of settlers and the British Empire's hold on North America: democracy versus oligarchy; local self-determination versus rule from London; emerging nationalism versus Empire; French versus English Canadians; traditional agrarian land-use versus capitalism; republicanism versus monarchy; and United States expansionism versus British imperial power. Many of these conflicts were symptoms of a deeper crisis in imperial governance that would also sweep through the Australian colonies.

In looking at immediate causes for the uprisings of 1837–38, liberal historians have given primacy to the constitutional crisis that simmered in both provinces for many years, a power struggle between Assemblies elected by Canadians and legislative councils appointed by the governors and therefore beholden to the British Crown. Two rebellions with very different underlying grievances were bound by this common constitutional standoff. In both provinces, politicians in the popular Assemblies wanted to wrest power from oligarchies that enjoyed economic, political and religious privilege legitimised by viceregal patronage. The vast majority of Canadians wanted to remain within the British imperial family, but believed they should be extended the rights to self-determination and liberty enjoyed by their fellow subjects in England. They had supporters in Britain as well, even in parliament from radical and some Whig, and especially Irish, MPs who believed in local self-government for the colonies of settlement.

The crisis in Canada was on a continuum with the push for greater democracy and post-colonial national assertion that stretched back through the American War of Independence (1775–1783) to the Irish rebellion of 1798. At root the rebellions in Canada were part of this longer struggle about what sort of empire the British were to have: one ruled from the centre like India and the plantation colonies of the West Indies or a collection of self-governing parliamentary democracies.[72] The outcome of the Canadian rebellion would therefore be of profound relevance to the Australian colonies that at this time were also beginning to debate the merits of popular control of their governments.

The British colonies of Lower Canada and Upper Canada were both carved out of the vast former French territory of New France in North America, under the new Canadian constitution of 1791. This land, home to ethnic French-Canadians and a diversity of the indigenous 'First Nation' peoples, was forfeited to the British Empire in 1763 after its victory against France in the Seven Years' War. Importantly, the terms of the *Treaty of Paris* of 1763 and the *Quebec Act* of 1774 had recognised the free practice of the Catholic faith and the use of French civil law for private matters. This protection of French custom was extended to the new province of Lower Canada. The sparsely populated Upper Canada was to have a different cultural and ethnic destiny, as loyalist refugees from the thirteen lost American colonies, that declared independence from Great Britain in 1776, and British immigrants flocked to the province. In Upper Canada, these settlers would be governed by wholly British institutions and laws, and the Church of England would enjoy its customary ascendancy as the established faith.

The constitution hammered out for both Canadian colonies in 1791 had at its centre an imperial leash that tethered popular Assemblies in each province to unelected legislative councils that reviewed their actions in the manner of the British House of Lords. The substantial business of government, however, was exercised by a British governor and an appointed Executive Council of advisers. The men who sat on both the Legislative and Executive Councils were chosen to ensure that British, rather than local, interests prevailed. As in Britain, the popular Assemblies were not representative of all the population, but were elected on a property franchise, and by the 1820s electoral and legislative contests were between factions of the bourgeois and landowning classes, with reformers coming disproportionately from the liberal professions. An even more authoritarian version of this imperial constitutional template was imposed on the infant Australian colonies.

During the 1830s reformist leaders emerged in the Assemblies of Lower and Upper Canada who agitated for an elected Legislative Council and parliamentary control of the appointed Executive Council through which the provinces were governed. Tory and Whig administrations in London were hostile to these demands for greater independence sensing in them the expression of an emerging local nationalism that threatened British interests and subjects in the colonies and the Empire's grip on North America. This refusal to countenance what would later be called 'responsible government' in the Canadian colonies was a principal cause for the first uprisings of 1837.

On the ground in each province this struggle between an elected 'commons' and an unelected executive became a matter of who had the right to raise and control taxes: the representatives of the Canadians or the representatives of a distant monarch? Here was a disturbing echo of the dispute that led to the American War of Independence. Empire does not come cheap, and after the Napoleonic Wars it became imperial policy to make colonies pay for their upkeep in terms of defence, public works and other governmental expenditure. The elected Assemblies were charged with raising taxes and rubber stamping its appropriation by the Executive Council. Daniel Heustis, an American who traded on both sides of the border, found the colonists' key grievance was that they 'were taxed, most exorbitantly, to support a host of proud, overbearing, insolent, and virtually irresponsible government-officers, in whose appointment they had no voice and over whose conduct they could exercise no control'.[73] That Heustis wrote this after serving a sentence as patriot prisoner in Van Diemen's Land does not make it any less valid. Finding intolerable a situation where colonists' taxes paid for a government they did not control, the Assemblies in both Lower and Upper Canada refused to approve the monies the governors needed to run the provinces. This blocking of supply lasted for four and a half years, leading to a paralysis in government that triggered rebellion.

As with the causes of the American Revolution the constitutional conflict in the Canadas was one between local autonomy and imperial control, democracy and oligarchy, about how the British Empire would be governed. Initially, the champions for popular government in Canada were much more accommodating to imperial sensibilities, asserting that Canadians wanted no more than the principal political right long enjoyed in England—parliamentary control of government. The Canadian Assemblymen could point to an English tradition of commonsense constitutional reform stretching back to the Glorious Revolution of 1688 and still very much alive. In this spirit the Whig Government had just pushed through the Great Reform Bill expanding the franchise for the House of Commons in the face of an intransigent House of Lords. If taxpayers in Britain could have a say over how they were governed, why not industrious, over-taxed Canadians? But as it became apparent that the British Government would not concede any of its prerogatives over the North American colonies, some Canadian reformers became radical, drawing inspiration from the British radical tradition stretching back to the Scottish Martyrs, and ultimately looked to the republic across the border as a model of anti-colonial national self-assertion.

But a constitutional deadlock does not of itself explain why otherwise loyal Canadian subjects of Britain became so discontented as to take up arms against their government. On closer inspection, other factors, not least problems arising from the abuse of power by an oligarchy in Upper Canada, the distinctive French character of Lower Canada and long-term grievances of an economic and cultural nature, sowed the seeds of revolutionary discontent. The crisis in imperial governance, though important of itself and for the future of other colonies, was in fact driven by simmering social struggles peculiar to each province.[74]

In Upper Canada a tightly bound group of leading notables, known as 'The Family Compact', divided economic privileges and political positions among themselves under the patronage of governors. Monopolising the Executive Council, and therefore the ear of the governor, controlling seats on the appointed Legislative Councils and hogging the principal administrative offices, the Family Compact aroused the hostility of democrats in the Assembly as a symbol of the unrepresentative character of the province's governance. Those who produced the wealth— professionals, merchants and small landowners—were excluded from shaping the economic policy of Upper Canada, and had little say over how the Executive Council spent their taxes. The Family Compact was authoritarian, nepotistic and ultimately bad for growth and modernisation, using its control of government to grant land to supporters, oppose immigration, impose limits on the press and free speech and, to harass its political opponents. New South Wales was dominated by a similar oligarchy at this time, the aptly named Exclusives, who also resisted moves to responsible government.

There was also a religious dimension to the clash between popular Assemblies and oligarchic government. As in Britain and Ireland, the Anglican Church in Upper Canada enjoyed the status of an established religion, having first call on some of the best land and charging tithes for its upkeep. Pybus and Maxwell-Stewart calculate that through the 'clergy reserves' the Anglican Church controlled a seventh of surveyed land and the wealth produced, even though it had a smaller flock than the Methodists and Presbyterians.[75] The Compact families were enmeshed with the hierarchy of the established Church, exacerbating the exclusion of the large number of non-conformist Protestants and Catholics. Meanwhile, in Lower Canada, where the French majority were able to practise their Catholic faith without persecution, the Church of England still accrued economic and political privileges that became a source of resentment.

In Lower Canada the political situation was more volatile, as the standoff between the French-dominated Assembly and British imperial authority was a shadow play for a deeper conflict between two vastly different ways of life that was coming to a climax in the 1830s. The distinct French character of Lower Canada brought an ethno-cultural dimension to the constitutional crisis reminiscent of the conflict between the subject Catholic Celtic tenant farmers and the Protestant Ascendancy in Ireland. Gallic custom, land use and civil law were increasingly under threat from an expanding mercantile economy that was at odds with a semi-feudal agrarian system favoured by the French landlords and their peasant tenants. Out of a political and economic struggle to preserve a traditional way of life against Anglicisation, French difference became something new: French-Canadian nationalism.

Following the original analysis of Lord Durham, the historians Gérard Filteau, L.O. David and Helen Taft Manning stressed the importance of an emerging French-Canadian nationalism as a cause of the rebellion in Lower Canada.[76] In his famous report to the British Government on Canadian governance in the aftermath of the crisis, Durham sheeted home blame for the rebellions 'in the main to arising French nationality within the shell of a British province'.[77] The sense of a distinctive French-Canadian identity certainly emerged in the speeches of radical politician and rebel leader Papineau, and percolates through the accounts of transported *patriotes* Prieur and Ducharme.

However, the groundswell of patriotism in Lower Canada must not be confused with the French revolutionary spirit of 1789. Instead many of the rustic rebels of 1837 manned the barricades to preserve the quasi-feudal social arrangements of the *Ancien Régime* that had been able to survive in the North American province. While the original mother country, France, had taken a decisive, world-changing journey into modernity, the French *habitants* had a deal with Britain that guaranteed preservation of their traditional religion, customs and rural forms of social organisation. Unhindered by guillotine or Napoleon's artillery, the status quo of 1763, characterised by peasants tilling land for seigniorial lords, was able to continue in Lower Canada into the nineteenth century. During the long wars with revolutionary France it had suited Britain to honour its undertakings and mothball French Canada in ignorant bliss. However, by the 1830s the *habitants*' agrarian way of life was under pressure from two seemingly irresistible forces that were the lifeblood of the Empire: British immigration and trade.

Britain's solution to land hunger and cyclical unemployment at home had long been immigration to the New World. The United States continued to beckon, but in the first half of the nineteenth century immigration to the Canadian colonies was actively encouraged by Crown land grants. Even US citizens from border states such as New York, Massachusetts and New Hampshire were sufficiently tempted by cheap farmland to swallow their republican ideals and become subjects of British monarchy. The huge province of Lower Canada, with its virgin land for farming and thriving timber industry, was an equally popular destination for British settlers who arrived in increasing numbers in the 1820s and '30s.

The French in Lower Canada viewed the influx of Britons with alarm. In the Assembly, Papineau spoke out against British demographic and economic takeover, contrary to the spirit of the *Quebec Act*. However, the governor and his imperial masters were unmoved, believing British immigrants not only helped secure the province for the Empire from predation by the United States, but that they had a more entrepreneurial character that would promote the colony's economic development. While such views were rooted in English chauvinism against the French, they also arose from a capitalist critique of traditional agrarian life.

For historians, such as D.G. Creighton, who look to materialist explanations of political events, the rebellion was a political expression of the clash between an older agricultural system and assertive capitalism.[78] The static peasant economy of Lower Canada was in the firing line of British merchants who had come to see it as an obstacle to commercial enterprise in the province. The irony was that after the defeat of France in the Seven Years' War, the victorious British had manipulated the introduction of the pound into French Canada so as to bankrupt Quebec's merchant class. Under pressure, the French-Canadian commercial bourgeoisie found it profitable to take their business to Europe, leaving the field clear for British investment, while the seigniorial agrarian system was allowed to persist along with the Catholic Church. But by the 1830s a new professional middle class composed of educated lawyers and doctors like Papineau and the Nelson brothers had emerged as political leaders of the French-Canadians, winning more and more seats in Lower Canada's elected Assembly. The largely English urban bourgeoisie in Lower Canada feared that if granted control of the government, the Assembly would erect a semi-feudal barrier across the trade routes of British North America. This would retard the colony's development and their own profit margins. As in Britain itself, traditional land rights and work practices could not be allowed to stand in the way of market forces.

Did the French-Canadian rebels use radical rhetoric and democratic constitutional principles to defend reactionary economic and social goals, as disillusioned British liberals later concluded? An examination of the demands from some of the French-Canadian rebels suggests a genuinely radical program to break up the great estates of the Châteaux landlords. Far from maintaining feudal arrangements the radicals wanted to provide freehold deeds to *habitants* for the land they cultivated on the Lords' estates. Doubtless this plan for a democracy of small farmers also seemed economically backward to British Whigs promoting large-scale capitalist agriculture at home. It suits English chauvinism and a crudely determinist type of history to think it inevitable that the Empire's modish market economy would supplant the older French farming communities, but the *habitants* did not see it that way, and were prepared to take up arms to protect their way of life. Predictions of the extinction of French Canada would prove premature.

There were other economic problems fuelling the fires of discontent. Both Canadas, as well as the United States and Britain, were in the grip of a prolonged depression and international financial crisis from 1837 that was at its worst in the years of rebellion.[79] Economic depression meant the hardship of unemployment, business failure and a dramatic market collapse in prices for wheat, a staple crop of both Canadas. The large seigniorial landowner gentry reacted to the downturn by squeezing their tenant peasants with higher rents, when they could have released more of their estate for subsistence crops.[80] But it was the English, who sat at the summit of government and the economy, rather than their own masters, who attracted the ire of the French peasants. Anxiety over declining economic conditions was directed at new British immigrants who competed for jobs and land as well as threatening the ethnic identity of the province.

Radical leaders in the Lower Canadian Assembly, such as Papineau, were able to harvest the discontent for the cause of French nationalism, directing anger at British businessmen and settlers rather than the traditional French land system.[81] For this reason many observers in London considered the rebellion in Lower Canada to be a 'French versus English' national struggle. But if we remove the educated political leaders from the equation, the peasant *patriotes* who rose in 1837 and '38 were not so different from the machine breakers and food rioters in Southern England in 1830—both resorted to force to preserve pre-modern rural custom from new forces unleashed by capitalism.

These long-festering disputes found political expression in the elected Assemblies of both Upper and especially Lower Canada, and came to a head in the constitutional crisis over supply.

Why did Britain's rulers refuse to make concessions to the Canadian reformers in the 1830s, and risk driving them to radicalism and rebellion? Canadian historian of the Empire, Peter Burroughs, tempers the traditional constitutional emphasis with insights into the geopolitical concerns and flawed policies of the British Colonial Office and a succession of Foreign Ministers and Cabinets.[82] His examination of government documents relating to the Canadian crisis reveals why both Tory and Whig administrations found it impossible to accede to Canadian demands for self-government in the 1830s. Burroughs seeks to counter the orthodoxy that criticises British ministers and officials as 'narrow-minded and indifferent to colonies' who ignored Canadian demands for reform until the rebellions brought them to their senses. Questioning the assumption that the achievement of responsible government was inevitable, he sees the outbreak of rebellion as the result of a genuine 'imperial dilemma' posed by the tension between British interests in North America and the desire of subjects in two very different colonies for greater self-government.

The older historical orthodoxy argued that because English public opinion was in favour of pulling out of expensive, turbulent colonies in the first half of the nineteenth century, their governments ignored the problems in Canada until it was too late. Burroughs disagrees, arguing that successive British Governments valued highly the prestige, wealth and strategic power that flowed from Empire.[83] This is why Britain kept acquiring colonial possessions in this period, such as South Australia, Victoria, New Zealand; why she tightened her grip on India; and why imperial policy makers were vitally concerned with keeping the Canadian colonies within the Empire.

One reason was trade. The long-established French-Canadian fur trade remained important, but since the Napoleonic Wars the timber industry in New Brunswick and the St Lawrence districts was a key supplier for British shipbuilding. The Canadas were also Britain's bread basket, exporting grain and other food stuffs to the mother country. Finally, in a period of rapid increase in population off the back of the industrial and agricultural revolutions, Britain reaped the economic (and political) benefit of mass emigration of its often poorest subjects to the Canadian colonies where land and demand for labour was plentiful. It was in this spirit of beginning a new life in a land of plenty that George Loveless and some of the other Tolpuddle Martyrs took their families to Canada. Likewise, the Canadas provided opportunities for Irish peasants fleeing hunger and persecution.

Of course the prairies, forests and rivers made available to waves of British settlers and investment were the birthright of the native North Americans, who in the Canadian southeast had organised themselves prior to European contact into what the Europeans termed the Iroquois Confederacy of Six Nations, composed of the Mohawk, Oneida, Cayuga, Onondaga, Senega and Tuscarora.[84] Their support for the British in the Seven Years' War led to treaties guaranteeing land and, following the loss of the American colonies, the creation of significant reservations over the border in Canada for the Confederacy Nations that remained loyal.

But despite service as shock forces in the British army, the Six Nations were gradually bought or pushed off their hunting and fishing grounds to make way for 'progress' and 'civilisation'.[85] The vast unsettled North American interior to the west still beckoned, and British businessmen looked forward to the economic bounty awaiting exploitation, provided they beat an expansionist United States to these resources.

British control of the Canadas was also of vital strategic importance. Britain was involved in a succession of trade disputes with the Americans in the 1830s, and many decision makers in London remembered that a trade war had become real war between the Empire and the upstart republic in 1812. Always at the back of the British Government's mind when thinking about ceding control to elected local Assemblies was the fear that the United States might try to annex nominally independent colonies, leading to the loss of the Empire in North America. This nightmare scenario was not so far fetched, given the recent intervention by American military adventurers in the Mexican territory of Texas. The objection of the US Government to piratical acts of war by its citizens did not stop Texas being absorbed by stealth into the union. During the 1820s a chain of forts was built by the British along their border with the United States as a deterrent and to ensure that any aggression could be swiftly met.[86] The invasions of Upper and Lower Canada by American 'patriot' militias in 1838 and 1839 demonstrated that far from paranoid, the republican zealots on the other side of the frontier were a clear and present danger to British rule in Canada.

British governments continued to pay lip service to their treaty commitment to guarantee the preservation of French custom, language, land use and religion in the province formerly known as Quebec. However, by the 1830s both Whigs and Tories believed that ultimately Lower Canadians would be Anglicised, for their own good. In the meantime the Whig Government of Lord Melbourne opposed granting control of government to the French-dominated Assembly for fear that the English minority would be persecuted, leading to civil strife and the blocking of Britain's trade routes through the province.

While acknowledging in 1836 that the Canadian constitution had ceased to function properly, Colonial Undersecretary James Stephen advised continued opposition to the Quebec Assembly's demands, as they must

lead to the virtual independence of Lower Canada—to the
consequent revolt of the other provinces—to a contest between the
French and English Canadians—and at no distant date to the
annexation of the Canadas to the United States.[87]

These fears were exacerbated in the second half of the 1830s with the capture of the movement for self-government, especially in Upper Canada, by more radical elements pledged to American-style republicanism and democracy.[88] The leading radicals were William Lyon Mackenzie and Dr Thomas Morrison, members of the Upper Canadian Assembly.[89] A firebrand Scot, Mackenzie was first elected to the Assembly in 1828 on the back of a campaign against the 'Family Compact' waged through his radical newspaper the *Colonial Advocate*. After the conservative forces led by the lieutenant-governor won a majority in the Assembly in 1836 Mackenzie launched a new periodical, the *Constitution*, to promote a republican break with monarchy and Britain.[90] The republicanism of Mackenzie and his supporters within Canada and later in the United States was in no way linked with socialism or working-class improvement, but was rather seen as a way to liberate the Canadian economy from exploitation by the Empire and local oligarchs so that its entrepreneurs might pursue free enterprise. Whereas industrialised Britain had a burgeoning union and Chartist movement, agrarian Canada had a preponderance of small landholders and independent artisans, encouraging a petit-bourgeois consciousness. While defenders of private property, the proposed break with British constitutional traditions divided Mackenzie's radical republicans from the moderate reformers, led by William and Robert Baldwin. The latter liberals remained committed to the British Westminster practice that would come to be called responsible government.[91]

Despite the rhetoric of the radicals, most Upper Canadian critics remained committed to reforming the province's British institutions, including the Crown, not replacing them with an American model. This loyalty suggested to London that incremental change was the best approach, for to do nothing in the face of Canadian demands might lead to rebellion anyway, as occurred in Ireland in 1798. Liberal Whigs in the Colonial Office, such as Undersecretary Lord Howick, son of the reforming prime minister, the 2nd Earl Grey (1830–34), advised compromise and devised schemes for moving the North American colonies towards self-rule. All through the 1830s and '40s a succession of British governments had to contend with a rump of radical MPs in the House of Commons critical of the unaccountable administrations running British North America, who viewed the Canadian reformers' demands for self-government with sympathy. For the radicals, ignoring the reasonable claims of the Canadians to enjoy English political rights threatened to provoke a repeat of the American War of Independence. MPs such as Hume, Roebuck, Warburton, Molesworth and Leader and even lords with a radical past, notably John Lambton, 1st Earl of Durham, ensured that the case for the Canadian Assemblies was given a hearing in the British Parliament, to the frustration of the prime minister, Lord Melbourne. To placate these critics and advisers, commissioners were dispatched and plans drawn up, to be debated in Cabinet and sometimes parliament, raising hopes in the colonies, before being thrown in the too-hard basket.

Despite much fact-finding and soul-searching on the question of how best to balance local autonomy and central control from London, Britain's imperial interests always won out. The result was policy inertia and half-hearted concessions that satisfied no one, leading inexorably to constitutional paralysis, rebellion and armed conflict.

* * *

'UP THEN CANADIANS!'
THE REBELLIONS OF 1837-38

REBELLION BROKE OUT IN LOWER CANADA ON 23 NOVEMBER 1837, and in Upper Canada on 4 December. Louis Joseph Papineau led the French *patriotes*, while in Upper Canada Mackenzie commanded a force that tried to seize Toronto. The rebellion by the French *patriotes* was expected by the Colonial Office and Cabinet, but the uprising in British Upper Canada was a surprise. The government had assumed that ties of custom and blood would bind the colony to the mother country, but it underestimated local discontent at the corruption of government by the Family Compact.

Who were the rebels? Most of the political and military leaders hailed from the professional bourgeoisie. Lawyers and journalists such as Papineau and Mackenzie were involved and medical doctors played a disproportionate role in both provinces. Physicians among the leading rebels included Doctors Charles Duncombe, E.B. O'Callaghan, Cyril Côte and Wolfred and Robert Nelson. This makes sense, as they represented a class with most to gain from an extension of political rights, currently monopolised by the self-serving colonial aristocrats of the Family Compact in Upper Canada and the viceregal Châteaux set in Lower Canada. However, most of the Canadians who fought in the rebellions were more humble farmers, skilled artisans, clerks and shopkeepers.

In Lower Canada the rebels unveiled a radical republican program that would have popular appeal among the ordinary people and contradicts the British portrayal of the French-Canadians as backward yokels. As well as the provision of smallholdings to the peasants who worked the big estates for the gentry were a series of measures that would end British privileges. The Church of England was to be disestablished, in order that the majority's Catholic faith would enjoy equality. The land reserved for the Anglican clergy was to be nationalised, along with the huge holdings of the British North American Land Company, the principal tool of imperial economic development. The death penalty was to be abolished except for murder, while imprisonment for debt was to cease. Significantly, the subsequent Declaration of Independence by Robert Nelson specified that in addition to equal rights for the French *habitants*, 'the Indians shall no longer be under any civil disqualification'. This was not just progressive but a strategic attempt at alliance building as the Six Nations had long been loyal to the British.

Rebellions broke out at Saint-Eustache, Saint-Benoît, Saint-Charles and Saint-Denis, this last providing a morale boost on 23 November when forces commanded by Dr Wolfred Nelson successfully repelled government troops. However, British regiments responded rapidly, under the command of Sir John Colborne, and the rebels' fortunes were reversed.[92] Colborne was an old adversary of the French nationalists. Until recently he had been the lieutenant-governor of Lower Canada, standing at the centre of the Châteaux Clique, and refusing to compromise with the Papineau faction as the crisis deepened. But first and foremost Colborne was a military man, distinguishing himself as a commander in the wars with revolutionary France, and decorated for his part in routing Napoleon at Waterloo. Now commander-in-chief of British forces in Canada, Colborne would be ruthless in defending the English ascendancy that was his life's work. The Lower Canadian *patriotes* were decisively beaten at Saint-Charles, then Saint-Eustache. Despite the long gestation of grievances and many years of crisis, the rebellions were hastily improvised and badly planned.[93] Their hope that the Canadian militias would come over to the rebellion proved to be naïve, as these part-time volunteers fell loyally in behind the red coats and enthusiastically put fellow Canadians to the sword. Even without the Canadian militias, the rebellions were easily suppressed by the superiority of the British Army in terms of firepower and especially discipline: 150 *patriotes* died at Saint-Denis compared to three British soldiers.[94] Against the might of the most powerful empire the world had yet seen and a determined commander, the rebels had little chance.

The rebels were not just routed in the battlefield. In an act of retribution reminiscent of state-sponsored violence in Ireland, British troops burned villages in Lower Canada suspected of supporting the uprising and specifically 'reduced to ashes' the property of known or suspected rebels.[95] Prieur grieved the 'useless and inhuman burnings of hundreds of dwellings' and noted that 'hundreds of families have found themselves out in the street as a result'.[96] Rudé assesses this wanton 'vandalism' as a deliberate strategy to 'terrorise' the French peasants. For destroying their property, the French-Canadians dubbed Colborne 'the Old Firebrand', and commenced a protracted campaign to claim damages.[97]

In Upper Canada the rebellion was centred on Toronto, backed by an uprising in the west led by Dr Duncombe, an American who had immigrated to the province. Mackenzie commanded a lightly armed force of about 500, assisted by officers Samuel Lount, Peter Mathews, Dr Morrison and Donald McLeod, a schoolmaster. Publican John Montgomery furnished the meeting place where the uprising was hatched. The rebellion opened with an 'Independence' proclamation from Mackenzie beginning with the rallying cry 'Up then Canadians! Get ready your rifles and make short work of it.'[98] But neither the people nor moderate reformers supported the poorly organised rebellion, which was routed on the streets of Toronto in what came to be known as the Battle of Yonge Street by British regulars and local Canadian militia.

With the insurrection in disarray the leaders from both provinces made a dash to the border hoping for asylum in the United States, at that time a refuge for democrats fleeing persecution. Papineau, Nelson and Côte escaped safely from Lower Canada into New York State. On 11 December Mackenzie crossed the Niagara River into Buffalo, followed by Duncombe.[99] Fleeing the rout on Yonge Street Upper Canadian rebel leader Dr Hunter hid, before crossing into the United States, but Samuel Lount and Peter Mathews were intercepted and hauled off to face trial for treason.[100]

When word of the 1837 rebellions reached the mother country the first reaction of some ministers was to cut the quarrelsome colonies loose, so shocked were they that not only the unruly Lower Canada, but also the previously loyal Upper Canada, could breed such treason.[101] However, the

Defeat of the French–Canadian insurgents by Sir John Colborne at Saint-Eustache on 25 November 1837. Colborne was henceforth nicknamed 'the Old Firebrand' by Lower Canadians.

wiser head of Prime Minister Melbourne prevailed, pointing out that the loss of Canada would mean the loss of office for the Whig Government.[102] A compromise that balanced imperial and colonial interests might still be brokered, but not at musket point, and not until the rebellions had been quelled and a lesson taught. Once the British army and Canadian militias had done their work, the gallows and transportation would provide the lesson.

George Arthur took over from the ineffectual Francis Bond Head as lieutenant-governor of Upper Canada in March 1838. Ten captured rebel leaders were tried and condemned to hang for treason. Arthur did not waste time once death sentences were handed down, executing Samuel Lount and Peter Mathews on 13 April 1838. Hoping to calm the province down by a terrible example, he had the two men hanged at the crossroads of Bloor and Yonge Streets in Toronto. Eight more awaited the hangman on death row. In Lower Canada, executions and the systematic burning of French-Canadian property was intended to quell any thought of further rebellion, but in fact had the opposite effect. As one French rebel declared at his court martial, his countrymen 'want revenge upon the authors of these attacks'.[103] The rebellions had not yet run their course.

It is wrong to portray the British Government as wholly hellbent on revenge. As Burroughs' research revealed, a vocal minority led by Howick now pushed a Colonial Office plan for a moderate reform of the Canadian Constitution to concede some degree of self-government. Once heads had cooled and the rebels of '37 were either dead or in prison, this was the approach the government took, in part to outmanoeuvre the extreme positions of the hard-line Tories and Radicals in parliament.[104] The eminent person chosen to fix the Canadian problem was the liberal Lord Durham, who arrived in Quebec on 29 May 1838. He immediately assumed the offices of Governor-General and High Commissioner charged with devising a constitutional solution that was expected to involve the union of the two rebellious provinces.

Durham was well regarded by radical MPs and was likely the most sympathetic ear that Canadian supporters of self-government could expect from within the imperial governing oligarchy. On his arrival in Quebec they were not to be disappointed. Of the 500 Lower Canadians imprisoned for rebellion and still awaiting trial, most were set free on bail, an exercise in what Rudé calls 'commendable moderation'.[105] Turning to the eight remaining Lower Canadian rebels awaiting execution, Durham sought to demonstrate Britain's capacity for clemency by instead exiling them to Bermuda, a move that won the support of reform-minded Canadians and even some of the banished rebels. 'Were it not for the fact that we were deported,' observed *partriote* exile Wolfred Nelson, 'we could be mistaken for some grand personages embarked on a pleasure cruise.'[106] Class distinction still mattered in 1838, so gentlemen political prisoners enjoyed a very different treatment to the farmers, tradesmen, labourers and clerks who did the fighting for them. Unfortunately for Durham, his magnanimous gesture in the tradition of aristocratic pardons proved his undoing, as it exceeded the limits of his legal authority to transport from one colony to another, and was disallowed in Britain by the Whig Government that commissioned him. Refused permission to disembark in Bermuda, the eight rebel leaders went into voluntary exile in the United States where Nelson, for one, began mobilising support for their cause.

Publicly humiliated, the mercurial Durham resigned as Governor-General, and with the fact-finding leg of constitutional review completed, departed North America to write his report recommending widespread constitutional change. A one-time radical sympathiser, Durham had arrived in Quebec sympathetic to arguments for an enhancement in local autonomy, but had become disillusioned that the root of the conflict appeared to be ethnic tensions rather than constitutional principles. His time in Lower Canada had persuaded him that the ongoing crisis had less to do with popular sovereignty than 'different races engaged in a national contest':[107] 'I had expected to find a contest between a government and a people ... I found a struggle not of principles, but of races'.[108] Durham did not find in Quebec the 'democratic party' that the Westminster radicals had conjured. The agenda of the so-called 'popular party' and cause of 'dissension' in Lower Canada was 'not the connection with England, nor the form of the Constitution ... but simply such institutions, laws and customs as are of French origin, which the British have sought to overthrow'. Yet a less chauvinist examination of the *patriotes'* cause could have led to the different conclusion that ethnic and constitutional self-determination go hand-in-hand.

On his return to London Durham spurned the radicals and set about devising a blueprint for the future governance of Canada that would further advance the political rights of English settlers at the expense of the French *habitants*. His prejudices seemed confirmed when on the eve of his departure on 1 November 1838 Lower Canada again erupted in rebellion.[109] Needing a hardliner to deal with the emergency, London turned to the *bête noire* of the French-Canadians, Sir John Colborne, and promoted 'the Old Firebrand' to acting Governor-General of British North America. He declared martial law and mobilised 7000 troops against rebels who were threatening Montreal and Quebec. As recounted, local *patriotes*, like the merchant François Xavier Prieur, put up a brave and principled fight, but the numbers were against them. The main force, commanded by the returned exile Dr Robert Nelson, was defeated at Odelltown, putting the rebels to flight and bringing the rebellion in Lower Canada to its conclusion. Colborne now had to decide what to do with 855 captured French *patriotes*.

✱   ✱   ✱

AMERICAN HUNTERS: PATRIOTS OR PIRATES?

WHILE THE REBELLION WAS OVER IN LOWER CANADA, UPPER CANADA came under renewed attacks by armed American militias seeking to reignite the republican uprising extinguished on the streets of Toronto in 1837. Far from ad hoc border skirmishes blundered into by hot-headed hordes, these incursions throughout 1838 were part of a sustained American underground movement sometimes termed 'the patriot war', carried out by local fighting battalions code-named Hunting Lodges, pledged to promote revolution in British North America. Although containing a fair share of trigger-happy frontiersmen, the so-called Patriot Hunters were often commanded by gentleman officers and drew on respectable American businesses and politicians for money, guns and ammunition.[110] For this reason Canadian historian Oscar Kinchen conceived of the Hunting Lodges as a 'vast secret revolutionary society'.[111]

What led United States citizens to risk their lives to liberate the people of a foreign country? With the failure of the original Canadian rebellions back in 1837, key leaders, notably Mackenzie, and Papineau, had evaded capture and found asylum in the United States. A stream of prominent Upper Canadian rebels crossed the border into the towns of West Rochester, Buffalo and Lockport. Among their number were James Hunter, John Montgomery, Donald McLeod and Assemblymen John Rolph, Thomas Morrison and Charles Duncombe, who evaded capture by disguising himself as a woman. Lower Canadians found refuge in New York and Vermont, and included Robert Nelson, T.S. Brown, Juline Gagaon, George Cartier, E.B. O'Callaghan, Cyril Côte and de Lorimier. Here their accounts of British tyranny found a receptive audience.[112]

On the run and condemned to death for treason *in absentia*, these refugee rebels concluded that the only way to rouse the slumbering Canadians to overthrow British 'tyranny' was to garner support and manpower from the freedom lovers on the other side of the border.[113] Public meetings were organised in towns and cities throughout the border states, notably Detroit, Cleveland and Buffalo, to foment support for the cause of Canadian liberation.[114] A newspaper in Jefferson County, New York reported that:

> [l]abourers leave their employ, mechanics abandon their shops, merchants their counters, magistrates official duties, husbands their families, children their parents, Christians their churches, and ministers of the Gospel their charges—to attend these meetings.[115]

Motions were passed condemning the Family Compact in Upper Canada and the use of 'bands of blood thirsty savages' by the British to help crush the rebellion.[116] The American democrats did not quite understand the rights accorded the Six Nations people by treaty with the British in the Canadas and their role in the army. Joining the refugees on the hustings were not just local firebrands, but also prominent local merchants and politicians who supported intervention as a moral crusade, but doubtless sensed profits and votes in the cause. Papineau claimed that his cause had the support of New York governor William L. Marcy and that New York banks had offered to loan the rebels $200,000.[117] American clergy, especially Baptists and Methodists, sympathised with their non-conformist brethren in Upper Canada enduring the Church of England Ascendancy.[118] The result was overwhelming enthusiasm to assist the Canadian rebels, whether through money, arms or men. Secret societies began forming in the border states and on the British side of the Great Lakes. They set about forming militias and trained openly in preparation for invasion to liberate Canada.

Illegal patriot militias seized guns and ammunition from the local sheriff in Buffalo and in Detroit 450 muskets were seized from a gaol.[119] But frequently arms were provided willingly. An American soldier reported that 'civil officers of the Republic have supplied arms in abundance and will continue to do so'.[120] In one sense the spontaneous call to action was an example of American democracy at its most participatory and its 'minute man' tradition of the citizen soldier's right to bear arms, but at another it showed the power of demagoguery to lead excitable crowds into folly.

Research by historians of the patriot armies suggest a number of reasons for the 'patriot' intervention in the Canadas. First, an almost missionary zeal to evangelise liberty to those denied republican government and to export the American revolution beyond its borders, if needs be by force. Second, there existed a long-standing enmity to Britain extending back to the War of Independence and the resumption of hostilities in 1812 but recently expressed through trade disputes and diplomatic incidents. Some Americans were influenced by an aggrandising state-sponsored patriotism committed to the expansion of US territory across the continent. The Hunting Lodges also harvested discontent resulting from the economic depression and consequent unemployment gripping the United States. The promise that patriots might be granted land in Canada in the wake of a revolution held out to many the hope of personal improvement. Finally, there was the romance of embarking on an adventure that was especially appealing to the young.

To understand the democratic zeal that fired the imagination of the young men who joined the patriot armies it is important to understand the youthful and still revolutionary American republic of the 1820s and '30s. According to Kinchen, many of the townsfolk and frontiersmen living along the border with Canada who responded to the speeches by Mackenzie and Papineau were 'nourished on Fourth-of-July oratory to the hatred of all things British'.[121] There was a disproportionate movement into the border states of New York, Ohio and Michigan by settlers from New England—at this time a centre of idealistic causes such as the abolition of slavery, temperance and democratic reform. Like the Canadian rebels these US insurgents called themselves 'patriots', but it was a patriotism attached to a uniquely American form of republican government assumed to be universal, a one-size-fits-all model to be imposed on other countries with little, if any, respect for local political traditions. Today we are accustomed to contemporary US rhetoric about extending the flame of liberty to despotic regimes in the Middle East and Asia, but this evangelism for American democracy has a long pedigree.

Far from an ally, in the early decades of the nineteenth century Britain was seen by many Americans as an enemy and tyrant, oppressing her own and other peoples around the world through her empire and dedication to aristocratic government headed by an hereditary monarch. The American colonies had prevailed against the world's greatest power in the War of Independence, proving that might was not always right, that the ideal of 'government of the people, by the people, for the people', if defended by determined military force, could overturn the divine right of kings and defeat armies led by lords. Britain's military and economic power frequently impinged on the United States, and this led to a bitterly fought war in 1812. Against the odds, American soldiers had performed well in that conflict, and many of its still-living veterans passed on to their sons and daughters a prejudice against British 'tyranny' and the idea that a revolution must be fought for and defended. The call to arms in Canada gave a new generation of young Americans, raised in the traditions of frontier democracy, the opportunity to march in the footsteps of the heroes of the American Revolution. A veteran of the Patriot Hunters looking back to his youth from old age in 1890 recalled that '[t]he movement on our side of the border was for the most part born of the old revolutionary sentiment, implanted in the breasts of their children by the fathers and mothers of Seventy-Six'.[122]

This revolutionary tradition was reinvigorated in the 1830s by President Andrew Jackson's emphasis on frontier democracy. It was invoked when a group of self-styled liberators without government backing, led by Sam Houston, crossed into the Mexican territory of Texas in 1835 in support of American settlers who had risen against the Mexican dictator Antonio Lopez de Santa Anna. Initial successes were reversed when a detachment of American defenders, led by Jim Bowie and Davy Crockett, suffered defeat and death after a siege by Santa Anna's army at the Alamo Mission. Their brave stand against overwhelming forces and massacre at the hands of the Mexicans rallied American settlers to Houston's cause. To the battle cry 'Remember the Alamo' the Texas troops routed the Mexican army, captured Santa Anna and expelled Mexico from the territory. The declaration of a Republic of Texas in 1836 would lead inexorably to the United States annexing the territory in 1845 and a war with Mexico out of which Washington would gain California as well. American patriots resident on both sides of the Canadian border were emboldened by the 'liberation' of Texas. Like Texas, Upper Canada had experienced an influx of American settlers in the decade prior to its rebellion, and many took an active role in the first uprising of 1837. The Canadian cause, according to transported patriot William Gates, was much more deserving of the American Government's intervention than that of Texas, as the latter introduced slavery, whereas the Canadian rebels wanted democratic rights for all.[123]

Notwithstanding the undoubted idealism of the American patriots, they should not be presented as simply altruistic liberators of colonials enduring the British yoke. The United States was a rising power pursuing its own advantage in what it considered its sphere of interest. The rival trade and territorial ambitions of the young republic and the world empire meant relations between the two powers frequently clashed. In the lead up to the rebellion of 1837 London and Washington locked horns over a disputed northeastern border between the state of Maine and the Canadian province of New Brunswick, a sore point for Americans as it was originally established as a haven for loyalists fleeing the American Revolution. America's own nascent imperial hubris was apparent at this time in a government ideology of territorial expansion that held it to be the 'manifest destiny' of the United States to control the North American continent from the Atlantic to the Pacific. A steady flow of US immigrants into Upper Canada enhanced the view that the province was becoming American by stealth and that its border was porous. Just as in Texas, American immigrants would play a disproportionate role in subsequent border raids. As in the Texas incident, the cause of liberty might be used to advance the geopolitical goals of Washington—this is certainly how London viewed the patriotic fervour on its Canadian border. The rustic radicals who breached the borders from New York State to Detroit may not have easily separated the idealistic mission to expand democracy and the northward expansion of the young republic's borders. Perhaps this is why they called themselves patriots rather than revolutionaries?

Economic depression and the hope for personal advancement in tough times also helped swell the ranks of the patriot militias. The Bank of England was a principal creditor to American businesses, and anger over the financial crisis could be directed against British capital and imperial trade restrictions.[124] Unemployed men, idle, transient and restless, filled the saloons of towns on the US side of the border, providing a receptive audience for demagogues peddling quixotic schemes. Alongside the respectable farmers, craftsmen and professionals who with sincerity took the pledge to liberate Canada were a good many wastrels, criminals and men who had fallen on hard times, who hoped to profit as soldiers of fortune. Even among self-avowed democrats there was a happy confluence of patriotism with the personal promise of romantic adventure and a nice plot of land. The popular image of Houston's heroic Texas liberators would have inspired many, but the catastrophe at the Alamo should also have served as a warning.

Men of means also flocked to the patriot cause, some to risk their own lives and many to risk their capital. '[M]any of the middle classes', observed the customs officer at Oswego, 'many persons of enterprise, industry and property, are now engaged heart and hand in the cause.'[125] The *Montreal Herald* concurred, reporting from across the border in Jefferson County, New York, that 'a large portion of the men, and among them persons of the highest standing and intelligence—gentlemen of princely fortunes and of every profession in life are leagued with the Patriots'.[126]

Back in Upper Canada, Lieutenant-Governor Arthur accused American businesses of playing both sides of the street for personal gain, noting that as well as secretly stoking intervention through covert aid, 'every store in Buffalo, Rochester, Detroit' legally sold goods to the British Army across the border. Making 'thousands of pounds from our commissary chest', he complained to Colonial Secretary Glenelg, 'they can well afford to be liberal contributors to the movement which proves so profitable to them'.[127] British Ambassador Fox suspected that American capital looked to the land waiting to be exploited on the Canadian frontier, alleging '[t]hese villains [US merchants] have a deep and permanent land-speculating interest in maintaining the [Patriot] movement'.[128] Patriotism and profit were not mutually exclusive and were fast becoming the American way.

By the time the patriot militias began to form in January 1838 much of the press, including *The Jeffersonian, Detroit Morning Post, Detroit Free Press, Daily Mercury* (Buffalo, New York State) and the *Philadelphia Public Ledger* were backing intervention. The *Philadelphia Public Ledger* editorialised that '[e]very people have the right to self-government. Therefore the Canadians have the right to follow our example, separate from the British Empire, and take a place among the nations'.[129]

A partisan patriot press also emerged in the United States to support the movement for intervention, with titles like *Canadian Patriot, Freeman's Advocate* (Lockport, New York State) and the *Bald Eagle*.[130] It is clear from the accounts left by the transported American patriots that they fervently believed the 'oppressed' Canadians would rise against British tyranny as they themselves had risen, and happily replace monarchical with republican institutions.[131] 'I entered the patriot service with the best of motives,' wrote Samuel Snow, 'only wishing that our Canadian neighbours might, in the end, enjoy the same civil, religious, and political rights, with which the citizens of the United States were blessed.'[132] A veteran of the 'Patriot War' recalled in 1861 that:

> *the Canadians were thought to be ripe for revolt, if only arms and supplies could be placed in their hands, that once the standard of revolt was erected there, thousands would flock from both sides of the line, and nothing more would be required but stout resolution and good commanders.*[133]

Not only good commanders, but also widespread Canadian discontent would prove to be in short supply.

On arriving in Buffalo in mid-December, Mackenzie found that volunteers had already begun organising, such was the enthusiasm for the rebellion in New York State. Daniel Heustis, who joined in Watertown after hearing the notorious Canadian orator, later wrote of being swept up in the enthusiasm for the crusade as '[t]he chivalry of the nation was roused, and thousands of our gallant spirits rushed to the battle-field'.[134] He noted that he was in sound company as '[t]he press was pregnant with good will; thronged assemblies were convened; loud huzzas answered to eloquent appeals; and the whole people were moved as by the upheaving of a volcano'.[135]

Unfortunately for hopeful young recruits like Heustis, the rapidly assembled patriot force chose as its military commander Rensselaer Van Rensselaer, an unstable character with a high opinion of his own military prowess. With Mackenzie in tow this small patriot army illegally occupied Navy Island on the Canadian side of the Niagara River. Here they proclaimed Mackenzie as president of a provisional government of Upper Canada. Van Rensselaer naïvely believed that if the Canadian rebels could win one battle with the help of the Americans, the population would rally against the British.

To inspire Canadians to rise up, Mackenzie announced a program of radical reforms for the new republic, which give a good insight into the political aims of the rebels and their American supporters. Reforms included equal rights for all, civil and religious liberty, the abolition of hereditary honours, a bicameral legislature, an executive elected by popular election and, as a symbolic touch, a flag for both Upper and Lower Canada depicting a new moon shining through the clouds.[136] Mackenzie's declaration also revealed the libertarian, open market and modernising policy settings of the rebels. In contrast to imperial preference for British capital and settlers and monopolistic trade practices, they wanted free trade on the St Lawrence River, unfettered immigration into the province and the opening of public lands to the 'industry, capital, skill and enterprise of worthy men of all nations'. To aid economic and social improvement the government would provide free public education for all children.

The other point to the stand on Navy Island was to attract American volunteers to the cause, and this met with greater success. The sweetener was the promise to reward all who enlisted in the army of the Canadian republic 300 acres (121 hectares) and 100 silver dollars.[137] Hubristic with the euphoria of having declared a revolutionary government, albeit one confined to a tiny island, the rebels even placed a price on the head of Lieutenant-Governor Sir Francis Bond Head. Not surprisingly, given such inducements and the mood on the border, 500 American volunteers had joined Mackenzie at Navy Island by January and began training for the assault on the mainland. One of these volunteers was twenty-four-year-old Robert Marsh from Detroit, who would later be transported to Australia.

The patriots' strategy depended on the rest of Upper Canada rising in support of Mackenzie's provisional government, but instead an uprising in the London district (of Canada) led by Dr Duncombe was quickly put down.[138] This left the provisional government exposed to attack by the British, leaving no choice but a hasty evacuation of Navy Island under hostile fire and recrimination over who was to blame for defeat.[139] Yet the debacle on Navy Island would still play into the patriots' hands, when British forces opened fire on the American steamer *Caroline*. The steamer was engaged in ferrying volunteers and supplies across to Mackenzie's rebels on Navy Island in the Niagara River.[140] According to Gates, British troops:

> *boarded her while under the protection of the American eagle, killing some and wounding others of the crew; when, cutting her loose and applying the torch, she was set adrift upon the foaming billows of the Niagara, with how many souls on board to take the awful plunge of that dreaded cataract.*[141]

The surprise assault on a ship of a neutral country in the dead of night within American waters became a national, then international, incident that strained diplomacy almost to breaking point. The attack was a bloody business, with the governor of New York, William Marcy, reporting that out of a crew of thirty-three 'probably a third of them were wantonly massacred'.[142] US President Van Buren informed Congress that 'an outrage of the most aggravated character has been committed, accompanied by a hostile though temporary invasion of territory, producing the strongest feelings of resentment on the part of our citizens'.[143]

As the incident escalated, Secretary of State Forsyth complained to Fox, the British ambassador in Washington, that 'the destruction of property and the assassination of citizens of the United States would necessarily form a subject for a demand for redress upon Her Majesty's Government'.[144]

The US Government mobilised the militia along the border, and the press called for retribution.[145] Yet Van Buren was unwilling to go to war on the basis of one incident and counselled caution amid sabre rattling. Patriots like Gates were incensed that 'instead of stoutly asserting American rights', the president 'crouched … at the feet of the British lion'.[146] Another war with the British Empire was not to be contemplated. The president took legal action to ensure that United States citizens respected the state of peace that existed between the two powers and refrained from intervening in Britain's Canadian troubles. Restraining the activities of private citizens whipped up by the rebel refugees was easier said than done.

The Patriot Executive Committee in Buffalo stepped up its efforts to enlist volunteers and commission officers. Similar organisations sprang up in Michigan, Rochester, Lockport, Detroit, Port Huron and Cleveland that were openly drilling men into armies for the purpose of invading British territory.[147] Fresh from Navy Island Robert Marsh observed

> [i]t was all excitement in Buffalo, Cleveland, Detroit and all along the frontier, as well as Lockport, Rochester, and in fact, the whole country was awake; many and strong were the inducements for young as well as married men, to engage in so glorious a cause.[148]

New commanders emerged. The refugee Canadian rebel leader Donald McLeod, a veteran of the war of 1812 before becoming a teacher, was sworn in as commander-in-chief of the Western Division of the patriot army. One group headquartered in Michigan and calling itself 'The Sons of Liberty' took a coordinating role and elected its leading light, Henry S. Handy, as commander of the northwest.[149]

The US Government condemned the vigilantism along the frontier, and prevailed on Congress to pass a *Neutrality Act* in March 1838 authorising the army to use force to maintain American neutrality along its border in the face of the Canadian troubles. But many patriots were determined to observe the border only in its breach, and at their meetings denounced the US Government as a tyrant for 'abridging our constitutional rights' by enforcing this law 'at the point of a bayonet'.[150] Gates depicted Van Buren as betraying the principles of the Founding Fathers, 'frightened by the roar of the royal whelp' and 'vying with that royalty itself to crush the rising of the oppressed for liberty's sake'.[151] Whereas his government had 'winked at' the armed citizen intervention in Texas, happily exploiting Mexico's weakness, it suppressed patriot support for the Canadian rebels for fear of Britain's might.[152] Far from deterring the patriots, the *Neutrality Act* seemed to dare them to action.[153]

The problem for the patriots was that their military prowess did not match their rhetoric. With British regulars backed by the Canadian militia on one side of the border and the US armed forces on the other it is not surprising that raid after raid on Canadian soil ended in defeat. In January 1838 the patriots seized Bois Blanc Island on the Detroit River and Pelee Island on the Canadian side of Lake Erie. Demonstrating that they were indeed capable of the piracy with which they were later accused, Americans captured the schooner *Anne* to make good the occupation of Bois Blanc.[154] However, the ship proved their undoing, for when using it to evacuate the island the Canadian militia easily disabled it with heavy gunfire and captured twenty-one Americans. Handy fared no better, occupying Sugar Island, and then having to be rescued by a boat provided by Michigan's Governor Mason. As these vanquished armies retreated across the border, they were invariably disarmed and dispersed by the legitimate US force patrolling the border under the command of Lieutenant-General Brady. When a raid was launched on Fighting Island in February under General McLeod, the Upper Canadian Garrison at Fort Malden was forewarned by Brady, and threw two Canadian militias and the 24th British regiment numbering 500 infantry at the Americans. Unable to withstand the force the American patriots retreated back into Detroit, where they were apprehended by US forces.[155]

In the states bordering Lower Canada the refugee rebels Nelson, Côte, de Lorimier and Julien Cagnon followed Mackenzie's example with plans for a republic and recruitment of a secret liberation army of American sympathisers. Papineau disagreed with this illegal scheme, advocating instead that the Canadians campaign for formal US support. As with the Navy Island declaration the interventionists drew up a constitution and program of reforms. Command of the force was given to a veteran of the Texas Revolution, C.G. Bryant, doubtless hoping to imitate on the northern border the insurgency that had proved a success on the southern frontier. But when the force launched into Lower Canada from Vermont it was easily repulsed by the local militia, and the patriots were rounded up by American forces as they retreated back across the border.[156]

As a pattern of brazen attack followed by inglorious retreat formed, the Canadian press published a mock heroic salute to the American liberators entitled 'Yankee Song of Triumph'.[157] One disillusioned American prisoner named Dodge wrote from captivity to General Sutherland to warn the patriot leaders of the folly of expecting an uprising from the Upper Canadians, a forlorn hope encouraged in America by 'false reports and misinterpretations'. He insisted that:

[t]o gain the point we aimed at is utterly impossible, to prevent further bloodshed is our duty. Nothing can be gained by further hostile operations … I again implore you to separate—to return home and to abandon a cause so utterly hopeless, and as I now perceive, so thoroughly unjust.

While this letter was widely circulated in the Canadian and American press, the regrouping patriots chose to ignore Dodge's insistent advice, possibly believing it was produced under duress at the hands of the British 'tyrants'.

This first cycle of skirmishes reached a bloody climax in late February 1838, when the patriots led by Sutherland and Van Rensselaer clashed with British and Upper Canadian forces on the frozen waters of Lake Erie near Pelee Island. The patriots had seized the island located 56 kilometres (35 miles) offshore, but were put to flight by a major force composed of four British companies, cavalry and the Essex militia backed by Six Nations warriors. The Empire's patience with this wanton infringement of its borders was now exhausted. As the patriots evacuated by sleigh a detachment of British troops blocked their exit on the ice, ensuring that there would be no easy retreat for the Americans. Backed by heavy fire the British infantry charged the trapped Americans with fixed bayonets. The 'Battle of the Ice' saw casualties on both sides, including the vainglorious Van Rensselaer, who was killed along with ten other Americans.[158] Eleven fleeing and injured patriots were captured and imprisoned as they scattered into the woods, including General Sutherland and his aide-de-camp.[159] One of these prisoners from the Battle of the Ice would end up among the convicts transported to Van Diemen's Land on the *Buffalo*. Those lucky enough to make it to the Ohio side of the border found Brady and the US Army waiting.

Undeterred, patriot leaders compared the defeats along the border to the early reversals suffered by their forebears in the American War of Independence.[160] Their diagnosis was that the invasion attempts failed due to their very openness, which exposed plans to the British and US governments. Greater secrecy was needed, and better-disciplined forces that could operate covertly across enemy lines and strike with surprise. Out of the shambles of the first patriot raids emerged the network of Lodges across the frontier states in May 1838, named 'Hunters' after the favourite pursuit of many of the frontiersmen who joined up. Like Irish groups such as the Defenders, these paramilitary secret societies were characterised by the use of rituals and oaths to bind the members to each other and to guard against betrayal. Members of one lodge swore

> *to promote republican institutions throughout the world ... and especially to devote myself to the propagation, protection and defence of these institutions in North America ... I promise, until death, that I will attack, combat and help destroy ... every power authority of Royal origin upon this continent; and especially never to rest until all tyrants of Britain cease to have any dominion or footing whatever in North America.*[161]

In northern Vermont, the *Frères Chasseurs*, one of the many lodges inspired by Dr Nelson, Côte and de Lorimier and aimed at French Lower Canada, imposed a more bloodthirsty oath. In language reminiscent of the Tolpuddle ceremony designed to instil fear in farmers, recruits knelt blindfolded and swore 'to observe the secret signs and mysteries of the society of Chasseurs' and 'never to write, describe, or make known in any way the things which shall be revealed to me by this lodge' lest I 'see my property destroyed and my throat cut to the bone'.[162] As already recounted, Prieur led the local chapter of this society in Beauharnais, holding the position of 'castor' (Captain)—the French hunting word for 'beaver'.[163]

In order to prevent detection the Lodges communicated through passwords, coded argot and hand signals drawn from the hunt.[164] Pybus and Maxwell-Stewart detail code names for different ranks such as 'snowshoe' and 'beaver' and pass phrases such as the question 'Are you a hunter?' to which the answer was the name of the previous day.[165] More crucially for raising arms and men, and in the spirit of American enterprise, the Hunters, with help from the exiled Nelson, created their own 'Republican Bank of Canada', in which the patriots bought shares that could be cashed in on the liberation of Canada, and minted dollar notes featuring the heads of the martyrs Lount and Mathews and the French revolutionary slogan '*Liberté, Égalité, Fraternité*'.[166]

In the context of mounting anger over the treatment of American prisoners from earlier raids, and the commencement of 'executions taking place in different parts of Canada', Robert Marsh described 'great preparations ... being made all over the country for renewing the war'.[167] Lodges were established in Port Huron, Rochester, Buffalo, Cincinnati and Detroit, and a 'Grand Lodge' in Cleveland attracted a membership of approximately 15,000.[168] Drawing on official Canadian and American sources Pybus calculates that the total membership of various lodges stood between 25,000 and 40,000 in 1838, though she notes that some believed that membership was as high as 100,000.[169]

Mackenzie became a formal member of a Hunters Lodge but remained aloof, perhaps sensing agendas and methods that would sit uneasily with the mass of Canadians. Due to their covert *modus operandi* and dalliance with sabotage, such as burning the steamer *Sir Robert Peel*, the Hunters' Lodges were closer in spirit to terrorist organisations. Pybus astutely perceives similarities between the Hunters in their secrecy, zeal and alienation from legitimate authority and the so-called 'prairie revolutionaries' of the 1980s and '90s—right-wing extremists who resorted to bombings to protest against what they perceived as a government conspiracy against ordinary white working-class Americans.[170]

By mid-year most of the various secret organisations had merged under the Hunters banner. Notwithstanding the humble caste of most of the foot soldiers, the elected officers tended to be professional and propertied gentlemen, only some of whom had military experience.

A new general, Ohio lawyer Lucius Verus Bierce, was installed as commander-in-chief to lead the invasion of Upper Canada that would spark the revolution, code named 'the hunt in the great north woods'.[171] Agents were dispatched across the border to form secret lodges among American immigrants in Upper Canada to prepare for a proposed invasion to be spearheaded by an attack on Windsor, scheduled for 4 July, American Independence Day.

Linus Miller, a twenty-year-old Pennsylvanian law student and zealous democrat, was sent across the border to provide intelligence and to ready US immigrants in Upper Canada for an invasion. Miller's reconnaissance in spring 1838 reinforced the patriot delusion that Canada was on the brink of revolt, with him reporting, 'I was universally assured that a large majority of the most respectable Canadians were more anxious than ever for independence ...'[172] However, the Hunters were also privy to contrary intelligence delivered by a patriot who escaped from prison in Quebec to warn his leaders of 'the utter folly and hopelessness of attempting an invasion of the western district [of Upper Canada] at that time'.[173] Foolhardy optimism prevailed, reflected in Heustis' belief that '[i]f we could take Fort Henry, a rallying-point would be established, where the Canadians could muster, provide themselves with arms, and prepare to meet the tyrants who were oppressing them'.[174]

The Hunters launched three major raids between June and December 1838, from which would be netted most of the Upper Canadian transportees. The first incursion occurred on 10 June when a party of thirty-five insurgents from the Patriot Army of the Northwest crossed the border and hid themselves at Short Hills, Niagara. The officers in charge were Colonel James Morreau, and Majors Benjamin Wait and Samuel Chandler, both of whom had business interests in Short Hills and could make some claim to be dual residents.[175] Among the party was Linus Miller, who had already reconnoitred the district. About half the men were Upper Canadians or Americans now resident in the province. The covert operation was meant to be a catalyst for rebellion in the area, and carried with it the names of 526 local supporters, a rebel flag (two stars on blue emblazoned with the word liberty) and a proclamation, that read in part:

NORTH AMERICAN PATRIOTS VS THE EMPIRE

Canadians:-

We have at last been successful in planting the standard of liberty in one part of our oppressed country—Fort George and Fort Massassauga are now in our possession. Canadians! Come to our assistance as you prize property, happiness and life … This is the hour of your redemption, rally to our standard of the Free, and the tyranny of England shall cease to exist in our land.[176]

This was wishful thinking. The locals failed to rally, and it appears the patriots had a rat in their ranks, a particularly nasty and mercurial character named Jacob Beemer. Dubbed 'the Prince of Traitors' by Miller, he was likely a paid informer. Perhaps to compensate for this treachery, Beemer cruelly threatened to hang seven captured British soldiers in retaliation for the execution of rebels, before his comrades restrained him from breaching the rules of war.[177] Unfortunately, the gentlemen patriots then took clemency a step too far, releasing the relieved red coats, who promptly rallied the local Canadian militia and nearby First Nations' warriors, including Mohawks, who hunted down the Hunters as they made their way back to the border.[178] In keeping with the pantomime unreality of this operation, Miller donned a variety of disguises to evade his pursuers, and was the last of his company to be captured.[179]

Wisely assuming that the patriot attack scheduled for 4 July would now be anything but a surprise, invasion plans were put on hold.[180] In September a convention of all the Hunters' Lodges took the somewhat presumptuous step of forming a republican government in exile for Upper Canada. The 'hunt in the great north woods' was reactivated on 12 November 1838 with the chaotic moonlight raid across the St Lawrence River on Prescott that culminated in the brave, yet doomed, stand at Windmill Point. As well as 121 Americans, the other prisoners from the windmill were a mixed bag of Canadians, Germans, Poles,

Site of the Battle of the Windmill where loyalist forces of the colonial government in British Upper Canada defeated a poorly-executed invasion attempt by insurgents, known as 'Patriot Hunters', based in the United States.

French, Spanish, English, Irish and a Scot, demonstrating the widespread support among new immigrants to Canada for the patriot militias.

The attack on Windsor finally occurred on 4 December 1838, and with only 180 armed men was more a raid than an invasion. Crossing Lake St Clair from Detroit, the Hunters under General Bierce captured the Windsor guard house and put a steamer, barracks and two houses to the torch, but the expected uprising of locals again failed to materialise.[181] 'Not a Canadian met us on our arrival,' recalled Cleveland volunteer Samuel Snow, 'save a few who joined us in Michigan and some of these turned traitor soon after.'[182] The local Canadian militia based in Essex advanced on the town in the early morning, engaging the Americans in battle, killing twenty-one and forcing them to retreat to Detroit. The British military machine had swung into ruthless action. The militia commander Colonel John Prince had no intention of extending to the pirates the conventions of war normally extended to enemy troops, as his terse report made clear:[183]

> Awoke at 6 a.m. by an alarm gun at Sandwich. Rose & saw a fire at Windsor. Proceeded there with the Militia & found it in possession of Brigands and Pirates. We attacked them & killed 27 and took 20 prisoners. I ordered the first 5 taken to be shot.[184]

In fact, he had allowed the five to make a run for it as his men shot at them, almost as sport. Colonel Prince was later brought to trial for these executions, the British Government keen to calm down ill feeling in the province and repair relations with its neighbour in the sober retrospection following the end of the patriot invasions.[185]

Bierce's withdrawal was the endgame of the rebellion in Upper Canada. The local newspaper reported with some glee that 'the fast footed pirates … fled with a velocity unexampled in the annals of locomotion'.[186] Patriots trapped in Canada were hunted down by British regulars assisted by mounted First Nations' warriors. Among the dead at battle's end was the second-in-command, a Canadian named William Putnam, and another officer, Colonel Harvell, while forty-four were taken in chains as prisoners to the nearby town of London.

262

In each encounter British troops and militia prevailed, though sometimes incurring significant casualties. What had gone wrong? Unfortunately for the American 'liberators' their aggrandising rhetoric was let down by incompetent military leadership, poor logistical back-up and an almost complete absence of Canadian support for revolution. Many of the raids throughout 1838 were poorly commanded by a mix of romantic adventurers, hucksters or martinets, who put easy glory and derring-do ahead of the hard slog of tactics.[187] Historian of the patriot hunters, John Carter, points to another problem confronting raw recruits in the field: they were not good soldiers.[188] Lacking discipline or experienced commanders, the Americans, often for very noble motives, were merely playing at war, and stood little chance against British regular soldiers, backed by loyalist Canadian militia and Six Nations' warriors. To make matters worse, the intelligence gathering across the border was inaccurate, and despite the oaths and secret codes used by the Hunters' Lodges, the patriot plans were frequently betrayed by informers.[189]

Finally, and most crucially, the American patriot insurgents had to their peril completely misread popular feeling in the two Canadian provinces. Their borders and sovereignty under attack, the overwhelming majority of Canadians remained loyal to the British Crown and its viceregal administration in their provinces. Many saw the American raids as a bid to force Upper Canada into the United States, as appeared to be happening with Texas. This explains why even the liberal press rallied against the American patriots as 'invaders', 'brigands' and 'pirates', as well as the local militia's enthusiasm in repelling the invaders. While radicals had embraced the republican solution, most politically active Canadians hoped that elected Assemblies might secure control over local affairs under monarchy and within the British Empire. As Pybus and Maxwell-Stewart argue, many of the Canadian rebels of 1837 had acted to stop the corruption of British institutions by colonial officials, not to abolish them.[190] As a result of the American attacks mainstream and left-of-centre political culture in Canada would henceforth take comfort in Westminster traditions and constitutional monarchy distinct from the aggrandising democracy over the border.[191]

The patriots, raised in their native republican culture, could not imagine that British political traditions also enshrined a notion of liberty, or that the rights of free Englishmen could co-exist with inherited monarchy. The invaders might have considered Britain's abolition of slavery throughout the Empire, while the United States continued to allow human beings to be owned as property. What the Americans knew was that unelected viceroys and aristocratic flunkies ruled Canada in the name of a distant queen. If anything, the entrance of the American patriots lost the rebel cause legitimacy in the Canadas, reinforcing the idea that the radical element in the reform movement was disloyal, prepared to sell out British people to a foreign power. The loyalist *Sandwich Western Herald* trumpeted:

> *Away ye American sympathizers with the ridiculous notion of imposing upon a few and loyal people the detestable bonds of Republicanism! We want none of your boasted self-eulogized Constitution. We want none of your laws and Sovereign Mob law breakers.*[192]

More moderate reformers saw the sense in sticking with the devil they knew—better to enjoy the prestige of being subjects of the greatest empire on earth, than annexed by their upstart neighbour.

* * *

TRIAL AND PUNISHMENT

BY THE TIME THE CANADIAN REBELLIONS AND AMERICAN RAIDS had ceased some 2200 men were in custody in gaols across the two provinces, awaiting trial in either military or civil courts on charges ranging from treason, sedition and insurrection to the new crime of 'piratical invasion' enacted to deal with the American threat.[193]

Of the 855 Lower Canadians imprisoned for their part in the 1838 uprisings at Montreal, Quebec, Sheerbrooke and Three Rivers most were released, but 108 were quickly tried by court martial in Montreal between 21 November 1838 and 6 May 1839.[194] All up twelve French *patriotes* were hanged, including a student and five farmers.[195] Fifty-eight were reprieved from the gallows for transportation beyond the seas. Rudé calculated that the ratio of convictions to prisoners for the 1838 Lower Canadian uprising was one in nine, which was quite lenient compared to the Swing Riots or disturbances in Ireland, though severe compared to Durham's amnesty for the rebels of 1837, which led to only one in 100 prisoners being convicted.[196]

By August 1838, 885 rebels had been imprisoned in Upper Canada from all the rebellions and raids. According to Rudé's calculations, these included 422 from Toronto itself, 163 from London, 90 from Gore, 75 from Midland and 43 from Niagara. The number of ring leaders who fled to the United States, and under sentence of death should they return, now numbered 61.[197] British action against the border raids had netted about 270 American prisoners and more would be added after the failed raids of November and December.

Some captured Americans may have thought their citizenship of another country rendered them immune from British jurisdiction, and that they would be repatriated across the border to face American justice, but in January 1838 the legislature of Upper Canada had passed the *Lawless Aggressions Act* 'to protect the inhabitants of this province against the lawless aggression from subjects of foreign countries at peace with her Majesty'.[198] Anticipating just such breaches of their sovereignty the British administration had made sure that Americans were warned by black letter law that if they crossed the border they would be tried and punished just like a Canadian subject. As examined in detail by Pybus and Maxwell-Stewart, most captured American citizens were tried for the crime of 'piratical invasion' established under this act.[199] In fact, the Act had not yet received royal assent at the time it was used, and Crown lawyers back in London had begun to raise concerns over its legality, but the trials proceeded regardless.[200] Americans who had already emigrated to Upper Canada could be tried as British subjects for treason. Notwithstanding the publication of warnings by Canadian authorities in early 1838, few American patriots would have understood the punishments at the disposal of the British Government in Upper Canada. Nor could the American patriots have anticipated just how impotent their own government would be to halt the grinding wheels of British justice.

While most of the prisoners were acquitted or pardoned there was little mercy for the ringleaders, whether British subjects or Americans, and the latter were especially singled out, beginning with the Short Hills captives. Lieutenant-Governor Arthur himself paid the Short Hills prisoners a visit at Niagara Gaol and made it clear the Americans would suffer the full force of the law for infringing British sovereignty.[201] Seventeen captured Americans and Canadians were found guilty in an ordinary civil court and sentenced to death. Public opinion, incensed at the breaching of the border, demanded severity and Arthur judged that quick exemplary justice might dissuade further American raids. However, following the hanging of Lount and Mathews the Secretary of State for the Colonies, Lord Glenelg, became anxious that the executions of the rebels reflected poorly on Britain's claims to be a civilising force, and pressured the lieutenant-governor to henceforth show leniency. 'Nothing would cause Her Majesty's Government more sincere regret', he advised Arthur, than further resort to the gallows.[202] Still, Arthur proceeded to execute the first of his Short Hills prisoners, Colonel Morreau. Far from defusing the unrest, the execution merely stirred up insurgents on the border. The sheer volume of trials and capital sentences, as well as the novelty of ethnic French and American citizens fighting a David and Goliath battle against the Empire, ensured that British justice, not to mention her global reputation, would be judged in the court of world opinion. Lord Glenelg's next directive left no room for viceregal discretion, disallowing the *Lawless Aggressions Act* and demanding 'no sentence of death, under any circumstances however extreme will be carried into effect'.[203]

Accordingly five Americans and eight Canadians on death row deemed to be more deserving were reprieved from execution, but in exchange for transportation to Van Diemen's Land, a prospect which greeted the men with almost as much terror. Arthur was intent that the four remaining condemned men would still hang, and it was only a last-minute intervention by the soon to depart Governor-General Lord Durham, backed by Glenelg, that saved them from the noose. Ultimately fourteen prisoners from the Short Hills raid marked for transportation to Van Diemen's Land were first shipped to the Thames hulks in England (along with nine still untried prisoners from the 1837 rebellion) for processing by the superintendent of convicts at the Home Office.[204]

Miller claimed that the patriots schemed to seize the ship, *Captain Ross*, en route, but their plot was betrayed once more by Beemer.[205] There was still some hope for the prisoners. The authorities in Upper Canada expected that once in England the men would be automatically confirmed in their sentences and be immediately transported to Australia, but this plan was jeopardised by proactive petitioning by the convicts and the intervention of radical supporters of the rebellion who spoke and wrote on the prisoners' behalf, challenging the legality of their courts martial under the *Lawless Aggressions Act*, and secured legal defence for them.[206] For radical MPs such as John Roebuck and Joseph Hume the arrival of the Canadian and American rebels was the perfect opportunity to promote the cause of constitutional reform in the Canadas.

Three of the Short Hills Fourteen, including Linus Miller, were selected to apply for writs of *habeas corpus* before the Queen's Bench in London to test the validity of their conviction. Debate in and out of the court hinged on the legality of the *Lawless Aggressions Act*. Meanwhile the remorseless wheels of the transportation machine ground on, and the other eleven patriots were transferred to the hulks. It was here, as the men had their heads shaved and clothes replaced with convict uniforms, that systematic dehumanisation began 'to assimilate us', according to twenty-five-year-old Benjamin Wait. He reports how shocked the patriots were to find themselves thrown in among common criminals, 'as much as possible to the condition, character and appearance of the "world's most degraded wretches" ...'.[207] Pybus and Maxwell-Stewart emphasise the ever-present threat of sexual assault that accompanied convict life on the hulks, quoting the vulnerable young Linus Miller's repulsion by '[v]ice and crime of the most revolting nature, such as called down the vengeance of heaven upon ancient Sodom and Gomorrah' that was 'prevalent to an alarming extent' due to 'herding depraved men together in such a system'.[208]

The situation of the prisoners became more hopeless when the application for *habeas corpus* failed, the court declining to overturn their detention or sentence of transportation. The *Lawless Aggressions Act* would stand, for now. While Miller and the other two remained in London to appeal, the Home Office wasted no time in transferring nine of the eleven political prisoners on the hulks to the *Marquis of Hastings*.

Despite behind-the-scenes protests by the US Ambassador about this cavalier disregard for the rights of American citizens, the ship sailed on 16 March 1839 for Van Diemen's Land. When the appeal also failed one young American was pardoned, as a concession to US overtures that were otherwise treated with contempt. Conceding American impotence in the face of the world's superpower, Ambassador Stevenson advised the President that the British 'seem to think that if they were to interpose as you suggest it might produce the state of things we all wish to avoid e.g. more bloodshed & excitement in Canada'.[209] On 22 September 1839 the remaining Short Hills men departed for Australia aboard the *Canton*. The *Marquis of Hastings* arrived on 18 July 1839, while the *Canton*, with four patriot prisoners, docked in Hobart on 12 January 1840. Tragically for convicts aboard the *Hastings*, scurvy took hold. Benjamin Wait, who fell ill, recorded that 'hospital victims were daily increasing, until salt waves closed over thirty unhappy victims of cruelty and starvation'.[210] While Wait and Chandler recovered, three patriot prisoners died of the disease shortly after arrival in Van Diemen's Land. The *Canton* made much better time, arriving in Hobart on 12 January 1840, its convict cargo in good shape thanks to the surgeon ensuring a healthy diet and regimen of exercise.[211]

The 140 prisoners from Windmill Point were tried by court martial for 'piratical invasion' at Fort Henry, Kingston from December 1838 to January 1839. The resort to a military court was deemed necessary due to the legal question marks then hanging over the *Lawless Aggressions Act*. After weathering the succession of American raids the Canadian justice system was in no mood for leniency and 135 men were found guilty and sentenced to hang. As already related, Arthur was determined that the sentences be carried out quickly, and eleven men, beginning with Colonel Von Schoultz, were hanged before London intervened and brought the executions to a halt.[212] Sixty of the condemned Windmill prisoners waiting in dread of the gallows learned that their sentences were to be commuted to transportation.

The American prisoners from the final battle at Windsor were likewise tried by court martial, with forty-three receiving the death sentence for 'hostile invasion of the province'.[213] While five were executed, eighteen left to anticipate their fate in Toronto gaol were eventually reprieved for transportation, including the young men Marsh and Snow. Another older prisoner, Elijah Woodman, recorded his refusal to be 'cast down' in the face of this punishment 'for I am only in the hands of men and am able to stand trials that are put upon me'.[214]

Having decided upon transportation for life, officials in Britain and the Canadas began conspiring to send these prisoners *directly* to the Australian colonies, circumventing the requirement that the prisoners must first be conveyed to London. The goal was to deny the rebels contact with the radicals in the British Parliament, who would seek writs of *habeas corpus* and hearings in open civilian courts as had occurred in the case of the Short Hills prisoners. The Tolpuddle trial had taught the Whig Government how easily a political trial might spiral into mass protest and martyrdom. Yet it was clear from Lord Durham's failed attempt to exile the rebel leaders of 1837 that viceroys did not have the authority to transport convicts from one colony to another. That incident made clear that this prerogative lay exclusively with the superintendent of convicts based in the Home Office. In authorising transportation for the Lower Canadian prisoners, Glenelg should have ensured that they would first be sent to Britain but instead they were to be sent directly to Van Diemen's Land and New South Wales.[215]

As Pybus and Maxwell-Stewart's research reveals, the legally dubious alternative of sending the prisoners from colony to colony originated with no less an authority than the Home Secretary John Russell, keen to deny the radicals ammunition when the government was under fire over the looming Durham Report.[216] Behind the scenes in early 1839, senior figures within the Colonial Office and the Admiralty, in concert with the colonial governors, secured the troop ship *Buffalo*, and in July dispatched the prisoners from Upper and Lower Canada onto the Atlantic bound for Australia. While precedent said that colonial governors could not compel another colony to accept convicts, it was a fair bet that the local convict administration in Van Diemen's Land would be unlikely to reject prisoners sent by its former warden-in-chief, George Arthur.[217] American prisoner Robert Marsh suspected that their direct transportation was illegal, and concerns over the rectitude of their direct transportation would continue to be raised by the patriots and their defenders in Canada and Britain.[218]

Why did the US Government acquiesce in this cavalier treatment of their citizens? Unknown to the public, no less an emissary than President Van Buren's own son had pressed the British prime minister for clemency for those marked for death or transportation, to no avail.[219] In a letter to Arthur, the British Ambassador Fox revealed his government's steely determination to resist any pardons being quietly urged by the Americans: 'A man must be blind who would expect that British authorities should be able by gentle means to repress the detestable crusade against Canada.'[220]

Unless they were prepared to risk war, the president and Congress were impotent, save for behind-the-scenes lobbying. The two powers were already at loggerheads over the disputed border between Maine and New Brunswick. Notwithstanding its territorial ambitions, the US Government had no interest in anarchy and violence on its border or in a conflict that would cost it dearly in blood and treasure. *Realpolitik* dictated patient diplomacy. Later after the dust of the rebellions had settled and the unrest on the border had quietened down, the US Ambassador in London would commence serious representations to Her Majesty's Government to secure pardons for the American transportees.

While the American patriots' journals caricature Arthur as a cruel tyrant with a fondness for the noose, Pybus and Maxwell-Stewart paint a more textured portrait of a not inhumane leader who reluctantly resorted to executions because he believed they would stem further loss of life. He had to balance the competing demands of fluctuating public opinion and demands of the government in London, composed of both soft and hardliners. In fact, many American patriots taken prisoner in Upper Canada were judged by Arthur to be minor foot soldiers or simply too young, and were quickly returned to the United States. In explaining this concession to the punitive Ambassador Fox, he confessed sympathy for '[s]o many of these poor creatures ... killed at Prescott—so many more at Windsor—besides those who suffered at the hands of the executioner ... I felt it a duty to extend mercy to the younger culprits.'[221]

Far from a monster, uneasy was the head that wore the crown.

✳ ✳ ✳

The patriots waiting on death row in prisons at Fort Henry, Toronto and Montreal only learned of their forced exile on the eve of their departure. Impotent in the thrall of their new British masters, the diarists make much of small, furtive acts of resistance into which they read great symbolic significance. For example, on 4 July 1839 the Americans at Fort Henry celebrated by making a flag out of 'pocket handkerchiefs', which Heustis reported 'as nearly representing the "star-spangled" banner as we could conveniently make it … We had faced the enemy as did the heroes of Bunker Hill.'[222]

Humiliation would have been difficult to avoid as the patriots were marched in chains through the street like trophies in a triumph, en route to a steamer that took them to Quebec. All up seventy-nine prisoners captured in Upper Canada at Windmill Point and Windsor joined the fifty-eight Lower Canadian prisoners below decks on the *Buffalo*, which sailed on 28 September.[223]

Some of the prisoners' accounts create the impression that they remained ignorant of the ship's destination until their eventual arrival, yet this seems more likely a dramatic device. A newspaper at the time published a letter from one of the American patriots, informing his brother they were bound for Van Diemen's Land.[224] Knowing the Australian colonies to be their destination would have intensified their fears, given the distances involved and the reputation of Van Diemen's Land in particular. Snow for one feared they 'should never return to their native land'.[225] As the *Buffalo* picked up speed, Gates records the sensation from below decks, of 'being carried farther and farther from our homes—our wives—our families—and all that we held dear and sacred in life'.[226]

Prisoners were packed between decks and below the waterline in rooms 23 metres (75 feet) by 10.5 metres (34 feet) by 1.5 metres (5 feet) high, composed of two-tier box berths each sleeping eight men.[227] 'This place was to be home of 140 prisoners, during a long and monotonous voyage at sea', complained Heustis:

> *It did not afford room for all of us to stand, and some were obliged to occupy the berths day and night, being relieved at suitable intervals. We had no air except what came down the hatchway.*[228]

As only one of the French prisoners had experience of the ocean, most men succumbed quickly to seasickness.[229] Heustis reported '[o]ur situation below was extremely nauseous and suffocating ... and two thirds of our number were vomiting' while Marsh recalled the *Buffalo* buffeted by a storm:

> *the sea beating against her sides, which often resembled thunder; the ship rolling and tumbling, throwing us from side to side; the tubs for use [for urinating] ... emptied of their contents, together with the effects of sea sickness, which cause the deck to be slippery, sending forth not a very agreeable smell.*[230]

On board the Lower Canadians were forbidden to mix with the Americans from Upper Canada, being locked in separate quarters on different sides of the ship. This made sense as the French-Canadians had little English, and were a tight group owing to their Gallic and Catholic cultural bonds. For example, from the first day on board, communal morning prayer was faithfully observed by the French speakers.[231] However, one American, Benjamin Mott, was locked with them as he was caught in their province, and likely suffered from being denied the fellowship of his countrymen. Having had family in Lower Canada with access to their prison, the French-Canadians had the advantage of being able to bring aboard chests of personal belongings, including clothes, but were perversely denied access to cutlery for meals, and were demeaned by having to tear at food with their teeth.[232] The Americans had little in the way of possessions but the clothes in which they were caught, and their identity as US citizens.

Like the fourteen rebels who had suffered the indignity of the London hulks, the published journals and letters of both groups of rebels aboard the *Buffalo* were at pains to stress their distinction from the common felons from Canada that had been shunted aboard the ship. Their status as political prisoners who had acted out of principle was important to their sense of self-worth and dignity amid their servitude, and might offer the best chance of special treatment or eventually a pardon. While on the *Buffalo* they were fortunate in being under the power of a generous ship's master, Captain Wood.[233] Assessing that the politicals were not 'very bad men', he allowed them freedom from the pain of leg irons while on board.[234]

Nevertheless, rumours of a plot among the Americans to seize the ship and take it to New York City inevitably reached the ears of the officers, and swift precautionary action was taken to nip it in the bud.[235] While the official ship's log is silent about this episode related in some of the prisoners' journals, one of the officers wrote in a letter from Sydney that '[i]t was reported before we left Quebec that some American sympathizers … intended fitting out two Baltimore clippers to intercept us; but we did not see … anything suspicious'.[236] Gates boasted that by 'seizing the arms at some opportune moment' and confining the soldiers below decks, the Americans were 'determined to make an effort to stop the course of the ship and head her for New York'.[237] Snow claimed a conversation was overheard between two Americans, saying

[h]ow easily this ship might be taken by us, if we were all agreed, and that too without killing a man. We could then run into some of the United States ports, as we have an old navigator among our number.[238]

Both French and American prisoners insist that the plot was betrayed in their midst, resulting in a search, confiscation of razors and suspension of privileges.[239] Prieur reported 'astonishment' when the French-Canadians' quarters were suddenly invaded by 'two officers, accompanied by strong detachments of the marines … armed with pistols and cutlasses'.[240] Snow alleged that the informer was the Upper Canadian prisoner John Tyrrell, who was subsequently 'hated by those he intended to betray, and despised by the whole ship's crew, for his story proved to be false'.[241] Pybus and Maxwell-Stewart conjecture that this mutiny was likely discussed but never seriously contemplated, and was exaggerated by some of the American pamphleteers to demonstrate their spirit of resistance.[242]

Conditions in the convicts' 'confined and airless quarters' became especially stifling as the *Buffalo* entered the tropics.[243] Exotic insect pests began to plague the men, who began to sicken.[244] While the patriots' accounts complain about the ship's food, they were transported at a time when the captain and medical officer had a monetary interest in landing as many convicts as possible alive and in good health.[245] Nevertheless, as fresh fruit and vegetables ran out during the long Atlantic crossing, prisoners began to lose their teeth, suggesting scurvy was stalking the ship.[246] Gates lost three teeth, yanked out by the surgeon's forceps. Prieur noted that the Americans and Upper Canadians were 'more unfortunate than ourselves' observing that the 'state of emaciation and of destitution of these poor unfortunates was extreme'.[247] In the end, only one rebel prisoner died during the four-and-a-half-month voyage. He was an American named Asa Priest, and at sixty was too old to withstand the privations of the voyage. The patriot from New York State was afforded the rites of a burial at sea in, according to Ducharme, a dignified and solemn ceremony.[248] Luckily the progress of scurvy was checked when the *Buffalo* docked at Rio de Janeiro, and supplies of fresh food and water were replenished.

Finally, on 8 February 1840 the *Buffalo* caught sight of Van Diemen's Land, described ambivalently by Snow as 'celebrated as well as notorious … on the very south-eastern outskirts of habitable creation'.[249] After so long at sea, the prisoners greeted the sight of land with a mixture of relief and foreboding. This echoed Miller's melancholic ambivalence when the *Canton* arrived in Hobart Town a month earlier. As the crew cheered at the sight of land he wondered:

> [b]ut the poor prisoner, the convict, where is he? … The future, its dark and cruel uncertainty, the years of hopeless misery and woe, shame, degradation and death, haunt his gloomy spirit, and he bitterly curses 'the land—the land!'[250]

* * *

TO PLOUGH VAN DIEMEN'S LAND

IN FOLLOWING THE TRAVAILS OF THE AMERICAN PATRIOTS IN VAN Diemen's Land we must approach their published journals with awareness of the authors' political intent. The narratives of the journals fall into what historian David Callahan identifies as an American tradition of capture, tribulation, righteousness and release.[251] As revealed through Pybus and Maxwell-Stewart's close reading, the Americans present themselves naturally free in their character as well as politically, while

British subjects are deferential, even servile.[252] Yet by becoming convicts the freedom fighters became in every sense of the word subject to the abstract tyranny they sought to overturn.[253] The idea of penal servitude across the oceans was for most Americans akin to slavery, and this theme threads through the published journals of the exiles. As Northerners most of the patriots were ideologically opposed to the practice of Negro slavery that existed in their own Southern states. Pybus and Maxwell-Stewart glean in the journals a tension between wanting to score a propaganda point exposing the depths of their subjugation as slaves of the British Empire, and their personal and political need to demonstrate their democratic and 'manly' refusal to bow to tyranny.[254] It also meant keeping a rhetorical distance from the 'desperate crowd of ruffians' who composed the bulk of the convict population in Van Diemen's Land. British historian Tim Causer has argued in relation to Miller's and Prieur's narratives that the 'isolation of a distinct convict Other is a common rhetorical technique used by prisoners who insist they had not forfeited their place in respectable society through association with "real criminals"'.[255] While the Americans might object to the 'slavery' and cruel punishments such as flogging to which the criminal convicts were subjected, their democratic principles never extended to divining a connection between crimes of property and British economic policies or to seeking political solidarity with common felons against a common enemy. The patriots' sense of self depended on their separation from the convict mass around them, and in this ambition they had some support from colonial authorities anxious to avoid cross-contamination.

A total of ninety-two Americans and Upper Canadians were delivered to Van Diemen's Land.[256] On landing at Hobart Town each ship-load of patriots was subjected to an identical bureaucratic induction to the system. A clerk who took down their particulars, including name, marital status, occupation and previous residence, interviewed each prisoner.[257] Significantly prisoners were quizzed as to their crime and sentence, and their answers were cross-checked against the official warrants to determine truthfulness. In an era before photographic mug shots and finger printing, meticulous descriptions were recorded for each prisoner, including identifying scars, birthmarks and deformities. 'By this method', noted Gates, 'such a minute description is obtained, that it is utterly hopeless for a prisoner to think of escaping from the infernal clutches of those petty tyrants …'[258]

Chief among the tyrants was the superintendent of convicts, William Gunn, who made it his business to personally assess each of his charges on board ship at their arrival in the colony. The original 'indents' would be supplemented by new information such as misdemeanours and punishments during the convict's time at sea and in the colony, placing at the hands of authorities and later historians some of the most detailed records for ordinary people yet compiled.[259] As the island colony's 'Lord of the Files', Gunn was able at a moment's notice to cross-check documents to locate a convict, identify absconders or assess behaviour for the award of tickets-of-leave. Gunn's data was the lifeblood of former Lieutenant Governor Arthur's system of rewards and punishments, designed with the best of intentions to promote good behaviour, even reform, by fast-tracking the obedient and hard working into easier berths, lighter work, greater freedom of movement and eventually a ticket-of-leave, while condemning the recidivist, immoral, insolent and the lazy to ever-harder labour, tougher discipline, flogging and confinement in penitentiaries of secondary punishment.[260] Notwithstanding the Christian principles of redemption and self-improvement that inspired Arthur, convicts confronted a fateful game of snakes and ladders, where luck played a bigger part than character. Having been bureaucratically defined, the dehumanisation process continued with all convicts issued standardised apparel, referred to ironically by Snow as 'the latest improved convict fashion'.[261]

At the apex of authority in Van Diemen's Land was Lieutenant-Governor Sir John Franklin, who insisted on addressing all new arrivals. In each of the American patriot narratives Franklin becomes the personification of all that is wrong with the British Empire. Reviewing the assembled patriot prisoners shortly after their arrival, the lieutenant-governor, sitting astride his horse in his feathered hat, is depicted as at once tyrannical and imbecilic, cruel yet a fool.[262] Gates ridicules the rotund Franklin as 'his bulkiness' and mocks his halting meandering speech to the assembled *Buffalo* men as unequal to the efforts of an 'American schoolboy'.[263] Franklin had already distinguished himself in the service of the Empire as a great Arctic explorer, who had captured the public's imagination by leading his men through a bitter ice-locked winter in which he was said to have eaten the leather on his boots. Pybus and Maxwell-Stewart analyse how it was important to the patriots to neuter this British hero in their narrative, by portraying him as an effete, childish blimp of a man, swollen with gluttony and pride, a caricature of the English upper class.[264] Against this straw tyrant the patriots contrast their own manly republican virtue, which is underscored by Franklin's alleged hostility to Americans as agents of revolution. According to Marsh, Franklin indulges this prejudice, telling the prisoners:

> [y]ou Yankee sympathisers must expect to be punished. I do not consider the simple Canadians, especially the French in Lower Canada, so much to blame, as they have been excited to rebellion by you Yankees.[265]

The lieutenant-governor stood doubly condemned in the eyes of the American prisoners, for he was the nephew of Benjamin Franklin, a hero of the American Revolution and founding father of their constitution. Some patriot accounts imply Franklin's anti-American prejudice stemmed from self-loathing, the consequence of rejecting his illustrious republican lineage to become supplicant to a female sovereign. As Pybus and Maxwell-Stewart's research makes apparent, the stereotyping of Franklin for political purposes by the patriots was unfair.[266] In fact, the lieutenant-governor was diligent in keeping them in their own work parties to spare the patriot prisoners from the worst excesses of the probation system and from harassment by the old lags.

The first patriots to arrive in Van Diemen's Land were the nine transported via London, who arrived on the *Marquis of Hastings*. These prisoners became part of the old system as devised by Arthur, where after an initial period performing hard labour for the state convicts were 'assigned' to private employers. As in New South Wales, transportees with skills relevant to the local economy could find their services in demand, and thereby exercise some bargaining power on the job.[267] Thus, the better-educated or skilled convicts frequently had an easier time thanks to this public–private partnership, regardless of the severity of their crime. The Vandemonian economy was not dissimilar to the frontier states and provinces from which the North American rebels came, and like the Swing convicts in New South Wales their skills as farmers and in rural trades were much sought after. Not surprisingly many of the Short Hills prisoners secured positions with good masters undertaking work to which they were accustomed. However, the assignment system, where convicts endured the indignity of being assessed like livestock while the wealthy and landed profited from a cheap labour supply, could reek of slavery, a view reflected in a melancholy folk ballad of the time:

> Oh! when that we were landed, upon that fatal shore,
> The planters they came flocking round full twenty score or
> more; They ranked us up like horses, and sold us out of hand,
> They yoked us to the plough, my boys, to plough Van
> Diemen's Land.[268]

The patriot prisoners who disembarked from the *Canton* in January and the *Buffalo* in February 1840 encountered a very different, and in many ways more brutal, regime of punishment in Van Diemen's Land, introduced in the new year just before their arrival.[269] Following strong agitation by reformers in Britain keen to remove the taint of slavery from the convict colony, it was decided by the same Commission that ended transportation to New South Wales to replace assignment with a system where all convicts were required to perform hard labour on government road gangs for a 'probationary' period of two years. As well as stopping wealthy settlers enriching themselves from free labour, the new system had the virtue of beginning all convicts on the same rung whatever their socio-economic position, removing the inequity where a convict's punishment was determined less by their crime and behaviour, than their economic utility to settlers or the state. But as Pybus and Maxwell-Stewart detail, the new system meant a much harder time for the *Canton* and *Buffalo* patriots, most of whom possessed agricultural, trades and clerical skills that would have seen them well placed in more comfortable jobs under assignment.[270] Now they were forced to undertake the same back-breaking work as all other prisoners, chained in gangs quarrying stone and building roads and bridges, labour that was so hard some of the men would not survive.

'Probation' was a textbook case of reformers' dreams designed in the abstract going wrong in practice. In theory, as Snow explained, 'the term of our servitude would be graduated by our good or bad behaviour'.[271] In reality, the patriots discovered it was common for petty tyrants and the corrupt among government overseers to magnify any transgression or failure to perform by over-worked prisoners into misdemeanours that extended probation indefinitely or, worse, condemned the weak, the rebellious or the absconder to the hell of secondary punishment.

The prisoners from the *Buffalo* faced the existential reality of hard labour cutting and carting stone from quarries, carrying heavy logs and working as beasts of burden on the construction of roads and bridges throughout the colony. Gates recounts how to convey the stone blocks four men were attached to great metal carts by leather collars, straining like oxen. One prisoner named Smith, who was a man of some wealth in America, could not cope with the strain of the road gang. Gates reports that:

> [h]is hands blistered so that the skin peeled from the whole palm and inner surface of the fingers ... And still he was compelled to work on without cessation, leaving the flesh upon the handle of his pick ... the blood trickling from his raw hands.[272]

Another American named Lysander Curtis sickened but was made to continue work until he died. Marsh and Wright were both hospitalised through the hardship of the gangs but survived.[273] It is at this point that the narratives make explicit that the British had transformed free men into slaves. Summarising the system erected by Arthur during his thirteen-year reign, Snow conjectures that 'Pharaoh of Egypt established a more moderate system of police, and governed the children of Israel with greater lenity'.[274]

The patriot prisoners clearly suffered terribly in Van Diemen's Land, though their hardships are at times embellished in the published narratives in order to depict the colony as 'Hell on earth', as Pybus and Maxwell-Stewart demonstrate through a careful comparison with official records. Putting exaggeration to one side, the labour exacted within the penal stations and the standards of housing, food and physical punishment were sufficient to prematurely kill a number of the men, and to break the spirits of many more. Altogether eleven American prisoners died in Van Diemen's Land while under sentence, together with two who perished en route (Asa Priest on the *Buffalo* and Elijah Woodman, in London on the way home).

As well as astutely perceiving transportation to be a system of enforced labour akin to the African slave trade, some of the patriots also condemned the British for the violent dispossession of the original inhabitants of Van Diemen's Land. Snow did not mince words about the bloody reality of what had occurred, and used this shameful episode in British colonialism to tarnish the reputation of Arthur:

> *Of the six thousand natives who used to live upon this island, the most of them were hunted down and exterminated during [Arthur's] residence there; only about eighty now remain of the whole number, and they are kept prisoner on a small island.*

Given that their crimes were 'political', the patriots could not manifest the contrition required by Arthur's system. Yet as generally honest and principled men it was within their grasp to evince the moral character that was required for advancement. At first the prisoners tried to find a balance between the good behaviour demanded by the system, and sticking up for what they considered to be fair. Led by Miller, a group of patriots organised a petition to the governor asking for pardons, which was promptly rebuffed. The mistake was to petition as a group, which threatened the very system of deference to authority in the chain of command that petitioning was meant to reinforce.[275]

After the failure of the petition, some of the patriots at Sandy Bay Station, near Hobart, decided they really had nothing to lose and began hatching plans to escape. Indeed, as the patriots thought of themselves as prisoners of war rather than felons, some reasoned it was their duty to escape. In September 1840 Linus Miller and Joseph Stewart fled the station and tried to make their way to the port at Hobart Town to stow away on a friendly American whaler.[276] While captains and ship owners faced heavy fines for harbouring escaped convicts, it was a fair bet that an American captain would take the risk to free a fellow countryman. This indeed happened in late 1841 when Benjamin Wait and Samuel Chandler escaped Van Diemen's Land after a prearranged rendezvous with an American passenger ship and were the first patriot prisoners to make it back to the United States. Miller and Stewart were not so lucky. After persuading a policeman to let them go, they were eventually caught, hauled before a magistrate and sentenced to hard labour at Port Arthur. But first they were put to work on a giant 'treadwheel' where the men were required to mill grain by stepping on the slats of a device resembling a paddle steamer propeller, literally grinding down their sense of self.[277] In this torturous confinement the men were thrown together at last with some of the island's most hardened convicts, and observed at close quarters the acts 'of the most revolting and diabolic character' that had given Van Diemen's Land an Empire-wide notoriety for sodomy.[278]

This escape bid also had consequences for Miller and Stewart's comrades at Sandy Bay, who found themselves relocated into the interior to Lovely Banks Station, away from passing ships, with their freedom of movement drastically curtailed. To mark them in case they should take to the bush, the men were dressed in parti-coloured, harlequin-like uniforms known as 'magpies'. Rather than succumb to what was intended to be a 'badge of the deepest disgrace', the patriots subversively broke into laughter and danced for joy before their captors in their grotesque costumes.[279]

Van Diemen's Land was notorious for its chain of prisons of secondary punishment for prisoners who committed crimes in the colony, all cut off from the outside world by natural and man-made barriers. The most infamous was Port Arthur, the very model of a modern penitentiary when its first buildings were erected in the 1830s on a peninsula approximately 60 kilometres (37 miles) from Hobart Town. Here was the last chance before the gallows for the ungovernable and incorrigible from other penal stations. The site was chosen for its access to timber that the prisoners could saw and lug and build into ships, but principally for the impregnable walls nature had provided—the rough seas of the Southern Ocean all around except for a tiny isthmus only 30 metres (98½ feet) across at Eaglehawk Neck that could be artificially cordoned off. As if inspired by the tales of Cerberus, the infernal hound who guarded the gates of hell, the narrow land bridge was blocked by a line of savage, half-starved dogs chained to barrels, spaced just far enough apart that one beast could not kill the other. The second line of defence was a brigade of red coats quartered at the isthmus, and connected to Port Arthur by an elaborate system of semaphore signals, designed to warn them if a convict bolted from the prison. New buildings such as the 'Separate', or 'Model', prison were added as the station grew in the 1840s and '50s, and reflect in their design a shift in penal punishment from the physical brutality of the lash to mental control favoured by reformers. Port Arthur's imposing stone parapets and labyrinthine passageways connecting damp dark cells reminded Marcus Clarke of gothic torture chambers, except the torments were modishly psychological, wearing down recalcitrants through a regime of solitary confinement, absolute darkness, enforced silence, humiliating uniforms and the masking of men to rob them of identity.

Arthur thought of his gaol as a natural panopticon, referring to the circular building devised by Jeremy Bentham for affording gaolers perpetual surveillance of their charges.[280] Nearby was a church to redeem souls, where men might look to the minister on his pulpit for salvation but were prevented from communing with the men seated either side by boards that divided the pews into private boxes, lest common prayer fester into something dangerous like solidarity. On the hill was later built an insane asylum for those the system drove mad.

It was into this man-made Hades that escapee patriots Linus Miller and Joseph Stewart sailed in chains on board the *Isabella* in 1841. Immediately they were confronted by the paradox of the penitentiary's natural and man-made beauty, from its harbour and wooded hills, to its neo-gothic buildings and gardens.[281] But in the 1840s this vision splendid was aurally punctuated by the snap of cat-o'-nine-tails and the groan of the work gangs straining in irons as they cut and carried massive logs. The reality was 'gloominess, despair and death'.[282] Miller and Stewart found themselves part of a 'centipede', the slang for the two-men abreast line formation used to carry the lumber. The greater height of the Americans meant that the weight of the burden bore down disproportionately on their shoulders, causing injury and threatening premature disability. Whether out of industrial efficiency or genuine compassion, the patriots were removed to easier duties, where their education and skills were soon recognised and put to use, putting them on the ladder to privileges in Arthur's fateful game of chance.[283]

While their hardships were many and varied, the patriots as a group had a much easier experience than the bulk of ordinary criminals sentenced to Van Diemen's Land. The narratives claim none of their number was flogged, though the men were certainly forced to watch other convicts suffer this punishment, including a boy who screamed at the first strike, and 'one starving dying man, subjected to seventy two cruel lashes on the bare back' from the cat-o'-nine-tails.[284] Pybus and Maxwell-Stewart reason that some separated from the main groups may have endured this punishment, but it was the exception to the experience of the Canadian prisoners, whereas for ordinary convicts it was far more common.[285] As lifers the political prisoners were not eligible for a ticket-of-leave until they had served a minimum of eight years, yet many won this privilege in 1841 after a mere two years. This was Franklin's doing, demonstrating he was far from the vindictive tyrant portrayed in the patriot narratives.[286]

Many of the Short Hills prisoners were granted significant liberty of movement once assigned to settlers. Even the men of the *Buffalo* who came through the probation system fared better than the average criminal convict. The chronic skills shortages within the colony meant that those with relevant craft skills were able to leverage themselves into jobs as carpenters and metal workers on public works projects. At Port Arthur, Stewart became a signalman and Linus Miller managed to parlay his skills as an educated legal clerk into book keeping for the commissariat officer, Thomas Lempriere, and then into a job as tutor to his children, living in the family home.[287] Furthermore, once patriots became eligible for tickets-of-leave after a minimum of two years' good behaviour, they were able to seek more congenial private employment. William Gates found himself engaged as the manager of two very large properties, responsible for sales and security and was trusted with large sums of money.[288] Some of the patriots' employers were men of substance within the colonial elite who, impressed by the Americans' abilities and work ethic, supported petitions to grant the men free pardons.

* * *

THE LAST OF NEW SOUTH WALES

IT WAS INTENDED THAT THE FRENCH *PATRIOTES* FROM LOWER Canada would endure an even tougher regime than the Americans, for they were to be sent to Norfolk Island. This isolated prison of secondary punishment in the Pacific Ocean 1675 kilometres (1041 miles) northeast of Sydney was reserved for recidivist or mutinous convicts who committed an offence in the colony. Since the early 1800s when insurrectionists from the Castle Hill Rebellion had served time there, Norfolk Island had been abandoned, only to be recommissioned in 1825 for those deemed a danger to the good order of the colony. In this second incarnation the island's reputation for systematic cruelty and arbitrary abuse of power by its officers was built on and even exacerbated, especially under commandant John Price in the 1840s. Prieur writes of the men's apprehension at learning they were to be sent to this 'Hell on Earth' to which were consigned 'the most depraved and incorrigible of the convicts'.[289] However the *patriotes* were spared this fate thanks to some divine intervention.

After Van Diemen's Land, the *Buffalo* docked in Sydney Harbour on 25 February 1840. Here the fortunes of the Lower Canadians at last began to improve, thanks to intercession on their behalf by the Catholic Bishop of Sydney, Monsignor Polding, who came on board the *Buffalo* with a French-speaking priest, met the *patriotes* and held Mass with them in a humble makeshift chapel.[290] Prieur reports that letters from the bishops of Canada to Polding had testified to the men's character and religious needs. Since Governor Bourke's time all religions were treated equally by the government in New South Wales, affording Catholics fairer treatment in the colony. The bishop made a strong case to the governor that the Catholic political convicts were devout men who needed to be able to take communion with priests of their faith, worship that would be denied them on Norfolk Island. He also guaranteed the prisoners' 'future good conduct'.[291] The captain of the *Buffalo* even intervened in negotiations, perhaps out of concern for the men's welfare, claiming he had no time to detour to Norfolk, as he had cargo that had to be taken to New Zealand. With God and commerce against him the governor relented and the *patriotes* were unloaded and conveyed up Parramatta River to the prison stockade at Longbottom near present-day Concord. Transportation to the colony would cease two months later, making the French-Canadian rebels some of the last convicts to be sent to the original penal settlement of mainland New South Wales.

While happy to have avoided Norfolk, the *patriotes* were nevertheless alarmed at being 'thrust into the midst of the major criminals of the United Kingdom' and concerned that their reputations had been blackened by press reports emanating from Montreal that they were 'bandits ... ready to carry out the greatest outrages without a shudder'.[292] Like the Upper Canadians and all transportees, the disembarking prisoners were subjected to questioning by officials as to personal details, offence and identifying features, though in the case of the interrogation of the French rebels, Prieur detected 'the most blind and most deep-rooted racial and sectarian prejudices'.[293] Thanks to 'prejudices, false reports and ill-will ... we were both objects of terror and of hatred in the eyes of the authorities'. A *Sydney Herald* correspondent reported that the convicts' 'whole career in Canada had been marked out by murder, pillage and arson'.[294] However, the missionary-priest Father Brady wrote to the same newspaper that, 'I cannot conceive how men so gentle, so modest and so good, whose conduct arouses the admiration of all those who are witnesses of it, can have deserved so terrible a punishment', and asked that amends be made 'by assigning them to good masters'.[295] Through deeds and character the French-Canadians were in time able to overturn the prejudice against them.

The *patriotes* originally performed hard labour for the government, hewing, crushing and carting stone from the nearby rocky shoreline for building the Parramatta and other roads. For a year they were kept together at Longbottom engaged on public works around the coves and bays of what is today known as the inner west of Sydney. The accounts by Prieur and Ducharme tell of their labile experiences at the hands of the corrupt superintendent at Longbottom, Henry Baddeley.[296] On one occasion after fighting with his guards in a drunken brawl, Baddeley ordered the *patriotes* to lock up the unruly gaolers, and placed the prisoners in charge of their own security![297] Anxious lest his prisoners betray that he had creamed off the proceeds of their work, the sleazy superintendent extended more and more privileges to them, elevating them to the positions of 'overseers', 'night warders' and 'cooks', while allowing them to do extra work on the side for income. The Canadians began collecting sea shells, which they sold to lime manufacturers, using the money to purchase superior food stuffs.[298] In pursuit of business opportunities, colonial Sydney was accustomed to turning a blind eye.

While the *patriotes* suffered daily the arbitrary tyranny wielded over them by small-time corrupt officials, they had a much easier time than the Americans and Upper Canadians who endured being part of road gangs in the probation stations. Effectively running their own prison, the men were soon cooking French stews, baking bread, and later even branched into wine making.[299] Only two French-Canadians died while serving their sentences in New South Wales—Joseph Dumouchelle and Ignace-Gabriel Chevrefils—compared to the eleven patriots who perished in Van Diemen's Land. Only one of them tried to escape—a merchant from Saint Césaire who was engaged as the clerk at Longbottom. He hid on a French whaler in September 1842 and made good his getaway.

Why were the *patriotes* less resistant to British authority than the Americans? The more tolerable conditions in Sydney, and their shared religious faith, stopped the *patriotes* from losing hope that their circumstances would improve. Notwithstanding their participation in rebellion, the French-Canadians were practised in the ways of

Etching depicting convicts pulling handcarts at Port Arthur—
some of the American patriots would not survive the hard labour
they were forced to endure in Van Diemen's Land.

deference and hierarchy, and kept their heads down in the hope that good behaviour would secure them pardons.[300] As British subjects, a pardon was the only way the Lower Canadians could return to their homeland, for to escape would mean permanent exile in the United States, another Anglo culture. By contrast, the Americans, coming from an activist democratic culture, were forthright in defending their rights, and regarded themselves as enemy combatants honour-bound to escape.

After working at Longbottom for less than a year, the Lower Canadians were eligible for assignment, and were distributed to private employers who were keen to harness men possessing a range of agricultural, trades and clerical skills. It was not long until good behaviour and industry earned all of them their tickets-of-leave, after which they sought jobs where they might earn money to pay for the journey back to Canada in the event of pardons being granted. Prieur found work as a baker, a candle maker and later went into business with other *patriote* exiles in the timber trade.

Despite their economic participation, the French-Canadians continued to suffer from cultural alienation within the Anglo-Celtic colony. The 'manner and habits of the people', observed Prieur, 'all appeared strange to us, and made us sigh for and wish for our native land'.[301] Ducharme was shocked by the random violence and drunkenness on the streets of Sydney. The one life raft of familiarity was the Catholic religion, which had 'the same doctrine, the same sentiments, the same charity, even the same language as in our Canadian clergy'. Nevertheless, the melancholy of homesickness began to weigh heavily on the *patriotes*.

✱ ✱ ✱

HOMEWARD BOUND

AS WITH THE TOLPUDDLE MARTYRS BOTH THE FRENCH-CANADIANS, the American and Upper Canadian prisoners had backers energetic in seeking their release. While never generating the mass rallies held in support of the Dorchester labourers, the *patriotes* had influential and skilled politicians, businessmen and diplomats working behind the scenes in the Canadas, the United States and Britain. They were eventually pardoned, but it was a piecemeal and tortuous process, frustrated by distance, poverty and the whims of officials back in the Australian colonies.

By the early 1840s United States diplomats were engaged in serious lobbying with British ministers to secure pardons for the American prisoners in Van Diemen's Land. Aaron Dressser and Stephen Wright won free pardons and a sum of money in June 1843 as a reward for capturing two notorious bushrangers.[302] In 1844 the US Ambassador, through a direct appeal to the British Tory prime minister, Sir Robert Peel, secured free pardons for half the patriots. But the actual pardons took many months to arrive in Australia, and when they did the new Vandemonian viceroy, Eardley-Wilmot, exercised his prerogative to withhold pardons from some of the men as punishment for misdemeanours committed in the colony. One of these was Linus Miller, but when he threatened to sue the authorities for wrongful detention the governor reconsidered and he was presented with his pardon the next day. But others, including William Gates, had to cool their heels.

Even when the pardons came the prisoners faced the problem of raising the fee for the passage back home from their parsimonious earnings. The colonial administration, supposedly so effective in tracking and identifying convicts, could be mysteriously inefficient when it came to setting its charges free. Poor John Berry, an Upper Canadian from Elizabethtown pardoned in October 1844, did not learn of his freedom until 1857, and was the last patriot to return home in July 1860. Interestingly given the antipathy to colonial Australia apparent in the published accounts, somewhere between ten and fifteen patriots captured in Upper Canada chose to remain in the Australian colonies, anchored here through marriage or opportunities for economic advancement. William Gates enjoyed working as a shepherd in Victoria, but when pardoned used his earnings to secure passage on a whaler bound for New England. He finally stepped back onto his beloved American soil on 31 May 1848, nearly a decade after setting off across the St Lawrence to liberate Canada:[303]

> ... here I was again, in the land of the free ... For almost ten long years ... had I been forced away—doomed to a life worse than slavery, compelled to bow to suffering that seemed to quite crush the

*spirit ... and still I had been spared—how miraculously!—to return
again to my kindred and my home.*[304]

Whereas the American journals are distinguished by a quite
strident and evangelical patriotism, the overriding tone in the journals
of the two French-Canadians, Prieur and Ducharme, is homesickness
for the Gallic village life they left behind, the loved ones pining for them
and the North American landscape. In New South Wales they find
themselves soul sick in an English culture they find to be materialistic,
irreligious and coarse. A folk song, *Un Canadien Errant*, about the exiled
patriotes composed in Lower Canada in 1842 by a young university
student evokes the same feeling of melancholia and nostalgia caused by
separation from community and environment.[305] The journals leave the
reader with a profound sense of the distinctiveness of French-Canadian
culture, balanced with the now-contrite authors' willingness to be loyal
subjects in their difference.

The *patriotes* in New South Wales owed their pardons to the tireless
agitation of the *Association de la délivrance* back in Canada.[306] Thirty-
eight pardoned French-Canadians who possessed resources to pay their
passage departed Sydney on the ship *Achilles* in 1844. But many could
not afford the steep fare, in part due to wages wrongfully withheld by
wealthy employers to whom they were assigned.[307] Prieur was one who
had insufficient funds to leave with his friends. He records how:

*[e]very Sunday, I would go and spend my afternoons on a rock in
an isolated little inlet in Sydney harbour, and there I dreamed of my
country and my family. It was as if my eyes followed in the wake
of the ship that carried away my lucky companions. My thoughts
accompanied that ship across the seas and up the St. Lawrence ...*[308]

In fact, money was raised by supporters back in Lower Canada via
the *Association de la délivrance*, to bring the exiles back home, but in
these pre-telegraph times it proved difficult to transfer these funds to
the colony.

By the late 1840s all fifty-five surviving *patriotes* had left New
South Wales, except for one man, Joseph Marceau, who elected to

remain behind.[309] A widower from Saint Cyprien whose uncle had been an officer under Napoleon, Marceau fell in love with an Australian girl, married and settled in the town of Dapto, in the Illawarra district 95 kilometres (59 miles) south of Sydney. The Marceaus became market gardeners and proprietors of a local grocery store, and had eleven children. Joseph died at the age of seventy-six in 1883, and was buried in the old Catholic cemetery, in rough scrub west of the town, where his grave and that of the wife he gave up Canada for are still visited by their legion of Australian descendants.

Prieur eventually secured passage back to Canada via London through the generosity of a French merchant for whom he worked in Sydney. It was certainly the case that while the French-Canadians suffered their share of prejudice and cruelty, they also won the respect and friendship of many leading people who became benefactors and tireless advocates for their freedom. He arrived in Montreal in September 1846, eight years after his imprisonment. Returning to the family home in the village of Saint-Polycarpe at 2 am in the dead of night, his overjoyed parents exclaimed at the door 'It's Xavier! ... It is he ... Yes, yes, our dear boy!' Noting candlelights moving around their neighbour's cottage, the villagers 'from miles around' lit their own candles, left their warm beds, dressed and made their way to the Prieurs', to welcome home the prodigal son. 'It is good to be here, my Canada, parish of my birth,' a grateful Prieur declared: 'Here I find again my parents, the friends of my childhood and my youth. O God full of kindness, blessed be thou!'[310]

*　*　*

CANADA AFTER THE REBELLIONS

YET THE *PATRIOTE* EXILES RETURNED TO A CANADA IN WHICH traditional French customs and institutions and the cyclical continuities of rural village life were under threat from Britain as never before. Lord Durham's *Report on the Affairs of British North America*, released on 4 February 1839, foreshadowed the assimilation of the French in Lower Canada into a larger Anglosphere, beginning with a new constitution designed to politically neuter French-speaking voters. Disillusioned with what he saw as the conservative character of French institutions, and sharing his countrymen's prejudice against the 'old enemy', Durham candidly welcomed the marginalisation of the French in Lower Canada, advising that:

> it must henceforth be the first and steady purpose of the British Government to establish an English population, with English laws and language, in this Province, and to trust its government to none, but a decidedly English Legislature.[311]

Colonial Secretary Lord John Russell and his government could not but agree, arguing that 'the end & consequence of the rebellion' must be 'the absorption of the French People & the destruction of their peculiar laws & institutions'. The prime minister cynically advised that a constitution must be devised that did not appear to be subjecting the French to a minority in Lower Canada. The solution recommended was a federal union of Lower and Upper Canada that would ensure that the predominantly British colonists from the other provinces had the numbers.[312] Durham dressed up the deal with the rhetoric of the liberal imperialist, intent on spreading the light of British civilisation to those less fortunate. Recycling arguments about progress that the Empire had already deployed against native Americans and Indigenous Australians, he condemned the 'hopeless inferiority' of the French *habitants*, explaining that it is 'to elevate them from that inferiority that I desire to give the Canadians our English character'.[313] While responsible government would eventually be the practical outcome of the constitution Durham put in train, the aim was the end of the separate Gallic identity in North America and the commercialisation of customary French land rights.

What was the constitutional make-over Durham recommended? To give the British a majority, Upper and Lower Canada were to be unified in the one province, by act of the imperial parliament. A single Assembly would draw from both Upper and Lower Canada. More progressively, Durham believed that the only way to end the continual clash of elected Assembly and the governor's Executive was to introduce to Canada the convention of Cabinet government that operated in Westminster, whereby the ministers who administered government must command the confidence of a majority in parliament.[314] But how to ensure self-government did not lead to the break-up of the Empire? First, Durham envisaged a powerful role for the governor as head of the Executive Council and arbiter-in-chief, commissioning ministers with the confidence of the house, analogous to the power still exercised at this time by the monarch in Westminster. This was responsible government lite, and during the 1840s London and her viceroys would have the wriggle room to frustrate the Assembly's control of Cabinet. Ultimately however, in the rough and tumble of Canadian Assemblies, the discretion of the governor was sidelined and the fuller version of responsible government became common practice.

Durham's second compromise was to divide power between the colonial and British governments, with London retaining control of matters of imperial concern such as foreign relations, trade, land grants and future constitutional change. This demarcation of responsibilities, while far short of what some vocal Canadian nationalists wanted, was far-sighted and would become a model for other colonies of settlement in the second half of the nineteenth century. Back in London, the Whig Government introduced into parliament legislation to unify the two provinces, but lost its nerve in July 1839 as incursions by the American patriot armies continued to destabilise Upper Canada.

In order to placate discontent on the ground and avoid further dissension in the two provinces, London embarked on a process of genuine consultation with the colonists' Assemblies.[315] The rebellions and hapless border raids may have been easily suppressed, but in the end they had succeeded in bringing a great empire to the constitutional bargaining table. For this sensitive task London appointed a Governor-General of liberal views, Whig politician Charles Poulett Thomson in place of the confrontational Colborne. Offering a mix of much needed social and municipal reform, and the carrot of a large British loan to pay for infrastructure, Poulett Thomson won the support of a majority in the Upper Canadian Assembly for union. The Lower Canadians remained unimpressed, but their views were not canvassed. At Westminster a bill unifying the two provinces into the United Province of Canada was passed into law in 1840 with the support of both Whigs and Tories.[316] While distinct provincial institutions continued in the former provinces, power in the new union rested with a new Assembly in which the now renamed territories of Canada East and Canada West had equal representation, notwithstanding the expectation that electors of British ethnicity would form the majority. But the assimilationist agenda was revealed in a law decreeing parliamentary business be conducted 'in English only'.[317]

Burroughs cautions against the view propagated with hindsight in Whig imperial histories that Durham's constitution resulted in the immediate achievement of responsible government.[318] In the aftermath of the rebellions, many aristocratic viceroys persisted in pushing their prerogatives and seeking to override the provincial legislatures. But colonial politicians had other ideas. Responsible government was achieved piecemeal in the 1840s by Canadian politicians backed by the voters insisting that Cabinets must be composed of members of the Assembly and survive or fall on votes of confidence in these popular chambers. Gradually the Executive Councils of Canada were recruited from Assemblymen who could command majorities and thus form a government. With popular control of Cabinets, governors and Governors-General became mere figureheads and party government analogous to that enjoyed in Britain emerged. Sir Robert Peel's new Tory Government and Queen Victoria were not amused, fearing responsible government would 'convert Canada into a republic', but bowed to evolving practice rather than provoke further civil strife.[319] That the Canadian colonies did secure responsible democratic government in the second half of the 1840s was unlikely to have occurred so speedily had not the rebellions persuaded London of the wisdom of reform and compromise. Despite forfeiting his freedom, William Gates was one who thought the rebellions 'wrought some good to the Provinces':

> *England saw plainly there was some disaffection amongst her colonists, and though she sent hordes of armed men to overawe them, still she was sensible enough to know, that unless she abated in some measure the rigor of her rule, there was little hope of long retaining them as attachments to her royal throne.*[320]

What of the hopes that the French would be swamped by British votes and MPs? Durham's constitution rapidly assumed a federal character, and ironically this provided an institutional safe haven for French-Canadians in Quebec to preserve their separate identity as part of an emerging nation.[321] Anglo-Celtic Canadians proved too divided between conservatives and reformers to form an ethnic majority, leaving the French to become a third political force, often holding the balance of power and welcomed into coalition governments.[322] In 1845 Queen Victoria pardoned Louis Joseph Papineau, who returned to his homeland and was elected to the Legislative Assembly of the United Province of Canada in 1848. The electoral clout of the French became apparent in 1849 when Governor-General Lord Elgin rubber-stamped the *Rebellion Losses Act*, authorising compensation for Lower Canadians, to the tune of £102,000, who suffered property damage at the hands of Colborne's rampaging British troops as they suppressed the rebellion.[323] The Nelson brothers were allowed to return from exile and became leading members of the Assembly, Wolfred even becoming Mayor of Montreal. In time French-Canadians, such as François Xavier Prieur's friend and one-time nationalist leader George Cartier, would even become prime ministers of the new Federal Dominion of Canada that brought together the various provinces and territories in 1867.

Durham's report had

> entertain[ed] no doubts as to the national character which must be given to Lower Canada; it must be that of the British Empire ... that of the great race which must, in the lapse of no long period of time, be predominant over the whole North American Continent.[324]

It did not work out that way, and the distinctive French culture of Quebec became a natural way to be a patriotic Canadian. Thus it was unremarkable, if ironic, when in 1875 the one-time notorious rebel and convict François Xavier Prieur was appointed Canada's Superintendent of Prisons.

*   *   *

CONCLUSION

THE INVASIONS BY THE PATRIOT HUNTERS REMIND US OF THE radical edge to the young republic when Americans had a zeal to export their revolution beyond its borders. This evangelism for the US version of democracy, rooted in the American exceptionalism and grandiose claims to lead the 'free world', still pervaded the rhetoric of its leaders in the late twentieth and early twenty-first century. It can be found in John F. Kennedy's logistical support for the ill-fated Bay of Pigs invasion of Cuba by anti-Castro refugees, in Lyndon B. Johnson's sacrifice of men and treasure in defence of South Vietnam, in Ronald Reagan's sabre rattling against the 'evil empire' of the Soviet Union, in George W. Bush's illegal invasion of Iraq to impose American-style 'freedom' and Barack Obama's pledge to stay the course to build democracy in Afghanistan.

As with more recent US crusades, the intervention by the patriot citizen armies in Canada was ambiguous, and could be read by the British subjects they came to liberate as merely a cover to advance the United States' territorial and economic ambitions. Whatever the motives, wishful thinking about Canada's potential for revolution proved a poor substitute for sound intelligence assessment and professional military planning. Historian John Carter dubbed the American patriot invasions of Canada 'uniformly disastrous'.[325] Sadly, the misreading of the Canadian popular mood by vainglorious and extremist leaders led to great suffering among the ordinary men who joined the patriot raids. Henceforth, Canadian nationalism would be framed against, rather than for, American-style republicanism, and embrace distinctively British traditions of liberty.

The failure of the rebels to win popular support confirmed that most Canadians wanted democracy on the Westminster model under monarchy and within Empire, rather than an imported and perhaps aggrandising American form of republicanism. By the end of the 1840s the liberal Lord Howick who had advised increased autonomy for the Canadas in the early 1830s had become the 3rd Earl Grey and Colonial Secretary in the Whig Government of Lord John Russell. He was confirmed in his youthful view that far from severing ties between a colony and the mother country, self-government was a way to strengthen imperial belonging.[326] He would prove much less obliging with the Australian colonies clamouring for more independence—perhaps because of their convict provenance—but still, the principle that colonies would achieve self-determination within the Empire and monarchical system was now established.

As the United States expanded ever westward across the continent, Canadian radicals would increasingly look to their local adaptation of British traditions as a mark of distinction and a political bulwark against the American way. Even the would-be president, William Lyon Mackenzie, who more than any other stirred up his own people and then Americans to risk all for Canadian republicanism, eventually made his peace with constitutional monarchy, and was welcomed back from exile to participate in the new Confederation of Canada.

As a result of the transportation of the North American rebels, the stories of Canada and Australia were for a time joined, but it is wrong to artificially separate the history of these sibling colonies of an interconnected global empire. While many in the eighteenth and nineteenth centuries never ventured beyond their villages, the local reality of staid rural hamlets was always in tension with the internationalising tendencies of discovery, war, imperialism, immigration and of course convict transportation. Empire, in particular, forged a strong bond between the colonies of Canada and Australia. In the late eighteenth century Captains James Cook and Arthur Phillip, the founding fathers of New South Wales, had both served in British wars in North America. Governor Arthur and his prisoner George Loveless lived for a time in both Australia and Canada. They were followed by the French and American patriots, and Governor Franklin would end his days stranded on the frozen waters of Polar Canada searching for the Northwest Passage. There were also political continuities between the North American and antipodean colonies. Like Lower and Upper Canada, New South Wales had a faction in its Legislative Assembly agitating for parliamentary control over the Executive Council, and three years before the Canadian rebels were exiled, Colonial Secretary James Stephen joked that the colony's democrats should be transported to Quebec to live with Papineau and his Gallic radicals.[327]

Like the transported rebels, the Canadian practice of responsible government would make its way to the Australian colonies, where it became a model for rabble-rousing democrats. The Canadian Patriot uprising spanning 1837 to '42 had an organisation and scope that dwarfs the stand taken by outraged miners on the Victorian goldfields in 1854, though in both uprisings American citizens would play a part, and democratic reforms would be gradually acceded in their wake. Britain's ready acquiescence in granting a significant degree of democratic self-government in its Australian colonies in the 1850s and '60s owes something to her experience in Canada, both of rebellion, but also the peaceful, piecemeal transition to responsible government under the post-Durham constitution in the 1840s. In the end, the hardships endured by the patriot convicts had not been in vain.

But does Australia remember the North American exiles? Owing to the superior education and literary abilities of political prisoners, historians know much more about them than ordinary criminal convicts. Yet paradoxically in popular culture Australia's transported rebels and martyrs are forgotten. The Canadian and American patriots are exemplars of this paradox, writing colourful journals of their exiles and travails to set the record straight and promote a political message, yet failing to make much of a dent on our contemporary consciousness about convict Australia. This is despite the revelatory scholarly work by Pybus and Maxwell-Stewart in Australia, and Canadians such as John Carter, in bringing the documentary record of the North American rebel exiles to life. However, the traces remain for those who wish to see.

The shores of Sydney Harbour, where the French *patriotes* collected shells to make lime, bear the names Exile Bay, France Bay and Canada Bay in remembrance of the exotic prisoners who laboured there. Visitors to the municipality of Canada Bay will come across Marceau Drive and Durham Street. In 1970, the Bicentennial Year of Cook's charting of the east coast of Australia, the Prime Minister of Canada, Pierre Trudeau, dedicated a stone plinth to the French-Canadian exiles where they had been imprisoned, at Bayview Park, Concord in Sydney. In Hobart monuments commemorating the patriots captured in Upper Canada may be found at Sandy Bay and Battery Point, the last proclaiming 'their struggle was a significant factor in the evolution of responsible government in Canada and Australia'.[328]

These humble memorials remind us that democracy in both former British dominions was not inevitable, but achieved through ordinary people making extraordinary sacrifices.

5

OUT OF IRELAND

TRANSPORTED MARTYRS AND THE MAKING OF A NATION

I am here to regret nothing I have already done, to retract nothing I have already said. I am here to crave, with no lying lip, the life I consecrate to the liberty of my country … To lift this island up—to make her a benefactor to humanity instead of being the meanest beggar in the world—to restore to her her native powers and her ancient constitution, this has been my ambition, and this ambition has been my crime. Judged by the laws of England I know this crime entails the penalty of death, but the history of Ireland explains this crime, and justifies it …[1]

THE SPEAKER WAS THOMAS MEAGHER, ONLY TWENTY-FIVE years old, yet one of the finest orators of mid-nineteenth century Ireland. He was speaking from the dock at his trial in Clonmel, Tipperary, having just been found guilty of treason for his part in leading the failed 1848 Young Ireland revolution. Uttered in the moments before the judge donned the black cap to pronounce sentence of death, Meagher's words, reminiscent of those delivered half a century earlier by another young radical, Thomas Muir, to a court in Scotland, were designed to live on and consecrate the defiant rebel's status as a martyr in the cause of Irish freedom. Though he had fired no shot at Her Majesty's forces, his treason rested in the actions his colourful words inspired in others. For the romantics of Young Ireland had gifted to their countrymen an idea of an independent Irish nation that would be difficult to kill. The British Government was mindful that Meagher not inspire the Irish people from beyond the grave, and so he would be spared the shocking traitor's punishment of being hanged, drawn and quartered. Along with six other Young Ireland leaders—William Smith O'Brien, John Mitchel, John Martin, Terrence McManus, Kevin O'Doherty and Patrick O'Donohoe—Thomas Meagher was to be transported to Van Diemen's Land, a place of both cruelty and opportunity, from where he and his fellow exiles would wage a spirited campaign to keep alive the cause of Irish nationalism.

Revolution returned to Ireland in 1848, fifty years after the United Irishmen's rising of 1798, and while the spirit of revolt was again sweeping

299

through Europe. But the decades in between had been far from placid. Beginning in the aftermath of the Napoleonic Wars, the common people waged a virtual guerrilla war over land rights. The Irish countryside was bloodied in violent protest against unfair rents, evictions and Church taxes, burdens that intensified as an industrialising England came to depend more and more on Ireland as a food basket and source of cheap unskilled labour. Land hungry and sometimes near starving peasants joined together in secret gangs, going by exotic names like 'Whiteboys' or 'Ribbonmen', to commit what the courts called 'outrages' against property and authority. Hundreds were tried and transported to the Australian colonies, cleared from their meagre tillages and delivered in chains to labour in the antipodean scrub. Alongside this 'primitive' rural resistance that historians have dubbed the 'land and tithe war' there emerged in the cities and towns a modern, almost respectable middle-class movement seeking constitutional independence for Ireland. Eschewing violence, this movement championed peaceful mass action to persuade the British Government to 'repeal' the Act of Union that had integrated Ireland at bayonet point into the United Kingdom in 1800. The failure of the 'Repealers'' reformist strategy, coupled with the devastating potato famine that cut a swathe through the rural population in the 1840s, provoked a breakaway movement that reluctantly came to countenance armed struggle to liberate Ireland.

Yet the revolution of 1848 would never quite escape its origins in the debating societies of the urban intelligentsia. Far from military tacticians, the rebel leaders were first and foremost journalists, publishers and orators—young university-educated professionals raised on stories of 1798 but untested in the heat of battle. The man at its helm was the most unlikely rebel of all. William Smith O'Brien was a wealthy aristocrat, an MP in the parliament at Westminster, and a Protestant who had everything to gain from Ireland remaining part of the United Kingdom. But as a direct descendant of the mediaeval Irish 'High King' Brian Boru, who fought the Danish invaders to unite Ireland, O'Brien felt a responsibility to end the suffering of the Irish people under what he saw as English economic exploitation.[2] His youthful commitment to the Union with Great Britain had not survived the government's tragic mismanagement of the famine. By 1851 at least a million and a half people had died of starvation and

Gentlemen revolutionaries: William Smith O'Brien (seated) and Thomas Meagher (right) under armed guard in Dublin's Kilmainham Gaol.

disease, while a further million emigrated.[3] As O'Brien saw it, Ireland produced enough other crops to feed herself, but too much was 'exported as tribute to absent proprietors' in England.[4] Animated by the spirit of *noblesse oblige*, the tall, somewhat aloof patrician believed the O'Brien family's privileged position required that he take a stand on behalf of ordinary people bearing the brunt of British misrule. Initially he worked to achieve Irish self-government through constitutional methods, but when this failed the middle-aged aristocrat forsook reformism for the radical path. At forty years of age O'Brien made common cause with Thomas Meagher and a circle of younger nationalist intellectuals who resolved that only a mass rising backed by the threat of force would free Ireland. Gathered around a succession of radical and rambunctious newspapers used to rally their cause, this new generation of Irish revolutionaries were fond of the romantic flourish, and called themselves 'Young Ireland'.

But the insurrection, embarked upon in the hopeful aftermath of a new revolution in France, ended in debacle, its key leaders arrested or forced to flee the country, the hopes for an independent Ireland seemingly crushed for a generation. The intellectual rebels of Young Ireland had invented a new cultural vocabulary of Irish nationalism to help their countrymen to once again imagine governing themselves, but when it counted proved incapable of the ruthlessness and military leadership required to make the new nation a reality. However, the real struggle with the British began *after* O'Brien, Meagher and the other five Young Irelanders were sentenced to transportation. For from their confinement in Van Diemen's Land, half a world away, the prisoners resurrected their cause by resisting at every turn the government's best laid plans to exile them into 'gentlemanly obscurity'. They marshalled their considerable skills as writers and publicists to bring their plight as 'prisoners of war', and therefore the Irish struggle, to the attention of the Empire and the world.

Through legal challenges, political lobbying, publishing projects and a succession of daring escapes, the Young Irelanders proved a constant thorn in the side of their gaolers and the government back in London, and won the moral and material support of the immense Irish-American diaspora. Most importantly for the future of Irish nationalism, the failed 'captain' of the uprising, William Smith O'Brien, was able to redeem himself through a dignified martyrdom, and earned the respect of his countrymen as an Irish hero. For a time he became Australia's most famous prisoner, the toast of colonial society and a catalyst for the colony's campaign to abolish transportation.

Occurring at the mid-point in nineteenth century Irish resistance to British rule, Young Ireland's bid to promote a spontaneous rising of the people brings to a climax problems of economics, governance and human rights simmering since the final suppression of the United Irishmen's rebellion in 1803, and its failure led to the emergence of the underground Fenian Brotherhood and the adoption of secretive, paramilitary tactics. While seeking to harvest the spontaneous rural discontent that filled the convict ships through the first half of the century, Young Ireland marked a decisive shift to a modern mode of resistance based in the cities that would reach its apotheosis in the Dublin Easter Rising of 1916. Crucially the movement pointed to the growing role for the intelligentsia in radical movements and the importance of cultural nationalism as a motive force inspiring colonised peoples to liberate themselves from over stretched empires. As much as fighters, revolutions need dreamers and martyrs, and this was to be Young Ireland's valuable contribution on the journey to Irish independence.

As educated men of means and leaders, the seven Young Ireland prisoners made a mark in history and are sometimes referred to as 'state prisoners' to designate their political status. However, with them to Australia came another five rebels, common foot soldiers from the working class who rallied to the cause and truly did disappear into the plebeian obscurity of the convict system. They were preceded by a constant stream of now-forgotten Irish protesters, largely tenant farmers and manual workers, whose acts of rural sabotage and formation of outlawed resistance groups were also political. Irish social protesters continued to be transported after the Young Irelanders, and Rudé calculated that altogether 2176 Ribbonmen, Whiteboys, cattle maimers, arsonists and assorted rural rebels arrived in Australia between 1814 and 1853.[5] The next big influx of purely political Irish prisoners followed the Fenian insurgency of 1867, yet another failed bid to achieve Irish independence by force that this time extended into the ranks of the army and onto English soil. Many of the sixty-two Fenian prisoners landed at Perth in Western Australia in 1868 were soldiers who had forsaken their oath to Her Majesty to clandestinely promote mutiny in the British Army as part of a conspiratorial Irish uprising. The Fenians were the last convicts to be transported to the Australian colonies, bringing to an end what Marcus Clarke described as 'a monstrous system of punishment, futile for good and horribly powerful for evil'.[6] Like the Young Irelanders, the Fenian prisoners would have the last laugh on their gaolers and the British Empire.

✳ ✳ ✳

IRELAND'S LONG LAND WAR

IRISH POLITICAL PRISONERS, IN COMMON WITH THOSE FROM Britain, divide into two broad categories: overtly political rebels, whether warriors or propagandists, such as the Young Irelanders and the Fenians; and social protesters, resisting hardships inflicted on them courtesy of their location in class relations vis-à-vis landlords, employers and local authorities.

While the political prisoners from the 1798 revolution came from all classes, those transported after the last United Irishmen insurgence tended to hail from the bourgeoisie and lower middle class. In Ireland, the nineteenth century social rebels come almost wholly from the countryside and were tenants or rural labourers and artisans—a big difference to Britain, where protest occurred in the cities as well as the agricultural areas, owing to activism among the urban working class, from machine-breaking to more modern trade unionism and Chartism. While the crimes in Ireland that may be considered social protest had similarities to those committed in the British countryside in the 1830s, there were some profound differences. As well as arson, sending threatening letters and attacks on houses, there was far more violence, including assaults on police, landlords and wealthy farmers, home invasions associated with these assaults, the forcible possession of another's land, armed assembly and murder.[7] Whereas industrialising Britain had a major problem with machine breaking in both the cities and the country, agrarian Ireland favoured 'cattle maiming' where stock was slaughtered, as a form of economic sabotage. More women, especially younger females, participated in arson and other acts of sabotage like cattle maiming than in Britain, and more females than men were convicted for protests involving fire in Ireland throughout the 1840s—perhaps out of anger and despair at seeing children go hungry in hard times.[8] But the truly unique feature of Irish rural protest was the preference for embittered Catholic peasants to form secret societies to terrorise enemies and deter informants. The Ribbonmen and Whiteboys in the nineteenth century owed their origins to the oath-bound gangs of the late eighteenth century. Their persistence must be attributed to the secrecy and collectivity demanded by the quasi-military occupation of Ireland after the uprising of 1798, which allowed the government to prosecute members of these secret societies using laws against the swearing of oaths and under general criminal laws against banditry.[9]

There is consensus among social historians that much of the rural dissent in Ireland should be analysed through the lens of British imperialism as a 'land and tithe war' between colonised and coloniser. Economic exploitation, especially by landlords, together with the tithes compulsorily collected from the mainly Roman Catholic peasants for the upkeep of the established Irish Anglican Church were common grievances directly stemming from British rule in Ireland. These causes underpinned the determination of many otherwise law-abiding farmers and labourers to pursue vendettas against neighbours and local authorities. Crimes like threatening letters, attacks on houses, arson and other activities often lumped together as Whiteboyism was deemed sufficiently 'political' for the government to invoke draconian 'Insurrection Acts' to bring whole districts to heel and troublemakers before the courts.

The seeds of nineteenth century Irish resistance were sown in both the political subjection and the economic exploitation of Ireland by Britain. Marxist historian T.A. Jackson stressed the interrelationship of constitutional union, commencing in 1800, and intensified economic imperialism. The failure of the Union may be traced to the continuation, and even exacerbation, of Britain's economic abuse of Ireland, which ensured that the colonial relationship persisted through the nineteenth century, contrary to the spirit of the Act of Union.

What were the economic causes of land distress in rural Ireland? Ireland's rural backwardness was collateral damage in Britain's accelerated industrialisation and domination of world trade. Throughout the nineteenth century Ireland was an economic supplicant, providing cheap food and a cheap source of labour to fuel England's industrial revolution.[10] Jackson points out that this essentially colonial relationship was no voluntary bargain of convenience, but a consequence of Britain using its trade muscle to retard Irish manufactures, protecting its own industries while ensuring minimal investment in Ireland outside agriculture. A steady flow of 'cheap as chips' Irish potatoes and other crops was necessary to fill the bellies of an English working class in the making.[11] The low prices paid to Irish farmers for their exported crops, and the predominance of English absentee landlords in this economy, ensured there was little surplus capital available in Ireland for investment. Return on investment dictated that even local landlords ploughed the surplus capital extracted from Irish peasants in rent back into the profitable English market.[12] The vicious circle was completed by the import of cheap English manufactured commodities that ruined Ireland's craft-based cottage industries in the cities and towns.

By remaining predominantly agrarian, Ireland remained poor, and for much of the population outside the few cities, pre-modern. Ireland's population increase from five million in 1800 to eight million just before the famine in the mid-1840s was almost exclusively in the countryside, with the biggest city, Dublin, only increasing by 50,000 people to 250,000 during the first half of the nineteenth century.[13] In the country, 500,000 peasant families still lived in mud huts in 1841. It is not surprising that even before the famine, poverty had compelled many to seek a new life elsewhere, and Ireland's migrating rural population helped swell the industrial cities of Britain and the United States. The British Empire's rather selective version of free trade systematically denied Ireland the fruits of mechanisation, urbanisation and improved standards of living, while simultaneously blaming the Irish for their own backwardness—an old imperialist's trick the British had used to malign the French in Canada, to justify their rule in India and to 'disperse' Aborigines in Australia.

Even Ireland's agriculture was retarded. According to Rudé, over the centuries of English rule, a semi-feudal system had been retained and refined in Ireland that 'ensured and perpetuated the poverty of the greater part of her population'.[14] As a comparatively recent and alien imposition, the Anglo-Ascendancy did not maintain traditional bonds between landlord and tenant farmers that persisted in Southern England. The harvest of rents was maximised by excessive subdivision, so that by 1841, 45 per cent of farms were under 5 acres (2 hectares).[15] Rents were high and landlords reluctant to provide even basic infrastructure such as fences and drains.[16] The capital flow to England meant that there was little investment in improving land and yield through 'scientific farming', such as the introduction of new technology or crop rotation and diversification.[17] Indeed, if peasants took the initiative to improve the land by means such as irrigation they would be charged higher rent commensurate with the land's increased value.[18] The small plots of tenant farmers led to a high dependence on the potato as a subsistence crop providing high nutrients for input.[19] The lack of crop variety would have devastating implications when the potato blight swept the land in 1845. Even in good years, so high were rents and so low the yields from the land, that often peasants faced the choice of feeding their families or defaulting on the rent, the latter resulting in swift eviction.

One of the great grievances of Irish tenant farmers was the 'Middle Men' system, whereby agents collected rents and their own cut on behalf of landlords, who washed their hands of any responsibility to their tenants. The persistence of this system from the eighteenth century demonstrated that while ceding political control to Westminster, there was no attempt to extend English tenant rights to all parts of the United Kingdom.[20] Contemporary commentator Edward Wakefield described the profiteering of Middle Men and other abusive land practices such as 'refusal of leases' as 'atrocities shocking to humanity and disgraceful to Empire' that led to 'the frequent risings of the people'.[21]

As if these grievances were not enough, all Irish farmers had to pay a tithe of one-tenth of the harvest to the established 'Anglican' Church of Ireland, even though less than one in twenty were of that faith. While this especially outraged and impoverished Catholics, it was a grievance they shared with Presbyterians. Tithes were also paid in rural Britain but in Ireland it smacked of the Protestant Ascendancy soaking the poor Catholics to build grand churches and keep its clergy in comfort, and was resented as a device of Anglicanisation contrary to the spirit of the Act of Union. Not surprisingly, one of the most despised functionaries in rural Ireland was the 'tithe proctors'.

The Land and Tithe War was a long, guerrilla-style conflict, lasting from the end of the Napoleonic Wars through to the 1840s. Protests and punishment in this period occurred in waves, upsurges in violence and disobedience usually coinciding with periods of economic distress and the imposition of draconian laws and aggressive policing.[22] Rudé tracked these patterns by examining trial records of arrests, charges and sentences, and transportation data such as muster rolls, ships' 'idents' and other Home Office records.[23] He divided disturbances in the 'land and tithe war' into four peak phases: 1812 to 1816 spanning the last years and aftermath of the Napoleonic Wars; 1821 to 1824; the early 1830s; and the greater part of the 1840s. These were periods of depression or recession throughout the United Kingdom, but the peculiarities of Ireland's backward agrarian economy and its exploitative system of land use exacerbated the hardship of small tenant farmers and rural workers. Wage reductions, unemployment and a decline in the price of crops occasioned by economic slumps exacerbated the burdens of rent and tithes. The sharp practices of landlords and Middle Men were especially resented in hard times. A collapse in the price of potatoes meant the grim choice of eviction or hunger. In these circumstances men and women undertook illegal activities to either obtain temporary relief or hit out at those they saw as the authors of their misery. Crunching the statistics, Rudé also noticed that agrarian protest subsided during periods of reform agitation, such as the successful campaign to extend political rights to Catholics, suggesting a safety valve for discontent.[24]

Trends in offences committed by protesters can be traced for each of the phases of the Land and Tithe War. Rudé dates the commencement of hostilities from acts of arson in Roscommon in 1812.[25] This was followed by an outbreak of armed assaults and stand-over tactics, reminiscent of the so-called Whiteboys of the 1770s and '80s. Thereafter, in 1813, Insurrection Acts were imposed on the counties of Westmeath, Meath, Clare and Limerick. These Acts were legislative innovations of the government of the United Kingdom designed to allow the Lord Lieutenant in Dublin Castle to selectively apply martial law to parts of Ireland as a precautionary measure in peace time, just as the original Insurrection Act had done in the lead-up to the 1798 uprising. Under these Acts, strict curfews were applied confining people to their homes after dark. Not surprisingly many Irish farmers and workers were arrested and transported for merely being out after sunset. For example, Philip Dwyer, a forty-two-year-old labourer who broke curfew, was transported for seven years.[26] Insurrection Acts were also imposed in the second peak period, 1821 to 1824, for rural resistance in the counties of Cork, Kilkenny, Kildare and Limerick. Again Whiteboy activity is cited in records that record charges of swearing oaths, carrying arms, as well as being out at night. Rudé criticised the arbitrary and malicious application of the curfew laws, noting the unfair case of a Limerick man named William Nix, who on going outside to write his name on his door in accordance with the Insurrection Act that had just come into force, was opportunistically arrested and transported for leaving his house.[27] On Rudé's calculations between 1813 and 1825, spanning the two peak periods when the Insurrection Acts were imposed, a total of 1160 rural Irish protesters were transported—571 to New South Wales and 589 to Van Diemen's Land. He broke down Irish rural social protesters from the later waves into 604 sent to New South Wales between 1827 and 1840, and 339 to Van Diemen's Land between 1840 and 1853, when transportation to that colony came to an end. To this he added 117 arsonists and thirty-five cattle maimers that appeared to be acts of protest.[28]

The third phase of rural protest from 1830 to 1836 is the 'Tithe War' proper, and coincided with the severe depression of the early 1830s that also triggered the Swing Riots in England. More often than not, tenant farmers paid the Church tithe with stock and crops, but as hardship began to bite peasants refused to surrender livestock. The first blow in the 'war' was struck in Graiguenamanagh, when yeomanry tried to compel seizure of cattle owned by a Catholic priest. Inflamed by sectarianism, resistance to seizures spread to Wexford, where police killed twelve protesters in the village of Bunclody. Resistance became more organised, with signals such as church bells being rung to warn farmers to hide livestock from confiscations. Violence flared throughout rural Ireland, measured in records for assault, murder, cattle maiming and destruction of property. Twelve police were killed in one pitched battle at Carrickshock in County Kilkenny and seventeen protesters died at Rathcormac, Cork. The conflict did not end until the government legislated in 1839 to reduce tithes by 25 per cent and have them collected from tenant farmers as part of their rent.

During these years Rudé found another spike in convictions for swearing oaths, carrying arms and compelling others to swear oaths. As in England in the 1830s, some of the offences relate to demanding increases in wages and decreases in rent through menacing letters, threats of and actual arson, and home invasions.[29] The resistance to tithes seemed to have opened the space for primitive collective bargaining to improve living standards in hard economic conditions. In Ireland in this period from the 1830s through to the mid-1840s violent gang activity directed to such ends was called Ribbonism, defined by Rudé as a 'catch as catch can' category like the label 'Whiteboyism' for all manner of 'outrages' by members of oath-based groups, such as assaults on police, landlords' Middle Men and tithe proctors, robbery, and even murder.[30] The authorities considered Ribbon societies to be Catholic gangs dedicated to ridding Ireland of the Anglo-Ascendancy. A note on the convict record of Francis McCanna, the last man sentenced to transportation for Ribbonism (in 1842), explained that

> *Ribbon societies are illegal combinations, sworn to obey their chiefs to take the arms of Protestants and turn them out of the country. Country delegates travel all over Ireland giving the ribbon men new signs of making appointments to meet at certain times.*[31]

More likely, the emergence of a new form of secret society in the records suggests a crisis in legitimate authority in the countryside, driven to violent extremity by intense poverty and colonialism, but seldom directed into a sophisticated modern political program of liberation.

Ribbonism persisted in the final peak phase of the Land War, from the late 1830s through the 1840s. The most rebellious counties were Tipperary, Limerick, Clare, Roscommon, Galway, Sligo and Longford and the calmest was the less-rural northern counties of Ulster. However with the onset of the famine in 1845, Ribbon societies began to peter out as a reported problem, and transportation statistics suggests a return to individual acts of protest related to the need to survive.[32] Order broke down in response to starvation, and the crime rate rose rapidly in the countryside, related to individual direct action, such as arson, thefts of livestock and the angry bashing or killing of landlords, rent collectors, police and those believed to be hoarding food.[33] Rudé concluded that rural protesters transported during the famine years were sentenced for 'individual acts of anger and despair rather than part of an organised movement'.[34] It was in this period that many women were arrested and transported for the opportunistic payback of burning houses and haystacks, especially in Cork, Kildare, Tipperary and Clare—areas hit hard by the famine.[35] Collective action, even the primitive sort practised by the Ribbon Societies, declines when basic subsistence cannot be found. Cecil Woodham-Smith, in her classic history of the famine, noted that '[a]part from terrible acts of individual vengeance, the mass of Irish people lay helpless and inert, indeed as blow after blow fell, they appeared too weak to protest'.[36]

This is not the place for an analysis of the causes of the potato famine but Britain's failure to address the problem, and determination to continue exporting Irish food stuffs throughout the 'hungry forties', helped de-legitimise her rule, especially in the eyes of a coming generation of educated political activists. One was the Young Ireland publisher and ideologue John Mitchel who described the misery of the blighted countryside in apocalyptic terms:

Children met you, toiling heavily on stone heaps, but their burning eyes were senseless, and their faces cramped and weasened like stunted old men. Gangs worked, but without a murmur, or whistle, or a laugh, ghostly, like voiceless shadows to the eye. Even womanhood had ceased to be womanly. The birds of the air carolled no more, and the crow and raven dropped dead upon the wing. The very dogs, hairless, with the head down, and the vertebrae of the back protruding like a saw of bone, glared on you from the ditch-side with a wolfish avid eye, and then slunk away scowling and cowardly.[37]

Historian T.A. Jackson, following Mitchel, observed that the potato crop failed across Europe but only Ireland was plunged into mass starvation, leading the Irish to lament, 'God sent the blight but the English landlords sent the Famine!'[38]

* * *

A COLONY UNDER OCCUPATION

THE OTHER SIDE OF IRELAND'S LONG LAND AND TITHE WAR WAS THE cranking up of the coercive power of the British state in Ireland. The 2176 social protesters transported to Australia were caught by new, permanent, paramilitary police forces and charged under draconian laws that would have been considered an unacceptable breach of liberty in England. Indeed, at the same time in the 1820s as the use of red coats to quell street disturbances and demonstrations was being phased out in England in favour of unarmed civilian policing, large tracts of Ireland remained under a form of martial law, and its police retained the military power to bear firearms.[39] The double standard owed a great deal to an English and Ascendancy prejudice about Irish Catholics that fanned a moral panic about the country's lawlessness. The Irish peasantry, as we saw in Chapter 2, were traditionally depicted in English discourse as depraved, and almost subhuman. Sir Robert Peel, when Home Secretary, referred to Ireland's 'national predilection for outrage and a lawless life which I believe nothing can control'.[40] That had not stopped him trying back in 1812 when he was appointed Chief Secretary for Ireland. Driven by a desire to reform the corruption and inefficiency he observed in the old system of magistrates, yeomanry, militias and ad hoc calls on the British Army, he used Ireland as a 'law and order' laboratory to trial a new civilian police force. This differed from the model he would later introduce into England in significant ways, justified by the renewed outbreak of rural unrest at this time.

Whereas the 'Bobbies' of London would only carry wooden clubs, the Irish constabulary were armed with guns. Where the English police detected and prevented crime, Ireland's new 'Peace Preservation Force' (PPF) were directed at lightning speed against public disorder and rebellion.[41] It was a mobile force directly responsible to Peel as Irish Secretary. As a sop to the local magistrates, they had the authority to request that districts be subjected to Insurrection Acts, calling in the PPF to effectively militarise troubled areas during the long land and tithe war from 1813 to the 1830s. Notwithstanding the 'primitive' (in Rudé's sense), isolated and frequently opportunistic nature of Whiteboy and Ribbon activity, the authorities both in Dublin Castle and back in London took these crimes as a political threat requiring this immediate and harsh military-style suppression. It was effective. In February 1822 alone, 300 people were arrested, faced trial and thirty-six were sentenced to death.[42] In 1836 the PPF was merged into a new Irish Constabulary that remained armed to the teeth and centrally controlled. Significantly police took an oath not to join any political or secret society, to guard against infiltration and to ensure that the Crown had undivided loyalty. It was this force that kept the peasantry in line during the famine, which brought the Young Ireland uprising to heel and was hailed as saviours of the country by the Lord Chief Justice.

*　*　*

REPEAL TO YOUNG IRELAND

WHEREAS IN BRITAIN INDUSTRIAL CAPITALISM PRODUCED CLASS conflict and the Chartist threat in the 1830s and '40s, in Ireland growing inequality was rightly attributed to colonial exploitation, and called forth a movement to end British rule.

Ireland's political integration into the one United Kingdom had failed to lift up Ireland's peasants. Despite Ireland electing MPs to the House of Commons in London, the Union failed to work because Britain's economic interests prevailed on the numbers. In the 1820s Irish Catholics still lacked the basic political right to stand for parliament, despite comprising 85 per cent of the population and promises of imminent reform at the time Ireland's parliament was dissolved. Many of the Protestant Irish MPs at Westminster were great or medium-size landowners, or their clients, who had a vested interest in the status quo. It was common for Irish representatives to be bought off with lucrative positions or even ministries so that they reflected the national British interest rather than those of their electors. Still a handful of Irish MPs were troubled by the persistence of colonial relations within the United Kingdom, and raised their voices for reform.

Young Ireland cut its teeth in the Repeal Association, led by the great Irish orator and pioneering Catholic parliamentarian Daniel O'Connell. Born in 1775, he was acclaimed as 'the Liberator' for his spirited campaign to secure for his fellow Irish Catholics the fundamental political rights to stand in elections and to hold high office in government and the civil service. After a five-year agitation as head of the Catholic Association, O'Connell placed himself at the centre of a national political crisis by standing for the seat of County Clare in 1828. He won, but as a Catholic was prevented by law from taking his seat in the House of Commons, thereby exposing the bare-faced discrimination at the centre of British governance. Escalating demonstrations throughout Ireland put the prime minister, the Duke of Wellington, under immense pressure. Fearing another rebellion in Ireland, the 'Iron Duke' and his Home Secretary, Peel, backed down and secured the passage of a law in 1829 allowing Catholics, Presbyterians and other Christian faiths throughout the United Kingdom to sit in parliament. 'Catholic Emancipation' reversed a century-long ban, and persuaded O'Connell of the power of what he called 'moral force'— peaceful agitation culminating in demonstrations of the popular will to achieve what seemed politically impossible. There were lessons here for achieving Irish independence without recourse to bloodshed—the genesis of the Repeal Association.

As an MP O'Connell held out the hope to his countrymen during the 1830s and '40s that the British Government might be persuaded by a mass movement of ordinary people to repeal the Act of Union and grant Ireland her own parliament and self-government within the Empire and under the Crown. He proved a canny political strategist, populist and institution builder, harnessing Catholic political empowerment to a new movement nurtured by the grass roots but reaching into the corridors of power in London. As a Catholic, he understood that the conservative Church hierarchy's acquiescence in the status quo was not shared by parish priests, and arranged that they would collect a small weekly 'rent' from worshippers to fund the organisation. From his seat in the House of

Daniel O'Connell (1775–1847), known as 'the Liberator' or
'the Emancipator', at a meeting in Trim, County Meath in 1843.

Commons he tirelessly advocated the repeal cause, while simultaneously organising mass rallies to demonstrate the groundswell of popular support for self-government within the Empire.

O'Connell agitated for liberal constitutional reform, not revolution. By the 1840s the Canadian colonies were on the way to responsible government, so why not the once independent Ireland? But whereas North American constitutional reform was triggered by violent, if unsuccessful, rebellion, O'Connell insisted no blood would be shed in securing Irish freedom. Like a Victorian era Gandhi, 'the Liberator' advocated the power of 'moral force', urging activists to turn away from a history of violent resistance and place their faith in popular actions such as 'monster rallies' and petitions. The English would be moved by the Irish people's overwhelming enthusiasm for repeal and their moral restraint and moderation in pursuit of independence. This optimism is explicable given that at Westminster he had participated in the passage of the Great Reform Act and the abolition of slavery, and by the 1840s had witnessed the impotence of the hard-line Chartist's resort to violence. O'Connell had the strength of his convictions, and was himself sentenced to one year's imprisonment for his campaign, only to be released after three months following an appeal, now a martyr to Repeal.

At the moment of the Repeal Association's greatest strength, O'Connell blinked. He had called for the largest 'monster' rally Ireland was yet to see, to take place at Clontarf as the penultimate signal that the people wished an end to the Union. But the government issued a proclamation banning the meeting, and O'Connell cancelled the event, fearing an attack by troops. Unfortunately, O'Connell's adherence to the letter of the law and abhorrence at the spilling of Irish blood meant he failed to take the tide at its height, and support for Repeal ebbed away. The limits of the strategy of peaceful protest were apparent.

Young Ireland had its origins in this failure. It was in this darkest hour for the Repeal Association that O'Connell secured the formal membership of O'Brien, who immediately became active in the movement's reform program.[43] From 1842 O'Connell had also made common cause with a network of bright young men making a mark as speakers and activists, notably Thomas Davis, Gavan Duffy and John Mitchel.[44] Through their talent as writers and journalists these men would help the Irish think of their country not as a colony but as a nation. The influx of new activists proved a mixed blessing for O'Connell, as they had their own ideas about how to win Irish self-government, and began questioning the ameliorist orthodoxy, especially the ban on violence. As well as Clontarf, the critics could point to the failure of the Chartist's version of moral force to persuade a determined government to accede to their six points.

There were other criticisms. While O'Connell strove to unite all the religions and classes of Ireland in this cause, the Repeal Association's reliance on parish priests led some Protestant supporters to fear a drift to Catholic sectarianism within the movement.[45] Clearly his nationalism had a strong Catholic flavour, and was pragmatically uncluttered by many of the philosophical and cultural issues beginning to concern the new nationalists. O'Connell was also seen to be too close to the Whigs in Westminster, a party that the younger radicals felt was as dismissive of Irish sovereignty as the Tories.[46]

The most bitter conflicts in politics are often to be found on one's own side, and before taking on the government, the putative Young Ireland tendency took on the Repeal Association. As the clamour for change became louder, the Liberator and his inner circle became resentful of the younger radicals, who in turn resented his dictatorial style. The generation gap was wide and contributed to mutual incomprehension and impatience. In 1842 O'Connell was nearly seventy, while Duffy, Davis and Mitchel were in their late twenties and student supporters Tom Meagher and Kevin O'Doherty were still only nineteen.[47] Over the next year they played court to O'Brien, who had an intellectual and increasingly political affinity with many of their positions, and shared their intolerance of O'Connell's high-handed interventions. At a vigorous forty O'Brien was attracted to the young radicals' energy and optimism. Frustrated by failing health, O'Connell responded to the challenge from the younger radicals by trying to remove them from the Repeal Association in 1846, but they happily seceded.[48] When presented with a petition by workers to bring the prodigals back to the fold, the Liberator cast it into the gutter.[49] O'Connell died in 1847 as division and recrimination engulfed the movement he had built, by which time the momentum was now with Young Ireland.

❋ ❋ ❋

The leading lights of this new movement were Thomas Davis, Gavan Duffy, James Finton Lalor and John Mitchel, ably assisted by the even younger Thomas Meagher and Kevin O'Doherty. There were women too, notably the nationalist poet-activists Mary Ann Kelly, known by the *nom de plume* 'Eva', and Jane Elgee, writing as 'Speranza', and later to be Lady Wilde, mother of Oscar.[50] The leaders were all propertied gentlemen by background, education and career trajectory but they were religiously an ecumenical network, combining Presbyterian non-conformists from the north with Catholics from Dublin and other urban centres. Divergence of origin suited this group's passion for a united rather than sectarian Ireland. At its best Young Ireland embraced their country's pluralism of faiths and cultures as a strength rather than a problem. Despite ultimately advocating 'physical force' as a means of achieving independence, for most of the group, violence was only sanctioned as a last resort and defensive show of strength. A careful reading of Young Ireland's published writings reveals a circle of liberal moderates befitting their origins in the constitutional repeal movement, pushed into extreme action by the government and their own naïve idealism.

Thomas Davis was founding editor and co-publisher of *The Nation*, a weekly periodical that was as ground-breaking in style as it was refreshing in ideas about an Irish national identity. *The Nation* was an early exponent of a style of partisan journalism that mixed opinionated politics with a literary and folk sensibility, appealing across the social divide through a discourse about what it meant to be Irish. Hailing from a Welsh father of English background and a mother claiming both Gaelic and Cromwellian ancestors, Davis was, in the words of cultural historian Terry Eagleton, 'the living symbol of ethnic diversity'.[51] Gavan Duffy was from Ulster and another talented journalist and publisher who took over the reins of *The Nation* after Davis's untimely death in 1845. James Lalor was a Catholic journalist and writer from a farming background who fell out early with the Repeal Association and used the pages of *The Nation* to advocate rural revolution based on a radical redistribution of the landed estates to the peasantry. His younger brother, Peter Lalor, would become leader of the Eureka Stockade uprising on the Victorian goldfields in 1854.

Another Ulsterman, John Mitchel, is often typecast as the most radical of the Young Irelanders because of his passionate antipathy to the English and disposition to what Irish historian Seán McConville calls 'a state of permanent opposition'.[52] Yet while Mitchel may have declared war on whatever establishment he happened upon, his weapons of choice remained the pen and printing press.[53] Like Davis, Mitchel was a Presbyterian, though his clergyman father left the non-conformist religion for the Unitarians. This was a still more dissenting and even secularising sect that had nurtured the counter-ethics of a number of radicals, including the Scottish Martyr Thomas Palmer. Mitchel's father had sworn the United Irish oath in his wild youth, and later raised eyebrows for charity work among Ulster's destitute Roman Catholics.[54] The son began courting controversy at age twenty-one, when he eloped with the sixteen-year-old daughter of an army officer and prominent Orangeman, leading to swift arrest and an eighteen-day gaol sentence for the young lawyer on a charge of kidnap. The bold flourish followed by internment would be a theme in Mitchel's life. Undeterred, the young romantic married Jenny Verner in secret in 1837.[55]

Mitchel was radicalised by first-hand experience representing Catholic victims of injustice in Belfast, and was persuaded by Daniel O'Connell to join the Repeal Association in 1843.[56] Still he had no regard for the Catholic Church, or any religion, being an equal opportunity secularist.[57] At Duffy's invitation he became co-editor of *The Nation* in 1845 where his provocative writing on matters such as English complicity in the Potato Famine and musings on violence caused an immediate stir, alienating the paper from the Repeal movement and even from moderate Young Irelanders. One article recommended that in the event of a rebellion, railway tracks be pulled up to derail trains carrying troops, anticipating (or inspiring) Ned Kelly's strategy at Glenrowan thirty-five years later. Mitchel became a defender of hungry and persecuted tenant farmers and labourers driven to violence by the avarice of landlords and Middle Men or caught up in draconian laws such as the curfew. He saw that the peasants were rebels engaged in a land war with the large estate owners who were agents of English exploitation.

For Mitchel the English deserved nothing but enmity, a prejudice that would be confirmed and deepened by his own maltreatment at their hands. Manifesting the romantic's allergy to rules and discipline, Mitchel found it difficult to remain part of a club that would want him as a member, and so his political and publishing career is littered with feuds, stoushes and resignations.[58] Breaking with Duffy, Mitchel established his own newspaper with a title designed to challenge the Anglo-Ascendancy as much as nationalist reformists: the *United Irishman*.[59] Through this vehicle he began promoting James Finton Lalor's case for a land strike by tenants as a harbinger to an agrarian revolution.[60] But he was no socialist. Dwelling in that wild border country on the political spectrum where left meets right, Mitchel's deep-seated hostility to modernity and a romantic enthusiasm for traditional agrarian society made him a radical conservative rather than a progressive liberal, though he was first and foremost an Irish nationalist.[61]

As befits the name, most of the second tier of Young Irelanders were younger still. Thomas Meagher, only 25 in 1848, was 'the boy most likely to' among the coming men of Young Ireland. He was born in 1823 into a wealthy and politically active Catholic family, his merchant father zealously asserting the newly won right of Catholics to stand for office by becoming both mayor and MP for the city of Waterford. Thomas received a Catholic education under the Jesuits at Stonyhurst College and went to Dublin in 1843 to study law.[62] While knocking around the pubs and public meetings of the capital discussing and arguing the great questions of the day, the young student found an outlet for his Irish patriotism and debating skills in Daniel O'Connell's Repeal Association. A good-looking, intelligent and charismatic man marked for the Irish Bar, Meagher quickly won a reputation as a stirring and formidable public speaker and ideas man. Ultimately disillusioned with Repeal's timidity and failure to seize the moment, the impatient idealist found a more amenable home as a writer at *The Nation* and in 1845 became a founder of Young Ireland.[63]

Historians of Young Ireland cast Meagher as the brilliant and dashing support star to O'Brien's dignified, patrician lead. For Eagleton, Meagher is the 'spinner of words and romantic in chief' while for Thomas Keneally, Meagher is 'the Young Tribune', a reference to the ancient champions of the Plebs in the Roman Republic, notably the two Gracchi brothers who were murdered and martyred while trying to redistribute land to the people.[64] Though a man of ideas and oratory, Meagher had drawn on the metaphor of a military sabre in defending the use of physical force to achieve Irish independence, and was henceforth known as 'Meagher of the Sword'.

Supporting the publishing ventures of Mitchel and Davis were John Martin, a doctor who had worked to relieve the suffering of the poor during the famine, and Kevin O'Doherty, a young medical student with a flair for journalism. Their stirring editorialising in support of revolution in the heady days of 1848 would see them marked for arrest. Standing alongside O'Brien in the field when rhetoric turned to rebellion were two young lieutenants, the merchant Terrence McManus and the law clerk Patrick O'Donohoe. Both men would share their captain's fate at revolution's end.

When events in 1848 propelled the Young Irelanders from words to action, there was no question that command would be vested in William Smith O'Brien, who could not be more removed from our modern stereotype of the rebel leader. In appearance, bearing and manner he was less Braveheart than Mr Darcy, a cultivated, influential and proud man who moved with ease in the very best society. In the aftermath of Cromwell's conquest of Ireland, O'Brien's ancestors had sworn loyalty to the English monarch and converted to the Church of England in order to maintain their lands and privileges, which included an hereditary peerage, a place in the House of Lords and guaranteed seats for family members first in the Irish Parliament and after 1800 in the House of Commons.[65] As stalwarts of the old Dublin administration, the O'Briens had opposed the Act of Union in 1800, but as Anglophones they quickly made Westminster their new power base.

Smith O'Brien was born in 1803 and raised in luxury at the family estate, Dromoland Castle, in County Clare and was educated in England following a predictable ruling class trajectory. He attended Harrow, studied classics and law at Cambridge and became a barrister, and then surprised his family by joining the Catholic Association in support of the emancipation cause. 'From my boyhood,' O'Brien explained amid the turbulence of 1848:

> *I have entertained a passionate affection for Ireland. A child of its most ancient race I have never read the history of their past—I have never witnessed the miseries and indignities which its people still suffer without a deep sentiment of indignation.*[66]

Taking up the family business, he won the family pocket borough of Ennis in 1828 and commenced his career as an Irish parliamentarian at Westminster.[67] There O'Brien came to support Catholic Emancipation and then O'Connell's crusade to repeal the Act of Union. In keeping with his class inclinations and in harmony with Repeal he passionately believed that an independent Ireland should remain a constitutional monarchy under the British Crown. This was small consolation to O'Brien's family. His increasing enthusiasm for Irish nationalism shocked his mother, the formidable Lady Charlotte, and his eldest brother Sir Lucius O'Brien (later Lord Inchiquin), and was a constant worry to his wife, Lucy, who was left alone at their run down but stately Georgian home, Cahirmoyle, to care for their six children, while William tarried in Dublin as first a Repeal then Young Ireland mover and shaker.

O'Brien confounded the usual path by becoming more radical as he aged. Originally a Tory, from 1835 he represented Limerick as an independent liberal, endorsed by Repeal and the Catholics, and voting with the Whig Government. He remained a supporter of the Empire, but joined with the 'Colonial Reform' MPs in championing mass emigration from Britain and Ireland to the colonies in Canada, Australia and New Zealand (paid for through the sale of land) and their gradual attainment of self-government under the Crown.[68] This conception of an Empire of semi-autonomous nations led O'Brien to favour a species of 'home rule' for the original colony, Ireland, and thus into the arms of the Repeal movement. Appalled at the government crackdown on the Repeal 'agitation' in 1843, O'Brien resigned his position as a local magistrate in protest, and came to attention throughout Ireland.[69] What galvanised his growing hostility to the Union was the mounting evidence of London's mismanagement of Ireland, exposed by the famine that accompanied the potato blight, though in the mid-1840s the Repeal leaders had little to say as this tragedy unfolded. O'Brien became a go-to man in the House of

Commons, first for Repeal, then Young Ireland, expending a great deal of his political capital in the 1840s to ensure that Irish independence could not be ignored as merely the cause of extremists and rabble rousers. Yet ultimately this was exactly how he himself came to be regarded by many of his parliamentary colleagues.

Over the centuries the O'Brien family had made the aristocratic English style their own, and William communicated this identity, so different from the Irish manners of his less august nationalist compadres, in his every movement and utterance. But in British power politics the value of these qualities should not be underestimated. As a scion of one of the land's foremost dynasties, the descendant of the last Irish King, O'Brien lent the otherwise bourgeois Young Ireland movement a mantle of nobility, even destiny.[70] One important practical consequence of this rank was an almost feudal loyalty he was able to excite in ordinary Irish men and women beyond the cities. At the other end of the social scale, his colleagues hoped he would attract other larger landowners to their cause. O'Brien had other qualities that would lift Young Ireland's stocks. As an MP whose family had represented their county for seven generations he brought legitimacy and valuable political connections in the imperial centre.[71] As an Anglican he contributed to Young Ireland's religious pluralism and appeal among other Protestants. Duffy was quite candid in his courting of O'Brien that he was 'providentially gifted with qualities for the time and place' which the other Young Irelanders lacked, explaining to him that:

> [t]he Protestants and the landed gentry must be won, and you, a man of property and family, and a Protestant, can and will win them. What chance of their listening to young men, most of whom are Catholics and all of them spring directly from the trading class.[72]

Later, when banished as a felon to Van Diemen's Land, O'Brien's pedigree and sense of entitlement ensured that he and his cause did not languish in obscurity. Yet Smith O'Brien's birthright meant he would never be a republican like his fellow Young Irelanders, and as their captain during the crisis of 1848, he remained at best a reluctant revolutionary, with tragic consequences.

*   *   *

INTELLECTUALS IN THE YEAR OF REVOLUTIONS

THE ADJECTIVE 'YOUNG' WAS ADOPTED IN PART TO DIFFERENTIATE the radicals from the older Irish ameliorists who opposed violence, but also as a voguish nod to the Young Italy movement inaugurated by Giuseppe Mazzini in 1831 to fight for an independent Italian republic. The late 1840s witnessed a revival in youthful hunger for change reminiscent of the mood for rejuvenation unleashed by the first French Revolution, when Wordsworth observed that to be young was 'very heaven'. For those on the barricades, 1848 would be a little like that too, as a new generation of idealists took a stand against the old way of doing things. This was more than the romantic pose of privileged bohemian youth flirting with a doomed cause. As the old empires were thrown on the defensive, young political activists were nurturing potent new ideas that were to gather force through the nineteenth century—nationalism, liberalism and socialism.

1848 is rightly marked in history as the year of revolutions. Across Europe nationalist, republican and even social rebellions shook the foundations of the conservative settlement imposed by the victors following the defeat of Napoleon at Waterloo. In February 1848 the people of Paris once again took to the barricades, toppling the Bourbon monarchy in favour of a new French republic. This was a signal to liberals, radicals and modernisers across Europe as discontent building up pressure under decades of repression erupted in armed uprisings and mass actions. From Manchester to Vienna subject provinces and classes demanded a say over how they were governed. By March the Germans and the Danes were in revolt against autocratic monarchs and the Poles had risen to expel the occupying Prussians. Next, revolution swept through the vast multi-ethnic empire of the Austrian Hapsburgs, with Czechs, Slovaks, Italians, Germans, Romanians, Serbs and the Hungarian Magyars fighting to throw off the yoke of Vienna to establish independent nations. In 1848 the Chartists again took to the streets of British cities, demanding working-class participation in government, clashing violently with police and the army. And in 1848 the Young Ireland leaders, inspired by people power on the Continent, sought to raise the Irish in revolution.

Ideas and media played a disproportionate role in the liberationist movements that emerged in the lead-up to 1848. Long before they took to the barricades, these ethnic revolutionaries were fighting a culture war with their colonisers for the right to imagine their communities as new nations, excavating folk traditions and refashioning the medium of the press to stake their claim for independence.[73] While modernisers, they looked back romantically to an organic, usually peasant community connected to the soil, reworking or contriving myths, legends and heroes in order to legitimise the new nation-states they conjured. The historian Eric Hobsbawm conceptualised this nineteenth century enthusiasm for divining an antiquity for a people or institution as 'inventing tradition'. The tartans of the Scottish clans, the craftsmanship of England's gothic cathedrals and Irish kings like Brian Boru were all reworked in the new age to authenticate contested national identities within the British Isles. Young Ireland, led by some of the country's best propagandists and a descendant of an ancient royal line should be seen in this context as first and foremost a phalanx of cultural warriors engaged in imagining an Irish nation.

To appreciate the innovation and implications of the Young Ireland challenge to British imperium it is necessary to locate its leaders in the development of new types of intellectuals in the nineteenth century. According to Terry Eagleton in his work *Scholars and Rebels*, the term 'intellectual' only began to be used as a noun in the nineteenth century, to describe the social application of knowledge.[74] The century witnessed a growing tension between applying knowledge to advance industrial modernity and its capacity to undermine old certainties, whether that be religion, social hierarchies or art. Science in the hands of intellectuals like Charles Darwin and Thomas Henry Huxley challenged the Bible's version of creation and discredited the idea of man as above nature. Economists extolled a free market that unleashed technological innovation to produce untold wealth while tearing up customary relations between classes and promoting advancement by merit. While many Victorian era intellectuals sat in the driver's seat of progress, the shock of the new also produced 'counter intellectuals' opposed to the new status quo, such as Marx, who analysed class struggle, and Ruskin who promoted a return to mediaeval crafts as an aesthetic revolt against industrialisation.

Whereas the radical thinkers of the eighteenth century were concerned with universal rights and principles and the spread of 'Enlightenment', their successors were worried about the problem of an accelerating modernity and the capacity of forces such as the free market, mechanisation and imperialism to dissolve communities and alienate individuals. Romanticism was one reaction, licensing poets and artists, but also political thinkers like Ruskin, to look back with nostalgia to earlier, pre-industrial times to provide the social and cultural glue to bond communities anew. For nineteenth century intellectuals, the obsession with community disintegration and restoration led to a focus on the local rather than the universal, to problems like industrialisation in England or British colonialism in Ireland, that seemed to have impoverished their country's people not only materially but also spiritually. For some the answer to this ennui of the soul was religion, but to many the answer was cultural nourishment, not just of the elite few, but of the whole people. Eagleton astutely observed that it suited intellectuals, whose stock in trade was culture, to elevate its importance.[75] Culture would reconnect communities, for some imagined as an empire of disparate peoples, but increasingly as nations based on land and ethnicity.

While a British intellectual like Mathew Arnold might equate these goals with a liberal imperial mission to spread the light of civilisation to subjects throughout the world, Irish intellectuals from outside the Anglo-Ascendancy viewed the Empire as itself a corrupting, divisive force, destroying traditions and robbing the people of cultural memory. The solution for colonised intellectuals was to rediscover and modernise indigenous cultural traditions, from language to land use, to help unite communities and guide them towards greater autonomy vis-à-vis the imperial polity. This was a project of French Canadian intellectuals alarmed at the impact of English migration and mercantilism in the 1830s ahead of their ill-fated rebellion, and this process was to be repeated in Ireland.

Anthony Smith argued that intellectuals played a disproportionate role in nationalist movements, their role being:

to mobilise a formerly passive community into forming a nation around the new vernacular historical culture that has been rediscovered … Nationalism … summon[s] intellectuals everywhere to transform 'low' into 'high' culture, oral into written, literary traditions, in order to preserve its fund of irreplaceable cultural values.[76]

The emphasis on culture and a people's unique identity as an 'imagined community' tied to country differentiates the cultural nationalists of the mid-nineteenth century from the more cosmopolitan 'rights of man' radicals of the late eighteenth century, such as the Scottish Jacobins. Ireland witnessed a flowering of cultural nationalism from the 1820s, ranging from the scholarly to the populist, the technocratic to the politically radical.

Nationalism was particularly attractive to colonial intellectuals because of the paradox of their predicament: necessarily conscripted into imperial state services designed to modernise the province, yet subjected to exclusion and condescension by the imperial elite.[77] National belonging was the balm to soothe alienation and frustrated ambition. In nineteenth century Ireland, intellectuals found developmental roles in the expansion of schools, tertiary education, the administration of the Poor Law and court system, and demographic and resource 'mapping' projects such as the 'Ordinance Survey'. After the emancipation of Catholics they enjoyed increased employment and promotion within the civil service and improved access to university education and the professions, feeding the growth of a secular Catholic intelligentsia in the 1840s.[78] But the Anglo-Irish Ascendancy continued to command the heights of the economy and government and kept Ireland from fully modernising because it suited England to have a source of cheap food and labour.

Technocratic state-building found a culture-building echo in Irish universities such as Trinity College, Dublin, where largely Anglo-Irish academics working in archaeology, literature and history undertook ground-breaking research into the country's Gaelic and Celtic past. Such work may have observed the conventions of scholarly detachment, but it legitimated the idea of an Irish nation with origins in antiquity and proved influential on critical young students, especially Catholics and

Presbyterians who felt they did not belong in the United Kingdom. A number of the Young Ireland radicals, including Duffy, Mitchel and Meagher, studied at Trinity College, Dublin, where they imbibed the emerging passion for Ireland's heritage.

Young Ireland accords with Gramsci's notion of organic intellectuals who in contrast to academics or technical state functionaries are activists in societies bound to a partisan cause.[79] Truly oppositional intellectuals, in Ireland and elsewhere, they plied their trade not in service of the state or the ivory tower of academia, but in the media, servicing a growing market for new styles of journalism from the 1830s.[80] Known to the Victorian era as 'men of letters' a new generation of well-educated young gentlemen (and some women) made their mark writing articles and essays on the issues of the day. Unlike jobbing journalists, they used the print media to promote ideas that, while partisan, drew on the writer's deep learning and skill as a stylist. Eagleton considered them as important as scientists and scholars to nineteenth century intellectual life, citing the influence of Thomas Carlyle, Arnold and Ruskin.[81] Far from crude propagandists, men of letters are analogous to twentieth century 'social commentators' or 'public intellectuals'. Some such as Mark Twain and Charles Dickens would move from journalism and essays to fiction and lecturing, while others moved into political theory and activism, such as Karl Marx who combined freelance journalism for the *New-York Daily Tribune* with writing *Das Kapital* and building the First Communist International. Some entrepreneurial 'men of letters', such as Davis, Duffy and Mitchel in Ireland, or Marcus Clarke in Australia, would try their hand at publishing and editing in order to enhance their freedom of expression and to champion innovation in the media itself.

One such experiment was the new weekly journal dedicated to the cause of Irish national identity and independence, titled *The Nation*, launched in October 1842 with O'Connell's blessing, but certainly not control. Duffy later explained the periodical's purpose: 'We desired to make Ireland a nation, and the name would be a fitting prelude to the attempt.' The prospectus was highly critical of the old liberal Irish journals, 'shackled by old habits, old prejudices, and old divisions'. *The Nation*'s argument for renewal took the first steps in setting out Young Ireland's mission:

The necessities of the country seem to demand a Journal able to aid and organise the new movements going on amongst us—to make their growth deeper, and their fruit 'more racy of the soil'—and, above all, to direct the popular mind and the sympathies of educated men of all parties to the great end of nationality.

To these romantics nationality meant more than governmentality and mere rational politics. They desired a safe haven for the Irish soul:

a nationality which will not only raise our people from their poverty, by securing to them the blessings of a domestic legislature, but inflame and purify them with a lofty and heroic love of country—a nationality of the spirit as well as the letter—a nationality which may come to be stamped upon our manners, our literature, and our deeds—a nationality which may embrace Protestant, Catholic, and Dissenter, Milesian and Cromwellian, the Irishman of a hundred generations, and the stranger who is within our gates; not a nationality which would preclude civil war, but which would establish internal union and external independence—a nationality which would be recognised by the world ...[82]

The Nation writers preferred the romantic fields of emotion, culture and spirit to institutional nation-building. For this reason, Seán McConville, the historian of Irish political prisoners, considered Young Ireland 'a textbook example of political romanticism'.[83]

The Nation was not only innovative in ideas, but also in its outreach among a new generation of Irish writers and poets working in both high and popular forms and combining them in ways that shook up the old hide-bound canon. In the still-divided Australian colonies the *Bulletin* would perform a similar rift on an emerging national identity, seeking talent 'racy of the soil' in the 1880s and '90s. Poetry and light verse were a crucial vehicle for helping readers imagine an Irish nation and became a powerful propaganda tool for the Young Ireland cause. In this literary firmament the most powerful pen belonged to Mary Ann Kelly, who became known simply as 'Eva of the Nation'. Historian Brega Webb reveals an oeuvre that ranged from the softly romantic to politically militant, such as the call to arms, 'The Awakening of the Sleepers':

Yes! The time is come!—it is the hour,
Warrior chiefs of Eire, now for your pow'r!
Lift those mail'd hands from brow— ... Now!—Now![84]

The Nation was the latest in a long line of periodicals, pamphlets, salons and societies that had helped to expand a new public sphere in the West since the eighteenth century. The public sphere was where oppositional intellectuals critically debated the emancipatory ideas that inspired the American and French revolutions, and where British and Irish radicals refined and promoted their competing ideas for political and economic reform.[85] While mainstream newspapers went hand in hand with the triumph of liberal democracy, it was partisan papers like the United Irishmen's *Northern Star* or the *Manchester Guardian*—often denied 'licences' to operate by the government—that pushed at the boundaries of what was acceptable to think and say, and ultimately to do. As we have seen, the borders of this 'republic of letters' were continually contested and breached by a British state that used censorship and the laws of sedition to curb free expression. It became clear with the punishment of Thomas Muir and the other Scottish Martyrs that transportation to the Australian colonies was a crucial weapon in the state's war against freedom to write, publish and disseminate ideas deemed dangerous to the political status quo. The events of 1848 in Ireland would demonstrate that the Crown's zeal to suppress media liberty was undiminished.

There were different 'national' traditions in Ireland. Should it be Gaelic and Catholic? What of the Presbyterian dissenters of the north, part of the Irish make-up for centuries, with a legacy of opposition to the Ascendancy as genuine as the toadying of the royalist Orangemen? The only way to harvest the best that the Irish had sown was to return to the United Irishmen's dream of a non-sectarian nation. This was a natural foundation for Irish nationalism given the diversity of ethnic and religious origins within Young Ireland itself. Yet the centuries of ill-treatment endured by the Catholic majority, lately revisited in the calamitous mismanagement of the famine, meant that Catholic Ireland would have a special place.

The problem for the romantic nationalists that composed Young Ireland was that they were not very good at the institutional and instrumental politics necessary to build a popular membership and move from words and ideas to action. A hopeful turn to the practical was the formation in January 1847 of the Irish Confederation following Young Ireland's break with Repeal.[86] As the name implies the Confederation sought connections to like-minded groups, and brought together various Irish clubs and groups that supported independence and even sought an alliance with fraternal rebels across the Irish Sea, the British Chartists. The Confederation was an open, not conspiratorial group, in keeping with the Young Ireland commitment to free debate and publicity, and a desire by its leaders to act with honour. According to McConville, this organisation ran a moderate line reminiscent of Repeal and in keeping with O'Brien's inclinations, in support of self-government under the British Crown, and of legal reform rather than revolution. Yet the Confederation would hothouse the revolutionaries of 1848.[87]

*   *   *

COUNTDOWN TO REVOLUTION

NO ONE HAD A HOTTER HEAD FOR REVOLUTION THAN MITCHEL. Outraged at the passage of a new Coercion Act, he lobbied the Confederation in January 1848 to prepare for a coordinated rural uprising. In order to change the 'stupid policy' of constitutional 'agitation' into one of 'guerrilla' insurgency the Confederation should:

> *employ themselves in promulgating sound instruction upon military affairs—upon the natural lines of defence which makes the island so strong—upon the construction and defence of field works, and especially upon the use of proper arms.*[88]

But the majority of member groups remained committed to the constitutional path believing the 'broken and divided' condition of

H. Warren.

J. Rogers.

the Irish people condemned an uprising to failure, and were backed in
this by Smith O'Brien. With his colleague John Martin, the incendiary
Mitchel took matters into his own hands and began publishing material
in the *United Irishman* designed to provoke the government into baring
its teeth.[89] He called for a political revolution and the establishment
of a republic but also a revolution in land ownership, demanding 'the
destruction of landlordism, and denial of all tenure and title derived
from English sovereigns'.[90] He resigned from the Confederation,
but could count on supporters within its member societies, especially
in Dublin.

Given the resolve of the Confederation that a call to arms was
doomed, what changed to persuade O'Brien, Duffy and Meagher to
embark on just such a course of action?[91] According to Young Ireland
historian McConville, the causes lie in the government's failure to
respond to the Potato Famine and the hope unleashed by the outbreak
of revolution in France.

As an almost wholly urban group, Young Ireland, like Repeal before,
had a poor grasp on the rural crisis and no solution to the suffering in
the countryside during the winters of 1846 and '47. Duffy conceded that
'[t]here were not many of us who would not have given his life
cheerfully to arrest this ruin, if only we could see a possible way …'.[92]
But the British Government's failure to halt the export of food from
Ireland, even as millions starved to death or emigrated, robbed it of
legitimacy and persuaded more moderates that Mitchel's solution was
morally righteous.

Duffy had joked to O'Brien that should Mitchel succeed in
provoking a 'peasant insurrection', either the country would 'be trampled
out under the feet of English soldiers' or in a new republic moderates
like the two of them 'will meet on a Jacobin scaffold, ordered for
executions as enemies of some new Marat or Robespierre'.[93] But then
the barricades once more went up in Paris and they stopped joking.

The fall of the monarch in France and the wave of rebellions it
provoked across Europe had an electrifying effect on the Young Irelanders

comparable to the impact that the earlier French Revolution had on first Scottish reformers and United Irishmen in the late eighteenth century and on rural rioters, machine breakers and other radicals in the early 1830s. Suddenly changes that seemed impossible appeared imminent. Ratcheting up his rhetoric for rebellion, Mitchel told the Confederation '[t]he news today announces that Vienna is in the hands of the people. Stand by us, citizens, and it shall be done'.[94] There occurred a decisive shift to a policy of physical force. O'Brien's conversion to direct action followed his typically romantic comprehension of events in France and beyond, which he described as:

> *characterised by alterations of moral grandeur and of moral beauty ... A passionate enthusiasm for liberty was preserved from excess by a universal love of order ... All Europe felt the electric sensation. Wherever oppression had been sustained by Power—there the shock produced a convulsion.*[95]

Had the aristocratic liberal surrendered his cool detachment for the rapture of the moment? O'Brien later claimed that he decided on revolution because it would cause fewer deaths than continuing Britain's tragic mismanagement of the famine.[96] He reversed his opposition to an uprising, claiming 'the state of affairs was totally different now'.[97]

Mitchel recalled that a

> *kind of sacred wrath took possession of a few Irishmen ... [t]hey could endure the horrible scene no longer, and resolved to cross the path of the British war of conquest, though it should crush them to atoms.*[98]

Like Thomas Muir bedazzled by the revolution of 1789, O'Brien and Meagher made a hasty pilgrimage to Paris in the Spring of 1848 to present congratulations to the latest French Republic. The message, moved by O'Brien at a meeting of 15,000 in Dublin, began 'As slaves we address freemen'.[99] They literally nailed the French colours to the Young Ireland mast, sailing back home waving an Irish tricolour.

Revolution across the channel, and the rapid reappearance of Chartist protest in the streets of England, was a signal to the military to be vigilant, especially in Ireland. While the government could rely on an extensive network of spies and informers, the Young Ireland leaders made no secret that they were preparing to call the people out.

The government may have been worried about France and the re-emergence of militant Chartism, but the Home Secretary had Young Ireland's measure. Intelligence on the ground assured him that the Confederation lacked the support of the Catholic Church, the propertied classes and even the peasants, who were supposedly providing the physical force in the coming rising.

The apocalyptic rhetoric of the *United Irishman* made Mitchel a marked man. One article bade tenant farmers consider the lethal arithmetic that there were 'more than a million' of them and only 'eight thousand' landed gentry, concluding 'it seems plain that you or they must die'.[100] But to silence Mitchel and others like him in Ireland and among the Chartists, the Home Office needed a new, more draconian law that mandated harsh punishment for urging rebellion in words and speech. The old crime of sedition under which so many radical publicists in the past were exiled to the Australian penal settlements would no longer do. Sedition was now a misdemeanour, not a felony, and only carried a short prison sentence, during which time someone else could step up to edit the offending publication. Nor did it outlaw speech likely to inflame rebellion. Mitchel, O'Brien and Meagher had been arrested, charged and bailed under the old sedition laws in March 1848, and promptly returned to their oratory and publishing. The serious crime of treason still carried the death penalty, but only related to actions such as taking up arms against the Sovereign or spying for a foreign power. Into this breach rode the *Treason Felony Bill*, proscribing both printed and spoken words promoting rebellion, and imposing the punishment of transportation, for seven to fourteen years.

There was opposition to the law in the House of Commons when the Bill was debated in April 1848, with liberal moderates as well as radicals appalled that a person could be arrested and transported for merely speaking. Some free speech advocates like Joseph Hume noted that the legislation would send sedition underground into conspiratorial cells while Sir William Gray worried that had the law been operating during the Great Reform debates, many parliamentarians may have been whisked off to the colonies.[101] It helped that Mitchel conveniently published his speeches in the *United Irishman*, so Home Secretary Sir George Grey could convey to the House the treasonous character of the words he had in mind. But the clinching argument for the government's law came from an unexpected quarter, when Smith O'Brien strode into the chamber fresh from Paris to speak against the *Treason Felony Bill*. He played up solidarity with the English Chartists, and answered accusations of treachery by declaring it was the government's ministers 'that are traitors to the country, the Queen, and the constitution'.[102] O'Brien lost the cause of Irish independence that badly needed support of moderate MPs and made pushing on to rebellion a matter of honour. His threatening, inflammatory language only served to demonstrate how far the Young Irelanders had progressed down the path of insurrection, and of the need for laws to temper such irresponsible oratory.[103] McConville notes how even in his battles at Westminster, O'Brien courted the romance of the noble defeat.[104] Voted onto the statute book, 'Treason Felony' would be used to suppress and imprison Irish dissidents into the twentieth century.

Mitchel could boast that a new law was enacted by a fearful government just to shut him up. On bail for sedition he told a Confederation rally, 'I did write seditious articles, and I write seditious articles. I will incite the people to discontent and disaffection.' The stage-struck firebrand was willing the government to follow through with its threats so he might use the court as theatre and his martyrdom to rally the Irish people.[105] The sedition charges against O'Brien and Meagher were dropped but Mitchel was once more hauled off to be the first person charged under the freshly minted *Treason Felony Act*. He was tried before a jury on 26 May 1848, where a guilty verdict was swiftly returned. The court applied the full force of the new law, sentencing Mitchel to fourteen years' transportation. Invoking the executed Christian martyrs of Rome, he threatened the court:

> *the Roman who saw his hand burning to ashes before the tyrant, promised that three hundred should follow the enterprise. Can I not promise for one, for two, for three, aye for hundreds.*[106]

Eva the poet echoed from Galway on the other side of Ireland:

> *For one—for two—for three—*
> *Aye! Hundreds, thousands, see!*
> *For vengeance and for thee*
> *To the last!*[107]

The instinctive anti-authoritarian had become the authority's plaything and began the martyrdom he craved. According to T.A. Jackson it was at this juncture, when the streets of Dublin seethed with indignation over their hero's treatment, that Young Ireland should have called the people to revolution. Into old age Eva believed that '[t]he people were then ready—were filled with rage and enthusiasm'.[108] O'Brien raised the prospect of a military action to liberate their comrade but like O'Connell at Clontarf the opportunity was not seized. Instead, in typical Young Ireland fashion, Mitchel's closest friend John Martin started a new paper, *The Irish Felon*, to continue the revolutionary rhetoric of the now defunct *United Irishman*, while the radical medical student Kevin O'Doherty launched the *Irish Tribune*. Frustrated that Mitchel's arrest had not occasioned action, Martin editorialised that:

> *[t]he transportation of a man, as a felon, for uttering sentiments held*
> *and professed by at least five-sixths of his countrymen, seems to me so*
> *violent and so insulting a national wrong, that submission to it must*
> *be taken to signify incurable slavishness.*[109]

Under armed military guard the political prisoner was speedily spirited out of Ireland, lest his supporters attempt a rescue. From there he was conveyed to a gaol on Spike Island, and then to the cruelly-named *Scourge*, bound for the British colony of Bermuda in the Caribbean. But no matter where he was sent—in an odyssey that would circumnavigate the Empire's more desolate outposts—this would not be the last Britain or Ireland heard of John Mitchel.

✻   ✻   ✻

THE CABBAGE PATCH REVOLUTION

IN QUICK SUCCESSION THE THREE SEDITIOUS PUBLISHERS
Martin, O'Doherty and Duffy were arrested under the *Treason Felony Act*,
and hauled off to Newgate Gaol. In the final issue of the *Irish Tribune*,
O'Doherty had reminded readers of the greatest wrong, the famine still
stalking the land: 'Every ditch has a corpse, and every lordling Moloch
his hetacomb of murdered tenantry. Clearly we are guilty if we turn not
our hand against the enemies of our race.'[110] A last issue of *The Nation*
carried the stirring words of Margaret Callan, Duffy's sister-in-law, daring
Irish men to battle: 'Now, indeed, are the men of Ireland cowards if this
moment for retribution, combat, and victory, was to pass by unemployed.
It finds them slaves, and it would leave them infamous.'[111]

At this point, in July 1848, Young Ireland leaders, notably Meagher
and O'Brien, commenced going among Confederate members and the
people in a series of rallies reminiscent of Repeal, seeking to prepare them
for a rising. O'Brien inspected 'ten thousand Confederates' at Cork he
judged to be the military equal of the Queen's finest.[112] Women too were
urged to the barricades, Eva beating the drum in a letter to 'The Women
of Ireland', asserting:

> *What is virtue in man is virtue also in woman. Virtue is of no sex.*
> *A coward woman is as base as a coward man ... It is not unfeminine*
> *to take sword, or gun, if sword or gun are required ... Plead not in*
> *this hour the miserable excuse—I am a woman.*[113]

In the midst of organising a mass rally to be held atop Slievenamon
Mountain in Tipperary, Meagher was arrested at home in Waterford
by a small army of British troops.[114] True to his reputation for oratory,
the 'Young Tribune' was charged for giving a seditious speech to the
townspeople of Rathkeale.[115] As the prisoner was taken under army
escort out of Waterford en route to Dublin the police carriage was
surrounded by an angry crowd blocking a bridge, determined to liberate
him. Incredibly, Meagher addressed his supporters and persuaded them
to stand down, once again squibbing an opportunity pregnant with
revolutionary potential. Keneally argues that Meagher's reluctance was

due to concern three warships moored nearby could reduce the town to rubble, but it reveals the reluctance of the Young Ireland intellectuals to roll the dice.[116]

The government, having removed Meagher from proximity to the rally, and concerned his internment might lead to a wider backlash, bailed him the next day. This was a mistake, for he met with Confederation members and immediately rode on horseback to Slievenamon Mountain, where a crowd of 50,000 supporters were gathering from Cork, Waterford, Wexford and Tipperary. Wearing a tricolour sash of green, white and orange, Meagher issued a proclamation on the rights of Irishmen and then rode on to rally supporters waiting in Carrick. He described the tumult and disorientation that greeted them as they entered the town:

> *A torrent of human beings rushing through lanes and narrow streets; surging and boiling against the white basements that hemmed it in; whirling in dizzy circles, and tossing up in dark waves, with sounds of wrath, vengeance, and defiance; clenched hands, darting high above the black and broken surface; and waving to and fro, with the wildest confusion, in the air; eyes red with rage and desperation, starting and flashing upwards through the billows of the flood; long tresses of hair—disordered, drenched, and tangled—streaming in the roaring wind of voices, and, as in a shipwreck, rising and falling with the foam.[117]*

Meagher's literary flourish betrays the shock of a young man first exposed to the chaos of the mob, unable to control events he was setting in train, tossed by exhilaration and fear. Carrick and Slievenamon persuaded the young man that the British would have to bow to the will of the people. As an older man, Meagher recalled his youthful optimism preparing to ride on to the capital:

> *flourishing a very handsome sword which belonged to a grand uncle of mine in the days of the … Warterford Volunteers' [giving] myself up to the gay illusion of a gallant fight, a triumphal entry, at the head of armed thousands, into Dublin, before long!*[118]

The catalyst for Young Ireland calling on the people to rise was the suspension of *habeas corpus* on 23 July and the swearing of warrants for the leaders still at large. Fearing their imminent arrest and detention the leaders fled the cities for the country to call the people 'out', in a fashion.

The strategy, to the extent that there was one, hinged on Mitchel's fantasy that the peasantry was on the verge of revolt and simply needed to be called out by the Young Ireland leaders. Great hopes, in particular, were placed on William Smith O'Brien's capacity as scion of a royal line to rally the people against the British. There had been some drilling of Confederacy members in the weeks leading up to the suspension of *habeas corpus*, but the rebel side had little of what counts in an uprising against a great military power—officers who had seen action, trained, disciplined fighters, guns, ammunition and international allies. Given these realities, O'Brien and the other leaders were counting on a sufficient show of popular opposition that the British would concede some measure of autonomy to Ireland—in effect the approach of Repeal but backed up with physical force.[119] Unlike Mitchel, with his schemes of sabotaged railways and land redistribution, O'Brien issued an edict that property and land rights were to be respected—hardly surprising given he was one of the country's largest landowners. He was determined to avoid 'a war of the poor against the rich'.[120] Peasants were expected to rise for an abstract notion of independence rather than against their immediate oppressors. If possible O'Brien wished to avoid bloodshed, to achieve what today we call a 'velvet revolution', but the greatest military machine on Earth would not be persuaded by pikes and fine words into conceding what it saw as the dismemberment of the United Kingdom. Leaving nothing to chance, overall political oversight for quelling the threatened rising was vested in no less a warrior than the Duke of Wellington, the Anglo-Irish Hero of Waterloo, former prime minister and at eighty still formidable.

O'Brien and the other Young Ireland leaders went out among people, mainly in the south, only to discover they were too demoralised by hunger to rally in all but a few counties. In Kilkenny the promised Confederate force of 17,000 turned out to be less than 1700.[121] Carrick, too, faced with the prospect of honouring its earlier pledge, backed down. Confederate clubs in other towns had radically exaggerated the strength and determination of local support. However, in Tipperary O'Brien had more luck, and 3000 men rallied to him on the common at Mullinahone.[122] Keneally likens O'Brien to a 'soldier-king' from Shakespeare going from camp fire to camp fire rousing the spirits of the peasants for combat.[123] Except the next day when they trapped a small party of police, O'Brien naïvely let them escape. There was to be more of this. Word came that cavalry were advancing on their position, barricades were erected by O'Brien's lieutenants and the troop blocked amid cheers from the rebels. Yet O'Brien agreed to let the cavalry pass if they promised not to arrest them, once more missing a chance for a morale-boosting battle, which the rebels would have won on the numbers.[124] At a council of war among the leadership, O'Brien resisted suggestions that the peasants be able to 'live off the enemy' and landed property be confiscated as spoils.

O'Brien's indecisiveness, a chivalric obsession with acting honourably, and distaste for spilling blood, combined to cripple his command. This ineptitude was on display when the two sides finally met on the Tipperary–Kilkenny border.[125] On Saturday 29 July, O'Brien, together with his lieutenants McManus and O'Donohoe, decided to take a stand at Ballingarry with a rebel force of 200 men and women against an advancing police column. Barricades were hastily erected, some men had guns but all the women and many men were armed only with pikes and stones. Just ahead of the roadblock, the approaching police force of forty-six men abruptly turned into a nearby field, and were pursued by O'Brien and the rebels, sensing they had the advantage. A skirmish ensued that was later dignified as the 'Battle of Ballingarry', though neither side would be covered in glory.

The police were well armed and took a defensive position in the nearby farmhouse of a local woman, named Mrs McCormack, a widow with small children. A standoff between the police and O'Brien's rebels was suddenly broken when Mrs McCormack appeared to grasp the chaotic scene, screaming that her children were inside the farmhouse. Ever the honourable gentleman, O'Brien accompanied the distraught mother to a window via her cabbage patch to secure the children's release, and asked the police to surrender. This parlaying came to an abrupt end when stones hurled at the house by rebels provoked an instant volley from the police guns. Two men fell and the rebels, on O'Donohoe's orders, returned fire. Simultaneously O'Brien and the widow retreated from the house through the hail of bullets. Attempts to smoke out the police failed, and their superior weaponry at close range ultimately put the ill-armed peasants to flight. On McManus's account, O'Brien was brave under fire and was the last man to leave, under pressure from his comrades, although some witnesses reported that the captain seemed to be seeking death.[126] However, the fact that only a handful of rebels were killed or injured owed much to O'Brien's restraint.

The image of the great noble stealing through a cabbage patch would be the defining image of the 'Battle of Ballingarry', a debacle that sealed the fate of O'Brien's 'kid glove revolution'. News of Ballingarry and the failure to raise the south cruelled attempts to bring reinforcements from Scotland and Belfast. The Young Ireland leaders were now on the run, protected by Confederation members, as the military fanned out across the country. McManus was arrested on 7 September, sitting in a cabin on board a steamer bound for New York. O'Brien was caught in a railway station in Thurles by a civilian who held him until police arrived. All his papers were seized.[127] Meagher, unable to raise supporters, tried to negotiate a surrender on condition that all rebels' lives would be spared, but he found unacceptable the authorities' demand that in return he confess to high treason.[128] He and O'Donohoe were caught by police at a roadblock in Tipperary and deposited with O'Brien and McManus in Dublin's Kilmainham Gaol.[129]

Young Ireland could spin words to evoke an Irish nation, but they were never competent to lead an armed struggle. McConville notes that:

> [t]he overthrow of firmly established authority is a rare event, and to have any chance of success, those who undertake it require conspiratorial experience, military skill, boldness, true ruthlessness, luck and some popular support.[130]

Lacking any of these prerequisites, the Young Ireland adventure was doomed before it began. It is likely that O'Brien realised this, but honour dictated they stay the course. The government played them for a trick, harassing them through legal persecution into taking a premature stand.

Whereas the Rebellion of 1798 was primarily a rural rising in which peasant soldiers drilled and fought battles under the command of land-holding United Irish officers, Young Ireland was an urban political movement lacking a base in the countryside. Confederacies had sprung up around the country, yet Young Ireland had no deep call on the loyalties of the peasantry, and this proved a strategic weakness when ultimately force was needed.[131] Young Ireland had a romantic view of the people as an abstract mass that they could unleash, rather than invite actual working people or tenant farmers to participate in the Confederation in any meaningful way, so that valuable insights were excluded. If the rebels did not know at the start that the still-famine-stricken peasants had no fight in them, they were quickly confronted by this reality.

The Catholic Church had opposed the Young Ireland cause, fearing anti-clerical excesses would be released by any breakdown in law and order. This conservative policy seemed confirmed when, on the eve of the arrests, the revolution in France took a bloody turn with a workers' rebellion against the new republic resulting in the death of the Archbishop of Paris.[132] Keneally points out that as the Young Irelanders moved about the countryside, stirring a particular community to action, the priests would then use their authority to calm down and disperse the Catholics.[133]

O'Brien, ever the honourable aristocrat, accepted responsibility as commander for 'this disastrous failure', especially for 'having totally misjudged the energies of the Irish People'.[134] Clearly he must shoulder blame for errors of timing and repeatedly failing to press Young Ireland's advantage in what Rudé ridicules as an 'impeccably courteous attempt to overturn the state'.[135] Keneally argues that O'Brien's failure to allow a starving people access to the food and the property of landlords was fatal for the revolution.[136] Duffy complained that O'Brien could never forget 'as Mirabeau and Lafayette forgot, that he belonged to the caste of gentlemen' and O'Donohoe reasoned that their captain lacked the necessary 'viciousness'.[137] The romantic rebel, like many officers in the Canadian uprisings, was too enamoured of the noble defeat and, nurtured on the classics, found solace in the heroic last stand of the Spartans against the Persian hordes at Thermopylae.[138] O'Brien's outdated code of chivalry left him no match for the Irish police, let alone soldiers. In a show of contempt for the cognitive capacity of the constabulary, Meagher had earlier boasted how 'an eloquent speech is enough, of itself, to disorganise the police force of Ireland'.[139] However, in the heat of battle words failed Young Ireland. Romanticism and student debates had provided inspiration for stirring speeches but in the field there was no substitute for the arts of war.

The failure of the uprising led inexorably to trial and punishment. The state's case against the accused men was easy to prove, given Young Ireland's commitment to an open revolution, and the publication of their intentions in newspaper articles and reported speeches that were tendered in court. First to be tried were Gavan Duffy, John Martin and Kevin O'Doherty, arrested for their publishing blitz in the lead-up to hostilities and charged with Treason Felony. Martin was found guilty of advising people to take up arms. Unbowed he told the court:

> *My object in all proceedings has been simply to assist in establishing the national independence of Ireland for the benefit of all people of Ireland—noblemen, landlords, clergymen, judges, professional men—in fact, all citizens, all Irishmen.*[140]

The twenty-four-year-old O'Doherty had to be tried three times before a jury would find him guilty. After five juries failed to convict Duffy, the authorities reluctantly released the rebel publisher, who wasted no time resurrecting *The Nation*. It was not all bleak for O'Doherty. Keneally's research reveals that the young medical student was visited by the poet Mary Ann Kelly, and the two 'glittering children of the revolution', as he called them, fell in love.[141] Both Martin and O'Doherty were sentenced to ten years' transportation beyond the seas. 'Eva' promised O'Doherty she would wait for his return.

In late September O'Brien, Meagher, McManus and O'Donohoe faced a special Judicial Commission in Clonmel, Tipperary accused of high treason. It was deeds, not words, for which they were charged, including 'lev[ying] war on our Sovereign Lady the Queen in her realm', marching 'in a warlike manner through diverse villages, towns, places and highways' and the attack on the 'dwelling house in which a large body of constables then were lawfully assembled'.[142] Each of the men was found guilty. In delivering their verdicts the jury asked the judge to show mercy in sentencing, for treason was a capital offence, and they expected that a man of O'Brien's stature and of Meagher's youth would be spared. However the court, determined that the Irish know the consequences of making war on the Sovereign, was in no mood for mercy.

Prior to sentencing on 23 October 1948, O'Brien addressed the Commission, with brevity declaring, 'I am perfectly satisfied with the consciousness that I have performed my duty to my country; that I have done only that, in my opinion, it was the duty of every Irishman to have done.'[143]

Then Chief Justice Blackburn turned to Smith O'Brien and delivered the traditional punishment for high treason, that the prisoner would be

> *drawn on a hurdle to the place of execution, and be hanged by the neck until you are dead; and that afterwards your head will be severed from your body, and your body divided into four quarters, and to be disposed of as Her Majesty shall think fit.*[144]

In quick succession this terrible sentence was imposed on each of the other three rebels, O'Donohoe, McManus and Meagher, all of whom refused to plead for mercy.[145] In his address to the court Tom Meagher had accepted his fate, confident that

> *it so happens, and it will ever happen so, that they who have tried to serve their country, no matter how weak the efforts may have been, are sure to receive the thanks and blessings of its people.*[146]

To applause from the gallery, the devout Catholic looked forward to a 'higher tribunal' where 'many of the judgements of this court will be reversed'.

But having demonstrated exemplary justice, the government did not want the prisoners to be executed, for that would certainly transform the bumbling rebels into martyrs.[147] Therefore as an act of mercy by the Sovereign, the death penalty was commuted to transportation for life. O'Brien was to be exiled from his beloved Ireland and family for the rest of his days, while Meagher and O'Doherty at the very least faced wasting their youth and potential confined at the ends of the Earth. The four men sailed together for Australia on the *Swift* and docked at Hobart Town on 27 October 1849. On board they were treated as gentlemen, though William Smith O'Brien had to make his own bed for the first time in his life.[148]

In *Protest and Punishment* Rudé assessed the Young Ireland revolution as a 'disaster and a dismal failure' and depicted O'Brien as a bungler.[149] The historian's sympathies lie more with the common men and women driven to commit acts of social resistance than gentlemen rebels who talked big and led their followers literally up a garden path. These criticisms echo those of the *London Times*, that decided the best way to neuter Irish nationalism was to mock, rather than demonise, its leaders. Smith O'Brien was continually depicted as an ineffectual martinet among Widow McCormack's cabbages, or as a pantomime fugitive trying to elude capture in disguise. Such lampooning was designed to unman the would-be rebels and now state prisoners, so as to deny them the status of Irish heroes. Otherwise they might become martyrs. Marcus Clarke passed this refrain to Australian readers in 1871, claiming there was 'something pathetic in an Irish rebellion stifled at its birth' and argued that if

> *the patriots ... had been shot down in the heat of battle, or executed on the scaffold the world would have accorded them the respect they merited ... but to be captured in a gooseberry garden and put in a Tasmanian corner like a naughty boy—most miserable!*[150]

But the well-connected Clarke, despite his sympathy for the plight of convicts, was no friend of the Irish, and he underestimated the impact the rebels' exile had on the wider Irish diaspora. Thomas Keneally, in his magisterial history of the Irish struggles of the nineteenth century, has a keen sense for the imaginative element of Irish nationalism, and a different assessment of the quixotic Young Ireland revolution. He argues it confirmed 'O'Brien and Meagher as two of the most admired Irish figures of the nineteenth century' and fed 'an Irish sense that it was always the irrepressible myth, not the potent battalion, which conquered in the end'.[151] The myth was made potent and lasting not in the half-hearted musters and failed skirmishes of 1848 but in Van Diemen's Land, where the Young Ireland prisoners waged a new war to keep their cause alive before the Irish people and the world.

* * *

RESISTANCE IN VAN DIEMEN'S LAND

THE MANNER IN WHICH THE YOUNG IRELAND REBELS BORE THEIR exile and confinement was an area over which they still had some control, due to the government's differential treatment of convicts on the basis of social class, and also a policy decision to spare them from the worst indignities of the probation system, lest the prisoners attract attention with allegations of official brutality. But this required that the exiles and their colonial warders accept the comfortable oblivion the government in London had prepared for them.

As soon as the *Swift* docked in Hobart, the prisoners were visited by the superintendant of prisons, who made an offer that was difficult to refuse. Lieutenant-Governor William Denison had been authorised by the Secretary of State for Colonies Earl Grey to offer each prisoner a ticket-of-leave immediately.[152] This meant that they could avoid the probation system to which all convicts, including 'politicals', like the American patriots had been subjected. Instead the men would be able to seek work on the free market, retain their pay, arrange their own accommodation, and be free agents within the colony, subject to conditions. Most onerously implied in the ticket-of-leave was a promise on their word of honour not to escape. They were on parole and this meant further restrictions based on the danger the colonial authorities feared they might pose. As well as reporting monthly to a magistrate and observing a 10 pm curfew, each man would be confined to a distinct district in Van Diemen's Land, no two of them allowed in the same one, lest they conspire.[153]

Denison and Grey were confident that the prisoners, anxious to avoid hard labour and the impact of probation on their health and peace of mind, would snatch the opportunity to retain a measure of autonomy. Historian of Young Irelanders' exile, Blanche Touhill, argued that Earl

Grey wanted to consign the rebels to 'gentlemanly obscurity' and to avoid at all costs creating martyrs yet again.[154] Wiser heads in the British Government would be mindful of the mistake made with the Tolpuddle labourers, where official overreaction created martyrs whose value to their cause was magnified through transportation. Indeed, Grey's father headed the government responsible for that error, and current Prime Minister Lord John Russell had worked hard back in the 1830s to salvage the public relations disaster and secure pardons for the exiled trade unionists. They knew it was important that the Young Ireland leaders not be subjected to a harsh regime that may attract sympathy. It is likely the government also wished to spare the prisoners indignities, especially that of mixing with the common criminals, out of genuine respect for the men's status as gentlemen. The preferential treatment of better-educated and culturally and economically upper-class convicts was especially imperative in the case of O'Brien, as a noble and political peer connected by kinship and politics to the most powerful men in the land. Grey was also mindful that the radical MPs in Westminster would be ever vigilant about what became of all the Young Irelanders, especially their former colleague William Smith O'Brien.

But the four prisoners, unable to leave the *Swift* until they made up their minds, knew the government's offer was a double-edged sword. Crucially, the ticket-of-leave posed a moral dilemma for men of honour such as the Young Ireland leaders. Once they had been given their parole, they could not, as gentlemen, try to escape, without suffering dishonour. To be dishonoured would jeopardise their martyrdom and discredit the Irish cause. There was another political implication that the subtle ruling-class mind of O'Brien immediately divined. It would be difficult for the Young Ireland exiles to attract attention to their suffering if they were allowed to be kept as well-fed birds in a gilded cage. Was not the onus on him, as the most pampered of the Young Irelanders and with the best call on outside supporters, to take the hard road?

After much interrogation of their captors as to their rights and obligations, Meagher, McManus and O'Donohoe each accepted the ticket-of-leave and Denison's conditions, consigned to the despondent reality that they could not escape. There were compelling reasons. They knew the dangers of being treated as a common criminal in terms of their physical and mental health. But it was also important to maintain their distinction from common criminals, in the eyes of the free colonial settlers and also the wider world. Martyrdom required that they refuse the definition of felon and the disgrace of criminality. The Victorian era had a terror of descent into the lower orders, which is explicit as a theme in the most famous convict novel of them all, *For the Term of His Natural Life*. On board ship the Young Irelanders had enjoyed their own cabins, ate with the officers and were not made to dress as convicts. The government's plan would save the Yong Ireland leaders from an unnecessary descent into shame and possibly harm.

They were allocated their districts: Meagher first to Campbell Town, then Ross; McManus went to Launceston, then later transferred to New Norfolk on the Derwent and O'Donohoe was allowed the privilege of living in Hobart, so that he might practise as a law clerk. When O'Doherty and Martin arrived four days later, they too chose the ticket-of-leave.[155] O'Doherty was sent to Oatlands, a village near Ross, where he attempted to put some of his medical training to use. Martin was sent to the farming district of Bothwell, north of Hobart.

However O'Brien was resolved to call their bluff. As the acknowledged leader, he refused the offer of a ticket-of-leave, insisting on his right as a prisoner of war to escape:[156]

> *having fully resolved to bind myself to no engagement whatsoever—a resolution not hastily formed but the result of long deliberation I replied without hesitation that I could not make any pledge that I would not attempt to escape.*[157]

Denison was furious. A no-nonsense military engineer who believed in the stick rather than the carrot, the governor worried that the politicals might seek to subvert Grey's concessions, and would have preferred to see the Young Irelanders on the road gangs.[158] As it was, O'Brien was conveyed by steamer to the isolated Darlington probation station on Maria Island, 4 kilometres (2 miles) from the east coast and a day's voyage north from Hobart. From this outpost escape would be difficult, but he had confounded the government's plan. Meagher, too, had secured some wriggle room, negotiating a provisional ticket-of-leave of only six months, implicitly establishing the precedent that his parole might be surrendered in advance should he resolve to escape.[159]

O'Brien had decided that the best way to prevent the world forgetting about the exiles and their cause was to pursue a strategy of resistance from within his confinement. Even before the prisoners had departed from Ireland, O'Brien, an astute lawyer, had entered into a legal cat-and-mouse game with the British Government and the judicial system. First he applied to the Queen's Bench in Dublin for a writ of error on seventeen objections prior to the verdicts, but these were overruled.[160] After learning of their exile, O'Brien then challenged the legality of transporting prisoners found guilty of treason, arguing that Ireland was not strictly a realm of the King as defined in the relevant Act of Edward III.[161] He sought a writ of *habeas corpus* to prevent transportation taking place, stating, 'I do not consent to be transported and if as I am assured is the case the law does not authorise the government to transport me, I claim the protection of the Law.'[162] As a group, the four men sentenced for treason then petitioned the House of Commons on the same grounds. The writ failed, but troubled by O'Brien's reasoning the Home Secretary had the Commons pass retrospective legislation—never a good look.[163] O'Brien demonstrated that he was a formidable opponent who had the capacity, even from a cell, to resist his gaolers and embarrass the government. This was a taste of things to come, as the Young Ireland prisoners would launch several legal challenges in Van Diemen's Land questioning the government's authority to hold them, with wide-reaching ramifications for the transportation system.

* * *

THE NOBLEMAN VS THE GOVERNOR

WILLIAM SMITH O'BRIEN WAS CONFINED TO A SMALL COTTAGE WITHIN the prison complex on Maria Island, but was initially allowed freedom of movement around the small outpost. He quickly won the respect of the superintendent at Darlington, Samuel Lapham, who was Irish, as well as many of the guards and the Catholic Priest.[164] O'Brien became a welcome visitor to the Lapham family home, enjoying the female company of his amiable wife and daughter. However, O'Brien's popularity with his gaolers caused unease for their superiors in Hobart, especially the Comptroller General, Dr John Hampton. O'Brien found his privileges removed, his rations reduced and was effectively placed in solitary confinement. Exercise was forbidden and he was denied all but perfunctory conversation with the prison staff. O'Brien likened his condition to being 'buried alive'.[165]

Colonial Secretary Grey would not have wished for the confinement of such a noble personage in this way, but Van Diemen's Land was a long way from London.[166] Hampton's justification was the need to prevent the prisoner, who was committed to escaping, from carrying out his threat. In reality he and Denison were toughening up O'Brien's conditions to compel him to accept the offer of a ticket-of-leave, which they persisted in dangling before him. This punitive attitude by the colonial administration was a miscalculation by Denison that gave O'Brien his opportunity to resurrect the Young Ireland cause from 'gentlemanly obscurity'.

As the government would not dare stop O'Brien writing and posting letters, he began an energetic correspondence campaign designed to attract local sympathy and bring the attention of the Commons and the press to his plight.[167] On 22 November he wrote to Irish MP Thomas Chilsolm Anstey, a man who had lived in the colony, explaining the reasons for his refusal of the ticket-of-leave, and complaining that the governor was exceeding his authority by imposing the unjustified punishment of solitary confinement. He explained to Anstey, and therefore the Commons where his letter was read out, that he considered it 'advisable not to fetter myself by an engagement which I should hold binding upon me as a man of honour but which an unscrupulous man would easily find some pretext of evading'.[168] O'Brien accused the governor of using inhumane methods to coerce him into accepting a ticket-of-leave. Letters expressing similar complaints were sent to powerful members of the O'Brien family, including his brother-in-law Charles Monsell, who brought it to the attention of his close friend William Gladstone, the rising Liberal politician in the Commons.[169]

By the 1850s the Australian colonies had a robust, at times rambunctious, press servicing a growing market for local and international news. O'Brien's confinement was both. The *South Australian Register* and the *Hobart Town Guardian* both came out in sympathy for the exile, the latter, reproving the government's 'unjust and irresponsible coercion in the case of Smith O'Brien'.[170] Surprised by the bad publicity the government's chief medical officer examined the now controversial prisoner, and increased his rations, using the opportunity to unsubtly advise that he accept the ticket-of-leave for his health's sake, which he refused.

In the New Year of 1850 O'Brien suffered chest pains related to a burgeoning heart condition, and his health began a downward spiral.[171] Denison relented and relaxed the restrictions on exercise and the prisoner was allowed outside with an overseer. Lapham then exercised discretionary powers given to commandants to preserve the health of prisoners, and ended the ban on staff conversing with the prisoner. O'Brien had a temporary respite from solitary confinement, during which time the rebel leader found support from an unexpected quarter. By the late 1840s Van Diemen's Land boasted a vigorous anti-transportation movement made up of free settlers determined that London should cease sending convicts to her shore. Anti-transportation acquired new momentum across Australia following Earl Grey's decision in 1848 to recommence transportation to New South Wales, including the Port Phillip settlement and districts yet to be separated as Victoria. The opponents of transportation were entwined with the campaign to win responsible government and greater independence for the colonies, as local autonomy seemed the only way to stop the convict ships. O'Brien was introduced into this movement when he sought legal opinion about the lawfulness of his confinement from the Hobart solicitor Robert Pitcairn and the barrister T. Knight, both leading anti-transportationists.[172] Knight advised O'Brien that he could bring a case that he was being illegally confined that would have implications for the wider convict system, but, more importantly, would bring the exile's case to the just formed Anti-Transportation League, sensing how the Young Irelanders might help their cause and vice versa.[173] The prisoner now had hope, but decided to keep his powder dry for the time being. Unlike Ballingarry, this was a battle that the politically sophisticated O'Brien was equipped to win.

From the start there was a groundswell of support in the colonies for the prisoners, especially among the Irish diaspora. When O'Doherty and Martin passed through Sydney Harbour en route to Hobart a meeting of the city's Irish hailed the unseen Young Irelanders as heroes rather than felons and established a committee to monitor the treatment of political prisoners.[174] In Van Diemen's Land the free Irish, even among guards, officials and priests, respected the patriots and sought to lend covert assistance. The anti-transportation advocates, on the other hand, tended to hail from the Protestant establishment, were anxious about the contamination of free settlers by the criminals in their midst and cared more about antipodean than Irish liberty.[175] Moving between these groups was Hobart businessman Richard Dry, a Protestant and Legislative Councillor, but also the son of the transported United Irish rebel-made-good of the same name. Both an Irish nationalist and leading opponent of convictism, Dry was one of the first men of influence to offer assistance to William Smith O'Brien.

Like Dry, most opponents of transportation looked forward to self-governing Australian colonies with economies free of the shackles of forced convict labour, and expected to play leadership roles in newly empowered representative institutions. Their cause had supporters in Westminster, but back in Van Diemen's Land, Denison was a staunch defender of both transportation and his Executive prerogatives.[176] Not surprisingly, anti-transportationists throughout the Australian colonies came to recognise in the Young Irelanders like-minded advocates for greater colonial autonomy. Significant newspapers in Van Diemen's Land and the mainland, such as the *Launceston Examiner*, were opposed to transportation too, and as they learned of O'Brien's plight, they took the Young Irelander's side in his conflict with Denison as a way to bring both the convict system and 'irresponsible' viceregal rule into discredit.[177]

Between April and June 1850 articles irked by O'Brien's treatment began appearing in the Irish and British press. The *Limerick Chronicle* set the tone, thundering that O'Brien's health was at risk 'from this tyrannous oppression, aggravated as it must appear when the Government of a great empire thus concentrates its giant force to crush a solitary individual'.[178] Many editorials admired his refusal to accept the offer of a ticket-of-leave. The collapse in O'Brien's health was centre stage when concerned MPs began quizzing the Home Secretary about the exile's condition in the House of Commons. Meetings were held in Cork, Limerick, Dublin and Kerry protesting O'Brien's treatment and expressing the deepest sympathy for the 'exiled patriot'.[179] Petitions were sent from Ireland to the Queen. The story was picked up by the American press and a meeting of over a thousand Irish-Americans was held at Tammany Hall, in New York. Amid parliamentary debate, Liberal and Radical members alike called on the Whig Government to pardon O'Brien.[180] The media and political discourse around O'Brien now presented him as a prisoner of war. A 'volley of dispatches' between Denison and Earl Grey investigated by Touhill reveal the Colonial Secretary's frustration that the policy of consigning the Young Irelanders to obscurity had failed.[181]

O'Brien had won an important victory. His stubborn refusal of a ticket-of-leave and campaign against his vindictive gaolers had stirred

Defeated but unbowed: the aristocrat William Smith O'Brien, prisoner at Kilmainham Gaol, Dublin on 31 August 1848.

the conscience of Westminster and reawakened the ire of the Irish people. Rallies were held in the streets of Dublin demanding O'Brien be released and supporters made pilgrimages to his home. Even the British newspapers that had earlier mocked O'Brien's ineffectual revolution now praised his dignity under intolerable repression, and wondered if pardons might be in order. In the Australian colonies the anti-transportation movement had made O'Brien their *cause célèbre*, using his case to attack the detested Denison and to expose the evil inherent in the convict system. Like South African political prisoner Nelson Mandela confined on Robben Island more than a century later, O'Brien had succeeded in becoming not just a martyr to a failed cause, but a cause himself, a leader of his people in the eyes of the world.

Most significantly for the future of the Irish struggle, O'Brien and the Young Ireland cause were now the toast of the Irish diaspora in America. Irish-American political leaders called on Britain to free William Smith O'Brien and his comrades, and the US Government, mindful of Irish electoral clout, was prevailed upon to request that Grey pardon the exile. Michael Doheny, one of the Young Ireland veterans of 1848 who escaped to America, declared at a mass rally '[i]f you wish to send comfort to Smith O'Brien, tell him there are a hundred thousand Irishmen in America ready to fight the battle of freedom'.[182] This was a promise of things to come, called into being by O'Brien's stand. As in Australia, the continuously replenished Irish community in the United States—numbering four million immigrants and their children—developed multi-identities and dual allegiances with the difference that in the young republic they enjoyed freedoms to act on their Irish nationalism that would have been seditious or treasonous on British territory.[183] A new organisation of Irish émigrés in New York City, going by the Francophilic name of the Irish Directory, began to hatch plans for direct action.

Meanwhile the convict John Mitchel had circled the globe like unwanted contraband. Arriving in tropical Bermuda, he was taken from the *Scourge* where he had enjoyed the status of a gentleman above decks and was confined in a 0.55 metre square (6 feet square) cell aboard the prison hulk *Dromedary*.[184] Here he found distraction from the tepid heat and crawling cockroaches by reading Homer.[185] Mitchel's 'odyssey' recommenced when he was among a group of convicts chosen to be shipped on the *Neptune* to a new penal settlement at the Cape colony in Southern Africa.[186] But here, as in Van Diemen's Land (and New South Wales a decade earlier), a political movement opposed to transportation was gathering momentum. Cape Town colonists were determined not to become another dumping ground for criminals, and resolved that the new prison would be starved of supplies. Loud protest greeted the ship's arrival, and the authorities deemed it unwise to unload the convicts, who instead endured five months detention on board while the ship lay at anchor offshore.[187] This stance was somewhat hypocritical given the Cape colony had transported its own subjects as felons to New South Wales and Van Diemen's Land, and used this punishment to expel indigenous Khoi and San who resisted removal from their lands and discriminatory labour practices.[188]

The *Neptune* eventually sailed for Van Diemen's Land, where, despite protest by the anti-transportationists on its arrival in April 1850, all prisoners bar controversial felon Mitchel were pardoned as compensation for their ordeal. Seriously ill from the voyage through the tropics, Mitchel had no choice but to accept the ticket-of-leave in the hope that he might convalesce. He was, however, allowed the concession of staying in Bothwell with Martin, who dutifully nursed his old friend to recovery. He sent word to his beloved wife Jenny in Ireland, who made the long journey with their children to be by his side.[189]

* * *

SNAKES AND LADDERS

FROM THE TIME OF THE ARRIVAL OF THE YOUNG IRELAND PRISONERS in Van Diemen's Land there was debate about the prisoners' status. Were they 'state prisoners' afforded privileges and freedoms allowed to prisoners of war, such as the right to escape? Or were they to be treated more like ordinary convicts, and subject to the carrots, sticks and petty torments of the probation system? The Young Irelanders insisted they be treated as prisoners of war, and the government back in London appeared to back this interpretation, given their special treatment on board ship and the instructions to Governor Denison specifying that the prisoners be granted tickets-of-leave. The prisoners hoped that by conducting themselves as prisoners of war, they ennobled their cause, and kept it alive. But it quickly became apparent to the prisoners on tickets-of-leave that Denison and his penal bureaucracy honoured the form, though not substance, of the deal. The Young Ireland prisoners might live as gentlemen while the money or employment lasted, but minor misdemeanours, often interpreted on a whim by surly officials, resulted in a loss of privileges, and more serious breaches would see them sent to a probation station to perform hard labour alongside the ordinary felons. For example, O'Doherty, who had resumed his medical studies in the colony, found his bid to practise medicine frustrated at every turn.[190]

Still, the prisoners found artful ruses to subvert the system's rules. Two and sometimes three of the prisoners in adjoining districts quickly discovered geographical points of intersection, such as the picturesque Lake Sorell, and began to regularly meet there. Soon, local worthies were lining up to be guests at these spirited soirees. Ever the gentlemen, Meagher and O'Doherty would thumb their nose at their careless keepers by ostentatiously setting up a table and dining on a bridge bordering their two districts.[191] It was important for the Young Irelanders to subvert Denison's system in these subtle ways, to ensure that they did not become cowered by authority. Gaols, even those with golden bars, extract conformity to their rules, and establish control of inmates by breaking a prisoner's spirit.

However, like their captain O'Brien, the ticket-of-leave men sought to exploit their relative liberty to embark on a more overt strategy of resistance. A natural field for the Young Irelanders to commence their fight back was the media. Staring Hampton and Denison in the eyes, the crazy-brave Patrick O'Donohoe had the temerity to begin publishing a newspaper in Hobart, titled *The Irish Exile*.[192] Here was a platform for the state prisoners to report their doings and problems, expose social ills and shape colonial public opinion in a liberal direction. It also proved a popular vehicle with erstwhile writers within the Irish diaspora in Van Diemen's Land, cultivating a community in exile. Incredibly the authorities allowed the newspaper to operate for a time, perhaps fearing a backlash, but Denison warned London that it represented an 'attempt to sow dissension among the people of the Colony'.[193] This news disturbed Grey more than any other, and he immediately advised Denison that should the state prisoners by any action 'create discontent and disturb the Society they should be immediately deprived of their ticket-of-leave'.[194] O'Donohoe was a marked man.

The authorities were in fact more vigilant than the prisoners suspected and things became tougher. When Mitchel and McManus met in an inn to discuss O'Brien's predicament, they were informed on and punished with temporary confinement. When O'Doherty, McManus and O'Donohoe were discovered in another district, they were each sent by Denison to a probation station for three months, decked out in prison uniforms and for the first time cast among the ordinary felons. O'Doherty wrote to Meagher, 'I am treated as a common convict, obliged to sleep with every species of scoundrel and to work in a gang from six o'clock in the morning to six o'clock in the evening being all the while next to half starved.'[195] Public meetings were held in Van Diemen's Land and the mainland demanding their release back into the community, while McManus had Knight seek his release through a writ of *habeas corpus* that challenged the authority of the governor to arbitrarily suspend an Irish convict's ticket-of-leave. To Denison's surprise, two judges of the Supreme Court ordered the release of McManus from the probation station until the Crown produced the legal documents proving that it had authority over the prisoner. Incredibly, it transpired that the administration in Van Diemen's Land lacked the key document, the Certification of Conviction, not just for McManus, but most convicts, and did not have copies of the Irish statutes on transportation.[196] Officials in Hobart and London scrambled to secure their paperwork lest the integrity of the transportation system be weakened by further court challenges. Once again Denison had underestimated the determination and ability of the Young Irelanders to work public opinion and the law in their favour.

O'Donohoe, turning to drink and increasingly unstable, began a downward slide into the nether lands of the system. When he attacked Denison directly in a letter to the *Launceston Examiner*, the governor immediately revoked O'Donohoe's ticket-of-leave. Calculating that the incorrigible publisher lacked the powerful friends of some of the other exiles, Hampton immediately dispatched him to six months' hard labour on a chain gang, forcing the sickly O'Donohoe into convict garb and the company of hard-bitten felons. From the governor down, the officials in the colony sought to keep the Young Irelanders' position ambiguous, following the letter of the Home Office's directions but at every turn compelling them to abide by the rules or suffer the punishments for incorrigibles, such as probation stations, solitary confinement, cuts to rations and work gangs. Denison resented the Young Irelanders' airs and their determination to resist conforming to the system. It was clear he would not grant them the courtesies of prisoners of war, but rather considered them criminals, traitors and troublemakers.

Around this time accusations began circulating in official circles that O'Brien had enjoyed an inappropriate sexual relationship with the thirteen-year-old daughter of the commandant, Susan Lapham, who was said to be smitten by the charming aristocrat. An official at Darlington claimed to have spied the two engaging in an indecent act.[197] Despite exhaustive research by Keneally and historian of Young Ireland, Richard Davis, it remains unclear whether this was a vindictive fabrication designed to discredit O'Brien at the moment of his public triumph, or whether the great man had succumbed to vanity and temptation and risked the ruination of an innocent girl.[198] O'Brien denied the accusation. It is impossible at this distance in time to know the truth of the matter, except to note that the government never pursued or publicised the allegations, and O'Brien remained a close friend of the Laphams for the duration of his time in the colony.

While the anti-transportationists began to rally colonial public opinion in favour of a pardon for the increasingly respected political exiles, an underground support group was also established, led by McManus and Meagher and assisted by local and American sympathisers. Its aim was to rescue O'Brien, who remained steadfastly committed to escape. The plan proceeded quickly. A whaler, the *Victoria*, was engaged under the command of a Captain Ellis to drop anchor off Maria Island on an appointed day. Father Woolfrey, the Catholic chaplain at Darlington, passed the information to O'Brien that on the appointed day while taking his regular walk on the beach with his overseer a long boat full of armed men would land, overpower the guard and row him to the waiting *Victoria*, that would convey him to the United States.[199] It did not work out that way. Hampton had been warned of the rescue attempt and the guard was forewarned and threatened to shoot O'Brien as he plunged into the waves. More curiously, those aboard the long boat made no attempt to rescue him but instead left him in the water for the guard.[200] It transpired that Ellis had betrayed O'Brien, doubly profiting from the money paid him by the plotters and whatever reward came his way.

O'Brien's privileges were now at an end. He was swiftly removed from Maria Island to the maximum security prison of secondary punishment at Port Arthur. As punishment for the near escape under his watch and his persistent fraternisation with his notorious prisoner, Superintendent Lapham, due to be promoted to commandant at Port Arthur, was dismissed from the post. O'Brien was confined once more, but to a two-storey cottage that exceeded the comforts available to most ordinary colonists at this time. Specially built to house the celebrity political detainee, it was so sturdy it still stands to this day. Yet O'Brien was back in solitary confinement, denied all but the most rudimentary intercourse with other human beings. Isolation was a Port Arthur specialty, designed to reform the miscreant where the whip failed, but actually just as effective in breaking a man's spirit. He concluded that this penal settlement had 'probably witnessed more of human suffering than almost any spot of equal size on the face of the globe'.[201] With his health once again failing and the fog of depression settling on his soul, O'Brien at last conceded to the government's request and accepted a ticket-of-leave. He could now accept the condition not to escape, having brought the exiles' cause to world attention, and having tried at great cost to flee his island prison. His family and political supporters back home and in the colony were overjoyed at this decision, as they feared he would perish at Port Arthur. Sent to the Derwent Valley district, O'Brien initially took lodgings at New Norfolk and tried his hand as a private tutor to a well-to-do-family.

Networking with anti-transportationist forces within the community, O'Brien continued to be a thorn in Denison's side.

He stepped up his letter writing war of words and remained the focus of a campaign that stretched from the colony to Britain, Ireland and the United States to secure pardons for the Young Irelanders. The *Launceston Examiner* condemned Denison's decision to consign three Young Irelanders to the work gangs as typical of his arbitrary rule, arguing that O'Brien had 'superior' credentials to be governor.[202] Representative but not responsible government came to Van Diemen's Land in 1850, with the granting of a Legislative Council in which two-thirds were elected on a property franchise and one third appointed by the Governor. Despite all elected positions going to candidates opposed to transportation, Denison remained very much in control.[203] Despite being a prisoner, O'Brien now found himself invited into the drawing rooms of newly elected MLCs, contributing ideas and consulted on tactics. Away from politics, the exiled aristocrat was now at liberty to enjoy what 'Society' Van Diemen's Land could offer, becoming a welcome guest in the homes of the wealthy and powerful, a favourite of the ladies and the toast of dinners and balls.[204]

It reveals much about class distinction in the convict system to contrast the treatment of the Young Ireland leaders with those of another five ordinary Confederacy fighters from Waterford who were convicted and transported for the aborted attack on a police barracks under O'Brien in 1848. Their names were John Walsh, Thomas Donovan, Cornelius O'Keefe, Thomas Wall and Edmund Sheafy and their sentences ranged from seven to fourteen years.[205] As they were all farm labourers or tradesmen and unlikely to attract international attention, they were accorded no special status as state prisoners and left to the petty tyrannies of the probation regime. Far from being offered an immediate ticket-of-leave, they had to wait the customary period in probation stations relative to the length of sentence. This accords with the treatment dished out to other political prisoners from working-class and lower-middle-class backgrounds, such as the Chartists.[206] Despite penalties for misdemeanours they acquitted themselves well and had secured free pardons by 1854. The success story was Tom Wall, who had a steep fourteen year sentence. He learned to read and write in a convict school, and through 'meritorious' service fighting bush fires was pardoned five years after his conviction.[207]

While the Young Ireland prisoners were pledged to liberate the Irish people in the abstract, up close and personal with real people who hailed from the 'lower orders' they exhibited prejudices typical of their class. The worst offender was Mitchel, who was scathing about colonial society. He later confessed to never shaking 'a violent horror of Australia and Van Diemen's Land', peopled as they were by 'detestable Savages, Savages *de*civilised'.[208] He reserved his worst vituperation for the ordinary convicts, mainly urban English, who tried to become farmers, complaining:

> *human they are not. Their training [in crime] has made them subterhuman, preterhuman; and the system of British 'reformatory discipline' has gone as near to making them perfect fiends as human wit can go.*[209]

Close proximity to the convict-settlers had bred not enmity but contempt. Believing them to be tainted stock made worse through the transportation system, he advocated only one reform: 'What a blessing to these creatures, and to mankind ... if they had been hanged.'[210] Mitchel was giving vent to the elitism, even proto-fascism, that underpinned his radical conservatism.

The liberal-minded O'Brien had more humane views about the convicts, wondering 'whether upon the whole the convicts as a class are not equal to the great majority of those who shrink from them with abhorrence', asking if 'the keeper of the criminal has not often exhibited as much ferocity as the criminal himself'.[211] Writing on the same theme, O'Donohoe was critical of the vulgar caste of the wider free society, complaining 'they do nothing but eating, drinking, whoring and backbiting—and the disease runs through all Classes, from the Merchant and Professional man down to the shoe boy!'[212] In his *Irish Exile* he exposed the arbitrary cruelties of the convict system, and making a connection with another conquered people, condemned the settlers for the theft of Aborigines' 'rightful heritage'.[213] O'Brien, also outraged by the killing and forced removal of the original inhabitants from the island, was moved to write '[p]erhaps in the annals of mankind there is no page more dark than that which records the extinction of the Aborigines of Tasmania'.[214]

But even the considered, empathetic O'Brien could be intolerant when the lower classes were elevated above their station—a common enough occurrence in the frontier society of Van Diemen's Land. He strongly disapproved when Meagher decided to marry 'a young governess' of no means whose father had been a convict and thus could never be presented in 'society'. In language reminiscent of Mr Darcy he made it known to the other gentlemen prisoners that while:

> it is not unnatural that [Meagher] should have united to himself the first nice girl that fell his way ... in a worldly point of view the connexion cannot be considered advantageous ... [i]t is hoped that Love will compensate to him the absence of all worldly advantages.[215]

Ultimately the 'people's Tribune', Thomas Meagher, at the height of his celebrity, also came to regret the match.

* * *

ESCAPE TO NEW YORK

WHAT DIFFERENTIATED THE YOUNG IRELAND LEADERS FROM THE Tolpuddle Martyrs was that as well as having influential supporters back home, improved communications meant they could publicise commentaries on their predicament within and from the colony to an eager market for journalism. They could also count on a growing international Irish liberation movement, based in the United States.

Despite the failure of O'Brien's rescue, escape remained very much on the other exiles' agenda. McManus and O'Donohoe dreaded a return to confinement in a probation station while the driven Meagher began to suffer ennui from the absence of purpose and initiative in his life, complaining that 'existence, thus harassed, deadened, drained, ceases to be a blessing—it becomes a penalty'.[216] Rescue became a credible option thanks to the intervention of the Irish Directory in New York, which was moved to act by the press reports of O'Brien's cruel confinement. It dispatched a cashed-up Irish-American agent, the colourfully named Patrick 'Nicaragua' Smyth, to Australia to plot with the ticket-of-leave prisoners and sympathetic citizens to secure their escape. Ships were booked and paid for, and measures taken to maximise security. The biggest hurdle for those prisoners tempted to escape would be the problem of honour, for they had given their word as gentlemen.

McManus took advantage of his release by the court, a hiatus during which his ticket-of-leave and therefore promise not to escape was still officially revoked. While police were distracted by an imposter pretending to be a bed-ridden, feverish McManus, the real prisoner covertly boarded a ship bound for California, the first Young Irelander to escape. His friends found an equally creative way around the problem of their honour. At the last possible moment prior to escape, the prisoner would formally return their ticket-of-leave and withdraw their parole. For honour to be preserved it was important that police had a chance to apprehend them, but in reality bribery, subterfuge and split-second timing would be used to confuse often ambivalent officials. Nevertheless, the very real danger remained that once authorities were informed of the prisoner's intent to escape, the prisoner risked being apprehended and detained in a penal station from which escape would prove difficult.

In quick succession between 1851 and June 1853 Meagher, O'Donohoe and Mitchel each fled their districts after resigning their ticket-of-leave, and made their way to waiting whalers that spirited them to the United States. There were some amusing moments. In order to leave no blemish on his honour, Mitchel entered the Bothwell Court House in great style with a gun-toting Nicaragua Smyth and passed a note to the astonished magistrate resigning his ticket-of-leave. As the bribed guards looked on, he stormed out, mounted his horse and rode into the bush to the cheers of the townspeople.[217] He hid in the mountains and returned some weeks later disguised as a priest and boarded the *Orkney Lass*, rendezvousing with his family in Tahiti. Meagher had the hardest time, left stranded for some time on the barren Waterhouse Island in Bass Strait among other escaped convicts, waiting for the ship that would take him to America.[218] It was apparent that for men with money and connections, even a prison as isolated as Van Diemen's Land could not prevent escape. Predictably, the anti-transportation Australian press sided with the escapees, blaming the 'vicious policy' of the governor and wishing them 'every success and a continuation of freedom'.[219]

Each of the prisoners arrived in America to a hero's welcome. There were speeches by local dignitaries, military parades by Irish-American brigades, brass bands and civic banquets held in their honour. The mayor of San Francisco toasted McManus with the words, 'Ireland gave him birth, England a dungeon; America, a home, with a hundred thousand welcomes.' Meagher was greeted by 7000 well-wishers on his arrival in New York.[220] Like a head of state, Mitchel was honoured with a thirty-one-gun salute as he entered Brooklyn, the heart of New York's Irish community. 'One slave less in Europe—one free man more, America to Thee!' he announced.[221] Fund raisers were organised and the escapees were put up in fine hotels as they crossed the country addressing supporters.

The dashing Thomas Meagher was the most celebrated of all. He inspected military parades and had a club, a military guard and a polka named in his honour.[222] He undertook a nationwide sell-out lecture tour that cemented the Young Ireland revolution in the Irish-American consciousness, and was even invited to the new president's inauguration.[223] The still-ambitious young man was embraced by the Irish-dominated New York Democratic Party based at Tammany Hall, and a new political career beckoned. But at the height of this euphoria, Meagher received the grim news that his three-year-old son had died of influenza, his little bones forever to lie buried in the soil of Van Diemen's Land.

Meagher's wife Catherine, who had never been beyond the island colony, now embarked on a great journey to America via Ireland. Arriving by sea into Dublin she was overawed to be greeted by thousands—there to honour the wife of Tom Meagher the Irish hero of 1848. The couple were reunited on free American soil and recommenced their life together, though Meagher's new found celebrity overwhelmed and then strained the intimate bond they had enjoyed in Van Diemen's Land. In retreat from the marriage, Catherine returned to Ireland, where she died of typhus following the birth of another baby, at age twenty-two. The Meaghers' surviving son was left in the care of his grandfather to be raised an Irishman, while the widower was admitted as a barrister and married the daughter of a successful New York lawyer with an impeccable Democratic Party pedigree.

The prisoners still in Australia were far from mere ghosts at the American banquets. One reception toasted 'William Smith O'Brien and his companions in exile. Rebels to their government, Patriots to their country, Martyrs to liberty; they lost the day, but they have gained immortality.'[224] Moved by the escapees' accounts, concerned Americans petitioned Congress and the President asking that the US Government lobby Britain to secure pardons for the remaining exiles. Overtures were duly made to Her Majesty's Government by Secretary of State Daniel Webster. President Fillmore himself guaranteed that if freed, O'Brien and the other prisoners would be offered 'safe asylum and full protection' in the United States.[225]

* * *

VINDICATION AND VALEDICTION

BACK IN VAN DIEMEN'S LAND, O'BRIEN'S PAROLE AFFORDED HIM the freedom to engage with local politics and return to his earlier parliamentary passion for colonial reform.[226] A reluctant republican, his preference had always been self-government under the British Crown, 'the restoration of the ancient Constitution of Ireland—the Queen, Lords and Commons of Ireland'.[227] Historian Richard Davis explored how O'Brien, like some other Young Irelanders, combined Irish nationalism with support for an empire Ireland had helped forge, but on the proviso that the imperial polity became more of a partnership between member nations.[228] Van Diemen's Land's most famous convict now sought to enter the Australian debate about imperial governance, writing the analytical work *Principles of Government, or Reflections in Exile*, and even drafting a constitution for the island colony, enshrining control of the Executive by a popular Assembly.[229] But responsible government would not come to Van Diemen's Land until transportation ceased.

In 1851 the colony's leading opponent of transportation, *Launceston Examiner* editor Reverend John West, took the lead in uniting with mainland activists appalled at the renewal of transportation to New South Wales and at the immigration of freed felons across Bass Strait to form the Australasian League for the Prevention of Transportation. As well as strengthening their voice in London, the League became a focus for radicals and liberals alike, threatening independence and even a republic, should the British Government refuse to grant the colonies domestic self-determination like the Canadians.[230] In the early 1850s views not dissimilar to O'Brien's were being promoted by newspapers such as the *Hobart Town Courier* that warned

> *[i]f the imperial Government shall continue to pour her criminals upon any part of shores of the States confederated for this purpose a constitutional reason for separation from the parent country will have been established ...*[231]

It did not come to that, as Grey's successor as British Colonial Secretary was persuaded to accede to the colonists' demands. The last convicts were transported to Van Diemen's Land in 1853, and in 1856 the colonists elected their first Legislative Assembly under a new constitution of their own design that replaced rule by the governor with a Cabinet drawn from and responsible to parliament. Though not O'Brien's exact model, it was his liberal vision of an empire of self-governing colonies, rather than Denison's preference for viceregal command and control, that would shape the newly named Tasmania.

Relief finally came to the remaining state prisoners in 1854, with the granting of conditional pardons to Kevin O'Doherty, John Martin and William Smith O'Brien by Lord Palmerston, Home Secretary in a new coalition government.[232] The one-time rebels were allowed to leave the colony and travel anywhere in the world outside Britain's dominions. They booked a vessel to Europe and made their base in France, where they were reunited with their loved ones. O'Doherty's revolutionary sweetheart Mary Ann Kelly, aka 'Eva', had waited faithfully for him to return and they were married according to Catholic rites in 1855. In 1856 O'Brien, O'Doherty and Martin were granted free pardons, and made a heroic return to Dublin to be greeted by crowds in the hundreds of thousands. Martin returned to the cause of Irish independence, albeit by parliamentary means, and in the early 1870s was elected to the House of Commons and held office in the Home Rule League. He died in 1875.

William Smith O'Brien refused all offers to stand for the British Parliament and never resiled from his view that the Revolution of 1848 was the morally correct course of action. However, henceforth he devoted himself as a writer and speaker to the cause of independence by constitutional means. In 1859 O'Brien visited New York, the city that had so rallied to his plight when all hope seemed lost, and found the Irish-American enthusiasm for the cause he ignited undiminished, if a little too radical for his tastes. O'Brien died in Wales in June 1864 at age 61 and was buried an Irish hero. A procession of 3000 accompanied his coffin through the streets of Dublin, where a statue of the unlikely revolutionary stands today.

Kevin O'Doherty was admitted to the Royal College of Physicians in Dublin, enjoyed rapid promotion through the hospital system and returned with Eva to Australia in 1860, perceiving the opportunities for the Irish in self-governing colonies to be quite favourable.[233] He established a thriving medical practice in Brisbane and the former felon was twice elected to the Queensland Legislative Assembly where he passed that colony's first Health Act and tried to abolish the shameful trade in indentured Kanaka labour, known as 'blackbirding'.[234] Eva, at first enthusiastic in her poetry about the new country's 'glorious future's rosy dawning', in time became homesick.[235] Another rebel of 1848, Gavan Duffy, long-time editor of the seminal *The Nation* who no jury would convict, immigrated to Australia just as his friends were being pardoned, and rose to become a leading politician in Victoria. Still committed to the Irish struggle, O'Doherty returned to Ireland in 1885 and was elected to the House of Commons for County Meath on a Home Rule platform. Back in Australia he found his stand on Irish Home Rule had damaged his medical practice, but was able to earn a living as an appointee to the Queensland Health Board and as supervisor of quarantine. O'Doherty passed away in Brisbane aged 82 in 1905, the last of the exiled Young Irelanders. 'Eva', his devoted soulmate in revolution, continued to write until death took her in 1910, aged eighty.

By escaping to America, the other four prisoners relinquished any chance of ever being pardoned, and so condemned themselves to permanent exile from Ireland. This was to be brief for O'Donohoe who, suffering the ill-effects of alcohol dependence, rapidly sank into obscurity in New York's borough of Brooklyn, and died in 1854. When McManus died in 1861, he experienced something of a triumphal homecoming, for his body was returned to Ireland by the Fenians for burial, where it was venerated like the holy relics of a saint. Meagher and Mitchel did particularly well in the United States, continuing their roles as writers, orators and leaders of men. Luckily in America they found a place where the Irish could thrive as free men. As well as advancing politically and in business as Americans, here enterprising Irish could enhance their cultural identity, albeit with a dash of Yankee enterprise.

On arrival in America, Mitchel declared, 'I am a professional revolutionist now, an adventurer, a seditious propagandist.'[236] He did not disappoint. In keeping with a long tradition of political prisoners exiled to Australia, Mitchel penned and published *Jail Journal* detailing his exile, and became an influential journalist, establishing newspapers, first in New York and then in the southern state of Tennessee where he settled his family for a time.[237] Here he shocked many in the Irish diaspora and supporters back home by defending negro slavery and then the Southern Confederacy in the American Civil War. Two of Mitchel's sons gave their lives as soldiers in the Confederate cause, and at the end of hostilities Mitchel became a prisoner of war yet again, this time at the hands of a republic.[238] For Mitchel the civil war was a contest between a traditional and noble agrarian society and a capitalist juggernaut. He believed the industrial north of the United States' bid to impose modernity on the South was no better than mercantile England raping rural Ireland.

Most Irish in America's Northern states did not see it this way, including Thomas Meagher who became a brigadier-general in the Union Army, heading up an Irish battalion. The boy intellectual had become a man of action, and he covered himself in glory—though thousands of Young Irish died on the battlefield. Still Meagher did not neglect the politics, raising his stocks still further within the Democratic Party and among America's Irish. After the war the one time prisoner of the British Empire was appointed acting governor of Montana, a frontier territory on the verge of statehood. Now an agent of the United States' irrepressible westward advance, Governor Meagher was charged with the paradoxical mission of civilising the wild west while depriving the Native Americans of their lands. Like his old adversary Denison, Meagher made many enemies as he sought to impose order, notably among self-styled Republican Party 'Vigilantes', a red-neck oligarchy who had enjoyed free rein in the lawless territory. There Meagher died in 1867, a still-youthful forty-four, drowning in suspicious circumstances after falling from a steamboat on the Missouri River. His body was never found.

Ever the rebel, Mitchel returned twice to Ireland in defiance of his exile, and ran for parliament on an independence platform in 1875. He won, but as an escaped felon his victory was declared invalid. He was then promptly re-elected, and made a great show of refusing his seat of Tipperary, claiming Westminster had no legitimacy in Ireland. Mitchel died on Irish soil after this last quixotic gesture, his long funeral procession stopping a nation not yet free.

✳ ✳ ✳

AFTERMATH: FENIAN RISING

FROM THE ASHES OF YOUNG IRELAND AROSE THE FENIAN PHOENIX. Unlike Young Ireland, the Fenian Brotherhood would be run by hard men along strict military lines. But like Young Ireland, the Fenians would embrace a national dream rich in symbols and grand gestures, and the suppression of their cause by exile would provide a stage for the new movement's greatest triumph.

Thanks to the martyrdom of its leaders, Irish nationalism—and the belief in 'Ireland on her own'—were strengthened by the Young Ireland adventure. The veterans of '48 chose different paths to achieve their goal. Duffy pursued a constitutional plan to elect MPs from a new Irish Parliamentary Party who would stage a strike of MPs at Westminster until an Irish Parliament was granted, or else secede and sit as a new Assembly in Dublin. His forty-eight Irish MPs elected in 1852 held the balance of power for a time, but its members were gradually bought off with government positions and its solidarity was lost. Yet others remained committed to so-called 'physical force', arguing that the problem with 1848 was not the revolution, but its poor organisation and leadership. The challenge was to take the energy unleashed by the Young Irelanders and the groundswell of support triggered by the martyrs and channel it into an effective new outfit.

The founder and first leader of the Fenian Brotherhood was James Stephens, who had served with William Smith O'Brien in the heady days of 1848. Together with John O'Mahony, Stephens had fled the British mop-up and taken refuge in France. There the two Young Irelanders experienced first-hand the revolutionary secret societies of Paris and came to appreciate that where a popular agitation failed a disciplined, underground vanguard might succeed.[239] Returning to Ireland in 1853 after the heat had died down, Stephens made contact with the remnants of the Confederacy, including O'Donovan Rossa's Phoenix Society.[240] Out of these disparate groups the Irish Revolutionary Brotherhood (IRB), popularly known as the Fenians, was inaugurated, first in New York, and then in Dublin on St Patrick's Day, 1858.[241] The name 'Fenian' was derived from the 'Fianna'—mythical warrior guardians of ancient Ireland whose deeds are told in fragments of Gaelic texts.[242] While part of one movement, the Irish and American branches remained structurally separate entities.[243] However, they were as one in their purpose, which was violent revolution to end British rule, brooking no compromise with constitutional reform or parliament. After an initial lull during which the movement's name was changed to the Irish Republican Brotherhood, the Irish Fenians received a burst of purpose and public support following public outpouring at the Irish funeral of McManus in 1861, leading to an influx of fresh young recruits inspired by the Young Ireland martyrs.[244]

From the 1848 debacle Stephens took away valuable lessons about structure, strategy and personnel. First and foremost, to succeed a revolution needed a conspiratorial, not an open, organisation. The perpetual problem for Irish political activism was betrayal by informers, infiltration by government spies and poor collective decision making. To correct these defects, Stephens established the new Fenian Brotherhood on military lines. Members were organised in circles, consisting of 820 men. At its 'centre' was a colonel, who appointed nine captains, who then chose nine sergeants, who in turn recruited nine men.[245] The Head

Centre, James Stephens, chose the 'centres' under him. Those in the lower ranks did not know those under other Sergeants, localising the impact of treachery. The year 1848 exposed a major limitation on Young Ireland as a revolutionary, as opposed to intellectual, society: it was all chiefs and very few Indians. Stephens' military model, by contrast, was a pyramid structure that emphasised central control by a small cadre and a large army of revolutionary 'soldiers'.

Young Ireland was always the plaything of dilettantes and gentlemen. The Fenians advocated recruitment from a much wider social stratum. 'We make no appeal to the aristocracy,' argued the Fenians. 'They are willing tools of an alien government whose policy it is to slay the people, or drive them like noxious vermin from the soil. The people must save themselves.'[246] Men and women from the working class and clerical occupations, and still-active Ribbonmen from the countryside, joined in great numbers and were welcomed into the upper ranks of the Brotherhood. This was a modern innovation, far removed from the Young Ireland idea of gentlemen generals simply rallying 'the people' like mediaeval serfs.[247] But as Keneally points out, recruiting from manual and white-collar workers was also a necessity as the bourgeoisie and nobility had abandoned the idea of violent revolution.[248] Nevertheless the greater egalitarianism of the Fenians reflected a more socialist orientation and the influence of Mitchel's ideas about evicting the large landlords and returning their holdings to the people.[249] Where O'Brien sought to protect landed estates from hungry rebels, the 'one simple object', claimed a Fenian publicist, was 'to rid the land of robbers, and render every cultivator of the soil his own landlord, the proprietor in fee simple of the house and land of his fathers'.[250] No mere liberal republic, the Fenians dreamed of social revolution.

To guarantee loyalty, Stephens introduced a traditional Irish method of enforcing group solidarity. Fenians in Ireland would swear an oath in the manner of the Whiteboys and Ribbonmen, just as the United Irishmen had done when they recruited among the people.[251] Like these traditional peasant fraternities, most Fenians were Catholics, though the Church hierarchy rejected the movement as it had Young Ireland, and the feeling was mutual from an organisation that promoted non-sectarian Irish patriotism.[252]

Significantly, the Fenians did not reject the Young Ireland commitment to cultural nationalism. Its leaders understood the importance of songs, poetry, flags and pageantry to rally its members and create an image of the nation different to Anglo-Ireland. The Fenians still believed that legitimacy for self-government required a great 'rising' of the Irish people against their oppressors. Most importantly the Fenians remained committed to the grand idea born in 1798 of the Irish nation won on the battlefield, its armies led by officers wearing Ireland's uniform and colours. In the 1860s the IRB was yet to commit to a strategy of guerrilla strikes and terrorism, anticipating conventional battles and the swift establishment of a revolutionary government. But unlike the dreamy Young Irelanders, the Fenians would plot and plan for that noble day, systematically testing out Britain's vulnerabilities and attending to practical matters such as the provision of men, guns, ammunition and transport.

McConville stresses that from the United Irishmen onwards, a key orthodoxy of Irish revolutionary strategic thinking was that the moment to strike was when Britain was preoccupied with a war elsewhere.[253] During the Crimean War, John Martin despaired at his countrymen's capacity to share in British Imperial patriotism, and saw this development as a threat to Irish nationalism. The Irish, sadly, were enthusiastic soldiers of empire. Where Martin lamented, Fenian leader John Devoy saw an opportunity. The Indian Mutiny of 1858, a two-year rebellion centred on the Indian 'Sepoys' within the British Army, had hit the Empire where it hurt. The quick escalation of the rebellion exposed the weakness of an overstretched imperium dependent on colonial soldiers for its defence.[254] If even part of the huge Irish personnel within the army—30 per cent on Keneally's calculations—could be persuaded to mutiny at an appointed time, the effects would be devastating for British rule in Ireland, and elsewhere.[255] Beginning in 1863 the Fenians, through their nuggetty chief organiser for the army, John Devoy, undertook a mass recruitment campaign of Irish soldiers within the British Army. This drive occurred not just in Ireland, but also in the British heartland, where the revolution would also be fought.[256] To this end, Irish immigrants in Britain were also cultivated. As in Ireland, members were also recruited in vital infrastructure such as the railways, ports and telegraphs.[257]

The end of the American Civil War in 1865 provided a unique opportunity to recruit, for the coming struggle in Ireland, battle-hardened Irish expatriates with no divided loyalty to the Queen. Jackson calculated that approximately 200,000 Americans and Irish immigrants had sworn the Fenian oath while fighting in that bitter conflict, sometimes in 'green' battalions like that commanded by Tom Meagher.[258] The United States chapter of the IRB would provide men, money and weapons. Drawing on huge reserves of cash and goodwill from Irish-Americans, the branch, based in New York, was robust and entrepreneurial. Given they did not have to operate under quite the same cloak of secrecy in the United States, they were given to parades, festivals and other displays of Irish national identity that enabled members to indulge a nostalgia for the old country. But the war between North and South had tested many American Fenians who were eager to use their fighting skills and guns to liberate Ireland. Indeed, the American Fenians had deliberately used the war to train its members and to win over new ones. Now the New York organisation recruited for the coming liberation of Ireland and arranged the veterans' passage. Commenting on Irish emigration to the new American republic in 1790, Lord Cornwallis predicted, 'They will embark with a spade, and return with musket.'[259] This they did en masse from 1865.

Plans firmed for a revolution to be launched in 1865 to take advantage of the Americans now streaming into Ireland. Fenians in the British Army were put on standby and sped up their swearing-in of new soldier recruits. However, the Fenian commitment to a general revolution made it difficult for the organisation to maintain secrecy, a confusion in Stephens' thinking about the differences between a mass and conspiratorial political organisation.[260] Another fatal mistake for an organisation that valued secrecy was to start a Fenian newspaper, the *Irish People*, staffed largely by the Irish central committee. In part, the paper was intended to carry on the culture war for Irish nationalism, promoting an alternative to both Englishness and the spell of docile collaboration cast by the Catholic hierarchy.[261] Government was alerted to the plan by spies at the newspaper and struck first on 15 September 1865, arresting most of the leaders, including Rossa, and many in the rank and file under the old standby, the *Treason Felony Act*.[262] This decapitation was reminiscent of the pre-emptive strikes against the

United Irishmen in 1798. Stephens, on the run, was himself arrested on 11 November. Thomas Keneally concluded that the taking out of the IRB leadership had long-lasting implications, setting in train an era of 'reckless' Fenian adventurism and tolerance of acts of terror that would 'set the tone of Anglo-Irish discourse for the remainder of the nineteenth and twentieth centuries'.[263]

The government's spirits were high as Special Commissions began trying the principals, when the Fenians sprang a surprise, rescuing Stephens from Richmond Prison.[264] He made his way to Paris, where the irrepressible John Mitchel, having recently joined the American IRB, was on hand as the Fenians' quasi-ambassador to France.[265] This daring escape revitalised the rebels, but the arrests had severely damaged their capacity to fight back, and Stephens decided to postpone the rising. Documents seized by the police from the *Irish People* not only helped secure prosecutions, but were released selectively to the press to fan fears that the Fenians were planning a terror campaign.[266] Then in February 1866 the authorities struck again. Claiming to have uncovered a conspiracy in the British Army, military police swept through army barracks in Ireland, arresting over 150 alleged Fenian members. The authorities' suspicions were not ill-founded, for these were the hard core of John Devoy's soldier 'sleepers', awaiting the signal to shed their disguise and offer their arms and lethal skills en masse to the wider Fenian rising.[267] From these ranks would come the nucleus of the Fenian transportees to Australia. Stephens' procrastination was blamed for the loss of the Fenian 'secret weapon', and he was dismissed as leader.

As more American insurgents poured into Ireland, the new Fenian leadership agreed to proclaim an Irish republic and the insurrection began in Dublin on 5 March 1867, and spread to Drogheda, Cork, Tipperary, Clare and Limerick.[268] The government suspended *habeas corpus* and used it to detain, without trial, the Americans. It was then left to the well-armed rapid response mobile police units to quickly suppress the rebellion. Despite all the talk and planning, the action when it finally came proved less impressive than the Young Ireland revolution. Still, both the Dublin rising and a nearly successful raid on a poorly guarded arms warehouse at Chester in England unnerved the British Government, that now turned its attention to punishing the captured rebels.[269]

Special Commissions tried the civilian rebels. The army 'mutineers' were tried by court martial for treason. The many condemned to death would be spared after pleas from the Catholic Church and the US Government. The prison sentences for both civilians and soldiers ranged from life to ten and five years. During the trials in September, the arrested Fenian leader, Colonel Thomas Kelly, was rescued in a daring raid in Manchester in which a police officer was shot dead. Such was the public outcry that of the twelve randomly apprehended Fenians convicted for this outrage, three were hanged.[270] At the public execution of the 'Manchester Martyrs', 2500 constables and 500 soldiers stood at the ready. The authorities were on notice that henceforth the war for control of Ireland would also be fought on English soil. Karl Marx observed:

> *Fenianism has entered a new phase. It has been baptised in blood by the British government. The public executions at Manchester ... open a new period in the struggle between Ireland and England.*[271]

* * *

VICTORY FROM DEFEAT: THE *CATALPA* COUP

MOST OF THE HUNDREDS OF FENIAN PRISONERS TRIED IN 1866 AND 1867 were civilians who served out their sentences in British and Irish prisons. Of the mutinous soldiers, seventeen deemed most dangerous were to be transported beyond the seas. This was because they might contaminate loyal troops with their beliefs, and out of concern the Fenians would seek to liberate them from a British prison at the first opportunity. The Chief Prosecutor warned the government that 'they entertain a firm conviction that they will be liberated from their prison by their friends'.[272] The Fenian rebels in the army were greeted with the same shock and anxiety as 'home grown' British-born Islamic terrorists have evoked in recent times. McConville points out that the 'mutineers' were considered 'double traitors', first to their oaths of loyalty as soldiers and secondly as British subjects.[273] That some of these Fenians were decorated and had seen years of service fighting the Empire's wars only magnified the betrayal.[274]

Before their exile, they would be publicly humiliated in front of their regiments by being stripped of their uniforms, forced into convict garb, discharged from the army and in some cases flogged.[275] The mutineers were then chained and marched through Dublin. The military hierarchy was especially offended at the abuse of trust, so important to the army's effectiveness, implicit in the planning of the mutiny. The commander-in-chief, HRH the Duke of Cambridge, was sufficiently incensed that he ensured that the soldiers were excluded from amnesties offered to Fenian prisoners in 1869 and 1871. But the mutineers held their heads high, considering themselves loyal soldiers for Ireland in the new Fenian republican army.

By the 1860s the era of transportation was coming to a close, and was used as a method of punishment and reformation only rarely. Convicted criminals were now incarcerated on home soil in the new 'separate' prisons, so called because prisoners were confined to their own cells for much of the time. Prisons like Dartmoor and Pentonville were the antecedents of the twentieth century penitentiaries, and by the 1860s were much harsher places to serve a sentence than in Australia as a transportee. Building on the Port Arthur experiment, these British prisons emphasised order, conformity and regimentation to bells and inspections in the manner of a modern army barracks. These prisons turned their back on the outside world—not only on the civilian community, but also the world of grass and sunshine and trees. The new prisons were 'industrial institutions' whose products were men and women, seldom reformed but frequently brutalised. Instead of the whip they were controlled by the restriction of rations, solitary confinement and searches. While the sentence of transportation still packed a punch and was calculated to teach the Fenian mutineers the enormity of their treachery, they were actually luckier than their many comrades who endured terrible torments for years in the domestic prisons.

Briefly incarcerated at Chatham Prison in England the mutineers were strip-searched four times a day, and it was common to move the Fenians from penitentiary to penitentiary. The authorities were wise to worry about security. While awaiting transfer to a transport ship, one of the soldiers, John Boyle O'Reilly, attempted to escape three times from three different prisons—Chatham, Dartmoor and Portsmouth. O'Reilly was no ordinary soldier, but a journalist, poet and something of an athlete who after joining the Fenians enlisted at age nineteen in the prestigious 10th Hussars Regiment, quartered in Dublin.[276] Here he deployed his diverse talents to winning over many of his fellow soldiers to the Irish revolutionary cause. It was not unusual for O'Reilly, a popular, gregarious man, to lead barracks sing-a-longs to rebel ballads.[277] Typical, too, was a poem he penned to inspire the new generation, that resurrected the spirit of the United Irish rebels of 1798 who

> *On many green fields where the leaden hail rattled,*
> *Through the red gap of glory they marched to their grave.*
> *And we who inherit their name and their spirit*
> *Will march 'neath the banners of Liberty, then—*
> *All who love Saxon law, native or Sassenach,*
> *Must out and make way for the Fenian Men.*[278]

Initially sentenced to death by firing squad, the twenty-two-year-old O'Reilly was sentenced to a lifetime of penal servitude. But a combination of intelligence, imagination and bravery made O'Reilly as formidable a prisoner as he was a rebel. To break his spirit the incorrigible escapee was placed on bread and water, and isolated in a 'punishment cell'.

Since transportation to Van Diemen's Land had ceased in 1853, Western Australia was the only colony still receiving convicts. Initially pleased to have a regular source of cheap labour, by the 1860s the West Australians had had enough of the convict stain, and were furiously campaigning to bring transportation to an end. They succeeded in 1868, but it was imperative that the Fenian soldiers be removed as far away from rescuers as possible. Such was the rising public anxiety about Fenianism that many of the civilian prisoners were given the choice of joining the soldiers in exile. Forty-Five Fenians took up the offer, bringing the number of transportees from the rebellion of 1865–67 to sixty-two. Along with the regular prisoners dispatched for Perth on the ship *Hougoumont* on 12 September 1867, the Fenians had the dubious honour of being the last convicts transported to Australia.

The Fenians enjoyed friendly relations with the ship's officers and crew, who treated them differently from the criminal convicts. The notorious revolutionaries even wrote and edited an on-board magazine, the *Wild Goose*, with verse contributions and journalism from O'Reilly.[279] Far from the monsters depicted in the press, the captain described their behaviour as 'exemplary'. Nevertheless, while en route Britain was rocked by an act of Fenian terrorism so wanton that the organisation's leaders apologised and disowned its authors, who were acting as lone agents. Attempting to rescue Fenian leader Richard O'Sullivan Burke in December 1867 from Clerkenwell Gaol in London a powerful bomb was detonated that destroyed much of the adjacent working-class neighbourhood, killing twelve and injuring 120 innocent people asleep in their beds. There was an outcry of anti-Fenian feeling across Britain and the empire, and by the time the *Hougoumont* docked, West Australians were implacably hostile to the importation of terrorists into their hitherto peaceful settlement. Following so closely after the Manchester killing, and with rumours circulating of Fenian pirates primed to rescue the prisoners, the new Governor of Western Australia, none other than Dr Hampton who had so harried the Young Irelanders, was forced to act. Hampton requested that the Commodore of the Australian Squadron protect Perth with a ship-of-war, and was duly sent the gunboat *Brisk* and two companies of troops. These fears briefly dissipated when the Fenians disembarked peacefully in February 1868 and displayed 'a quiet demeanour'.

All bets were off, however, when an assassination attempt was made in Sydney on the visiting son of Queen Victoria, Prince Alfred, Duke of Edinburgh. The shooter was an Irish Catholic and claimed to be following orders from the Fenian Brotherhood, triggering a nasty anti-Catholic, anti-Irish and anti-Fenian moral panic throughout the Australian colonies. But it transpired O'Farrell was a mentally unstable lone gunman, who cleared the Fenians of blame just prior to his execution. Yet once inflamed West Australians could not easily shake the paranoia over the terrorists in their midst—such was the public perception of Fenianism since the killings in England. Hampton continued to request military support, convinced the American Fenians would try to liberate their comrades.

On arrival the hard core of soldier Fenians were quickly dispersed to different parts of the colony to stop them conspiring, while the civilian rebels were allowed to work together. In Australia, they enjoyed a much greater degree of liberty than they experienced in British prisons. The exile from family, friend and home was considered punishment in itself. By the 1860s the worst excesses of the system had passed, though as former soldiers they could still be flogged. Be that as it may, they were able to work outside in the daylight, and organise their own work parties with minimum supervision. After a period spent on probation in the work gangs, that varied according to length of sentence, the men would enjoy the even greater liberty of a ticket-of-leave. The short-sentence men rapidly attained tickets-of-leave, one in only seven months. Still, these largely working-class men endured a much harder regime than the gentlemen Young Irelanders. In particular they were mixed up with the ordinary criminal convicts while on probation.

As the first sentences began to end and a general amnesty was extended to some of the civilian Fenians in early 1869, a support fund was established by pro-Fenian Irish in the colonies to assist the freed men make their way home. Ten returned to Ireland and fifteen sailed for the United States, but nine decided they quite liked Western Australia, and made it their home. In March 1871 under another amnesty all civilian Fenians still in Western Australia were pardoned, and all but one left the colony. But the 'mutineers' were another matter, and would remain until their sentences were served. Those soldiers serving life sentences had little to lose, and focused on escape.

Not surprisingly, the first mutineer to take flight was the enterprising John Boyle O'Reilly, who escaped a year into his sentence. With the help of a sympathetic Catholic priest he boarded a whaler in February 1869 and arrived in Philadelphia in November. Placing as much distance between himself and the long arm of British law as he could, O'Reilly promptly took out American citizenship, settled in Boston and recommenced his career as a journalist, becoming editor and publisher of *The Boston Pilot*.[280] The one-time mutineer and convict enjoyed literary success in his new home, and even wrote a fictionalised account of his experiences as an exile in Western Australia.[281] While for him America was a land of opportunity, O'Reilly quickly realised that the home of the brave offered little protection for the weak who fell through the cracks, including the many poor, uneducated Irish immigrants forced into the most menial occupations in barely habitable ghettoes.[282] Here was one of many causes for *The Boston Pilot*'s crusading brand of journalism. Although he increasingly came to favour independence for Ireland by the constitutional means advocated by the Home Rule movement rather than violence, O'Reilly remained a critical friend of the American Fenians, a movement growing in numbers and influence.

Since the Clerkenwell atrocity, it had increasingly fallen to the Americans to exercise the Fenian leadership. In this spirit they even approached John Mitchel to take over the presidency, but he declined. The man to step up to the plate was John Devoy, who was released under Prime Minister Gladstone's 1871 amnesty on condition he leave the United Kingdom. He was a careful and energetic leader, and took charge of the Fenian sub-branch called Clan na Gael. The Fenian headquarters in New York wanted a grand gesture. A replay of the 1839–40 American incursions into Canada had been on the drawing board since the American Civil War, and enthusiasm remained undiminished despite a series of failed Fenian border skirmishes in the aftermath of that conflict.[283] The plan was to threaten Britain in North America in order to force concessions in Ireland. So on 25 May 1870 a raiding force of Irish-Americans crossed the Canadian frontier to renew anti-British revolution in North America. Only 200 of the promised 2000 men showed up, and even *The Nation* headlined its article on the bungled adventure 'Fenian Fiasco'. Arriving in New York, Devoy realised the Fenians were in danger of becoming a laughing stock.

By 1876 there were only eight Fenian 'lifers' left in Western Australia, all but one being the feared 'mutineers', and now concentrated in the high-security Fremantle Prison. The Duke of Cambridge, commander-in-chief of the army, scotched any plans for pardons, and was said to have declared that 'releasing these Fenian soldiers would be subversive of discipline. They must—and shall—die in chains'.[284] Desperate, and fearing they were forgotten by the cause for which they sacrificed their freedom, one of the prisoners, James Wilson, wrote to their old comrade Devoy—responsible for the mutiny strategy—explaining their suffering over the past decade and asking to be rescued. The missive ended,

'Remember this is a voice from the tomb ... Think that we have been nearly nine years in this living tomb ... In the name of my comrades and myself, [I] ask you to aid us ...' As a soldier, Wilson had served in India, Syria and America and had been a prized recruit to the Fenians.[285] Reading the plea in New York, Devoy's guilt over the men's abandonment combined with the sensing of an opportunity. With the help of John Boyle O'Reilly he persuaded Clan na Gael to fund a rescue mission on a scale never attempted by the Fenians before.[286] They purchased the 200 ton, 27 metre (90 foot) ship *Catalpa*, and outfitted and crewed it as a commercial whaler, no less. Smith O'Brien's failed rescue demonstrated the importance of a captain who could be trusted. Devoy found his man in George Anthony, a thirty-one-year-old Bostonian, who, though a Protestant, was a democrat and man of high integrity and some bravery. Only one Fenian was put on board so as to ensure the authenticity of the whaling masquerade, and the *Catalpa* made its slow way to faraway Western Australia operating as a genuine working whaler.

Meanwhile, Devoy dispatched an agent named John Breslin to Perth, acting as a businessman exploring investment opportunities in the bustling city. Breslin had been pivotal as the Fenians' inside man in Stephens' escape from prison, and was now a New York journalist and member of Clan na Gael.[287] The Irish-American impressed local worthies keen to cultivate a potential investor, was not suspected by officials and at Fremantle made contact with the Fenian prisoners via the local priest. So unsuspecting were the authorities of Breslin's impersonation that the Fenian was given a tour of the prison, and even invited to dine—along with the captain of the visiting American whaler *Catalpa*—with the viceroy at Government House![288] This was despite warnings to Governor Sir William Robinson, from the colonial secretary in London, Lord Carnavon, that intercepted intelligence suggested he should be vigilant lest an attempt be made to liberate the Fenians.[289] Lacking Hampton's insights into Irish patriots, Robinson dismissed these concerns on 13 April 1876, confident he could secure the small group still in his charge. Four days later on the quiet morning of the Easter Monday holiday, six of the mutineers—James Wilson, Thomas Darragh, Martin Hogan, Michael Harrington, Thomas Hassett and Robert Cranston—absconded from their work groups and bolted for

Rockingham Beach, 32 kilometres (20 miles) from their prison. An alarm was sounded but the Fenian agents had cut the telegraph wires between Fremantle and Perth, delaying pursuit.

A whaleboat captained by Anthony met the men and Breslin at the beach, and began a race against time as its crew rowed out to rendezvous with the *Catalpa*, hovering some 26 kilometres (16 miles) offshore, beyond British territorial waters. Meanwhile the *Georgette*, a large state-of-the-art British steamship urgently pressed into government service, was sent to search the *Catalpa*, but was rebuffed and returned to port to refuel and arm. With a small government cutter on the tail of the whaleboat, Captain Anthony and the escaped prisoners on board loaded their guns determined to fight rather than surrender.[290] The winds were with the fugitives and they beat the police boat to the *Catalpa*, which promptly sailed off into international waters. But the *Georgette* was back in pursuit, carrying armed soldiers and police. On 19 April it intercepted the ship, demanded the convicts be handed over and fired a warning shot across its bows.

The Fenian soldiers anticipated a battle at sea, but knew they were outgunned. But now on the Indian Ocean well outside the 5 kilometre (3 mile) limit, the captain was not for turning, and hoisting high the American flag, insisted that Britain had no jurisdiction over his vessel. Through a loud-hailer the superintendent of the water police warned, 'If you don't give them up, I will fire into you and sink you or disable you', eliciting the bold riposte from Anthony, pointing aloft to his country's ensign: 'I don't care what you do, I'm on the high seas, and that flag protects me.'[291] To attack the *Catalpa* would provoke an international incident. The Fenians had won. Robinson sheepishly wrote to Lord Carnarvon, 'it is my painful duty to report that six of the convicts in question have escaped from the Imperial Prison at Fremantle, and gone to sea'.[292]

The nail-biting chase, the *Catalpa*'s brave defiance of British might at sea and the spectacle of the 'Stars and Stripes' awing a great empire quickly became the stuff of legend.[293] The bold rescue was reported around the globe, and the British set up a Committee of Inquiry. Like O'Brien and the Young Irelanders, the Fenians had exploited the flaws in the transportation system to enhance the reputation of the Irish cause, snatching victory from the jaws of defeat. Disembarking in New

York on 18 August 1876, the six liberated Fenians and Captain Anthony were given a hero's welcome. Beginning with an article by O'Reilly, the American press was overwhelmingly on the side of the escapees and the brave New Bedford captain.[294] The *Catalpa* coup strengthened Devoy's leadership and won him a place in the Fenian pantheon. The six men, broken by their nine years of captivity, left the limelight to Devoy. The dramatic rescue humbled the British and revived Fenianism to enter into a new stage. The way forward would be conspiracy, terrorism, symbolic victories and guerrilla-style insurgency.

While the Fenians were born out of the frustrated nationalist hopes of Young Ireland, the movement's military character, uncompromising republicanism and readiness to take up arms against the British connects it to the revolutionary tradition of the United Irishmen. Indeed the actions of the Irish Republican Brotherhood helped restore the legacy of 1798 to the heart of Irish nationalism. The movement also gave pride of place to ordinary working- and middle-class people, renovating the clandestine ganglands of the rural Whiteboys and Ribbonmen for an era of modern urban warfare.[295] Seán McConville argued in his recent history of Irish political prisoners that despite the failures of its insurgencies of the 1860s, Fenianism ultimately succeeded in most of the aims it set itself, thanks in part to its skilful exploitation of the theatre afforded by trial and punishment.[296] Notwithstanding a drift into 'irrational hate and an irresponsible readiness for violent deeds', T.A. Jackson in his classic work judged the Fenians 'one of the most remarkable and enduring revolutionary secret societies in history.'[297] Certainly a line of activism for an independent Irish nation may be traced from the Fenians' founding in the late 1850s through the rebellion of 1865–67, resistance to punishment in Britain and Australia, the American diasporic ascendancy and the 1916 rising to the republic and its methods and values continued to inspire Sin Fein and the IRA in Northern Ireland throughout the twentieth century. John Devoy lived long enough to support the civil war launched by the Fenians with the seizing of Dublin Post Office at Easter 1916, and was welcomed as a hero by the new Irish Free State in 1924. A song written during these latter-day struggles acknowledged the debt the new generation owed to the first Fenian rebels and their martyrdom at home and in exile, remembering:

Some died by the glenside
Some died amid strangers,
And wise man have told us
Their cause was a failure;
But they stood by dear Ireland
And never feared danger,
'Glory O, glory O,
To the Bold Fenian men!'[298]

✳ ✳ ✳

CONCLUSION: THE REBEL LEGACY

BY TURNING THE TABLES ON THEIR GAOLERS, THE FENIANS AND Young Ireland transportees had used the theatre of imprisonment well. The defiant martyrdom of William Smith O'Brien and the daring escapes of the Young Irelanders and Fenians contributed more to the future of Irish nationhood than the disastrous 1804 rebellion at Castle Hill.

The stories of Young Ireland and the Fenian rebels highlight key themes confronting political prisoners transported to Australia, notably the resort to draconian laws, especially treason, to suppress not only violence but freedom of expression; the tension between the British Government's use of transportation to silence opponents and the power of martyrdom; growing opposition to transportation in the Australian colonies; the double-standards applied to the punishment of political prisoners determined by their social class; penal authorities' increasing difficulty holding political prisoners determined to escape; and the continued role of US citizens in lending support to dissidents within the British Empire, especially the growing importance of the Irish diaspora in New York as sponsors of rebellion in Ireland and rescues in Australia.

Young Ireland represented a turning point in Celtic nationalism. Young Ireland's intellectual rebels did not just recover indigenous Irish cultural traditions; they used them to create a modern form of Irishness distinct from Englishness and imperial belonging, to legitimise Ireland's claim for independent nationhood and, if necessary, to mobilise the people against British rule. The inspiring and community-building cultural nationalism they promoted in Ireland would later have influence in other colonies emerging from Empire, such as India and Australia. The tragedy for Young Ireland was that revolutions and nations are not built of culture alone. Its disinterest in the nitty-gritty of modern organisational politics or actually building a mass movement of the people meant that once the British started shooting there were few people to fire back. However, no future revolution would succeed without Young Ireland's important work in imagining an Irish nation. That Young Ireland's ideas ultimately achieved widespread legitimacy among the Irish people and internationally owed a great deal to how its leaders handled their defeat.

The Young Ireland exiles, particularly their 'captain', William Smith O'Brien, more closely resembled the experience of the six unionists from Tolpuddle than the Scottish Jacobins. In the late eighteenth century so isolated was the fledgling penal colony of Sydney that Muir and his fellow radicals were effectively removed from debate about political reform, and rendered out of sight, out of mind. Even their escapes and attempts to return home after serving their terms were hampered by the perilous nature of sea transport in a war-torn world. Not so the Young Irelanders, who through a spirited campaign of letter writing, legal manoeuvres, local publishing initiatives and the courting of colonial and international opinion disappointed the British Government's hopes to consign its enemies to what Blanche Touhill terms 'gentlemanly obscurity'. Indeed, the exiles continued to be active participants in the debate about Irish independence. Thanks to well-executed escapes to the United States, William Smith O'Brien's refusal to accept his parole and dignified and well-publicised endurance of solitary confinement, the exiles' stature as Irish leaders was greatly enhanced.

Transportation had ceased to be an effective method of silencing political enemies. Modern communications, the emergence of a rambunctious unfettered Australian press, a local colonial movement hostile to transportation, and the determination of an international Irish liberation movement to rescue prisoners perforated the ramparts of Britain's feared penal colonies. Rescue from Van Diemen's Land seemed to be only a row boat and a passing whaler away. Once gold was discovered in Ballarat and the Victorian gold rush had begun the

British Government had no alternative but to end transportation to Van Diemen's Land, now re-named as Tasmania by a relieved citizenry.

Of the 39,000 Irish men and women transported to Australia from the eighteenth to nineteenth centuries, at least 2250 can be classed as political prisoners. Most of these were rural protesters involved in a bloody war for land rights. As poor tenant farmers, tradesmen and labourers few have made a mark in the history books, but most never returned to their homeland, making their new home in Australia, where they have etched deep song lines.

Unlike America and Ireland there is little public commemoration of the Irish political prisoners. At Rockingham beach there is a graceful sculpture dedicated to the *Catalpa* escape and at Port Arthur visitors can walk through William Smith O'Brien's cottage and see a cardboard cut-out of the noble martyr. Australia has no public commemoration of the thousands of victims of the Land and Tithe War brought in chains to our shore. However, the legacy of their resistance lives on in a rich tradition of folk ballads, poetry and a larrikin instinct to thumb one's nose at authority. The spirit of the Whiteboys and Ribbonmen may also be gleaned in the ganglands of our political culture, especially in the Labor Party where the party pledge, factional loyalty and solidarity are ruthlessly enforced, and 'rats' forever ostracised. Irish Catholic ambivalence about the British Empire's wars played a part in the defeat of the referenda to introduce conscription during the First World War, and the subsequent expulsion from the ALP of Prime Minister Billy Hughes and those who supported conscription against party policy. Almost a century later the Catholic Church in Australia keeps alive the flame of Irish nationalism, as a cherished ingredient of our own.

In the late nineteenth and early twentieth centuries Irish Catholic Australians told each other the tales of rebel heroes, martyrs and wild colonial boys unfairly exiled. Today we honour Irish resistance through the Australianised legend of Ned Kelly, the son of a convict, who claimed to be continuing the old country's struggle against English oppressors. Perhaps when Australians once more turn their hearts and minds to leaving the British monarchy behind and becoming a republic, the stories of the Irish rebels who lived among us will resonate once more?

CONCLUSION

TRACES OF LIBERTY

THE DEFIANT DEPARTURE OF THE *CATALPA* **WITH HER CARGO OF SIX** Fenian terrorists brings to a close the story of the political prisoners that the British Empire exiled to its far-flung Australian colonies. It is a story spanning eighty-two years, from 1794 to 1876, from the Jacobin radicals who demanded political liberty in Scotland, to the Fenian Brotherhood, unleashing revolution and terrorism to achieve Irish freedom. The constant stream of radicals, rebels, social protesters and nationalists exiled to Australia coincides with almost the entire life of the transportation period, that formally stretched from 1788 to 1868, though prisoners continued to serve out their sentences as 'old lags' into the late 1800s.

This was a period that witnessed revolutionary change: in economics, technology, society and politics in Britain and throughout her vast empire. For the years of transportation also coincided with the expansion of British imperium around the globe, on all continents and climes, buttressed by military, mercantile, industrial and cultural power on a scale the world had never before witnessed. Yet great power carries great dangers, not least hubris and deafness to the pleas of those dominated by or excluded from power. Surveying Britain's triumph at the end of the wars unleashed by the first French Revolution, a circumspect Edmund Burke observed 'it was a close run thing', by which he meant the threat of revolution at home as much as the danger posed by Napoleon. For the British imperial state, the threats from those unhappy with its rule would not go away, and transportation confronted the passions of dissent as both a deterrent and a safety valve.

The rate of change, combined with the opportunities and *realpolitik* of empire, sowed the seeds of dissent, but also optimism that things could be improved through political activism. In the late 1900s capitalist modernity came up hard against a traditional elite and way of life that had its roots in feudalism. In America and then France, the dogs of revolution were unleashed. Britain fought both revolutions, and with difficulty set about suppressing the revolutions in its own backyard. The triumph of capitalism called forth liberal reformers and radical idealists from the ranks of the rising bourgeoisie, who wanted greater participation in government and a say over how taxes were spent through the extension of political rights and the cleaning up of corruption. The old rural-based oligarchy's implacable opposition to reform turned some liberals into radical republicans, a seditious act in a time of war with the Jacobin revolutionaries of France.

CONCLUSION

The extension of cold market logic and machines to England's agricultural bread basket tore up centuries of customary rights, and provoked a backlash from peasants thrown into unemployment and penury. The dark satanic mills of the Industrial Revolution transformed peasants and artisans into proletarians, whose only strength vis-à-vis employers was in solidarity. The English working class, like the middle class before it, wanted to protect its material wellbeing and gain a greater say over government. The march of trade unionists and Chartists through the factories and streets of Great Britain was an unstoppable advance for human rights and political liberty, but to the ruling and business classes the agitation of common men and women threatened the prerogatives of property and good order, and needed to be nipped in the bud through draconian laws against combinations, free speech and sedition.

In the provinces of Empire, first and foremost in Ireland, but extending to the formerly French province in Canada, subject peoples came to resent English rule dismissive of indigenous custom and representation. Mindful of the example of the United States, they promoted, plotted and executed nationalist and republican revolutions. Deemed traitors by an imperial government that still smarted over the loss of its North American colonies, nationalist rebels were treated with the greatest severity of all, running the gauntlet of specially concocted laws for treason and sedition. Imperial misrule in Ireland hurt ordinary peasants the most, and the British justice system was especially brutal punishing random resistance from below. These largely uneducated farmers and labourers buckling under economic exploitation and a maladministered famine hit back at their oppressors through individual and gang violence, a prelude to the urban terrorism that would bloody Anglo-Irish relations into the late twentieth century.

Transportation to the colony of New South Wales, Britain's latest imperial possession seized from the Aboriginal people on the continent of Australia, was invented to soak up the wave of criminality caused by the tectonic shifts in traditional British social relations. But very early in the life of transportation it was embraced as the best way to excise from the body politic both radical malcontents who wanted to import foreign systems of government like republicanism, and dissenters from the lower orders who threatened the King's peace and property. By the 1790s transportation was also seized upon as the solution to Irish lawlessness and habit of rebellion.

The British Government reasoned that as an alternative to execution, exile would avoid creating martyrs, and that the troublemakers would be safely out of sight and out of mind. That this was not to be in a shrinking world became clear with the escape of Thomas Muir, the rising of the United Irishmen at Castle Hill and the international campaigns to pardon the martyred Tolpuddle Unionists and Young Irelanders. Spirited legal action and a virtual library of published convict memoirs and pamphlets ensured their contemporaries and history learned of the struggles and sufferings of the exiles. Finally, and returning to Muir's spirited odyssey around the globe, a succession of derring-do rescues climaxing in the *Catalpa* revived hopes for political comrades back home and demonstrated how permeable were the walls of the Australian prison.

A state fashioned in more parochial and authoritarian times also had difficulty coping with a revolution in communications that had greatly expanded the public sphere, a 'republic of letters', in which intellectuals and other ideas entrepreneurs used the discourse of journalism and academia, and the convivial spaces of cafés and pubs, to debate and promote new ways of seeing and doing. With technical improvements and growing literacy came a proliferation and diversification of publishing: newspapers, pamphlets, treatises, manifestos and proclamations. In these media innovations, new rights, new classes, new systems of government and new nations were first imagined. Reforms codified in black letter law and revolutions won or lost with sabres and bullets were borne of the thoughts and ideals traded in this rambunctious free market of ideas stretching from Britain to the colonies in Ireland, North America and even to the new prison provinces of Australia. Yet a government dedicated to the gospel of free trade in property resisted freedom to write and speak, imposing onerous licences, and when that failed laws of sedition that allowed writers, journalists, poets and pamphleteers to be dragged off to gaol in the dead of night. These illiberal laws lasted well into the mid-nineteenth century, and ensured that many of the political prisoners transported to Australia were some of the finest orators, wordsmiths and propagandists of their age.

On the sidelines mocking Britain's crisis of authority and imperialism were radical democratic citizens of the still-young American republic. Throughout the period of transportation, the United States was the beacon of hope to Britain's liberals and radicals, providing a safe haven for refugees of failed revolutions, and diplomatic pressure where it believed the great empire was stamping on the rights of man. But some citizens went further. American democratic zealots together with liberals of goodwill provided material and moral support for Britain's rebels. There were those Americans such as the Patriot Hunters and the Irish diasporic nationalists who went further still, boldly rescuing political prisoners from Australian gulags and invading British territory in Canada and Ireland. To imperial Britain, the United States was an exporter of revolution and terrorism. Unsurprisingly, when captured in Canada, American 'privateers' were also banished to the Empire's maximum-security prison at the ends of the Earth—Van Diemen's Land.

Political prisoners received a mixed reaction in the Australian colonies. Sometimes they were feared as an importation sure to provoke sedition and rebellion, but employers and administrators welcomed their higher levels of education and relevant trade skills. For the most part honest and free of the alleged contagion of the 'criminal class', political convicts were sought after as teachers, clerks, tradesmen, overseers and farm workers in colonies that began life with severe labour and skills shortages. Convicts like the Swing Rioters who arrived on the *Eleanor* took to farming in New South Wales, enjoyed a standard of living denied them in the miserly home counties of England and often prospered. So too did many of the Irish peasant rebels assigned to farms, public works and officers in the growing colonies. Most British and Irish protesters settled in Australia and made a life. At the extremes, a tiny few became wealthy through business and government service while a marginalised minority, like the Kelly family in Victoria's northeast, saw their children replay the land wars of Ireland.

Today there is little official acknowledgment of the debt our democracy owes to the Scottish and Tolpuddle Martyrs, the Chartists and machine-breakers, and the North American patriots. Commemoration of political convicts remains strongest among Australians of Irish ancestry. Interest among citizens in the Irish rebel tradition has grown, with 12,000 attending a spirited re-enactment of the battle at Castle Hill in 2004 to mark its bicentenary, memorials raised to the victims of the Famine in Sydney and Melbourne, and a bronze sculpture of six wild geese in flight honouring the *Catalpa* Fenians dedicated on the Rockingham shore near Fremantle. Even so, the transported political prisoners have remained captives of the national histories of their countries of origin and the empire that is no more, rather than entering popular memory as part of the Australian story.

This is surprising, as Australia was bequeathed an inspiring legacy. Liberalism, republicanism, trade unionism, working-class politics, democracy, responsible government and post-colonial nationalism all arrived in the colonies in chains. Yet through the alchemy of martyrdom, spirited resistance, canny campaigning back home and in the colonies and dramatic escapes these radical ideas broke free of convict fetters to disseminate around the world. They became the common sense of liberal nation-states and left strong influences in Australia's political culture. It is not surprising that New South Wales boasted robust liberal radicals so early in its history, when the seeds were sown by the defiant Scottish Martyrs and officers of the United Irishmen.

Responsible government was achieved in New South Wales, Victoria and Tasmania in the 1850s, and this was surely in part a consequence of the stand taken by the Canadian patriots. The adoption of universal male suffrage decades ahead of Britain comes directly from the Chartist program, as did other Australian innovations such as short parliaments and the secret ballot. The early embrace of trade unionism by the colonial working class owes much to the brave stand taken by the Tolpuddle Martyrs, and in creating one of the world's first Labor parties the unions were following in the tradition of working-class political action pioneered by so many of the Chartists exiled for their activism. The principled stand taken by political prisoners in defence of fairer pay, lower rents, the right to bargain collectively and secure rights to land and shelter are manifest in the still vital ethos of egalitarianism expressed as the 'fair go'.

Young Ireland's cultural efforts to imagine a new nation, even before it was a political reality, was adopted in Australia with gusto, in the *Bulletin*, an antipodean version of *The Nation* that sang and versified a new Australian nation, racy of the soil, of mates and larrikins ahead of Federation and ANZAC. The many dissident journalists and writers transported to our shores lived on in a cultural sense well beyond the nineteenth century, in a succession of feisty libertarian and larrikin journals that fought for the right to think, write and publish freely—the same cause for which Thomas Muir and John Mitchel were dispatched to our shores.

Surveying the living Australian traditions that the transported radicals, rebels and protesters fertilised, some with their bones, one legacy remains unborn. The seeds of republicanism, liberal and abstract in the pamphlets of the Scottish Martyrs, passionate and romantic in the speeches of Thomas Meagher and John Mitchel, populist and democratic in the memoirs of the American patriots, was ploughed into our colonial soil but is yet to bear fruit. All of these rebels and reformers agreed that a republic was more than simply replacing the monarch with a president. A republic was about liberty, extended to all citizens through thoroughly democratic institutions and bills of rights. This plant, which republican poet Henry Lawson called the Young Tree Green, broke the soil in the 1880s but was trodden down in the rush to Federation and an imperial war. It grew a little again in the 1990s, only to wither and die.

'Death or Liberty!' was the call to arms of so many of the revolutionaries, rebels and reformers transported as political prisoners to Australia. Scottish radicals, Irish and Canadian republicans, seditious pamphleteers and publishers, English Chartists, rural protesters and the martyred trade unionists from Tolpuddle had no reason to idealise the British state that had exiled them to our fatal shore, and saw themselves first and foremost as defenders of freedom *from* government. Liberty can sit oddly with modern parties and movements of the left, that as collectivists often uncritically embrace the government as the sole provider of public goods. But in the late eighteenth and nineteenth centuries 'progressives' looked to themselves and their communities to provide social bonds and safety nets, rather than just to the state, which was seen as the defender of vested interests, and the opponent of emerging or marginalised social movements. The rebels and reformers transported to Australia agitated to make the government more liberal, more democratic, by insisting on their human right to govern themselves. Back home and in exile they agitated to open up the then oligarchic British state by extending the franchise to the middle and then 'lower' classes, entrenching rights of freedom of assembly and speech, and winning self-government in the colonies. Once liberal rights were achieved working-class reformers fought for the producer rights to form a union and strike and for the representatives of labour to stand for parliament. From the 1890s in Australia and Britain both liberal and social democracy worked hand in hand to inaugurate a century of reform, to extend civil liberties and human rights, but the work is never over.

Oligarchy has a tendency to regroup, and the commons needs not only to be defended, but also regularly returned to the people, so that it may serve new times and the newly disenfranchised. Yet many modern progressives forget the centrality of liberty to our cause, and instead embrace government as the great and powerful friend, surprised when its ministers and officials curb our freedoms to protest, favour big business mates or cruelly lock up refugees. Instead of retooling democracy for the twenty-first century, Australia's leaders across the political spectrum have indulged a national talent for bureaucracy-building and managerial surveillance—an illiberal tendency in our public life that is perhaps a colonial hangover from the vast convict apparatus erected on our shores to catalogue, control and coerce human beings.

In thinking about the rebels and protesters exiled from their friends, loved ones and everything familiar we should pause and ask: Is there a cause today for which I would lay down my liberty? There is much still to put right, from the threat of global warming and the persistence of poverty, to Australia's detention of refugees and stubborn, habitual marginalisation of her Indigenous people.

So strange in times like these that we seldom pause to remember the political rebels, protesters and martyrs who sacrificed their freedom and sometimes their lives for rights we take for granted. There are few monuments. Their stories—swashbuckling, noble, inspiring, tragic—are not taught in our schools and seldom recalled in our museums. While we stop for the Eight Hour Day, the Melbourne Cup and the Queen's Birthday, there are no national holidays here for the principles for which our colonial-era martyrs forfeited their freedom. Perhaps the greatest tribute we can offer is to imagine an Australian republic with liberty and democracy at its heart.

ENDNOTES

INTRODUCTION

1   J. Gerrald, Court Transcript, 17 May 1795, quoted on sign marking the 200th anniversary of the death of Joseph Gerrald, Royal Botanic Gardens and Domain, Botanic Gardens Trust, 1996.

2   A. Curthoys, 'Does Australian History Have a Future?', *Australian Historical Studies*, vol. 33, no. 118, 2002, p. 146.

3   F. Clune, *The Scottish Martyrs: Their Trials and Transportation to Botany Bay*, Angus and Robertson, Sydney, 1969; N. Curtin, *The United Irishmen, Popular Politics in Ulster and Dublin*, Oxford University Press, Oxford, 1994; A. Whitaker, *Unfinished Revolution: United Irishmen in New South Wales 1800–1810*, Crossing Press, Sydney, 1994; C. Costello, *Botany Bay: The Story of the Convicts Transported from Ireland to Australia, 1791–1853*, The Mercier Press, Cork, 1987; J. Marlow, *The Tolpuddle Martyrs*, Andre Deutsch Limited, London, 1971; D. Kent and N. Townsend, *Convicts of the Eleanor: Protest in Rural England, New Lives in Australia*, Pluto Press, Annandale, 2002; C. Pybus and H. Maxwell-Stewart, *American Citizens, British Slaves: Yankee Political Prisoners in an Australian Penal Colony 1839-1850*, Melbourne University Press, Carlton South, 2002; R. Hughes, *The Fatal Shore: A History of the Transportation of Convicts to Australia 1787–1868*, Pan Books in Association with Collins, London, 1987.

CHAPTER 1

1   T. Muir, *An Account of the Trial of Thomas Muir, Esq. Younger, of Huntershill, before the High Court of Justiciary, at Edinburgh. On the 30th and 31st days of August, 1793, for sedition*, Edinburgh, 1793, p. 130. (*First Pamphlet*.)

2   T. Muir, *The Trial of Thomas Muir, Esq. Younger of Huntershill; Before the High Court of Justiciary, Upon Friday and Saturday the 30th and 31st days of August. On a Charge of Sedition, 1793*, Edinburgh, 1793, pp. 1–2. (*Second Pamphlet*.)

3   J. Earnshaw, 'Muir, Thomas (1765–1799)', *Australian Dictionary of Biography*, Volume 2, Melbourne University Press, Carlton South, 1967, pp. 266–267.

4   H. Cockburn, *Examination of the Trials in Scotland for Sedition*, cited in F. Clune, *The Scottish Martyrs: Their Trials and Transportation to Botany Bay*, Angus and Robertson, Sydney, 1969, p. 9.

5   ibid., pp. 9–10.

6   T. Muir, *Second Pamphlet*, p. 14.

7   ibid., p. 14.

8   For example the Seditious Writings Bill.

9   T. Muir, *Second Pamphlet*, p. 2.

10   N. Leask, 'Thomas Muir and *The Telegraph*: Radical Cosmopolitanism in 1790s Scotland', *History Workshop Journal*, issue 632007, pp. 49–51.

11   T. Muir, Court Transcript, cited in T. Muir, *First Pamphlet*, p. 5.

12   See discussion by N. Leask, op. cit., pp. 55–56.

13   ibid., p. 130.

14   R. Hughes, *The Fatal Shore: A History of the Transportation of Convicts to Australia 1787–1868*, Pan Books in Association with Collins, London, 1987, p. 176.

15   T. Muir, Court Transcript, cited in T. Muir, *First Pamphlet*, p. 139.

16   H. Cockburn, op. cit., p. 13.

17   ibid., p. 36.

18   R. Hughes, op. cit., pp. 2, 43.

19   ibid., p. 36.

20   T. Muir, Court Transcript, cited in *First Pamphlet*, p. 138.

21   T. Muir, Court Transcript, cited in *Second Pamphlet*, p. 107.

22   T.F. Palmer, *The Trial of the Rev. Thomas Fyshe Palmer, before the Circuit Court of Justiciary, held at Perth, on the 12th and 13th September, 1793*, Edinburgh, 1793, p. 7.

23   Lord Abercrombie, Court Transcript, quoted in T.B. Howell and T.J. Howell (eds), *A Complete Collection of State Trials and Proceedings for High Treason and Other Crimes and Misdemeanors*, Vol. XXIII, London, 1817, p. 340.

24   T.F. Palmer, Court Transcript, quoted in ibid., p. 375.

25   Quoted by H. Cockburn, cited in F. Clune, op. cit., p. 26.

26   ibid., p. 28.

27   W. Skirving, quoted in ibid., p. 29.

28   M. Roe, 'Margarot, Maurice (1745–1815)', *Australian Dictionary of Biography*, Volume 2, Melbourne University Press, Carlton South, 1967, pp. 206–207.

29   H. Cockburn quoted in F. Clune, op. cit., p. 32.

30   ibid., p. 33.

31   M. Margarot, Court Transcript, cited in F. Clune, op. cit., p. 34.

32 J. Gerrald, 'Politics for the People: or, a Salmagundy for Swine', vol. 1, no. xiv, London, 1794–95, p. 204, quoted in ibid. p. 40.

33 ibid. p. 40.

34 Braxfield, quoted in Michael Fry, 'Macqueen, Robert, Lord Braxfield (1722–1799)', *Oxford Dictionary of National Biography*, Oxford University Press, 2004. Website: http://www.oxforddnb.com/view/article/17738

35 J. Gerrald, Court Transcript, quoted in F. Clune, p. 44.

36 R. Hughes, op. cit., p. 177.

37 Maconachie, quoted in F. Clune, op. cit., p. 19.

38 C.J. Fox, *An Impartial Report of the Debates that Occur in the two Houses of Parliament ... by William Woodfall and Assistants*, Volume II, London, 1794, p. 263.

39 M. Roe, quoted in F. Clunes, op. cit., p. 31.

40 G. Rudé, *Protest and Punishment: The Story of Social and Political Protesters Transported to Australia 1788–1868*, Clarendon Press, Oxford, 1978, pp. 1, 10.

41 ibid., pp. 2–10.

42 E. Hobsbawm, *The Age of Revolution: Europe, 1789–1848*, Weidenfeld and Nicholson, London, 1962.

43 E.P. Thompson, *The Making of the English Working Class*, Victor Gollancz Ltd, London, 1964, pp. 189–199, 198–204.

44 R. Owen, *Observations on the Effect of the Manufacturing System*. 2nd edn, R.A. Taylor, London, 1817; F. Engels, *The Condition of the Working Class in England*, Blackwell, Oxford, 1958.

45 H. Fielding, *An Inquiry into the Late Increase of Robbers ...*, quoted in R. Hughes, op. cit., p. 25.

46 M. Clarke, 'Port Arthur', in M. Wilding. (ed.), Marcus Clarke; *Portable Australian Authors*, University of Queensland Press, St. Lucia, 1976, p. 530.

47 R. Hughes, op. cit., p. 29; E.P. Thomspon, *Whigs and Hunters: the Origin of the Black Act*, Allen Lane, London, 1975.

48 D. Hay, *Albion's Fatal Tree: Crime and Society in Eighteenth Century Britain*, A Lane, London, 1975.

49 M. Clark, 'The Origins of the Convicts Transported to Eastern Australia, 1787–1852', *Historical Studies*, vii, no. 26, May 1956, pp. 121–135 and vii, no. 27, November 1956, pp. 314–327.

50 R. Hughes, op. cit., p. 175.

51 G. Rudé, op. cit., p. 10.

52 E.P. Thompson, op. cit., pp. 78–79.

53 ibid., pp. 78–80; J. Hirst, 'Empire, State, Nation', in D. Schreuder and S. Ward (eds), *Australia's Empire*, Oxford University Press, Oxford, 2008, p. 141.

54 E.P. Thompson, op. cit., p. 78.

55 *Anti-Jacobin*, 1 January 1798, quoted in ibid., p. 79.

56 M. Margarot cited by F. Clune, op. cit., p. 31.

57 T. Hardy, cited in F. Clune, op. cit., p 31.

58 W.O. Henderson and W.H. Chardoner, 'Notes to F. Engels' in F. Engels, op. cit., p. 259, Note 2.

59 *Declaration of Independence*, The unanimous Declaration of the thirteen United States of America, In Congress, 4 July 1776.

60 W. Wordsworth, *The Prelude*, X, 1805; S.T. Coleridge, *France: An Ode*, 1798.

61 Description in H. Cockburn, cited in F. Clune, op. cit., p. 42.

62 John Brimms, 'From Reformers to "Jacobins": the Scottish Association of the Friends of the People', in T.M. Devine (ed.), *Conflict and Stability*, John Donald Publishers Ltd, Edinburgh, 1990, pp. 31–50.

63 E.W. McFarland, *Ireland and Scotland in the Age of Revolution*, Edinburgh University Press, Edinburgh, 1994; See discussion of historiography by N. Leask, op. cit., pp. 48–49.

64 T. Muir, quoted in ibid., p. 51.

65 T. Pain, *Rights of Man*, quoted in ibid., p. 91.

66 Lord Braxfield cited in F. Clune, op. cit., p. 28.

67 Quoted in ibid., p. 3.

68 M. Roe, cited in F. Clune, op. cit., p. 31.

69 M. Margarot, cited in ibid., p. 34.

70 T. Muir, quoted in ibid., p. 11.

71 T. Palmer, quoted in ibid., p. 17.

72 Quoted in ibid., p. 17.

73 ibid., p. 31.

74 ibid., pp. 2–3.

75 H. Cockburn, quoted in F. Clune, op. cit., p. 7.

76 G. Mealmaker, quoted in ibid., p. 17.

77 Lord Abercrombie, quoted in ibid., p. 20.

78 M. Margarot and T. Hardy, quoted in ibid., p. 31.

79 ibid., p. 5.

80 Lord Braxfield quoted in R. Hughes, op. cit., p. 176.

81 F. Clune, op. cit., p. 19.

82 N. Leask, op. cit., pp. 52–53.

83 ibid., pp. 53–54.
84 ibid., p. 54.
85 ibid., p. 50.
86 Lord Abercrombie, quoted in F. Clune, op. cit., p. 20.
87 N. Leask, op. cit., p. 51.
88 ibid., p. 65.
89 T. Muir, quoted in ibid., p. 56, from *First Pamphlet*, p. 100.
90 J. Hartley, *Popular Reality: Journalism, Modernity, Popular Culture*, Hodder Headline, London, 1996, pp. 8–13.
91 T. Muir, quoted in N. Leask, op. cit., p. 56, from *First Pamphlet*, p. 107.
92 H. Cockburn, cited in F. Clune, op. cit., p. 10.
93 Lord Braxfield, quoted in T. Muir, *The Trial of Thomas Muir, Esq. Younger, of Huntershill; Before the High Court of Justiciary, Upon Friday and Saturday the 30th and 31st days of August, 1793. On a Charge of Sedition*, Edinburgh, 1793, p. 65.
94 Lord Swinton, cited in F. Clune, op. cit., p. 29.
95 H. Cockburn, cited in F. Clune, op. cit., p. 35.
96 W. Godwin, *Enquiry Concerning Political Justice*, February 1793.
97 W. Godwin, cited in F. Clune, op. cit., p. 21.
98 R. Sheridan, cited in ibid., p. 61.
99 R. Burns, 'Scots wha hae wi' Wallace bled', poem cited in ibid., p. 14.
100 M. Margarot, 'Letter to H. Dundas', 27 March 1794, quoted in ibid., p. 37.
101 *A Narrative of the Sufferings of T.F. Palmer and W. Skirving During a Voyage to Botany Bay, 1794*, London, 1797, quoted in ibid., p. 68.
102 M. Margarot, cited in F. Clune, op. cit., p. 37.
103 Under Secretary King, Home Office, *Historical records of New South Wales, Vol. II*, 14 February 1794, cited in ibid., to p. 23.
104 T. Palmer and W. Skirving, cited in ibid., p. 67.
105 ibid.
106 R. Hughes, op. cit., p. 178.
107 T. Palmer and W. Skirving, cited in F. Clune, op. cit., p. 71.
108 T. Palmer, *Narrative*, quoted in R. Hughes, op. cit., p. 35.
109 Registrar-General's Certificate, cited in F. Clune, op. cit., p. 95.
110 D. Collins, *An Account of the English Colony in New South Wales, 2 Volumes*, London, 1798, cited in ibid., p. 94.
111 T. Palmer, 'Letters', 23 April and 5 May 1796, cited in ibid., p. 97.
112 T. Muir, *The Telegraph; A Consolatory Epistle from Thomas Muir, Esq., of Botany Bay, to Hon. Henry Erskine, Late Dean of Faculty*, quoted in R. Hughes, op. cit., p. 178.
113 T. Palmer, 'Letter to Reverend Jeremiah Joyce', 15 December 1794, cited in F. Clune, op. cit., p. 77.
114 T. Palmer, 'Letters', 23 April and 5 May 1796, cited in F. Clune, op. cit., p. 78.
115 T. Palmer, 'Letter to Dr John Disney', 13 June 1795, cited in ibid., p. 85.
116 T. Palmer, 'Letter to Anon.', 16 September 1795, cited in ibid., pp. 88, 96.
117 T. Palmer, 'Letter to Reverend Theophilus Lindsay', 15 September 1795, cited in ibid., p. 88.
118 Calculated by C. Riley, 'The 1804 Australian Rebellion and Battle of Vinegar Hill', Hawkesbury Historical Society, 2003, p. 16. Website: http://www.hawkesburyhistory.org.au/articles/Battle_of_Vinegar.html
119 Lieutenant McKellar, quoted in M. McKenna, *The Captive Republic: A history of Republicanism in Australia 1788–1996*, Cambridge University Press, Oakley, 1996, p. 14.
120 *The Telegraph*, quoted in R. Hughes, op. cit, p. 179.
121 ibid.; N. Leask, op. cit., p. 59. As an example of a recent British history that accepts Muir's authorship, Leask cites Tom Devine, *Scotland's Empire, 1600–1815*, London, 2003, pp. 160–161.
122 N. Leask, op. cit., p. 59.
123 Muir, *The Telegraph*, quoted in R. Hughes, op. cit., p. 179.
124 R. Hughes, op. cit., p. 178.
125 ibid., pp. 65–66.
126 ibid., p. 65.
127 Told in great detail over four chapters in F. Clune, op. cit., pp. 99–130.
128 T. Muir, 'Letter to Washington', in ibid., p. 116.
129 R. Hughes, op. cit., p. 181.
130 M. Margarot and Governor King, 'Letter to Under-Secretary King', 14 August 1804, quoted in ibid., p. 13.
131 Great Britain, Parliament, *Report from the Select Committee on Transportation*, Parliamentary Papers, House of Commons, no. 314, 1812.
132 Women of Western Australia or the territories were not included initially and many Indigenous and non-British immigrants were not able to vote.

CHAPTER 2

1   G. Rudé, op. cit., pp. 9, 73; T.J. Kiernan in C. Costello, *Botany Bay: The Story of the Convicts Transported from Ireland to Australia, 1791–1853*. Cork-Dublin, Mercier, 1987, p. 34. Kiernan calculates the larger figure of 750.
2   P. Lenihan, *Confederate Catholics at War, 1641–49*, Cork University Press, Cork, 2001, p. 112.
3   G. Rudé, op. cit., p. 27.
4   Arthur Wellesley, 1st Duke of Wellington, quoted in ibid., p. 28.
5   C. Woodham-Smith, *The Great Hunger*, London, Hamish Hamilton, 1974, pp. 23–25; G. O'Tuathaigh, *Ireland Before the Famine, 1798–1848*, Dublin, 1972, pp. 5–6.
6   T.A. Jackson, *Ireland Her Own*, Lawrence and Wishart, London, 1991, p. 97.
7   C. Costello, op. cit., p. 10.
8   J. Swift, *A Modest Proposal*, in P. Pinkus (ed.), *Johnathan Swift: A Selection of his Works*, Macmillan, Toronto, 1965.
9   T.A. Jackson, op. cit., p. 102.
10 R. O'Donnell, 'Dwyer, Michael (1772–1825)', *Australian Dictionary of Biography*, Supplementary Volume, Melbourne University Press, Carlton South, 2005, p. 110.
11 G. Rudé, op. cit., pp. 91–92; G.C. Bolton, 'Holt, Joseph (1756–1826)', *Australian Dictionary of Biography*, Volume 1, Melbourne University Press, Carlton South, 1966, pp. 550–551.
12 Quoted in N. Curtin, *The United Irishmen, Popular Politics in Ulster and Dublin*, Oxford University Press, Oxford, 1994, p. 247.
13 'Address from the Society of United Irishmen of Dublin, 30 Dec. 1791', quoted in ibid., p. 21.
14 G. Rudé, op. cit., p. 37.
15 D. Gahan, *Rebellion: Ireland in 1798*, O'Brien Press, Dublin, 1998, p. 17.
16 ibid., p. 14.
17 N. Curtin, op. cit., pp. 6, 10–15, 283.
18 ibid., p. 283.
19 *Northern Star*, 4 January 1792 and 7 April 1792, quoted in ibid., p. 21.
20 D. Gahan, op. cit., p. 16.
21 T.A. Jackson, op. cit., p. 120.
22 ibid., p. 95.
23 ibid., p. 96. This power was established by Poynings' Law, 1494 and a special Act of the English Parliament in 1720.

24 ibid., p. 93; G. Rudé, op. cit., p. 28. *See also* C. Woodham-Smith, op. cit.; G. O'Tuathaigh, op. cit., pp. 1–7.
25 G. Rudé, op. cit., p. 28.
26 T.A. Jackson, op. cit., p. 95.
27 D. Gahan, op. cit., p. 15.
28 A. de Tocqueville, *The Old Regime and the Revolution*, Harper and Brothers, New York, 1856.
29 J. Swift, 'Fourth Drapier's Letter', quoted in T.A. Jackson, op. cit., p. 102.
30 ibid., p. 102.
31 D. Gahan, op. cit., p. 17.
32 Reverend J. Porter, *Billy Bluff and the Squire, or a Sample of the Times*, 1st edn, 1796, quoted in N. Curtin, op. cit., pp. 185–186.
33 Earl of Westmoreland, 'Letter to William Pitt', 10 December 1792, in ibid., p. 193.
34 'The Jovial Friend', quoted in N. Curtin, op. cit., p. 194.
35 Alexander Knox, 'Letter to Peter Burrowes', 3 March 1797, in ibid., p. 197.
36 D. Gahan, op. cit., p. 18.
37 ibid., p. 24.
38 Dublin Castle Administration, quoted in T.A. Jackson, op. cit., p. 126.
39 T.W. Tone, quoted in ibid., p. 139.
40 N. Curtin, op. cit., p. 61.
41 T.A. Jackson, op. cit., p. 145.
42 C. Costello, op. cit., p. 10.
43 T.D. Williams (ed.), *Secret Societies in Ireland*, Gill and Macmillan, Dublin, 1973, pp. 13–25, 36–40, 58–67.
44 T.A. Jackson, op. cit., p. 102.
45 G. Rudé, op. cit., p. 71.
46 A.G.L. Shaw, *Convicts and the Colonies: a study of penal transportation from Great Britain and Ireland to Australia and other parts of the British Empire*, Faber, London, 1966, p. 171.
47 *Collection of '98 Songs*, compiled by E.R. Williams, in N. Curtin, op. cit., p. 198.
48 ibid., p. 283.
49 *Paddy's Resource*, quoted in ibid., p. 195.
50 C. Costello, op. cit., p. 10.
51 *Irish House of Commons, Parliamentary Register, Ireland*, 1796, quoted in A.G.L. Shaw, op. cit., p. 169.
52 C. Costello, op. cit., p. 25.
53 N. Curtin, op. cit., p. 262.
54 W. Orr, 1797, quoted in R. Hughes, op. cit., p. 185.
55 D. Gahan, op. cit., p. 27.
56 Quoted in N. Curtin, op. cit., p. 167.
57 Colonel Bagnell, 'Letter to Dublin Castle', 28 June 1797, quoted in ibid., p. 170.

58 Thomas Pelham, 'Letter to Gen. Gerard Lake', 27 April 1797, quoted in ibid, p. 172.
59 ibid., p. 172.
60 R. Abercromby, 'Letter to William Pitt', 28 January 1789., in ibid., p. 162.
61 R. Abercromby, 26 February 1798, quoted in ibid., p. 256.
62 N. Curtin, op. cit., p. 257.
63 D. Gahan, op. cit., p. 34.
64 N. Curtin, op. cit., p. 258.
65 ibid., p. 258.
66 Viscount Castlereagh, 'Letter to Thomas Pelham', 8 June 1798, quoted in N. Curtin, p. 254.
67 Earl Camden, 'Letter to Thomas Pelham', 6 June 1798, quoted in ibid., p. 260.
68 G. Rudé, op. cit., p. 40.
69 ibid., p. 40.
70 T. Pakenham, *Year of Liberty: The Story of the Great Irish Rebellion of 1798*, Hodder and Soughton, London, 1972, p. 263.
71 N. Curtin, op. cit., p. 261.
72 Reverend Edward Lascelles, 'Letter to Marquess of Downshire', 4 June 1798, in ibid., p. 261.
73 ibid., p. 263; R.R. Palmer, *The Age of Democratic Revolution: a Political History of Europe and America, 1760–1800*, Princeton University Press, New Jersey, 1964, pp. 293–421.
74 Curtin calculates that if the various actions of rebels across Ulster are taken into account approximately 22,000 'turned out', in 1798. See N. Curtin, op. cit., p. 267.
75 D. Gahan, op. cit., p. 70.
76 R.M. Young, *Ulster in '98: Episodes and Anecdotes*, Belfast, 1893, p. 68.
77 ibid., p. 87.
78 N. Curtin, op. cit., p. 275.
79 Marquis Cornwallis, 'Letter to Major-General Ross', 1798 quoted in R. Hughes, op. cit., pp. 185–186.
80 G. Rudé, op. cit., p. 92; C. Costello, op. cit., pp. 9, 35. T.J. Kiernan in Costello calculates the larger figure of 775.
81 Witness quoted without citation in ibid., p. 35.
82 R. O'Donnell, op. cit., p. 110.
83 ibid.
84 *Freeman's Journal*, quoted in C. Costello, op. cit., p. 66.
85 Dr. E. Trevor, quoted in ibid., p. 67.
86 N. Curtin, op. cit., p. 269.
87 A. Rowan, quoted in ibid., p. 284.
88 ibid., p. 284.
89 G. Rudé, op. cit., p. 37.
90 'The Attractions of a Fashionable Irish Watering Place', Father Prout (attributed to Rev. Francis Mahony), in A.P. Graves (ed.), *Songs of Irish Wit and Humour*, Chatto and Windus, London, p. 259. Website: http://www.archive.org/stream/songsofirishwith00gravrich/songsofirishwith00gravrich_djvu.txt
91 Quoted in C. Costello, op. cit., p. 16.
92 ibid., p. 16.
93 G. Rudé, op. cit., pp. 8–9.
94 ibid., pp. 72–73.
95 C. Costello, op. cit., p. 29.
96 ibid., p. 30; G. Rudé, op. cit., p. 73.
97 C. Costello, op. cit., p. 20.
98 G. Rudé, op. cit., pp. 9, 73; T.J. Kiernan, quoted in Costello, op. cit., p. 34.
99 Quoting figures by A.G.L. Shaw, op. cit., p. 171. See also G. Rudé, 'Early Irish Rebels in Australia', *Historical Studies*, vol. xvi, no. 62, April 1972, pp. 17–23.
100 Hughes opts for a higher figure of 775 just for politicals sent in the aftermath of the rebellion. See R. Hughes, op. cit., p. 186.
101 G. Rudé, op. cit., p. 74.
102 ibid., p. 35.
103 C. Costello, op. cit., pp. 35, 40–50.
104 Father P. O'Neil, quoted in C. Costello, op. cit., p. 47.
105 ibid., p. 47.
106 J. Hunter, 'Letter to Portland', 3 March 1796, quoted in ibid., p. 19.
107 P. King, 'Letter', 29 August 1802, quoted in Rudé, op. cit., p. 73.
108 Convict informer quoted in C. Costello, op. cit., pp. 19–20.
109 Quoted in ibid., p. 28.
110 D. Collins, *An Account of the English Colony in New South Wales*, 1802, Vol. I, pp. 380–381, quoted in ibid., p. 21.
111 R. Hughes, op. cit., p. 185.
112 Quoted in Costello, op. cit., p. 22.
113 R. Hughes, op. cit., p. 184.
114 G. Rudé, op. cit., p. 163.
115 C. Costello, op. cit., p. 45.
116 ibid., pp. 56–57.
117 Quoted in ibid., pp. 56–57. Betts was acquitted of the killings during the mutiny but found guilty of the manslaughter of Pendergast for which he was fined.
118 ibid., p. 36.
119 ibid., p. 12; J. Hirst, *Freedom on the Fatal Shore: Australia's First Colony*, being *Convict Society and its Enemies: a History of Early New South Wales* (1983) and *The Strange Bird of Colonial Democracy: New South Wales 1848–1884* (1988), Black Inc, Melbourne, 2008, pp. vii–ix, 71–75.

120 J. Hirst, *Sense & Nonsense in Australian History*, Black Inc, Melbourne, 2005, p. 4.

121 ibid., pp. 5, 111.

122 J. Boyce, *Van Diemen's Land*, Black Inc., Melbourne, 2008.

123 R. Hughes, op. cit., p. 181.

124 J. Hunter, 'Letter to Portland', 12 November 1796, quoted in R. Hughes, op. cit., p. 184.

125 S. Marsden, 'A Few Observations on the Toleration of the Catholic Religion in New South Wales', quoted in ibid., p. 188.

126 D. Collins, *An Account of the English Colony in New South Wales*, 1802, Vol. II, p. 57, in Costello, op. cit., p. 23.

127 R. Hughes, op. cit., p. 181.

128 C. Costello, op. cit., p. 18.

129 Quoted in ibid., p. 18.

130 J. Hunter, quoted in ibid., p. 19. *See also* Hunter, 'Letter to Portland', 10 January 1798, in R. Hughes, op. cit., p. 186.

131 P. King, quoted in C. Costello, op. cit., p. 46.

132 G. Rudé, op. cit., p. 167.

133 J. Hirst, *Freedom on the Fatal Shore*, pp. vii–viii, 32–34.

134 Anonymous, quoted in C. Costello, op. cit., p. 48.

135 G. Rudé, op. cit., p. 157.

136 C. Costello, op. cit., p. 34.

137 J. Hunter, 'Letter to Portland', 20 March 1800, quoted in C. Costello, op. cit., pp. 37–38.

138 ibid.

139 R. Hughes, op. cit., pp. 428–430.

140 C. Riley, 'The 1804 Australian Rebellion and Battle of Vinegar Hill', *Hawksbury Historical Society Website*: http://www.hawkesburyhistory.org.au/articles/Battle_of_Vinegar.html. November 2003, p. 5.

141 S. Marsden, quoted in C. Costello, op. cit., p. 38.

142 J. Holt, 'Life and Adventures of Joseph Holt', in R. Hughes, op. cit., p. 189.

143 S. Marsden, quoted in C. Costello, op. cit., p. 41.

144 R. Hughes, op. cit., p. 187.

145 Quoted in C. Costello, op. cit., p. 41.

146 S. Marsden, 'A Few Observations on the Toleration of the Catholic Religion in New South Wales', quoted in R. Hughes, op. cit., p. 188.

147 J. Holt, *Memoirs of Joseph Holt, General of the Irish Rebels in 1798*, T.C. Croker (ed), H. Colburn, London, 1828, vol 1, pp. 119–121.

148 S. Marsden, quoted in ibid., p. 38.

149 'King's Court of Inquiry into Irish Insurgents', 1 October 1800, in R. Hughes, op. cit., p. 189.

150 J. Fouveaux, 'Letter to Duke of Portland', 17 September 1801, quoted in R. Hughes, op. cit., p. 117.

151 Rudé, op. cit., pp. 179–180. Flogging ceased in New South Wales and Van Diemen's Land in the 1840s.

152 ibid., p. 176.

153 P. King, 'Letter to Portland', quoted in C. Costello, op. cit., p. 46.

154 ibid., p. 48.

155 J. Holt, quoted in ibid., p. 51.

156 G. Rudé, op. cit., p. 183; R. Hughes, op. cit., p. 181.

157 A. Moore, 'Phil Cunningham: a Forgotten Irish–Australian Rebel', *The Hummer*, Sydney Branch, Australian Society for the Study of Labour History, vol. 4, no. 2, 2004. Website: asslh.org.au

158 C. Riley, op. cit., J. Hirst, *Sense & Nonsense in Australian History*, p. 33.

159 ibid., p. 2.

160 ibid., p. 9.

161 R. Hughes, op. cit., p. 191.

162 C. Riley, op. cit., p. 8.

163 E. Macarthur, quoted in C. Flower, *Illustrated History of New South Wales*, Rigby Publishers, Sydney, 1981, pp. 54–55.

164 C. Riley, op. cit., p. 10.

165 ibid., p. 11.

166 C. Costello, op. cit., pp. 51–52; A. Moore, op. cit.

167 C. Riley, op. cit., p. 15.

168 P. King, quoted in C. Costello, op. cit., p. 53.

169 J. Holt, *Memoirs*, vol 2, p. 228.

170 R. Hughes, op. cit., p. 194.

171 P. King, in C. Costello, op. cit., p. 52.

172 A. Whitaker, *Unfinished Revolution: United Irishmen in New South Wales, 1800–1810*, Crossing Press, Sydney, 1994, p. vii; A. Moore, op. cit.

173 R. O'Donnell, '"Liberty or Death"; The United Irishmen in New South Wales 1800–04', in T. Bartlett, D. Dickson, D. Keogh and K. Whelan (eds), *1798. A Bicentenary Perspective*, Four Courts Press, Dublin, 2003, pp. 607–619.

174 H.B. Hayes, quoted in C. Costello, op. cit., p. 60.

175 G. Rudé, op. cit., p. 93.

176 M. Dwyer, July 1805, quoted in C. Costello, op. cit., p. 69.

177 Captain Sainhill, 2 August 1805, quoted in ibid., p. 70.

178 M. Dwyer, quoted in ibid., p. 70.
179 P. King, quoted in ibid., p. 72.
180 G. Rudé, op. cit., p. 186. He cites Musters 1806 and 1822 and Census of NSW 1828.
181 P. King, quoted in C. Costello, op. cit., p. 72.
182 Secretary of Dublin Castle, 'Letter to Governor King', 17 August 1805, quoted in ibid., p. 71.
183 Rudé, op. cit., pp. 186–187.
184 ibid., pp. 219–220.
185 ibid., p. 174.
186 ibid., p. 185.
187 Muster, 1806, in ibid., p. 186.
188 G.C. Bolton, op. cit., pp. 550–551.
189 R. Hughes, op. cit., pp. 181–183.
190 T.M. Perry, 'Meehan, James (1774–1826)', *Australian Dictionary of Biography*, Volume 2, Melbourne University Press, Carlton South, 1967, pp. 219–220.
191 Rudé, op. cit., p. 167.
192 Rudé, op. cit., p. 186.
193 See also J. Waldersee, *Catholic Society in New South Wales, 1788–1860*, University of Sydney Press, Sydney, 1974, pp. 254–255.
194 G. Rudé, op. cit., p. 187.
195 ibid., p. 187.
196 W. Sorell, quoted in ibid., p. 189.
197 ibid., p. 189.
198 W.V. Teniswood, 'Dry, Richard (1771–1843)', *Australian Dictionary of Biography*, Volume 1, Melbourne University Press, Carlton South, 1966, pp. 328–329.
199 Rudé, op. cit., p. 189; J. Waldersee, op. cit., p. 235.
200 V. Parsons, 'Redmond, Edward (1766–1840)', *Australian Dictionary of Biography*, Volume 2, Melbourne University Press, Carlton South, 1967, p. 371.
201 R. Ward, 'The Australian Legend Revisited', *Historical Studies*, vol. 18, no. 17, Oct., 1978; V. Palmer, *The Legend of the Nineties*, Melbourne University Press, Carlton South, 1958.
202 'The Croppy Boy', quoted in R. Hughes, op. cit., p. 191.
203 ibid., p. 185.
204 ibid., p. 187.
205 Quoted in C. Costello, op. cit., p. 73.
206 A. Moore, op. cit.
207 D. Gahan, op. cit., p. 129.
208 R. O'Donnell, 'Dwyer, Michael', op. cit., p. 110.
209 G. Rudé, op. cit., p. 71.
210 E.G. Whitlam, *Memorial to Battle of Vinegar Hill, Dedication*, 5 March 1988.

CHAPTER 3

1 G. Loveless, *The Victims of Whiggery. A Statement of the Persecutions Experienced by the Dorchester Labourers; with a Report of their Trial; Description of Van Diemen's Land, and Reflections Upon the System of Transportation*, Central Dorchester Committee and Cleave, Shoe Lane, Fleet Street, London, Eighth edn, 1838, p. 29.
2 ibid., p. 29.
3 J. Marlow, *The Tolpuddle Martyrs*, Andre Deutsch Limited, London, 1971, p. 19.
4 G. Loveless, op. cit., p. 10.
5 ibid., p. 28.
6 J. Marlow, op. cit., p. 15.
7 E. Halévy, *The Birth of Methodism in England*, Chicago University Press, Chicago, 1971.
8 J. Marlow, op. cit., p. 15.
9 ibid., p. 36.
10 G. Rudé, op. cit., pp. 53–54.
11 From W. Henderson (ed.), *Victorian Street Ballads: A Selection of Popular Ballads Sold in the Street in the Nineteenth Century*, Country Life Ltd, London, 1938, in J. Marlow, op. cit., p. 40.
12 G. Loveless, op. cit., p. 6; R. Owen, *Address to All Classes in the State*, Association for Removing the Causes of Ignorance and Poverty by Education and Employment, London, 1832.
13 Derbyshire, quoted in J. Marlow, op. cit., p. 87.
14 Quoted in ibid., p. 44.
15 Quoted in *Dorset County Chronicle*, 27 February 1834, quoted in ibid., pp. 44–45.
16 ibid., pp. 30–31.
17 ibid., p. 45.
18 ibid., p. 36.
19 ibid., p. 60. J. Marlow's research indicated Legg himself was no spy, simply a weak and simple man who cracked under pressure from the authorities.
20 Lord Melbourne, 'Letter to Sir Herbert Taylor', 24 November 1831, quoted in ibid., p. 54.
21 ibid., p. 53.
22 ibid., p. 52.
23 57 Geo. III, c. 19 (1817) and 39 Geo. III, c. 79 (1799).
24 G. Rudé, op. cit., pp. 183–184.
25 37 Geo. III, c. 123 (1797).
26 J. Marlow, op. cit., pp. 59–60.
27 Quoted in W. Citrine (ed.), *The Martyrs of Tolpuddle*, TUC, London, 1934, pp. 12–13.
28 J. Marlow, op. cit., p. 62.

29 James Brine, quoted by G. Loveless, op. cit., p. 6.
30 ibid., p. 6.
31 ibid., p. 6.
32 G. Loveless, op. cit., p. 7.
33 J. Marlow, op. cit., pp. 65–66.
34 G. Loveless, op. cit., p. 6.
35 J. Marlow, op. cit., p. 67.
36 ibid., p. 67.
37 J. Marlow, op. cit., p. 76.
38 *Law Magazine*, vol. XI, May 1834, quoted in ibid., p. 79.
39 ibid., p. 69.
40 G. Loveless, op. cit., p. 8.
41 Justice B. Williams, quoted in ibid., p. 8.
42 'The Song of Freedom', quoted in ibid., p. 8.
43 G. Rudé, op. cit., pp. 53–58.
44 ibid., p. 58.
45 E.P. Thompson, op. cit., p. 194.
46 ibid., pp. 194–195.
47 ibid., p. 9.
48 ibid., p. 9.
49 G. Loveless, op. cit., p. 28.
50 E.P. Thompson, op. cit., pp. 90–91.
51 ibid., pp. 93–94.
52 ibid., p. 28.
53 G. Rudé, op. cit., p. 54.
54 ibid., p. 61.
55 ibid., p. 67.
56 E. Hobsbawm and G. Rudé, *Captain Swing*, Lawrence and Wishart, London, 1969, p. 26.
57 E. Hobsbawm, *Labouring Men: studies in the history of labour*, Weidenfeld & Nicolson, London, 1964, pp. 5–17; E. Hobsbawm and G. Rudé, op. cit., p. 26.
58 E.P. Thompson, op. cit., p. 315.
59 G. Rudé, op. cit., p. 52.
60 W. Blake, 'Jerusalem', 1804.
61 M, Löwy and R. Sayer, *Romanticism Against the Tide of Modernity*, trans. C. Porter, Duke University, London, 2001, pp. 7, 10, 15.
62 W. Morris, *News From Nowhere, or, An Epoch of Rest: Being some Chapters from a Utopian Romance*, Routledge & Kegan Paul, London, 1970.
63 Rudé, op. cit., p. 17.
64 ibid., p. 24.
65 E. Hobsbawm and G. Rudé, op. cit., pp. 106, 209; G. Rudé, op. cit., p. 53.
66 ibid., p. 94.
67 P.B. Shelley, 'The Mask of Anarchy: Written on the Occasion of the Massacre at Manchester', in E. Aveling and E.M. Aveling (eds), *Shelley's Socialism and Popular Songs*, The Journeyman Press, London, 1979, p. 47.
68 E.P. Thompson, *The Making of the English Working Class*, Victor Gollancz, London, 1964, p. 703.
69 ibid., p. 700.
70 G. Rudé, op. cit., p. 95.
71 P. Ellis and S. Mac A'Ghobbain, *The Scottish Insurrection of 1820*, Victor Gollancz, London, 1970, p. 255.
72 G. Rudé, op. cit., p. 65.
73 ibid., p. 65.
74 ibid., p. 66.
75 J. Marlow, op. cit., p. 32.
76 G. Rudé, op. cit., p. 114.
77 J.L. and B. Hammond, *The Village Labourer, 1760–1832*, Longmans, London, 1911. See discussion E. Hobsbawm and G. Rudé, op. cit., pp. 13–14, 35.
78 J. Marlow, op. cit., p. 24.
79 E.P. Thompson, op. cit., p. 218.
80 E. Hobsbawm and G. Rudé, op. cit., p. 97; E.P. Thompson, op. cit., p. 62.
81 Interview with Henry Hunt, *The Times*, 17 November 1830, quoted in J. Marlow, op. cit., p. 33.
82 ibid., p. 28.
83 ibid., pp. 27–29.
84 ibid., p. 29.
85 Magistrate, 'Letter to Home Office', quoted in ibid., p. 37.
86 E.P. Thompson, op. cit., p. 817.
87 G.D.H. Cole, *The Life of William Cobbett*, Collins, London, 1927.
88 W. Cobbett, *Rural Rides*, quoted in D. Kent and N. Townsend, *Convicts of the Eleanor: Protest in Rural England, New Lives in Australia*, Pluto Press, Annandale, 2002, p. 68.
89 W. Cobbett, quoted in ibid., p. 68.
90 W. Cobbett, quoted in J. Marlow, op. cit., p. 32.
91 W. Cobbett, quoted in ibid., p. 32.
92 Attorney-General, 1831, quoted in D. Kent and N. Townsend, op. cit., p. 124.
93 W. Cobbett, *Rural Rides*, quoted in J. Marlow, op. cit., p. 30.
94 ibid., p. 33.
95 ibid., p. 34.
96 D. Kent and N. Townsend, op. cit., pp. 87–90.
97 W. Oakley, quoted in ibid., pp. 32–33.
98 ibid., p. 101.
99 ibid., p. 103. This is what Joseph Mason did after the Hampshire men had concluded their drinks.
100 ibid., p. 34.
101 J.L. and B. Hammond, op. cit., pp. 98–99.

102 Quoted in G. Rudé, op. cit., p. 119.
103 G. Rudé and E. Hobsbawm, op. cit., p. 16.
104 D. Kent and N. Townsend, op. cit.,
pp. 46–47.
105 J. Marlow, op. cit., p. 56.
106 ibid., p. 33.
107 ibid., p. 33.
108 D. Kent and N. Townsend, op. cit., p. 113.
109 ibid., p. 113.
110 J. Marlow, op. cit., p. 36.
111 D. Kent and N. Townsend, op. cit., p. ix.
112 R. Hughes, op. cit., p. 199.
113 ibid., p. 200.
114 G. Rudé, op. cit., p. 117. Rudé paraphrases
The Times, 3 December 1830.
115 D. Kent and N. Townsend, op. cit., p. 18.
A typical smallholder might have four
acres and a cow to provide for a family and
a surplus for market.
116 G. Rudé, op. cit., p. 115; D. Kent and
N. Townsend, op. cit., p. 18.
117 ibid., p. 125.
118 G. Rudé, op. cit., p. 115.
119 D. Kent and N. Townsend, op. cit., p. 125.
120 Quoted in ibid., p. 125.
121 ibid., p. 101.
122 ibid., pp. 101, 125.
123 G. Rudé, op. cit., p. 115.
124 D. Kent and N. Townsend, op. cit., p. 131.
125 ibid., p. 131.
126 G. Rudé, op. cit., p. 115.
127 E. Hobsbawm and G. Rudé, pp. 265–266.
128 G. Rudé, op. cit., p. 119.
129 The Times, quoted in J. Marlow, op. cit.,
p. 35.
130 D. Kent and N. Townsend, op. cit., p. 5.
131 ibid., pp. 166–168.
132 Quoted in J. Marlow, op. cit., p. 38.
133 R. Dillingham, 'Letter to Parents', quoted
in R. Hughes, op. cit., p. 200.
134 J. Hirst, Freedom on the Fatal Shore,
pp. 32–33, 42, 100.
135 R. Hughes, op. cit., p. 200.
136 G. Rudé, op. cit., pp. 199–200.
137 ibid., p. 119; T. Cook, The Exile's
Lamentation; or Biographical Sketches of
Thomas Cook, Sydney, 1841. Republished
Library of Australia History, North
Sydney, 1978.
138 Quoted in R. Hughes, op. cit., p. 201.
139 G. Rudé, op. cit., p. 246.
140 The Times, 6 December 1830, quoted in
J. Marlow, op. cit., p. 37.
141 E.P. Thompson, op. cit., pp. 228–229.
142 R. Hughes, op. cit., p. 201.
143 D. Kent and N. Townsend, op. cit., p. 241.
144 R. Hughes, op. cit., p. 200; G. Rudé,
op. cit., p. 119.

145 ibid., p. 120.
146 ibid., p. 122.
147 ibid., p. 26.
148 ibid., pp. 26, 123.
149 G. Loveless, op. cit., p. 29.
150 G. Rudé, op. cit., p. 56.
151 ibid., p. 55.
152 J. Marlow, op. cit., p. 108. They were first
referred to as 'martyrs' in April 1834.
153 ibid., p. 92.
154 ibid., p. 107.
155 G. Rudé, op. cit., p. 56.
156 J. Marlow, op. cit., p. 107.
157 J. Loveless, J. Brine, T. Standfield and
J. Standfield, A Narrative of the Sufferings
of Jas. Loveless, Jas. Brine and Thomas
and John Standfield. Four of the Dorchester
Labourers. Displaying the Horrors of
Transportation. Written by Themselves. With
a Brief Description of New South Wales by
George Loveless, London, 1838.
158 True Sun, 31 March 1834, quoted in
J. Marlow, op. cit., p. 119.
159 G. Loveless, op. cit., p. 10.
160 G. Loveless, 'Letter Read in Parliament
by T. Wakley', Debate, July 1835,
Parliamentary Debates, vol. xxvii, quoted
in J. Marlow, op. cit., p. 104.
161 Mr Scott, quoted in J. Loveless, et. al.,
op. cit., p. 11.
162 ibid., pp. 11–12.
163 ibid., pp. 11–12; J. Marlow, op. cit., p. 146.
164 J. Loveless, et. al., op. cit., pp. 11–12;
J. Marlow, op. cit., p. 145.
165 ibid., p. 145.
166 ibid., p. 146.
167 J. Hammett interviewed in Dorset County
Express, 23 March 1875, in ibid., p. 147.
168 Report, Select Committee of the House of
Commons on Transportation, 1837–1838,
with Minutes of Evidence, Appendix and
Index, 2 vols, 1838.
169 G. Loveless, op. cit., p. 12.
170 ibid., p. 12.; Corroborated in The
Tasmanian by J. Marlow, op. cit., p. 154.
171 G. Loveless, op. cit., p. 13.
172 ibid., p. 13.
173 ibid., pp. 19–20.
174 ibid., p. 23.
175 ibid., p. 26.
176 J. Marlow, op. cit., p. 107.
177 Morning Herald, 2 April 1834 in ibid.,
p. 108.
178 ibid., p. 111.
179 The Times, 22 April 1834, quoted in
J. Marlow, op. cit., pp. 127, 290.
180 ibid., p. 130.
181 ibid., p. 115.

182 ibid., p. 113.
183 ibid., p. 109.
184 Reprinted in the *True Sun*, 7 April 1834 in ibid., p. 114.
185 J. Marlow, op. cit., p. 66.
186 ibid., p. 64. Hammett later admitted the subterfuge.
187 ibid., p. 209.
188 ibid., p. 248.
189 ibid., p. 248.
190 ibid., p. 55.
191 G. Rudé, op. cit., p. 20.
192 *Representation of the People Act* 1832.
193 E.P. Thompson, op. cit., pp. 807–809.
194 G. Rudé, op. cit., pp. 95–96.
195 Different Acts were passed conferring similar electoral reform in Scotland and Ireland for the election of their members to the House of Commons.
196 G. Rudé, op. cit., p. 26.
197 Joseph Rayner Stephens, 24 September 1838 speaking at Kersal Moor, Manchester, quoted in M. Bloy, *The Victorian Web, Literature, History and Culture in the Age of Victoria*. Website: http://www.victorianweb.org/history/chartism.html
198 G. Rudé, op. cit., p. 9.
199 G. Rudé, op. cit., p. 139.
200 Ben Wilson, Yorkshire Chartist, in D. Vincent, *Testaments of Radicalism: Memoirs of Working Class Politicians 1790–1885*, Routledge, 1977, p. 198.
201 G. Rudé, op. cit., p. 62.
202 ibid., pp. 65–66.
203 *Northern Star*, May 1842.
204 G. Rudé, op. cit., pp. 23, 68, 215.
205 K. Marx and F. Engels, 'The Communist Manifesto', in *Selected Works*, Lawrence and Wishart, London, 1970.
206 G. Rudé, op. cit., p. 142.
207 ibid., p. 144.
208 ibid., pp. 9, 213–218.
209 ibid., p. 213.
210 ibid., pp. 214–215.
211 ibid., p. 218.
212 ibid. p. 70.
213 W.K. Hancock, *Australia*, Jacaranda, Brisbane, 1966, p. 71.
214 P. Cochrane, *Colonial Ambition: Foundations of Australian Democracy*, Melbourne University Press, Carlton South, 2006, p. 10.
215 M. McKenna, op. cit., p. 42; J. Hirst, *Sense & Nonsense in Australian History*, Black Inc., Melbourne, 2005, pp. 210–211.
216 ibid., pp. 253–254.
217 H. Collins, 'Political Ideas and Practices', in N. Meaney (ed.), *Under New Heavens: Cultural Transmission and the Making of Australia*, Heinemann Educational Australia, Port Melbourne, 1989, p. 101.
218 P. Cochrane, op. cit., p. 249.
219 James Smith, quoted in M. McKenna, op. cit., pp. 92–93.
220 This innovation followed the granting of female suffrage in South Australia (1894), NSW (1902) and was followed by Victoria (1908). The vast majority of Indigenous Australians of both sexes were denied the vote, and citizenship was racially limited by the *Immigration Restriction Act* 1901 (Cth).
221 G. Rudé, op. cit., p. 218.
222 Hobart *Mercury*, 11 August 1870, in ibid., p. 218.
223 J. Hirst, 'Empire, State, Nation', pp. 141–162; N. Meaney, 'In History's Page: Identity and Myth', in D. Schreuder and S. Ward, op. cit., pp. 363–389; H. Collins, op. cit., pp. 83–107.
224 G. Loveless, op. cit., p. 23.
225 C.H. Pearson, *National Life and Character: a Forecast*, Macmillan, London, 1894.
226 P. Kelly, *The End of Certainty: Power, Politics and Business in Australia*, Allen & Unwin, St. Leonards, 1994.
227 A. Metin, *Socialism Without Doctrine*, trans. R. Ward, Alternative Publishing Cooperative, Chippendale, 1977.
228 In a speech at Mansion House, 5 November 1895.

CHAPTER 4

1 *Les Mélanges Religieux*, 15 September 1846, quoted in F.X. Prieur, *Notes of a Convict of 1838*, translated from the original with an introduction and notes by George Mackaness, *Australian Historical Monographs*, no. 18, Sydney, 1949, p. 9.
2 G. Mackaness, 'Introduction', in ibid., pp. 5–6.
3 ibid., p. 13.
4 G. Mackaness in ibid., p. 6.
5 ibid., p. 6.
6 *Déclaration d'indépendance du Bas-Canada*. Website: http://www.republiquelibre.org/cousture/NELSON.HTM
7 F.X. Prieur, *Notes of a Convict of 1838*, translated from the original, with an introduction and notes by George Mackaness, *Australian Historical Monographs*, no. 18, Sydney, 1949, pp. 11, 13.

8 Dr E. Falardeau, 'Prieur l'Idéaliste', quoted in ibid., p. 7.
9 Although the title Chevalier was a French equivalent of the British Knighthood, in de Lorimier's case it was simply a given name.
10 F.X. Prieur, op. cit., p. 14.
11 ibid., p. 15.
12 ibid., p. 18.
13 ibid., p. 21.
14 ibid., p. 25.
15 ibid., p. 35.
16 ibid., p. 37.
17 ibid., pp. 29, 37–38.
18 ibid., p. 38.
19 ibid., p. 32.
20 ibid., p. 43.
21 ibid., p. 43.
22 ibid., p. 47.
23 ibid., p. 42.
24 C. Hindenlang, quoted in ibid., p. 47.
25 ibid., pp. 6, 48. The twelve rebels executed between 21 December 1838 and 15 February 1839 were Cardinal, Duquette, Decoigne, Robert, Ambroise and Charles Sanguinette, Hamelin, de Lorimier, Hindenlang, Narbonne, Nicolas and Daunais.
26 ibid., p. 56.
27 ibid., p. 56.
28 ibid., p. 48.
29 W. Gates, *Recollections of Life in Van Diemen's Land*, edited with an introduction, notes and commentary by George Mackaness, in two parts, *Australian Historical Monographs*, no. 40, 1961 (first published 1850), p. 9.
30 D. Heustis, *A Narrative of the Adventures and Sufferings of Captain Daniel Heustis*, Redding & Co. by S.W. Wilder, Boston, 1847, pp. 1, 8, quoted in C. Pybus and H. Maxwell-Stewart, *American Citizens, British Slaves: Yankee Political Prisoners in an Australian Penal Colony 1839–1850*, Melbourne University Press, Carlton South, 2002, p. 8.
31 W. Gates, op. cit., p. 12.
32 C. Pybus and H. Maxwell-Stewart, *American Citizens, British Slaves: Yankee Political Prisoners in an Australian Penal Colony 1839–1850*, Melbourne University Press, Carlton South, 2002, p. 1.
33 ibid., p. 2.
34 W. Gates, op. cit., p. 14.
35 ibid., p. 14.
36 ibid., p. 16.
37 C. Pybus and H. Maxwell-Stewart, op. cit., pp. 1, 36.

38 W. Gates, op. cit., p. 9.
39 ibid., p. 10.
40 ibid., p. 10.
41 ibid., pp. 15, 17.
42 ibid., p. 18.
43 ibid., p. 19; C. Pybus and H. Maxwell-Stewart, op. cit., p. 2. Pybus and Maxwell-Stewart estimate thirteen Americans killed and twenty-eight wounded.
44 S. Wright, *Narrative and Recollections of Van Diemen's Land During Three Years Captivity of Stephen S. Wright*, New York, 1844, quoted in ibid., p. 3.
45 ibid., p. 39.
46 W. Gates., op. cit., p. 21. We only have Gates's word for this.
47 ibid., p. 22.
48 C. Pybus and H. Maxwell-Stewart, op. cit., pp. 3, 38.
49 W. Gates, op. cit., p. 22.
50 D. Heustis, quoted in C. Pybus and H. Maxwell-Stewart, op. cit., p. 2.
51 S. Wright, quoted in ibid., p. 36.
52 ibid., p. 14.
53 ibid., p. 20. The relevant Act is Vic. 1 c. 10.
54 ibid., p. 39. Seventeen patriots captured at the Windmill agreed to give evidence against the 140 in exchange for their freedom.
55 ibid., p. 38.
56 W. Gates, op. cit., p. 28.
57 ibid., p. 42.
58 Only ninety-two caught in Upper Canada actually arrived in Van Diemen's Land owing to the death of one on board the *Buffalo*.
59 C. Pybus and H. Maxwell-Stewart, op. cit., p. 3.
60 ibid., p. 3.
61 G. Rudé, op. cit., pp. 42–51, 82–88, 202–204; O. Kinchen, *The Rise and Fall of the Patriot Hunters*, Bookman Associates, New York, 1956; J.C. Carter, 'Rebellious Acts in the Western District of Upper Canada: Precursor to Transportation to Van Diemen's Land', *Australasian Canadian Studies*, combining vol. 22, no. 2, 2004, and vol. 23, no. 1, 2005, pp. 33–36; C. Pybus and H. Maxwell-Stewart, op. cit.
62 F. Mackey, 'Bound for Australia', *Horizon Canada*, October 1986, vol. 7, no. 84, p. 2009; T. Causer, '"On British Felony the Sun Never Sets": Narratives of Political Prisoners in New South Wales and Van Diemen's Land, 1838–53', *Cultural and Social History*, vol. 5, no. 4, pp. 425–426.

63 L.L. Ducharme, *Journal of a Political Exile in Australia, 1845*, translated from the original French with an introduction and notes by George Mackaness, *Australian Historical Monographs*, no. 9, D.S. Ford, Sydney, 1944.

64 C. Pybus and H. Maxwell-Stewart, op. cit., p. 5.

65 ibid., p. 5.

66 S. Wright, quoted in ibid., p. 50.

67 W. Gates, op. cit., p. 31.

68 C. Pybus and H. Maxwell-Stewart, p. 6.

69 D. Heustis, quoted in ibid., p. 3.

70 ibid., p. 6.

71 R. Frances, Review of 'American Citizens, British Slaves', *Australian Humanities Review*, September–December 2002, p. 1. Website: http://www.australianhumanitiesreview.org/archive/Issue-September-2002/frances.html

72 S. Schama, *A History of Britain: 1776–2000 The Fate of Empire*, Vol. 3, BBC Books, London, 2007, pp. 240–241.

73 D. Heustis, quoted in C. Pybus and H. Maxwell-Stewart, op. cit., p. 8.

74 P. Borroughs, *The Canadian Crisis and British Colonial Policy, 1828–1841*, Edward Arnold, Ltd, London, 1972, p. 95.

75 C. Pybus and H. Maxwell-Stewart, op. cit., p. 8.

76 Quoted in P. Burroughs, op. cit., p. 94.

77 Quoted in O. Kinchen, op. cit., p. 13.

78 P. Burroughs, op. cit., p. 94.

79 ibid., p. 95.

80 ibid., p. 95.

81 ibid., p. 95.

82 ibid., pp. 1–8.

83 ibid., p. 1.

84 'Iroquois' was a French term. The members of the Six Nation confederacy referred to themselves as Haudensosaunee, meaning 'People of the Longhouse'.

85 The North American chapter of the Seven Years' War is also known as the 'French and Indian War'.

86 P. Burroughs, op. cit., pp. 1–3.

87 ibid., p. 84.

88 ibid., pp. 11–13.

89 C. Pybus and H. Maxwell-Stewart, op. cit., p. 9.

90 ibid., p. 9.

91 ibid., p. 9.

92 G. Rudé, op. cit., p. 82.

93 J.C. Carter, op. cit., p. 9.

94 G. Rudé, op. cit., p. 82.

95 F.X. Prieur, op. cit., p. 49.

96 ibid., pp. 49, 55.

97 ibid., p. 49.

98 Quoted from, 'The Canadian Rebellion of 1837', excerpted from H.W. Hill, dd. *Municipality of Buffalo, New York, A History. 1720–1923*. Lewis Historical Publishing Company, Inc. New York. Website: http://www.buffalonian.com/history/articles/1801-50/canrebellion.html

99 C. Pybus and H. Maxwell-Stewart, op. cit., p. 9.

100 ibid., p. 9; O. Kinchen, op. cit., p. 31.

101 P. Burroughs, op. cit., p. 107.

102 ibid., p. 96.

103 *Report of State Trials held Before a General Court Martial, 1838–39*, 2 vols, Montreal, 1839, pp. 1, 537–540.

104 P. Burroughs, op. cit., pp. 97–98; The Canada Government Bill was passed by the House of Commons on 29 January 1838.

105 G. Rudé, op. cit., p. 83.

106 F. Mackey, op. cit., p. 2007. Other rebel leaders exiled to Bermuda included Henri Gauvin and Bonaventure Viger.

107 Lord Durham, 'Letter to Glenelg', 9 August 1838, quoted in P. Burroughs, op. cit., p. 100.

108 J.G. Lambton, Earl of Durham, *The Report on the Affairs of British North America* (known as the *Durham Report*), 4 February 1839, published with Despatches, Ridgways, London, 1839, pp. 8, 306–307.

109 P. Burroughs, op. cit., p. 99. Lord Durham resigned as Governor-General 19 September 1838.

110 G. Rudé, op. cit., pp. 82–83; C. Pybus and H. Maxwell-Stewart, op. cit., pp. 15, 35. Pybus and Maxwell-Stewart show that officers were elected and embraced a range of backgrounds, from skilled trades to an *émigré* nobleman.

111 O. Kinchen, op. cit., p. 11.

112 ibid., p. 5.

113 G. Rudé, op. cit., p. 83.

114 J.C. Carter, op. cit., p. 57.

115 *Buffalo Daily Mercury*, 8 December 1838, quoted in O.A. Kinchen, op. cit., p. 21.

116 Carl Wittke, 'Ohioans and the Canadians—American Crisis of 1837–38', *Ohio Archeological and Historical Quarterly*, vol. LVIII, pp. 26–37, quoted in ibid., pp. 17–18.

117 ibid., p. 25.

118 ibid., p. 20.

119 ibid., p. 17.

120 *Report of State Trials*, II, op. cit., p. 556.

121 O. Kinchen, op. cit., p. 5.

122 *Detroit News*, 30 January 1890, quoted in ibid., p. 14.

123 W. Gates, op. cit., pp. 14–15.

124 O. Kinchen, op. cit., p. 11.

125 George H. McWhorter (Collector of Customs, Oswego) to Secretary of the Treasury, 14 September 1838, quoted in ibid., p. 19.

126 *Montreal Herald*, 12 November 1838, quoted in ibid., p. 19.

127 G. Arthur, 'Letter to Glenelg', 2 January 1839, quoted in ibid., p. 19.

128 H.S. Fox, 'Letter to Arthur', 6 December 1838, quoted in ibid., p. 20.

129 Reprinted in the *Buffalo Daily Mercury*, 8 December 1838, quoted in ibid., p. 21.

130 ibid., p. 21.

131 C. Pybus, 'Introduction to Samuel Snow's Narrative', *Convict Narratives*, International Centre for Convict Studies, University of Tasmania, 1999. Website: http://iccs.arts.utas.edu.au/narratives/pybusintro.html

132 S. Snow, *The Exiles Return or Narrative of Samuel Snow who was Banished to Van Diemen's Land, for Participating in the Patriot War in Upper Canada in 1838*, Smead and Cowles, Cleveland, 1846, edited and annotated by C. Pybus, *Convict Narratives*, International Centre for Convict Studies, 1999. Website: http://iccs.arts.utas.edu.au/narratives/snow.html

133 L. Bishop, 'Recollections of the Patriot War of 1837–38', Detroit Historical Society, 28 March 1861, quoted in O. Kinchen, op. cit., p. 22.

134 C. Pybus and H. Maxwell-Stewart, op. cit., p. 12.

135 D. Heustis, quoted in ibid., p. 11.

136 Listed in O. Kinchen, op. cit., p. 22.

137 ibid., p. 23.

138 ibid., p. 23.

139 J.C. Carter, op. cit., p. 35.

140 O. Kinchen, op. cit., p. 15; W. Gates, op. cit., p. 11.

141 ibid., p. 11.

142 O. Kinchen, op. cit., p. 15.

143 President M. Van Buren, quoted in ibid., p. 15.

144 H.S. Fox, quoted in ibid., p. 15.

145 C. Pybus and H. Maxwell-Stewart, op. cit., p. 10.

146 W. Gates, op. cit., p. 11.

147 J.C. Carter, op. cit., p. 35.

148 R. Marsh, quoted in ibid., p. 35.

149 ibid., p. 35.

150 Fort Covington Resolutions, 17 November 1838, quoted in O. Kinchen, op. cit., p. 18.

151 W. Gates, op. cit., p. 11.

152 ibid., p. 11.

153 ibid., pp. 11–12; C. Pybus and H. Maxwell-Stewart, op. cit., p. 11.

154 J.C. Carter, op. cit., pp. 36–39.

155 ibid., p. 41; O.E. Tiffany, *The Canadian Rebellion of 1837–1838*, Buffalo Historical Society, Buffalo, 1905, pp. 140–141.

156 O. Kinchen, op. cit., p. 25.

157 *Toronto Patriot*, 2 March 1838, quoted in J.C. Carter, op. cit., p. 41.

158 C. Pybus and H. Maxwell-Stewart, op. cit., p. 12.

159 J.C. Carter, op. cit., pp. 48–49.

160 Adjutant General R.W. Ashel, 'Letter to Bond', 1 March 1838, quoted in ibid., p. 46.

161 Quoted in C. Pybus and H. Maxwell-Stewart, op. cit., p. 13.

162 Quoted in O. Kinchen, op. cit., p. 32.

163 G. Mackaness, 'Introduction', in F.X. Prieur, op. cit., p. 7.

164 O. Kinchen, op. cit., p. 31.

165 C. Pybus and H. Maxwell-Stewart, op. cit., p. 13.

166 ibid., p. 13.

167 R. Marsh, quoted in J.C. Carter, op. cit., p. 51.

168 ibid., p. 52.

169 C. Pybus, End Note 2 in S. Snow, op. cit.

170 C. Pybus, 'Introduction to Samuel Snow'.

171 O. Kinchen, op. cit., p. 31.

172 L. Miller, *Notes of an Exile to Van Diemen's Land*, Fredonia, W. McKinstry and Co., New York, 1846, p. 3.

173 Edward Theller, 1905, quoted in J.C. Carter, op. cit., p. 54.

174 D. Heustis, quoted in C. Pybus and H. Maxwell-Stewart, op. cit., p. 14.

175 ibid., p. 17.

176 Quoted in ibid., p. 17.

177 ibid., pp. 17–18.

178 ibid., p. 19.

179 ibid., p. 19.

180 ibid., p. 15.

181 ibid., p. 42.

182 S. Snow, 1846, quoted in J.C. Carter, op. cit., p. 55.

183 G. Rudé, op. cit., p. 82.

184 Colonel J. Prince, quoted in J.C. Carter, op. cit., p. 56; G. Rudé, op. cit., p. 82. Rudé puts the number of patriot deaths at twenty-four.

185 ibid., p. 82.

186 *Sandwich Western Herald*, quoted in J.C. Carter, op. cit., p. 56.

187 ibid., p. 58.

188 ibid.
189 C. Pybus and H. Maxwell-Stewart, op. cit., p. 17.
190 ibid., p. 14.
191 C. McKenna, 'The Impact of the Upper Canadian Rebellion on Life in Essex County, Ontario, 1837–42', Unpublished Research, 1985, discussed by J.C. Carter, op. cit., p. 58.
192 *Sandwich Western Herald*, 23 January 1838, quoted in ibid., p. 41.
193 G. Rudé, op. cit., pp. 82–83.
194 ibid., p. 83.
195 ibid., p. 84.
196 ibid., p. 84.
197 ibid., p. 85.
198 *Lawless Aggressions Act*, quoted in ibid., p. 85.
199 C. Pybus and H. Maxwell-Stewart, op. cit., p. 6.
200 ibid., p. 20.
201 ibid., pp. 19–20.
202 Glenelg, 'Letter to Arthur', 30 May 1838, quoted in ibid., p. 21.
203 Glenelg, 'Letter to Arthur', 23 June 1838, quoted in ibid., p. 21.
204 ibid., p. 25.
205 ibid., p. 26. Fellow patriot prisoner Benjamin Wait claims that Beemer concocted the story of a plot to curry favour.
206 ibid., p. 26.
207 B. Wait, quoted in ibid., p. 30.
208 L. Miller, op. cit., p. 237.
209 Stevenson, 'Letter to Van Buren', quoted in C. Pybus and H. Maxwell-Stewart, op. cit., p. 29.
210 B. Wait, *Letters from Van Diemen's Land Written During Four Years Imprisonment for Political Offences Committed in Upper Canada*, A.W. Wilgus, Buffalo, 1843, p. 251.
211 C, Pybus and H. Maxwell-Stewart, op. cit., pp. 32–33.
212 G. Rudé, op. cit., pp. 84–86.
213 ibid., p. 86.
214 ibid., p. 87.
215 C. Pybus and H. Maxwell-Stewart, op. cit., p. 48.
216 ibid., pp. 47–48.
217 ibid., p. 70.
218 ibid., p. 54.
219 ibid., p. 43.
220 Fox, 'Letter to Arthur', 31 January 1839, quoted in ibid., p. 41.
221 G. Arthur, 'Letter to Glenelg', 21 March 1839, quoted in ibid., p. 51.
222 D. Heustis, quoted in G. Rudé, op. cit., p. 87.
223 C. Pybus and H. Maxwell-Stewart, op. cit., p. 54. Pybus and Maxwell-Stewart found a discrepancy between the names of eighty-two Upper Canadian prisoners listed as shipped on the *Buffalo* in the Home Office records and those recorded as arriving in Van Diemen's Land.
224 ibid., p. 52. Elijah Woodman's diary of 1 April records being informed they were to be transported to Van Diemen's Land.
225 S. Snow, op. cit.
226 W. Gates, op. cit., p. 34.
227 F. Mackey, op. cit., p. 2008.
228 D. Heustis, quoted in C. Pybus and H. Maxwell-Stewart, op. cit., p. 55.
229 F.X. Prieur, op. cit., p. 64.
230 D. Heustis and R. Marsh, quoted in C. Pybus and H. Maxwell-Stewart, op. cit., pp. 57, 60.
231 F.X. Prieur, *Journal of a Political Exile*, p. 63.
232 L.L. Ducharme, op. cit., p. 15; S. Snow, op. cit.
233 E. Woodman, quoted in C. Pybus and H. Maxwell-Stewart, op. cit., p. 55.
234 S. Snow, op. cit., p. 3.
235 F.X. Prieur, op. cit., p. 66.
236 Unnamed officer on the *Buffalo*, quoted in F. Mackey, op. cit., p. 2009.
237 W. Gates, op. cit., p. 36.
238 S. Snow, op. cit.
239 ibid.; F.X. Prieur, op. cit., p. 67.
240 ibid., p. 67.
241 S. Snow, op. cit.
242 C. Pybus and H. Maxwell-Stewart, op. cit., pp. 61–62.
243 F.X. Prieur, op. cit., p. 69.
244 ibid., p. 69.
245 W. Gates, op. cit., p. 36.
246 ibid., p. 37.
247 F.X. Prieur, op. cit., p. 70.
248 L.L. Ducharme, op. cit., p. 19.
249 S. Snow, op. cit.
250 L. Miller, op. cit., p. 254; C. Pybus and H. Maxwell-Stewart, op. cit., p. 33.
251 D. Callahan, University of Aveiro, Portugal, quoted in R. Frances, op. cit.
252 C. Pybus and H. Maxwell-Stewart, op. cit., pp. xiv, 50, 61, 181.
253 ibid., p. 81.
254 ibid., op. cit., p. xiv.
255 S. Snow, op. cit.; T. Causer, op. cit., p. 426.
256 Discounting Asa Priest, who died at sea, but including the three from the *Hastings* who died on shore in hospital after disembarkation.

257 W. Gates, op. cit., p. 39.
258 ibid., p. 40.
259 C. Pybus and H. Maxwell-Stewart, op. cit., p. 84.
260 ibid., p. 85.
261 S. Snow, op. cit.
262 ibid.
263 W. Gates, op. cit., p. 45.
264 C. Pybus and H. Maxwell-Stewart, op. cit., pp. 78–81.
265 R. Marsh, *Seven Years of My Life, or a Narrative of Patriot Exile*, Faxon and Stevens, Buffalo, 1847, pp. 72–73.
266 C. Pybus and H. Maxwell-Stewart, op. cit., p. 82.
267 ibid., pp. 83–85.
268 Van Diemen's Land. Website: http://folkstream.com/091.html
269 C. Pybus and H. Maxwell-Stewart, op. cit., p. 88.
270 ibid., pp. 92–94.
271 S. Snow, op. cit.
272 W. Gates, op. cit., p. 48.
273 ibid., p. 58.
274 S. Snow, op. cit.
275 C. Pybus and H. Maxwell-Stewart, op. cit., p. 126.
276 W. Gates, op. cit., p. 61.
277 C. Pybus and H. Maxwell-Stewart, op. cit., p. 155.
278 L. Miller, op. cit., pp. 320, 347.
279 W. Gates, op. cit., p. 62.
280 C. Pybus and H. Maxwell-Stewart, op. cit., p. 68.
281 ibid., p. 156; L. Miller, op. cit., pp. 326–327.
282 ibid., pp. 327, 347.
283 W. Gates, op. cit., p. 61.
284 ibid., p. 71.
285 C. Pybus and H. Maxwell-Stewart, op. cit., pp. 113–114.
286 ibid., op. cit., pp. 159–160.
287 ibid., p. 157.
288 W. Gates, op. cit., vol. 2, pp. 17–19.
289 F.X. Prieur, op. cit., p. 80.
290 ibid., p. 78.
291 ibid., p. 82.
292 ibid., p. 80.
293 ibid., p. 81.
294 *Sydney Herald*, quoted in ibid., p. 88.
295 Father J. Brady in *Sydney Herald*, quoted in ibid., p. 88.
296 ibid., p. 85; L.L. Ducharme, op. cit., pp. 36–38.
297 ibid., p. 90.
298 ibid., p. 92.
299 ibid., p. 91.
300 F. Mackey, op. cit., p. 2009.

301 F.X. Prieur, op. cit., p. 86; L.L. Ducharme, op. cit., p. 48.
302 C. Pybus and H. Maxwell-Stewart, op. cit., pp. 190–191.
303 W. Gates, vol 2, op. cit., p. 47.
304 ibid., p. 47.
305 *Un Canadien Errant*, attributed to Antoine Gérin-Lajoie, Lyrics on Songs for Teaching. Website: http://www.songsforteaching.com/canada/uncanadienerrant.htm
306 G. Mackaness, 'Introduction', p. 8.
307 L.L. Ducharme, op. cit., pp. 40–41.
308 F.X. Prieur, op. cit., p. 123.
309 G. Mackaness, 'Introduction', p. 9.
310 F.X. Prieur, op. cit., p. 140.
311 P. Burroughs, op. cit., p. 103.
312 Lord Melbourne, 'Letter to Russell', 2 September 1838 and, 11 and 23 December 1838, quoted in ibid., p. 101.
313 Earl of Durham, *Durham Report*, p. 216.
314 ibid., p. 105.
315 ibid., p. 107.
316 Often just termed the Province of Canada.
317 P. Burroughs, op. cit., p. 108.
318 ibid., pp. 108–109.
319 Lord Stanley, Colonial Secretary, House of Commons, 'Letter to Peel', 27 August 1842; *Hansard*, 3rd Series, LXXV, 30 May 1844, quoted in ibid., p. 112.
320 William Gates, op. cit., p. 9.
321 P. Burroughs, op. cit., p. 108.
322 ibid., p. 108.
323 ibid., p. 114; G. Rudé, op. cit., p. 82.
324 P. Burroughs, op. cit., p. 103.
325 J.C. Carter, op. cit., p. 33.
326 P. Burroughs, op. cit., p. 116.
327 J. Stephen, 1836, quoted in F. Mackey, op. cit., p. 2006.
328 The Concord memorial ends with: 'Measures taken as a result of the uprisings in Lower and Upper Canada represented significant steps in the evolution of responsible government and parliamentary democracy in Canada and Australia.' Website: http://www.canadainternational.gc.ca/australia-australie/bilateral_relations_bilaterales/battery_point.aspx?lang=eng

CHAPTER 5

1 T. Meagher, 22 October, 1848 quoted in T. Keneally, *The Great Shame, A Story of the Irish in the Old World and the New*, Random House, Millers Point, 1998, p. 182.

2   R. Davis, 'William Smith O'Brien: Irish
    Rebel and British Colonial Reformer',
    *Bulletin of the Centre for Tasmanian
    Historical Studies*, Irish Edition, vol. 2,
    no. 3, 1989, p. 2.
3   There is dispute over actual numbers of
    deaths caused by the famine, as record
    keeping was poor. British census figures
    in 1841 record an Irish population of
    8,175,124, which should have increased to
    9 million by the census of 1851 but had in
    fact been reduced to 6,552,385. William
    Smith O'Brien later estimated that Ireland
    had lost approximately two million people,
    and reasoned at least one million had
    perished. See O'Brien, 'Journal', pp. 5,
    18–20, 11 November 1851, quoted in
    B. Touhill, *William Smith O'Brien and His
    Revolutionary Companions in Penal Exile*,
    University of Missouri Press, London,
    1981, p. 136.
4   ibid., p. 137.
5   G. Rudé, op. cit., p. 8.
6   M. Clarke, 'Port Arthur', p. 530.
7   G. Rudé, op. cit., p. 4.
8   ibid., p. 5.
9   ibid., pp. 8–9, 38–39.
10 T.A. Jackson, op. cit., p. 205.
11 ibid., p. 209.
12 G. Rudé, op. cit., p. 27.
13 ibid., p. 27.
14 ibid., p. 27.
15 ibid., p. 27.
16 E. Wakefield, quoted in T.A. Jackson,
    op. cit., p. 206.
17 G. Rudé, op. cit., p. 56.
18 T.A. Jackson, op. cit., p. 208. Except in
    Ulster where tenants had a property right
    in improvements made.
19 G. Rudé, op. cit., p. 28.
20 G. Rudé, op. cit., p. 27.
21 E. Wakefield, *Survey of Ireland*, vol. 1,
    quoted in T.A. Jackson, op. cit., p. 209.
22 G. Rudé, op. cit., pp. 38–39.
23 ibid., p. 8. Home Office records included
    lists of people apprehended and sentenced
    under the Insurrection Acts, that appeared
    in *Hansard*.
24 ibid., p. 38.
25 ibid., p. 38.
26 ibid., pp. 38, 106.
27 ibid., p. 105.
28 ibid., p. 8.
29 ibid., pp. 108–110.
30 ibid., pp. 108–110.
31 Note on Francis McCanna, 1841, Tas.
    Arch, CON 33/18, quoted in ibid., p. 110.
32 ibid., p. 29.

33 C. Woodham-Smith, op. cit., p. 326.
34 G. Rudé, op. cit., p. 39.
35 ibid., p. 145.
36 C. Woodham-Smith, op. cit., p. 329.
37 J. Mitchel, *United Irishman*, quoted in
    T. Eagleton, *Scholars and Rebels in
    Nineteenth Century Ireland*, Blackwell
    Publishers, Oxford, 1999, p. 139.
38 T.A. Jackson, op. cit., p. 244.
39 G. Rudé, op. cit., p. 71.
40 Sir R. Peel, quoted in ibid., p. 71.
41 ibid., p. 74.
42 ibid., pp. 76–77.
43 R. Davis, op. cit., p. 3.
44 S. McConville, *Irish Political Prisoners,
    1848–1922: Theatres of War*, Routledge,
    London, 2003, pp. 14–15.
45 ibid., p. 18.
46 ibid., p. 18.
47 ibid., p. 13, drawing on Cardinal Tomas
    O'Fiaich, 'The North and Young Ireland',
    Tipperary Historical Journal, 1998, p. 20.
48 ibid., pp. 12–13.
49 ibid., p. 20.
50 B. Webb, 'Eva of *The Nation* and the
    Young Ireland Press', in L.M. Geary and
    A.J. McCarthy, *Ireland, Australia and New
    Zealand: History, Politics and Culture*, Irish
    Academic Press, Dublin, 2008, pp. 78–79.
51 T. Eagleton, op. cit., p. 141.
52 S. McConville, op. cit., p. 15.
53 ibid., p. 15.
54 K. Molloy, 'An Irish Radical and his
    Nephew: the papers of John Mitchel and
    Sir William Hill Irvine', *Latrobe Journal*,
    no. 84, Spring 2009, pp. 37–38.
55 ibid., p. 42.
56 ibid., p. 42.
57 D. Gwyn, *Thomas Francis Meagher*,
    Dublin, 1949, p. 53.
58 S. McConville, op. cit., p. 16.
59 K. Molloy, op. cit., p. 42.
60 ibid., p. 42.
61 ibid., p. 141.
62 G. Rudé, op. cit., pp. 46–47.
63 ibid., p. 46.
64 T. Eagleton, op. cit., p. 141.
65 S. McConville, op. cit., p. 13.
66 R. Davis, op. cit., p. 2.
67 S. McConville, op. cit., p. 14.
68 W.S. O'Brien, *O'Brien's Retrospect*, 1848,
    quoted in R. Davis, op. cit., p. 1. The
    immigration plan, advocated by Edward
    Gibbon Wakefield, failed to recognise the
    ownership and continued use of the land
    by indigenous populations.
69 S. McConville, op. cit., p. 14.
70 ibid., p. 13.

71 ibid., p. 13.
72 G. Duffy, 'Letter to O'Brien', 26 December 1846, quoted in ibid., p. 15.
73 See discussion about culture and nationalism in B. Anderson, *Imagined Communities: Reflections on the Origin and Spread of Nationalism*, Verso, London, 2006, pp. 1–8.
74 T. Eagleton, op. cit., p. 4.
75 ibid., p. 18.
76 A. Smith, *National Identity*, University of Nevada Press, Reno, 1991, pp. 64, 84.
77 T. Eagleton, op. cit., p. 5.
78 ibid., pp. 30–31.
79 ibid., pp. 36–37; A. Gramsci, *Selections from the Prison Notebooks of Antonio Gramsci* (ed.) and Trans. Q. Hoare and G.N. Smith, Lawrence and Wishart, London, 1971, pp. 3, 6, 16.
80 ibid., p. 36.
81 ibid., p. 5.
82 *Nation*, 'Prospectus', quoted in *Life of John Mitchel*, P.A. Sillard, James Duffy and Co., Ltd, Dublin, 1908, p. 3.
83 S. McConville, op. cit., p. 7.
84 'Eva', *nom de plume* of M.A. Kelly, 'The Awakening of the Sleepers', *The Nation*, 23 February 1845, quoted in B. Webb, op. cit., p. 79.
85 ibid., p. 2.
86 S. McConville, op. cit., p. 18.
87 ibid., p. 19.
88 J. Mitchel, 'Letter to *Nation*', 8 January 1848, quoted in ibid., p. 19.
89 ibid., p. 19.
90 J. Mitchel, 'Letter to a friend', 20 June 1858, in ibid., p. 21.
91 M. Doheny, *The Felon's Track*, M.H. Gill & Son, Dublin, 1920, p. 124, quoted in ibid., p. 20.
92 G. Duffy, *Four Years in Irish History, 1845–1849*, Melbourne, 1883, quoted in ibid., p. 21.
93 G. Duffy, 1883, in ibid., p. 22.
94 J. Mitchel, quoted in ibid., p. 32.
95 W.S. O'Brien, National Library of Ireland, O'Brien Papers: MS. 449, in ibid., p. 22.
96 W.S. O'Brien, 'Letter to T.C. Anstey', 20 August 1850, quoted in B. Touhill, op. cit., p. 81.
97 W.S. O'Brien, *Freeman's Journal*, 21 March 1848, 2d., quoted in S. McConville, op. cit., p. 23.
98 J. Mitchel, 1869, quoted in ibid., p. 23.
99 W.S. O'Brien, 1848, quoted in ibid., p. 22.
100 *United Irishman*, vol. 1, no. 3, 4 March 1848, 56a–c, in ibid., p. 31.
101 W. Grey, quoted in ibid., p. 28.
102 W.S. O'Brien, 3 *Hansard*, XCVIII, cols. 74–80; 10 April 1848, in ibid., p. 29.
103 ibid., p. 30.
104 ibid., p. 29.
105 J. Mitchel, 1848, quoted in ibid., p. 31.
106 J. Mitchel, 1848, quoted in T. Keneally, op. cit., p. 150.
107 'Eva', aka M.A. Kelly, quoted in ibid., p. 151.
108 M.A. O'Doherty (nee Kelly), quoted in ibid., p. 174.
109 J. Martin, *The Irish Felon*, 1848, in ibid., p. 153.
110 K. O'Doherty, *Irish Tribune*, 1848, quoted in ibid., p. 154.
111 M. Callan, *Nation*, 1848, quoted in ibid., p. 154.
112 W.S. O'Brien, quoted in ibid., p. 157.
113 'Eva', aka M.A. Kelly, 'The Women of Ireland', *Nation*, 25 March 1848, quoted in B. Webb, op. cit., p. 80.
114 T. Keneally, op. cit., p. 155.
115 ibid., p. 155.
116 ibid., p. 156.
117 T. Meagher, quoted in A. Griffith (ed.), *Meagher of the Sword: Speeches of Thomas Francis Meagher in Ireland, 1846–1848*, M.H. Gill and Son, Dublin, 1916, pp. 227–228.
118 Meagher, quoted in T. Keneally, op. cit., p. 157.
119 R. Davis, op. cit., p. 5.
120 W.S. O'Brien, 'Letter to T.C. Anstey', 20 August 1850, quoted in B. Touhill, op. cit., p. 81.
121 T. Keneally, op. cit., p. 159.
122 ibid., p. 161.
123 ibid., p. 161.
124 ibid., p. 163.
125 G. Rudé, op. cit., p. 39.
126 T. Keneally, op. cit., pp. 164–166.
127 ibid., p. 169.
128 ibid., p. 172.
129 ibid., p. 172.
130 S. McConville, op. cit., p. 23.
131 G. Rudé, op. cit., p. 40.
132 T. Keneally, op. cit., p. 155.
133 ibid., p. 159.
134 W.S. O'Brien, 'Motives which induced William Smith O'Brien to take up arms against the British Government', quoted in B. Touhill, op. cit., p. 133.
135 G. Rudé, op. cit., p. 40.
136 T. Keneally, op. cit., p. 167.
137 P. O'Donohoe, c. 1858, quoted in ibid., p. 168.
138 ibid., p. 183.

139 T. Eagleton, op. cit., p. 139.
140 J. Martin quoted in Keneally, op. cit.,
    p. 175.
141 ibid., p. 174.
142 Quoted in ibid., p. 177.
143 W.S. O'Brien, 1848, quoted in ibid., p. 179.
144 Quoted in ibid., p. 179.
145 S. McConville, op. cit., p. 43.
146 T. Meagher, 1848, quoted in ibid., p. 182.
147 S. McConville, op. cit., p. 43.
148 William Smith O'Brien, 'Journal', quoted
    in T. Keneally, op. cit., p. 197.
149 G. Rudé, op. cit., p. 39.
150 M. Clarke, Old Tales of a Young Country,
    Mason, Firth & McCutcheon, Melbourne,
    1871, republished Sydney University Press,
    1972, p. 199.
151 T. Keneally, op. cit., p. 159.
152 ibid., pp. 187, 200; B. Touhill, op. cit.,
    p. 35; J.M. Ward, 'Grey, Henry George
    (1802–1894)', Australian Dictionary
    of Biography, Volume 1, Melbourne
    University Press, Carlton South, 1966,
    pp 480–484. Henry George Grey
    succeeded his father as the 3rd Earl Grey
    in 1845, and had previous experience
    in colonial affairs—he served as the
    undersecretary for Colonies (under
    the title Viscount Howick) during the
    Canadian crisis. He is not to be confused
    with his father, the Great Reform Bill
    prime minister of the 1830s, nor with
    his uncle, Sir George Grey, the Home
    Secretary responsible for security in
    Ireland and administration of justice at the
    time of the Young Ireland rising.
153 Touhill, op. cit., p. 35.
154 ibid., p. xi.
155 G. Rudé, 'O'Doherty, Kevin Izod (1823–
    1905)', Australian Dictionary of Biography,
    Volume 5, Melbourne University Press,
    Carlton South, 1974, p. 355.
156 Rudé, op. cit., p. 124.
157 W.S. O'Brien, To Solitude Consigned:
    the Tasmanian Journal of William Smith
    O'Brien, 1849–1853, edited by R. Davis,
    et. al., Crossing Press, Darlinghurst, 1995.
158 B. Touhill, op. cit., p. 35. Touhill quotes a
    letter from Lady Denison, confirming her
    husband's views, 29 October 1849.
159 ibid., p. 36.
160 S. McConville, op. cit., p. 45.
161 T. Keneally, op. cit., p. 191.
162 W.S. O'Brien, 'Letter to Sir Colman
    O'Loghlen', 5 June, 1849, quoted in
    B. Touhill, op. cit., p. 43.
163 T. Keneally, op. cit., p. 193;
    S. McConville, op. cit., p. 44.
164 ibid., p. 47.
165 W.S. O'Brien, 'Letter to Ellen O'Brien',
    1 January 1850, quoted in B. Touhill,
    op. cit., p. 53.
166 ibid., p. 47.
167 ibid., p. 49.
168 W.S. O'Brien, 'Letter to C. Anstey',
    22 November 1849, in Touhill, op. cit.,
    pp. 49–50.
169 ibid., p. 50.
170 South Australian Register, 12 December
    1849 and Guardian, 14 December 1849,
    quoted in ibid., p. 51.
171 ibid., p. 52.
172 ibid., p. 54.
173 ibid., pp. 54–55; J.M. Ward, op. cit.,
    pp. 480–484. The League was established
    in 1849.
174 T. Keneally, op. cit., p. 199.
175 B. Touhill, op. cit., p. 32.
176 ibid., p. 33; J.M. Ward, op. cit.,
    pp. 480–484. As undersecretary for
    Colonies Viscount Howick, Earl Grey
    had supported increased self-government
    for the Canadian colonies, and ultimately
    aimed for an end to transportation to Van
    Diemen's Land, but had to administer,
    and if possible improve, the policy as it
    stood.
177 For example the Launceston Examiner.
178 Limerick Chronicle, c. 14 June 1850,
    quoted in B. Touhill, op. cit., p. 63.
179 ibid., p. 62.
180 Great Britain, Hansard Parliamentary
    Debates, 3rd Series 112:786–95, quoted
    in ibid., p. 64.
181 ibid., p. 56.
182 New York Tribune, quoted in Nation,
    29 June 1850, in ibid., p. 62; T. Keneally,
    op. cit., p. 253.
183 A. Curthoys, 'Does Australian History
    Have a Future?', Australian Historical
    Studies, vol. 33, no. 118, 2002, p. 149.
    Curthoys discusses new 'diasporic
    histories' emphasis on 'multiple identities'.
184 T. Keneally, op. cit., p. 171.
185 ibid., p. 171.
186 B. Touhill, op. cit., p. 23; G. Rudé,
    'Mitchel, John (1815–1875)', Australian
    Dictionary of Biography, Volume 2,
    Melbourne University Press, Carlton
    South, 1967, pp. 234–235.
187 ibid.
188 L.C. Duly, '"Hottentots to Hobart and
    Sydney": The Cape Supreme Court's Use
    of Transportation, 1828–38', Australian
    Journal of Politics and History, vol. XXV,
    no. 1, 1979, p. 39.

ENDNOTES

189 J. Mitchel, *Jail Journal of Five Years in British Prisons*, *The Citizen*, New York, 1854, p. 256.

190 B. Touhill, op. cit., pp. 41, 68.

191 ibid., pp. 41, 42.

192 Provocatively launched on the anniversary of Britain's establishment of the first penal settlement at Sydney Cove, 26 January 1850.

193 W. Denison, 'Letter to Grey', 6 December 1849, quoted in ibid., p. 56.

194 Earl Grey, 'Letter to Denison', 29 April 1850, quoted in ibid., p. 59.

195 K. O'Doherty, 'Letter to Meagher', 1 January 1851, quoted in ibid., p. 103.

196 ibid., pp. 110–111.

197 T. Keneally, op. cit., pp. 221–223.

198 ibid., p. 223; R. Davis, op. cit., p. 7.

199 B. Touhill, op. cit., pp. 76–77.

200 W.S. O'Brien, 'Journal', 3:19–21, 14 August 1850, p. 143.

201 ibid., 8:7–8, 13 November 1849.

202 *Launceston Examiner*, 4 and 11 January 1851, quoted in B. Touhill, op. cit., p. 105.

203 ibid., p. 140.

204 See R. Davis, *William Smith O'Brien, Ticket of Leave*, New Norfolk, Sassafras Books, Hobart, 2006.

205 G. Rudé, op. cit., p. 101.

206 W. Denison, 'Letter to Grey', 11 December 1849, quoted in B. Touhill, op. cit., p. 57.

207 G. Rudé, op. cit., pp. 226–267.

208 J. Mitchel. *Jail Journal*, p. 192. *See also* illuminating discussion of Mitchel's attitudes to ordinary convicts in T. Causer, op. cit., pp. 423, 426–429.

209 ibid., p. 256.

210 ibid., p. 256.

211 W.S. O'Brien, *Journal*, and *Hobart Town Courier*, 29 January 1853, quoted in R. Davis, 'William Smith O'Brien', pp. 7–8.

212 P. O'Donohoe, 'Letter to O'Doherty', 9 November 1849, in B. Touhill, op. cit., p. 44.

213 P. O'Donohoe, *Irish Exile*, 28 September 1850, quoted in R. Davis, op. cit., p. 9.

214 W.S. O'Brien, *Hobart Town Courier*, 29 January 1850, quoted in ibid., p. 9.

215 W.S. O'Brien, quoted in B. Twohill, op. cit., p. 117.

216 T. Meagher, 'Letter to O'Brien', 16 December 1849, quoted in B. Touhill, op. cit., p. 40.

217 T. Keneally, op.cit., p. 266.

218 ibid., pp. 249–250.

219 For example, the *Argus* (in Melbourne), 20 March 1851; *Launceston Examiner*, 26 March 1851; *Hobart Town Guardian*, 10 January 1852, quoted in B. Touhill, op. cit., pp. 114, 142.

220 T. Keneally, op. cit., p. 252.

221 Mitchel Banquet, *New York Times*, 20 December 1853, quoted in ibid., p. 275.

222 ibid., pp. 255, 262–263.

223 ibid., p. 262.

224 Civic reception for T. McManus, San Francisco, June 1851, reported in *Sydney Morning Herald*, 24 August 1851, and quoted in B. Touhill, op. cit., p. 123.

225 ibid., pp. 144–145.

226 R. Davis, 'William Smith O'Brien', p. 1.

227 W.S. O'Brien, 'Letter to T. C. Anstey', 20 August 1850, quoted in B. Touhill, op. cit., p. 81.

228 R. Davis, *The Young Ireland Movement*, Gill and Macmillan, Dublin, 1987, pp. 206–208.

229 W.S. O'Brien, *Principles of Government or Meditations in Exile*, James Duffy and Co. Ltd, Dublin, 1856; R. Davis, 'William Smith O'Brien', p. 9.

230 J. Reynolds, 'West, John (1809–1873)', *Australian Dictionary of Biography*, Volume 2, Melbourne University Press, Carlton South, 1967, pp 590–592; M. McKenna, op. cit., pp. 44–47.

231 *Hobart Town Courier*, 27 January 1853, quoted in M. McKenna, op. cit., p. 73.

232 T. Keneally, op. cit., p. 278.

233 B. Webb, op. cit., p. 86.

234 G. Rudé, 'O'Doherty', op. cit., p. 355; T. Keneally, op. cit., p. 566.

235 E.A. Kelly, *Freeman's Journal*, 30 January 1861, quoted in ibid., p. 87.

236 Mitchel Banquet, *New York Times*, 20 December 1853, quoted in T. Keneally, op. cit., p. 275.

237 *The Citizen* and *Southern Citizen* were among the many newspapers Mitchel edited or wrote for in America; J. Mitchel, *Jail Journal*.

238 G. Rudé, 'Mitchel, John', op. cit., p. 235.

239 T.A. Jackson, op. cit., p. 276.

240 ibid., p. 275.

241 T. Keneally, op. cit., p. 324.

242 ibid., p. 324.

243 ibid., p. 324.

244 T.A. Jackson, op. cit., p. 281.

245 S. McConville, op. cit., p. 117.

246 *Irish People*, extract included in *Indictment of Fenian leaders*, 1865, quoted in T.A. Jackson, op. cit., p. 293.

247 ibid., p. 118.

248 T. Keneally, op. cit., p. 419.
249 T.A. Jackson, op. cit., p. 294.
250 *Irish People*, extract included in *Indictment of Fenian Leaders*, 1865, quoted in ibid., p. 294.
251 T. Keneally, op. cit., p. 419.
252 ibid., p. 421; C.J. Kirkman, quoted in T.A. Jackson, op. cit., p. 294.
253 S. McConville, op. cit., p. 114.
254 ibid., p. 15.
255 T. Keneally, op. cit., p. 429.
256 ibid., p. 429.
257 S. McConville, op. cit., p. 122.
258 T.A. Jackson, op. cit., p. 284.
259 Lord Cornwallis, 1790, quoted in S. McConville, op. cit., p. 121.
260 ibid., p. 118.
261 T. Keneally, op. cit., p. 422.
262 ibid., p. 431.
263 ibid., p. 427.
264 ibid., p. 429.
265 ibid., p. 450.
266 T.A. Jackson, op. cit., p. 285.
267 ibid., p. 439.
268 ibid., p. 477.
269 S. McConville, op. cit., p. 130.
270 T.A. Jackson, op. cit., p. 288.
271 K. Marx, quoted in S. McConville, op. cit., p. 135.
272 Col. W. Fielding, ibid., p. 166.
273 ibid., p. 165.
274 T. Keneally, op. cit., pp. 440–441.
275 S. McConville, op. cit., p. 126.
276 T. Keneally, op. cit., pp. 429, 438.
277 Wendy Birman, 'O'Reilly, John Boyle (1844–1890)', *Australian Dictionary of Biography*, Volume 5, Melbourne University Press, Carlton South, 1974, p. 371.
278 J.B. O'Reilly, quoted in T.A. Jackson, op. cit, p. 296.
279 T. Keneally, op. cit., pp. 485–486.
280 Wendy Birman, op. cit., pp. 371–372.
281 J.B. O'Reilly, *Moondyne; A Story of Convict Life in Australia*, Kennedy, New York, 1879.
282 T. Keneally, op. cit., p. 537.
283 ibid., pp. 454–457.
284 Quoted in S. McConville, op. cit., pp. 208, 303; P. Fenell and M. King (eds), *John Devoy's* Catalpa *Expedition*, New York University Press, New York City, 2006, p. 30.
285 T. Keneally, op. cit., p. 440.
286 ibid., p. 372.
287 T. Keneally, op. cit., p. 557.
288 ibid., p. 573.
289 ibid., p. 563.
290 ibid., p. 585.
291 Reported in *The Fremantle Herald*, 22 April 1876, quoted in ibid., pp. 589–560.
292 Quoted in S. McConville, op. cit., p. 210.
293 For a detailed account of the aftermath see T. Keneally, op. cit., pp. 597–601.
294 ibid., p. 594.
295 T.A. Jackson, op. cit., pp. 290, 293.
296 S. McConville, op. cit., p. 114.
297 T.A. Jackson, op. cit., pp. 275, 289.
298 P. Kearney, 'Down by the Glenside' (Bold Fenian Men). Written in the aftermath of the 1916 rebellion.

SELECT BIBLIOGRAPHY
PRIMARY SOURCES

Cook, T., *The Exiles Lament; or Biographical Sketches of Thomas Cook*, Sydney, 1841.

Ducharme, L.L., *Journal of a Political Exile in Australia*, 1845, translated from the original French with an introduction and notes by George Mackaness, *Australian Historical Monographs*, No. 3, D.S. Ford, Sydney, 1944.

Gates, W., *Recollections of Life in Van Diemen's Land*, (first published New York, 1850), edited with an introduction, notes and commentary by George Mackaness, *Australian Historical Monographs*, No. 40 (in two volumes), Sydney, 1961.

Godwin, W., *Enquiry Concerning Political Justice*, G.G & J. Robinson, London, February 1793.

Graves, A.P. (ed.), *Songs of Irish Wit and Humour*, Chatto and Windus, London, no date. Website: http://www.archive.org/stream/songsofirishwith00gravrich/songsofirishwith00gravrich_djvu.txt

Great Britain, Parliament, *Report from the Select Committee on Transportation*, Parliamentary Papers, House of Commons, No. 314, 1812.

Griffen, A. (ed.)., *Meagher of the Sword: Speeches of Thomas Francis Meagher in Ireland 1846–1848, His Narrative of Events in July 1848, Personal Reminiscences of Waterford, Galway and his Schooldays*, Gill, Dublin, 1916.

Heustis, D., *A Narrative of the Adventures and Sufferings of Captain Daniel Heustis*, Redding & Co. by S.W. Wilder, Boston, 1847.

BIBLIOGRAPHY

Howell, T.B., and Howell, T.J. (eds), *A Complete Collection of State Trials and Proceedings for High Treason and other Crimes and Misdemeanors*, Vol. XXIII, Bagshaw, London, 1817.

Loveless, G., *The Victims of Whiggery. A Statement of the Persecutions Experienced by the Dorchester Labourers; with a Report of their Trial; Description of Van Diemen's Land, and Reflections Upon the System of Transportation*, Central Dorchester Committee and Cleave, Shoe Lane, Fleet Street, London, Eighth Edition, 1838.

Loveless, J., Brine, J., Standfield, T., and Standfield, J., *A Narrative of the Sufferings of Jas. Loveless, Jas. Brine and Thomas and John Standfield. Four of the Dorchester Labourers. Displaying the Horrors of Transportation. Written by Themselves. With a Brief Description of New South Wales by George Loveless*, London, 1838.

Marsh, R., *Seven Years of My Life, or a Narrative of a Patriot Exile*, Faxon & Stevens, Buffalo, 1847.

Marx, K. and Engels, F., 'The Communist Manifesto', in *Selected Works*, Lawrence and Wishart, London, 1970.

Miller, L., *Notes of an exile to Van Diemen's Land: comprising incidents of the Canadian Rebellion in 1838, trial of the author in Canada ... ; also, an account of the horrible sufferings endured by ninety political prisoners during a residence of six years in that land of British slavery*, Fredonia, New York, 1846.

Morris, W., *News From Nowhere, or, An Epoch of Rest: Being some Chapters from a Utopian Romance*, Routledge & Kegan Paul, London, 1970.

Muir, T., *An Account of the Trial of Thomas Muir, Esq. Younger, of Huntershill, before the High Court of Justiciary, at Edinburgh. On the 30th and 31st days of August, 1793, for sedition*, Edinburgh, 1793 (First Pamphlet).

Muir, T., *The Trial of Thomas Muir, Esq. Younger of Huntershill; Before the High Court of Justiciary, Upon Friday and Saturday the 30th and 31st days of August On a Charge of Sedition*, Edinburgh, 1793 (Second Pamphlet).

Muir, T., *The Trial of Thomas Muir, Esq. Younger of Huntershill; Before the High Court of Justiciary, Upon Friday and Saturday the 30th and 31st days of August, 1793. On a Charge of Sedition*, Edinburgh, 1793 (Third Pamphlet).

O'Brien, W. S., *Principles of Government, or: Meditations in Exile*, James Duffy and Co., Ltd, Dublin, 1856.

O'Brien, W.S., *To Solitude Consigned: the Tasmanian Journal of William Smith O'Brien, 1849–1853*, edited by R. Davis, et. al., Crossing Press, Darlinghurst, 1995.

Owen, R., *Observations on the Effect of the Manufacturing System*, 2nd edn, R & A Taylor, London, 1817.

F. Engels, *The Condition of the Working Class in England*, Blackwell, Oxford, 1958.

Palmer, T.F., *The Trial of the Rev. Thomas Fyshe Palmer, before the Circuit Court of Justiciary, held at Perth, on the 12th and 13th September, 1793*, Edinburgh, 1793.

Pearson, C.H., *National Life and Character: a Forecast*, Macmillan, London, 1893.

Prieur, F.X., *Notes of a Convict of 1838*, translated from the original with an introduction and notes by George Mackaness, *Australian Historical Monographs*, No. 18, Sydney, 1949.

Shelley, P.B., 'The Mask of Anarchy: Written on the Occasion of the Massacre at Manchester', in Aveling, E. and Aveling, E.M. (eds), *Shelley's Socialism and Popular Songs*, The Journeyman Press, London, 1979.

Snow, S. *The Exiles Return or Narrative of Samuel Snow who was Banished to Van Diemen's Land, for Participating in the Patriot War in Upper Canada in 1838*, Smead and Cowles, Cleveland, 1846 Edited and annotated by C. Pybus as part of *Convict Narratives*, International Centre for Convict Studies, 1999, p. 1. Electronic Version Website: http://iccs.arts.utas.edu.au/narratives/snow.html

Swift, J., 'A Modest Proposal', in Pinkus, P. (ed.), *Johnathon Swift: A Selection of his Works*, Macmillan, Toronto, 1965.

Wait, B., *Letters from Van Diemen's Land Written During Four Years of Imprisonment for Political Offences Committed in Upper Canada*, A.W. Wilgus, Buffalo, 1847.

Whitlam, E.G., *Memorial to Battle of Vinegar Hill, Dedication*, 5 March 1988.

Wilding, M. (ed.), *Marcus Clarke: Portable Australian Authors*, University of Queensland Press, St. Lucia, 1976.

Wright, S., *Narrative and Recollections of Van Dieman's Land During Three Years Captivity of Stephen S. Wright*, J. Winchester, New York, 1844.

Declaration of Independence, The unanimous Declaration of the thirteen United States of America, In Congress, July 4, 1776.

SECONDARY SOURCES
BOOKS

Boyce, J., *Van Diemen's Land*, Black Inc., Melbourne, 2008.

Burroughs, P., *The Canadian Crisis and British Colonial Policy, 1828–1841*, Edward Arnold, Ltd, London, 1972.

Citrine, W. (ed.), *The Martyrs of Tolpuddle*, TUC, London, 1934.

Clune, F., *The Scottish Martyrs: Their Trials and Transportation to Botany Bay*, Angus and Robertson, Sydney, 1969.

Cochrane, P., *Colonial Ambition: Foundations of Australian Democracy*, Melbourne University Publishing, Carlton South, 2006.

Costello, C., *Botany Bay: The Story of the Convicts Transported from Ireland to Australia, 1791–1853*, The Mercier Press, Cork, 1987.

Curtin, N., *The United Irishmen, Popular Politics in Ulster and Dublin*, Oxford University Press, Oxford, 1994.

Davis, R., *Revolutionary Imperialist: William Smith O'Brien, 1803–1864*, Crossing Press, Sydney, 1998.

Davis, R., *William Smith O'Brien, Ticket-of-Leave, New Norfolk*, Sassafras Books, Hobart, undated.

de Tocqueville, A., *The Old Regime and the Revolution*, Harper and Brothers, New York, 1856.

Eagleton, T., *Scholars and Rebels in Nineteenth-Century Ireland*, Blackwell Publishers, Oxford, 1999.

Flower, C., *Illustrated History of New South Wales*, Rigby Publishers, Sydney, 1981.

Gahan, D., *Rebellion: Ireland in 1798*, O'Brien Press, Dublin, 1998.

Halévy, E., *The Birth of Methodism in England*, Chicago University Press, Chicago, 1971.

Hammond, J.L. and Hammond, B., *The Village Labourers, 1760–1832: A Study in the Government of England Before the Reform Bill*, Longmans, London, 1920.

Hancock, W.K., *Australia*, Jacaranda, Brisbane, 1966.

Hay, D., *Albion's Fatal Tree: Crime and Society in Eighteenth Century Britain*, A Lane, London, 1975.

Hirst, J., *Freedom on the Fatal Shore, Australia's First Colony*, Black Inc, Melbourne, 2008.

Hobsbawm, E., *The Age of Revolution: Europe, 1789–1848*, Weidenfeld and Nicholson, London, 1962.

Hobsbawm, E., *Labouring Men*, Weidenfeld and Nicholson, London, 1964.

Hobsbawm, E., and Rudé, G., *Captain Swing*, Lawrence and Wishart, London, 1969.

Jackson, T.A., *Ireland Her Own*, Lawrence and Wishart, London, 1991.

Keneally, T., *The Great Shame: A Story of the Irish in the Old World and the New*, Random House, Milson Point, 1998.

Kinchen, O.A., *The Rise and Fall of the Patriot Hunters*, Bookman Associates, New York, 1956.

Lenihan, P., *Confederate Catholics at War, 1641–49*, Cork University Press, Cork, 2001.

Löwy, M. and Sayer, R., *Romanticism Against the Tide of Modernity*, trans. Porter, C., Duke University, London, 2001.

Kelly, P., *The End of Certainty: Power, Politics and Business in Australia*, Allen and Unwin, St. Leonards, 1994.

Kent, D. and Townsend, N., *Convicts of the Eleanor: Protest in Rural England, New Lives in Australia*, Pluto Press, Annandale, 2002.

McFarland, E.W., *Ireland and Scotland in the Age of Revolution*, Edinburgh University Press, Edinburgh, 1994.

McConville, S., *Irish Political Prisoners, 1848–1922: Theatres of War*, Routledge, London, 2003.

McKenna, M., *The Captive Republic: A History of Republicanism in Australia 1788–1996*, Cambridge University Press, Oakley, 1996.

Marlow, J., *The Tolpuddle Martyrs*, Andre Deutsch Limited, London, 1971

Metin, A., *Socialism Without Doctrine*, trans. Ward, R., Alternative Publishing Cooperative, Chippendale, 1977.

O'Brien, P.K. and Quinault, R. (eds), *The Industrial Revolution and British Society*, Cambridge University Press, Oakley, 1993.

O'Tuathaigh, G., *Ireland Before the Famine, 1798–1848*, Gill and Macmillan, Dublin, 1972.

Pakenham, T., *Year of Liberty: The Story of the Great Irish rebellion of 1798*, Hodder and Soughton, London, 1972.

Palmer, R.R., *The Age of Democratic Revolution: a Political History of Europe and America, 1760–1800*, Princeton, New Jersey, 1964.

Palmer, V., *The Legend of the Nineties*, Melbourne University Press, Carlton South, 1958.

Pybus, C. and Maxwell-Stewart, H., *American Citizens, British Slaves: Yankee Political Prisoners in an Australian Penal Colony 1839–1850*, Melbourne University Press, Carlton South, 2002.

Rudé, G., *The Crowd in History: A Study of Popular Disturbances in France and England, 1730–1848*, Wiley, New York, 1964.

Rudé, G., *Protest and Punishment: The Story of Social and Political Protesters Transported to Australia 1788–1868*, Clarendon Press, Oxford, 1978.

Schreuder, D. and Ward, S. (eds), *Australia's Empire*, Oxford University Press, Oxford, 2008.

Schama, S., *A History of Britain: 1776–2000 The Fate of Empire*, Vol. 3, BBC Books, London, 2007.

Shaw, A.G.L., *Convicts and the Colonies*, Faber, London, 1966.

Sillard, P.A., *Life of John Mitchel: with an Historical Sketch of the '48 movement in Ireland*, James Duffy and Co., Ltd, Dublin, 1908.

Thompson, E.P., *The Making of the English Working Class*, revised edn., Penguin, Harmondsworth, 1980.

Touhill, B., *William Smith O'Brien and His Irish Revolutionary Companions in Penal Exile*, University of Missouri Press, Columbia, 1981.

Vincent, D., *Testaments of Radicalism: Memoirs of Working Class Politicians 1790–1885*, Routledge, London, 1977.

Waldersee, J., *Catholic Society in New South Wales, 1788–1860*, University of Sydney Press, Sydney, 1974.

Whitaker, A., *Unfinished Revolution: United Irishmen in New South Wales 1800–1810*, Crossing Press, Sydney, 1994.

Watson, R.A., *The Life and Times of Thomas Francis Meagher: Irish Exile to Van Diemen's Land*, Southern Holdings, Rosny Park, 2001.

Williams, T.D. (ed.), *Secret Societies in Ireland*, Gill and Macmillan, Dublin, 1973.

Woodham–Smith, C., *The Great Hunger*, Hamish Hamilton, London, 1974.

Young, R.M., *Ulster in '98: Episodes and Anecdotes*, Belfast, 1893.

ARTICLES AND CHAPTERS

Birman, W., 'O'Reilly, John Boyle (1844–1890)', *Australian Dictionary of Biography*, Volume 5, Melbourne University Press, Carlton South, 1974, pp. 371–372.

Bolton, G.C., 'Holt, Joseph (1756–1826)', *Australian Dictionary of Biography*, Volume 1, Melbourne University Press, Carlton South, 1966, pp. 550–551.

Brimms, J., 'From Reformers to "Jacobins": the Scottish Association of the Friends of the People', in T.M. Devine (ed.), *Conflict and Stability*, in *Scottish Society 1700–1800, Proceedings of the Scottish Historical Studies Seminar*, John Donald Publishers, Edinburgh, 1990.

D. Callahan, Review, 'American Citizens, British Slaves', *49th Parallel*, no. 17, Spring 2006, p. 1. Website: http://www.49thparallel. bham.ac.uk/back/issue17/Callahan.pdf

Carter, J.C., 'Rebellious Acts in the Western District of Upper Canada: Precursor to Transportataion to Van Diemen's Land', *Australasian Canadian Studies*, combining vol. 22, no. 2, 2004 and vol. 23, no. 1, 2005, pp. 33–66.

Causer, T., '"On British Felony the Sun Never Sets": Narratives of Political Prisoners in New South Wales and Van Diemen's Land, 1838–53', *Cultural and Social History*, vol. 5, no. 4, pp. 423–435.

Clark, M., 'The Origins of the Convicts Transported to Eastern Australia, 1787–1852', *Historical Studies*, vii, no. 26, May, 1956, pp. 121–135 and vii, no. 27, November, 1956, pp. 314–327.

Collins, H., 'Political Ideas and Practices', in Meaney, N. (ed.), *Under New Heavens: Cultural Transmission and the Making of Australia*, Heinemann Educational, Port Melbourne, 1989.

Davis, R., 'William Smith O'Brien: Irish Rebel and British Colonial Reformer', *Bulletin of the Centre for Tasmanian Historical Studies, Irish Edition*, vol. 2, no. 3, 1989, pp. 1–10.

Earnshaw, J., 'Muir, Thomas (1765–1799)', *Australian Dictionary of Biography*, Volume 2, Melbourne University Press, Carlton South, 1967.

Frances, R., 'Review of American Citizens, British Slaves', *Australian Humanities Review*, September–December 2002, p. 1. Website: http://www. australianhumanitiesreview.org/archive/ Issue-September-2002/frances.html

Fry, M., 'Macqueen, Robert, Lord Braxfield (1722–1799)', *Oxford Dictionary of National Biography*, Oxford University Press, 2004. Website: http://www. oxforddnb.com/view/article/17738, accessed 18 Jan 2010

Leask, N., 'Thomas Muir and *The Telegraph*: Radical Cosmopolitanism in 1790s Scotland', *History Workshop Journal*, issue 632007, pp. 48–69.

Mackey, F., 'Bound for Australia', *Horizon Canada*, October, 1986, vol. 7, no. 84, pp. 2006–2011.

Molloy, K, 'An Irish Radical and His Nephew: the Papers of John Mitchel and Sir William Hill Irvine', *La Trobe Journal*, no 84 Spring, 2009, pp. 34–47.

Moore, A., 'Phil Cunningham: a Forgotten Irish–Australian Rebel', *The Hummer*, Sydney Branch, Australian Society for the Study of Labour History, vol. 4, no 2. Website: asslh.org.au

O'Donnell, R., 'Dwyer, Michael (1772–1825)', *Australian Dictionary of Biography*, Supplementary Volume, Melbourne University Press, Carlton South, 2005, p. 110.

O'Donnell, R., '"Liberty or Death"; The United Irishmen in New South Wales 1800–04', in Bartlett, T., Dickson, D., Keogh D. and Whelan, K. (eds), *1798. A Bicentenary Perspective*, Four Courts Press, Dublin, 2003.

Parsons, V., 'Prieur, François Xavier (1814–1891)', *Australian Dictionary of Biography*, Volume 2, Melbourne University Press, Carlton South, 1967, pp 352–353.

Parsons, V., 'Redmond, Edward (1766–1840)', *Australian Dictionary of Biography*, Volume 2, Melbourne University Press, Carlton South, 1967, p. 371.

Perry, T.M., 'Meehan, James (1774–1826)', *Australian Dictionary of Biography*, Volume 2, Melbourne University Press, Carlton South, 1967, pp. 219–220.

Riley, C., 'The 1804 Australian Rebellion and Battle of Vinegar Hill', Hawkesbury Historical Society, 2003, p. 16. Website: http://www.hawkesburyhistory.org.au/articles/Battle_of_Vinegar.html

Roe, M., 'Margarot, Maurice (1745–1815)', *Australian Dictionary of Biography*, Volume 2, Melbourne University Press, Carlton South, 1967, pp. 206–207.

Rudé, G., 'Early Irish Rebels in Australia', *Historical Studies*, xvi, no. 62, April 1972, pp. 17–23.

Teniswood, W.V., 'Dry, Richard (1771–1843)', *Australian Dictionary of Biography*, Volume 1, Melbourne University Press, Carlton South, 1966, pp 328–329.

Ward, R., 'The Australian Legend Revisited', *Historical Studies* 18, 17 October 1978.

Webb, B., 'Eva of *The Nation* and the Young Ireland Press', in Geary, L.M. and McCarthy, A.J., *Ireland, Australia and New Zealand: History, Politics and Culture*, Irish Academic Press, Dublin, 2008.

WEBSITES

Australian Folk Songs: http://folkstream.com/

M. Bloy, *The Victorian Web, Literature, History and Culture in the Age of Victoria*: http://www.victorianweb.org/history/chartism.html

Convicts to Australia, A Guide to Researching Your Convict Ancestors: http://www.convictcentral.com/

Museum of Australian Democracy: http://moadoph.gov.au/exhibitions/

Tolpuddle Martyrs Museum: http://www.tolpuddlemartyrs.org.uk/mus_frms.html

IMAGE CREDITS

Australpress: p. 242

Corbis: pp. 20–21

Getty Images: cover (top), pp. 190–191, 310, 318–319, 330–331, 352

Irish Weekly Independent, Courtesy of the National Library of Ireland: p. 95

Library and Archives Canada, Acc. No. 1955-128-17: p. 260

National Library of Australia: cover (bottom), pp. 39, 72, 122–123, 212

Photolibrary: pp. 4, 27, 69, 153, 160, 186–187, 188, 296

Tasmanian Archive and Heritage Office, Allport Library and Museum of Fine Arts: p. 286

ACKNOWLEDGMENTS

Every book is a collaborative effort, and *Death or Liberty* could not have been completed without the support of numerous institutions, academic colleagues and publishing professionals.

I wish to acknowledge the invaluable assistance provided at the commencement of the project by the NSW Government and Arts NSW in awarding me the NSW History Fellowship in 2007. This enabled research, travel and time to write. My special thanks to the judges Professor Erik Eklund, Dr Alison Holland and Associate Professor Melanie Oppenheimer for their vote of confidence.

Monash University's Faculty of Arts generously assisted the book through grants for research assistance and travel in 2009. Special thanks to Professor Jenny Hocking and Linda Butler for their support via the School of Humanities and Social Science Research Committee and to Professor Bruce Scates, Director of the National Centre for Australian Studies for encouraging my research.

I am also grateful to the University of Sydney's Faculty of Arts and School of Philosophical and Historical Inquiry for kindly making available workspace and library access during the early stages of research and writing in 2008.

The most rewarding time for a historian is spent in the archives and library. I single out for special mention the Tolpuddle Martyrs Museum in Dorchester, the Trades Union Congress Library in London, the Tasmanian Government Archive, Concord Heritage Society, the NSW Botanic Gardens Trust, the Sydney and Monash University Libraries and the State Libraries of NSW and Victoria. My perception of the rebel convicts was enhanced through investigating a number of key sites of protest and punishment. A big thank you to Derek Pride for his engaging tour of Dorchester, 'the original home of rough justice' where the Tolpuddle Martyrs were tried.

The idea for *Death or Liberty* originated with Diana Hill, Publisher at Murdoch Books. I thank Diana for choosing me to author the book, and for her unflagging support, enthusiasm and flexibility in what proved to be an eventful couple of years. It fell to Paul O'Beirne as editor to crack the whip and herd the chapters together and I am grateful for his attention to detail, patience, commitment and acquaintance with Irish geography. Paul worked closely with designers Katy Wall, Emilia Toia and Peter Long, and I thank them for the striking styling of the book. Thanks also to the wider team at Murdoch Books for pushing and promoting *Death or Liberty*, particularly Kate Mayor, Mary-Jayne House and Jacqui Smith.

This book benefits from the input and advice of two PhD students who worked as research assistants on the first two chapters, Jamie Agland and Jenny Coats. Professor Geoff Gallop, Sydney University, kindly allowed me to read his doctoral thesis on British radical thought; London-based labour activist Paul Smith helped me get my bearings for Chapter 3; Bryce Webber and Janet Purkis provided valuable Canadian feedback on Chapter 4; and Dr Val Noone of Melbourne University kindly read and scrutinised the two Irish chapters (Chapter 2 and Chapter 5). I am especially grateful to my colleague at the University of Sydney, historian Dr Kirsten McKenzie, for taking time to read and comment so astutely on the draft manuscript and for her words of encouragement. I also thank Pam Dunne and Tim Learner for carefully proofreading the typeset pages. Any mistakes that remain are my own.

Thomas Keneally—essayist of the Irish–Australian story and passionate republican—kindly reviewed proofs before publication, and I thank him for his generous endorsement. Dr Peter Cochrane's scholarly narrative history of colonial New South Wales sets the bar high, and his words about *Death or Liberty* are greatly appreciated by his old student.

I gratefully acknowledge the Historic Houses Trust of NSW, the National Centre for Australian Studies at Monash University, and the Menzies Centre for Australian Studies at King's College London for assistance in promoting the book to readers.

I pay tribute to my recently deceased mother Jean, who encouraged in her children a sense of the fair go, and who never failed to enthuse about my projects, including this one. Finally, I thank my wife Lizbeth and children Joseph, Eliza and Samuel for patiently living with my latest obsession.

INDEX

430

Published in 2010 by Pier 9, an imprint of Murdoch Books Pty Limited

Murdoch Books Australia
Pier 8/9
23 Hickson Road
Millers Point NSW 2000
Phone: +61 (0) 2 8220 2000
Fax: +61 (0) 2 8220 2558
www.murdochbooks.com.au

Murdoch Books UK Limited
Erico House, 6th Floor
93–99 Upper Richmond Road
Putney, London SW15 2TG
Phone: +44 (0) 20 8785 5995
Fax: +44 (0) 20 8785 5985
www.murdochbooks.co.uk

Publisher: Diana Hill
Editor: Paul O'Beirne
Designers: Katy Wall, Emilia Toia and Peter Long

National Library of Australia Cataloguing-in-Publication Data

Author: Moore, Tony.
Title: Death or Liberty : Rebels and radicals transported to Australia 1788–1868 / Tony Moore.
ISBN: 978-1-74196-140-9 (pbk.)
Notes: Includes index. Bibliography.
Subjects:
    Convicts--Australia--History--18th century
    Convicts--Australia--History--19th century
    Revolutionaries--Australia--History--18th century
    Revolutionaries--Australia--History--19th century
    Political prisoners--Australia--History--18th century
    Political prisoners--Australia--History--19th century
    Transportation of convicts--Australia--History
    Exiles--Australia--History--18th century
    Exiles--Australia--History--19th century
    Penal colonies--Great Britain.
    Great Britain--Politics and government--History.
Dewey Number: 365.450994

A catalogue record for this book is available from the British Library.

PRINTED IN AUSTRALIA by Ligare Pty Ltd.

Page 4 image caption: Chartist rioters fire on the magistrates at the Westgate hotel but are
dispersed by the military, 4 November 1839. Eight of the ringleaders were transported for
high treason.